T0314122

Social Change and
Sustainable Transport

Social Change
and
Sustainable Transport

Edited by

William R. Black and Peter Nijkamp

Indiana University Press / Bloomington and Indianapolis

This material is based upon work supported by the National Science Foundation under Grant No. 9901271. Any opinions, findings, and conclusions or recommendations expressed in this material are those of the author(s) and do not necessarily reflect the views of the National Science Foundation.

This book is a publication of

Indiana University Press
601 North Morton Street
Bloomington, Indiana 47404-3797 USA

http://iupress.indiana.edu

Telephone orders   800-842-6796
Fax orders   812-855-7931
Orders by e-mail   iuporder@indiana.edu

The paper used in this publication meets the minimum requirements of American National Standard for Information Sciences—Permanence of Paper for Printed Library Materials, ANSI Z39.48-1984.

Manufactured in the United States of America

Library of Congress Cataloging-in-Publication Data

Social change and sustainable transport / edited by William R. Black
and Peter Nijkamp.
p.   cm.
"Papers from a conference on Social change and sustainable transport."
Includes bibliographical references and index.
ISBN 0-253-34067-5 (cloth : alk. paper)
1. Transportation—Social aspects—Europe—Congresses.
2. Transportation—Environmental aspects—Europe—Congresses.
3. Social change—Europe—Congresses.
I. Black, William R. (William Richard), date
II. Nijkamp, Peter.
HE242 .S65 2002
388—dc21

2001005864

1 2 3 4 5   07 06 05 04 03 02

Contents

Acknowledgments

The Social Change and Sustainable Transport (SCAST) Conference at the University of California in Berkeley was supported by the National Science Foundation (NSF) in the United States and the European Science Foundation (ESF) based in Strasbourg, France. We appreciate the support of these two organizations. In particular, we are grateful for the assistance given by Thomas R. Leinbach of NSF and John Smith of ESF. NSF also supported the preparation and publication of this volume of papers originally presented at the SCAST conference.

The editors were assisted in the preparation of this volume by Bobbi Diehl, Marian Ezzell, and Jane Lyle, all of Indiana University Press. Each of these individuals did an exceptional job with her particular part of the task. Our very sincere appreciation goes to each of them.

Introduction:
Pathways to Sustainable Transport and Basic Themes

William R. Black
and Peter Nijkamp

Setting aside the early prognostications of Thomas Malthus and others, the idea that there are limits to the human occupation of this planet has been recognized for perhaps five decades. The notion that components of this occupancy could be sustainable dates back to the Brundtland Commission report (World Commission on Environment and Development, 1987), which established the tenet that development could be sustainable. Since that time we have seen similar arguments made for sustainable manufacturing (Roome, 1998), urban sustainability (Alberti, 1996), sustainable forestry (Jenkins and Smith, 1999), sustainable tourism (Middleton and Hawkins, 1998), and sustainable transport or mobility (Nijkamp et al., 1998; Whitelegg, 1993). Our concern here is the last of these: sustainable transport.

For more than a decade, there has been a recognition that transport as it is offered today is non-sustainable. This non-sustainability was initially viewed as stemming from excessive use of petroleum, a finite resource, and the resultant global air pollution that use of this fuel produced. While these continue to be important, other factors are also recognized as contributing to the non-sustainability of transport (Black, 1995). Sustainable transport is inhibited in the major cities of the world by local air quality problems that are exacerbated by transport emissions. Each year, crashes on our transport systems take hundreds of thousands of lives and injure millions more. Finally, existing transport systems are approaching gridlock due to congestion in developed and developing nations of the world, particularly in our largest cities. We cannot view a transport system with these problems as even approaching sustainability.

The twenty-first century will see a variety of new social and technological trends that will influence the way in which transport is supplied and utilized. At present a wide range of social phenomena, including rising incomes, increased leisure time, new communication technologies, an aging population, and a declining role for the traditional family, are changing the nature of the demands we place on transport. In response to new techniques of production, shipping, and the growth of markets, economic activities are also changing. Institutional reforms such as privatization and deregulation have changed transport in ways that are not yet well understood. At the same time, increasing use of petroleum resources for travel and transport has raised concerns about the eventual depletion of this fossil fuel as well as its contribution to global warming and inferior urban air quality. Europe and the United States are the world's major energy consumers and transport users. However, the long-term sustainability of current transport systems is increasingly being questioned as rates of motor vehicle fatalities and injuries as well as congestion continue to rise. These trends raise questions about whether our current transport systems are sustainable beyond the next half-century.

Recently the social dimensions of the sustainable transport problem have begun to receive the attention of scholars from around the world. Most of the proposed solutions will succeed or fail on the basis of the social response to these different initiatives. These initiatives may require changes in behavior or changes in attitudes, or giving up a certain amount of mobility. At the same time, changes are occurring in our society that exacerbate the sustainability problem, including an increase in the number of single-parent households, more local and global leisure travel, and industrial globalization.

Recognizing the social dimension to the transport sustainability problem and realizing that little research attention had been given to this aspect of the problem, the European Science Foundation and the National Science Foundation in the U.S. sponsored a transatlantic research conference at the University of California at Berkeley on the topic of "Social Change and Sustainable Transport" (SCAST) in March of 1999. The present volume includes less than a quarter of the papers initially submitted for the conference. The authors of the papers included here represent geography and regional science, economics, political science, sociology, and psychology, and come from twelve different countries in Europe and North America.

Transport research can be viewed as a prime example of a research field in which the promotion of an interdisciplinary research approach is needed. Traditionally, transport research has been seen as an applied field dominated by engineering and logistics research approaches. There is a need to highlight the contribution of the social, economic, and behavioral sciences to the theoretical and methodological development of research in the transport field. These issues played a role at the Berkeley conference.

Prior to the SCAST conference, workshops were held in Europe and the United States to identify major research themes worth pursuing by interdisciplinary, transatlantic research teams. Criteria for identifying such themes included the following: (1) the themes must be international in nature; (2) they should involve common methodological approaches; (3) they must be feasible or tractable; and (4) they should involve long-term problems and findings.

International themes, it was thought, should be the focus of these joint undertakings. This would include such topics as international trade and transport, but also case studies that compared situations in North America and Europe. Alternative solutions to problems faced on both continents were also important and worth pursuing. The need for common methods should be apparent if generalizations were to flow from the research that would be valid in both areas. This implied the use of common models, databases, and methods. Recognizing that many research projects lead to a conclusion that more research is necessary or that better methods need to be developed, participants were eager to see problems addressed for which answers could be identified. Thus the concern with feasibility and tractability. Finally, there was a concern that the problems addressed should have long-term impacts. The problems should focus on issues such as the long-term consequences of international action or inaction. This would include, *inter alia,* topics such as the environmental, social, and economic consequences of globalization, approaches to reducing and eliminating motor vehicle crashes, and the social and economic consequences of global warming and the contribution of transport to this problem. Using the above criteria, a series of five research themes or problem clusters were identified:

- *Sustainability.* This is a central theme and includes not only environmental and resource concerns, but also social, political, and economic dimensions.
- *Social change.* Many of today's problems have come about because of changes in society, such as population growth, more workers outside the home, and an aging, motor vehicle–oriented population.
- *Globalization.* Significant changes are occurring in the developed world as industries strive for increased productivity and different labor-to-capital ratios. From the transport side, this begins to seriously impact the global networks and flows and raises questions regarding the externalities created by these activities.
- *Information technology.* In Europe and the U.S., Intelligent Transport Systems (ITS) are a common ingredient in attempts to solve contemporary transport problems. An objective assessment of the contribution of ITS to solving these problems raises many questions, chief among them whether information and communication technology can reduce the demand for travel.
- *Institutional considerations.* Although different approaches to transport are offered by different governmental units, research into the most efficient forms should be pursued. Should these be centralized or decentralized, regulated or deregulated, public or private? Although we have taken action in this area over the past twenty years, assessments of their success have often been from an economic perspective as opposed to a transport or mobility perspective.

Research teams, consisting of one European and one North American, were asked to prepare papers identifying these themes in more detail. These were subsequently published (Giuliano and Gillespie, 1997; Greene and Wegener, 1997; Hodge and Koski, 1997; Janelle and Beuthe, 1997; and Stough and Rietveld, 1997).

The first chapter in Part I of this volume introduces the reader to the basic themes of the SCAST effort. The second chapter, a paper from one of the plenary sessions at the conference, examines social trends and research needs in the area of social change and sustainable transport. The papers on the major research themes noted above (social change, sustainable transport, the role of information and communication, globalization, and the role of institutions) have been updated and appear next.

The social ramifications of a shift toward sustainable transport as a policy initiative are the subject of the first chapter in Part II. This policy aspect is also pursued in the following chapter, which looks at scenario building as a way of viewing alternatives. A method of viewing policies in Europe and North America is offered, followed by case studies that examine edge cities of the U.S. and comparisons between Chicago and Stockholm. The latter comparative, transatlantic studies are viewed as important in this research area; there is a belief on the part of many scholars that such studies have findings that provide deeper understanding than single-continent studies can provide.

A critical problem in the U.S. and a growing problem in Europe is the problem of automobile dependency. Privatization and deregulation in the passenger transport sector have resulted in a loss of transport service in many areas, and this has necessitated a need for automobiles. This topic is pursued in Part III, a set of four chapters that look at automobile dependency from its social impacts to the fact that in some cases it represents learned behavior.

Sustainability of transport implies that future generations will not be negatively affected by our actions. This has opened a discussion on equity as it currently exists. This topic is introduced in Part IV, where issues of location, aging, and gender equity are addressed.

One need only look at some recent statistics to see that automobile ownership is increasing in nearly every country in the world. The chapters in Part V address the travel and transport that result from increased recreational travel, tourism, company car use, and simple economic growth. These all exist for very good reasons in today's society, but we must endeavor to understand the situation more fully if transport is to become sustainable.

Although non-sustainability is viewed primarily as a problem resulting from excessive use of automobiles, it is also a general transport problem. Agreements that eliminate trade barriers, such as tariffs, encourage additional trade over longer distances, and such shipments are not sustainable, although they may be desirable for other reasons. Part VI looks at freight flows and what is being done and can be done to make these more sustainable.

Cultural perspectives on social change and sustainable transport are examined in Part VII. The three chapters in this part examine society's growing preoccupation with speed, the tendency for transport to result in a different type of urban landscape, and similarities between transport networks and communication networks.

Finally, Part VIII identifies some solutions to the problems of transport sustainability, but it also recognizes that these "solutions" may not be rapidly accepted. Among the notions examined here are the use of "intelligent transport" as it can influence land use, the role of pricing measures, the future of e-commerce and its role in the sustainable transport realm, and the difficulty of having new ideas and technologies adopted by users of the transport system. The volume concludes with some thoughts and glimpses of the future.

REFERENCES

Alberti, M. 1996. "Measuring Urban Sustainability." *Environmental Impact Assess Rev.,* 16, 381–424.

Black, W. R. 1995. "Sustainable Transport: A U.S. Perspective." *Journal of Transport Geography,* 3, 159–166.

Giuliano, G., and A. Gillespie. 1997. "Research Issues Regarding Social Change and Transport." *Journal of Transport Geography,* 5, 165–176.

Greene, D., and M. Wegener. 1997. "Sustainable Transport." *Journal of Transport Geography,* 5, 177–190.

Hodge, D., and H. Koski. 1997. "Information and Communication Technologies and Transportation: European-U.S. Collaborative and Comparative Research Possibilities." *Journal of Transport Geography,* 5, 191–198.

Janelle, D., and M. Beuthe. 1997. "Globalization and Research Issues in Transportation." *Journal of Transport Geography,* 5, 199–206.

Jenkins, M. B., and E. T. Smith. 1999. *The Business of Sustainable Forestry.* Washington, D.C.: The Island Press.

Middleton, V. T. C., and R. Hawkins. 1998. *Sustainable Tourism: A Marketing Perspective.* London: Butterworth-Heinemann.

Nijkamp, P., S. Rienstra, and J. Vleugel. 1998. *Transportation Planning and the Future.* Chichester/New York: John Wiley.

Roome, N.J. 1998. *Sustainability Strategies for Industry: The Future of Corporate Practice.* Washington, D.C.: The Island Press.

Stough, R., and P. Rietveld. 1997. "Institutional Issues in Transport Systems." *Journal of Transport Geography,* 5, 207–214.

Whitelegg, J. 1993. *Transport for a Sustainable Future: The Case for Europe.* New York: Belhaven Press.

World Commission of Environment and Development. 1987. *Our Common Future.* New York: Oxford University Press.

PART I

An Overview

CHAPTER ONE

Social Change and Sustainable Transport

A Manifesto on Transatlantic Research Opportunities

Marina van Geenhuizen,
Peter Nijkamp,
and William R. Black

THE CHANGING SCENE OF TRANSPORT

The late twentieth and early twenty-first century was an important period of social change. Demographic trends, new lifestyles, flexible production and work, new policy priorities, new requirements in policy-making, and technology advances all contribute to social change at the same time that they are influenced by this change. As a result of this interplay, we are witnessing developments that can best be summarized as concentration and uniformity at one level and spread and differentiation with increased cooperation at other levels. Transport and communication are important factors in the realization of spread, differentiation, and cooperation.

Transport and communication are the most visible manifestation of a modern network economy. Bridging distances—whether physically or virtually—reflects economic progress and a modern way of life. Spatial interaction contributes to efficient economic development and offers actors a strong competitive position in an open and increasingly global network society. Transport also has a clear social function (e.g., civic and educational participation and family visits) and satisfies particular social-psychological desires (such as the intrinsic need to be mobile), although the latter function is not well under-stood. However, it is also increasingly recognized that a mobile society incurs high social costs and causes a variety of negative externalities of various kinds, including traffic congestion, accidents and fatalities, pollution and noise annoyance, destruction of visual landscape (town-scape) beauty, waste in the use of resources, raw materials, and energy, and so forth. In general, social costs are charged not to the user of transport, but to other social categories. At the same time, the demand for transport is increasing, especially in those sectors that are relatively most polluting, viz. road and air (ECMT, 1997). For example, over the past twenty-five years, private car use in Europe has more than doubled, while in the same period road freight has risen by 160 percent. Transport by air has shown an even more spectacular increase. Extrapolation of current trends into the future would lead not only to critical bottlenecks and a high level of environmental decay, but also to serious disparities in accessibility of regions and cities. Accordingly, the overall picture of the transport sector is a rather negative one: the demand for transport services is rapidly rising, causing increasing stress on the environment and quality of life.

Not surprisingly, against this background increasingly

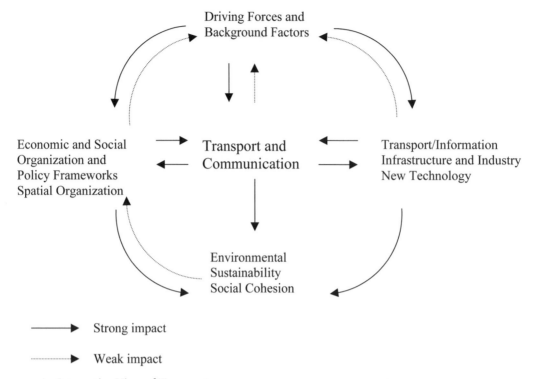

Figure 1.1   An Integrative View of Transport

louder voices are being heard, demanding a change in these trends. This has culminated in the concept of sustainable transport, which expresses the need for transport to be brought into balance with the requirements imposed by the protection of the environment, now and in the future, globally. The concept of sustainability does not immediately offer operational guidelines and testable frameworks for assessing and evaluating environmental, land use, and transport policies. For this reason, we have witnessed in recent years the emergence of the delinking criterion, which states that the annual growth in transport demand should be less than the average growth in Gross Domestic Product (GDP). But one needs to realize that transport is narrowly interwoven with many other activities in our society, and that it is therefore largely a derived demand. Thinking in terms of delinking means paying attention to driving forces from economic behavior and how these might be changed. Policies on delinking therefore require a broad portfolio of different initiatives, instruments, and regulations. Because of the many cause-and-effect relationships, such policies also require an integrative approach.

SOCIAL CHANGE AND SUSTAINABLE TRANSPORT: AN INTEGRATIVE FRAMEWORK

Knowledge about the complexity of transport systems is still limited. A transport system may show rather unexpected turbulence as a result of interacting forces between dynamic behavior and limits to capacity. This may hold for daily traffic flows, but also for changes in patterns of international trade, although the latter display more inertia. Unexpected behavior also happens as a result of policy-making. There is a shortage of insights into how actors in transport respond to policy measures, particularly cost measures, at the same time that there is a need to fine-tune goals, measures, and social acceptance.

Whereas much past research had a strong emphasis on engineering principles, it is beyond doubt that future research needs an interdisciplinary approach, rigorously including concepts from the social sciences and the humanities, while it also needs to address issues of policy implementation and process management. Transport cannot be properly analyzed in isolation from its context; on the contrary, the driving forces in mobility and communication are a direct result of broader social, economic, technological, and policy developments. Figure 1.1 demonstrates the integrative approach by including in a comprehensive way major direct and indirect influences on transport and communication from driving forces in the economic and social system and policy frameworks. The figure equally underlines the interaction of the spatial organization of society, transport infrastructure and industry, and new transport technology with transport and communication. Furthermore, it makes explicit reference to the natural environment, which is strongly influenced by land use, transport and transport infrastructure, and new technology solutions, but has only weak reverse impacts. The same is true for social cohesion (exclusion) on various geographical scales.

This chapter utilizes the systematic scheme above as a frame of reference for identifying the driving forces behind changes in transport and communication. Within the integrative approach, we will focus on economic and social behavior, policy and process management, and new technology solutions to transport problems. In the realm of behavior, we can identify the following driving forces: an increased need for self-realization of individuals, leading to new lifestyles, demographic trends such as the growing number of elderly and of one-parent families, flexible organization in the workplace, flexible production organization, and globalization in the spatial organization of production. In the field of policy and process management, the driving forces are the following: changing institutions, the involvement of a wide range of actors and interests in policy-making, an increased need for flexible and adaptive governance, and an increased need for integrative policy-making, including various sectors and spatial levels. Finally, with reference to technology, we can identify various factors that influence the adoption of new transport technology, such as the complexity of the technology itself and actor complexity in process management of technology introduction. In addition, there is the widespread influence of information and communication technology (ICT) on transport and transport technology.

Clearly, transport and communication contribute to trends for spread and differentiation and for cooperation at the same time that the global network society induces new forms of cooperation, communication, interaction, and mobility. Some interesting examples of the implications of this interplay with often antagonistic develop-

ments are sketched below, dealing with economic organization (logistic concepts), spatial organization and infrastructure (suburbanization), and the transport industries.

In freight transport, new logistics are increasingly being applied by firms, thereby impacting on the aggregate spatial pattern of physical movement. Increasing the level of customer services is a major quality aim, often leading to thinner and more dispersed, yet faster and more frequent flows of goods. In addition, a persistent international division of labor implies that the transport of mass-produced goods or components tends to be over longer distances. At the same time, a new element in future logistics is the recycling of products and waste materials. Far-reaching principles such as integrated product-chain management and reversed logistics will, however, meet fierce resistance because of the need for a new landscape of production, distribution, collection and treatment of waste materials, and energy conversion and storage systems.

Driving forces such as individualization and preference for suburban lifestyles are important in influencing the rising mobility of households and individuals. There seems to be an ongoing move toward the mobile society away from the homebound society, although there still seems to be a difference between the rich and the poor. High-income groups and the well-educated are usually more mobile, exhibiting a persistent preference for living in suburban locations aside from a few respectable inner-city quarters. The growing constraints in physical infrastructure, evident mainly in road and air traffic congestion, will, however, inevitably lead to the collapse of major traffic routes and the loss of attractiveness of particular suburban locations. Adequate policy solutions are still to be found, but they may entail a combination of measures, such as more efficient use of existing transport systems and a selective increase in physical infrastructure. In improving the role of public transport, there is the dilemma between rising housing densities in order to make public transport feasible and the desire among suburbanites for low-density living in a countryside environment.

Transport industries play an important role in the force field of transport, because they contribute significantly to employment in manufacturing and services. Accordingly, the automobile and aviation industries are often used as a showpiece by national governments. However, today nationally based industries are becoming part of a

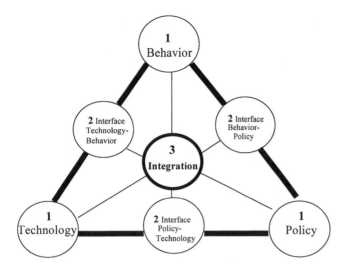

Figure 1.2   SCAST Research Triangle

field, the next sections will elaborate the so-called SCAST Research Triangle.

THE RESEARCH TRIANGLE OF SCAST

Using the Research Triangle of SCAST (Figure 1.2), we can identify various interesting research themes on social change and sustainable transport. The corners of this triangle represent Behavior, Policy, and Technology (Level 1). In addition, a second category of emerging themes can be found at the interface of each pair of corners, between Behavior and Policy, Policy and Technology, and Technology and Behavior (Level 2). A third category comprises themes that relate the three corners in an integrative way (Level 3). All three categories together sufficiently cover research in transport fields relevant for social change and sustainable transport (SCAST), in terms not only of basic research, but also of applied and strategic research.

The remainder of this chapter discusses various emerging research themes at different positions in the Research Triangle. Themes located in the individual corners of Behavior, Policy, and Technology are discussed first, followed by themes at the three interfaces in between and the integrative themes related to all three corners. In the selection of themes, emphasis is placed on relatively new issues that might be jointly pursued by scholars from North America and Europe, including issues put forward at the SCAST conference. However, no attempt has been made to be totally inclusive. The final section concludes with the gains of collaborative action between Europe and North America in this important research area.

larger globalization process, preferring to locate footloose segments of their chain where costs are lowest. The importance of the transport industry rests also on its ties with other manufacturing sectors, such as textiles and metalworking, and complementary services such as finance, insurance, and fueling. At the same time, the production of transport hardware is an extremely important segment for the application of new technology that supports sustainable transport, such as new types of systems for converting and storing energy, new lightweight construction and lightweight materials, and advanced sensor and identification systems. However, the main focus of large transport industries is technologies that advance the full mobility of individuals; new technologies for sustainable transport are kept low-profile in the belief that these can be activated if markets grow. It is difficult to predict the conditions that foster the uptake of new technologies, such as social-psychological factors, financial conditions and legal (liability) aspects, and prescriptive measures.

The previous examples sufficiently illustrate the many questions about strategic policy research that go far beyond conventional transport research, but they also cover industrial dynamics, resource management, regional development, telecommunication, environmental sustainability, and safety. In order to cope with this multifaceted

BEHAVIOR

Behavior encompasses many forms of mobility and interaction of actors on various geographical scales. There are four observable driving forces with far-reaching behavioral impacts and a number of (weaker) influences (Table 1.1). First, there is an increasing trend toward self-realization among individuals by means of consumption of differentiated products and services. Second, there are important demographic changes, such as the decreasing incidence of the traditional nuclear family and the growth in the proportion of the elderly. Third, there is additional flexibility in the organization of work and in the organization of production. A final trend to be mentioned here is the increased globalization in the spatial organization of production, due largely to global outsourcing. The central question is how these new behavioral patterns influence sustainable transport.

New research themes include household-related changes (new lifestyles) and concomitant new consumer demand in living and transport, and workplace-related changes. There has been an increase in the number of single-parent and single-person households. The net result is a growing number of trip-making units. In addition, patterns of residential choice have led to a further decentralization of the population in metropolitan areas, with an increase in home-work trips (including cross-commuting). However, there are also signs of a growing preference for living in downtown redevelopment areas and edge cities. A further theme concerns consumer wishes in transport and related transport behavior. Particularly, in order to make public transport services more attractive, there is a need for a coherent set of knowledge covering issues such as preferred time schedules, travel duration including waiting time, comfort, convenience, and so forth, and willingness to pay. The differentiation among various types of consumers, particularly their time valuation, is still insufficiently understood. A thorough understanding of consumer wishes is also important for the design of smart combinations of private and collective transport in commuting. With regard to workplace-related changes, jobs for life are becoming less common. There is an increasing trend toward flexible work organization, including part-time work, freelancing, outsourcing, mobile working, and flexible retirement schemes. These trends seem likely to have a significant influence on home- and work-related travel demand. Another emerging research theme is the behavior of employers. This category of actors may significantly influence travel patterns by supplying company cars, company parking, collective transport for commuters, and financial incentives for carpooling.

Care work in society and its impact on sustainable transport have been largely ignored by researchers. There is scant knowledge of the mobility needs of care work, which consists mainly of caring for children (by women) and caring for the elderly. Patterns may differ between Europe and North America, because North America has more extensive systems of school transport and daycare at schools for children, and Europe has a stronger emphasis on caring for the elderly in their homes (instead of nursing homes or institutions). There is, however, one common trend based on the growing number of women

Table 1.1 Behavioral Forces in Transport

Driving forces

- Self-realization of individuals
- Demographic trends
- Flexible organization of work and production
- Globalization in the spatial organization of production

Other forces

- Car appeal
- Preferences for suburban living
- Increased traveling by women
- Increased traveling for leisure purposes
- Consumer preferences for new and fashionable goods
- Increasing power of global players in trade and transport

who are entering the workforce, and that is joint caring for children by women and men. A further common trend is that women are increasingly becoming involved in travel because they live longer than men and become increasingly "car-oriented." Accordingly, there is a need to focus research more on travel behavior that seems to be typical for women, and on the potential for reducing their travel miles. This would include attention to decisions about purchases and shopping (food), multipurpose trips, and security as a central issue in traveling. Conventional notions, often based only on men's travel behavior, need to be reconsidered.

Recently, there has been increasing attention to leisure, tourism, and mobility patterns. Tourism and recreational participation have risen as a result of increased personal mobility, increases in income and time, and demographic factors, particularly the growing number of elderly with discretionary income. There is an ongoing differentiation in leisure activities based on the need for self-realization, but there remains an emphasis on rural destinations, particularly seashores. Specific coastal areas seem to suffer from congestion during peak times, although there may be a difference in impacts from short-stay (daily) tourism and long-stay tourism. Here is a field urgently in need of research aimed at the identification of sustainability conflicts, including underlying consumer behavior. A

Table 1.2   Policy Forces in Transport

Driving forces

- Institutional changes
- Involvement of a wide range of interests and stakeholders
- Need for flexible and adaptive governance
- Need for integrated policy-making, including various fields and levels

Other forces

- New roles and relations between public and private sectors
- Need for enhanced efficiency in management of (formerly public) transport systems

---

further unexplored theme is the influence on travel behavior of access to green areas. There is scant evidence on differences in leisure travel between people who live in the countryside and people who live in cities at a distance from green areas.

In connection with mobility behavior itself, an emerging theme is the type of mobility (e.g., car culture) and underlying human desires. Relevant variables include gender, age, and social class, and possibly several other culturally based differentiating factors. We know that Americans drive more than Europeans, but are they driving more than is necessary? This touches upon whether it is possible to identify some optimum (minimal) level of traffic or minimum requirements approach to travel (Black, 1997). Such an approach would enable planners to set realistic levels of travel reduction. An equally unexplored field is the appeal of automobiles beyond merely utilitarian transport purposes. Such an appeal would, for example, satisfy the need to divert aggression or enjoy freedom. An associated theme is the influence of car access during childhood on later adult travel behavior.

A final theme would include questions on the ethics of ever-increasing mobility, regarding both persons and goods. Is there a limit to the self-understanding of increased mobility, and is there a differentiation for particular categories of persons and goods in the definition of such a limit?

An important behavioral theme connected with the transport of goods (logistic chains) is changes in consumer demand. In particular markets there is a trend toward buying based on fast-changing fashion and taste, as well as quick delivery of goods. This development has contributed to a shift toward flexible production systems, such as that apparent in flexible sourcing, customized production runs, zero inventory, and so forth. At the same time, companies increasingly source on a global scale and find new customers in emerging markets. The result of these changes is an increasing number of thin flows covering larger and larger distances, while using less sustainable modes such as air freight and motor carriers. Accordingly, how producers react with their logistic strategies and services to new customers' demand is an important research theme. In generic terms, the theme can be addressed under the heading of ways and policies to delink economic growth and transport.

Furthermore, corporate behavior of carriers and shippers is important because of its influence on global patterns of trade and traffic flow. There is an ongoing market concentration (mergers) among global multimodal carriers and shippers, whereas it remains unknown to what extent the connected strategies will influence the future growth of particular seaports and airports. This is an urgent research theme because many European seaports (e.g., the ones in the Le Havre–Hamburg range) plan large increases in capacity without knowing the stability of the routings currently in use (Janelle and Beuthe, 1997). The same holds true for airports.

POLICY

Policy encompasses a broad range of fields, including regulation, process management of change such as the design of policy-making models and decision-support tools, the (daily) management of transport systems, and the nature of new policy solutions. A crucial role is played by institutions (as rule-based structures), because these underlie many forms of policy. Moreover, the past decades have seen three new driving forces in transport policy-making: the involvement of a wider range of stakeholders, pressure for more flexible and adaptive governance, and pressure for integrated policy (Stough and Rietveld, 1997) (Table 1.2).

The involvement of a wider range of interests and stakeholders means that in pursuing transport goals, one has to consider a broad range of constraints and externalities (such as societal equity and environmental impacts), causing more complexity in decision making and consensus formation than ever before. Research is needed on how these new requirements can be respected without losing too much time in obtaining implementable decisions. In addition, transport policy typically finds itself in a multi-layer situation, with policy-making at various geographical scales (e.g., local, metropolitan/regional, national, and European). This means, for example, that improving the efficiency of a transport system at a specific level (say, the metropolitan) needs to match interests at various related levels. There is not much experience in this respect, causing a need to identify appropriate models of policy-making with different actors (levels) involved, leading to systems of integrated transport supply and management. A further research theme stems from the need to transform transport organizations (formerly in the public sector) into demand-responsive and flexible structures aimed at efficiency, but also sustainability gains.

Various important research needs stem from the increased actor complexity in transport policy-making. A number of shortcomings in the policy-making process (policy cycle) can be observed, such as in the design of alternative options for sustainable solutions. What often happens is a situation of "forgotten" alternative options, due to a quick (or a priori selective) generation of options. If there is no systematic and transparent generation of alternatives, hidden agendas may be put forward. More important, it is apparent that cost-benefit analysis may need to be improved along various dimensions. There is little recognition of how large a benefit must be before it is significant. There is also a lack of valuation criteria with respect to specific impacts (such as societal and equity costs and environmental costs), but there is a need to systematically include these impacts in the analysis. Another point of improvement is the treatment of uncertainty, in particular how benefits are assigned to gradual project development and flexibility in implementation. A relatively new element would be to let stakeholders participate in cost-benefit analysis in order to improve the quality of the results as well as increase the support for

those results. A final point to be mentioned here is the need to learn from past (and present) policy implementation, particularly from a causal analysis of success and failure in transport policy. Accordingly, there is a need for solid monitoring based on adequate data.

In general, research is needed on how information bases and user-friendly software can be used as dynamic decision-support tools to simulate and compare future outcomes under different policy assumptions. Such tools create opportunities in the entire process of policy-making to enrich the information of different stakeholders and increase their support. In addition, there is a need to further improve tools such as gaming and scenario analysis. The results of different types of these tools must be validated in order to identify the conditions under which they obtain the best results in supporting policy-making.

One does have to realize that different countries have different steering cultures, values, and institutions (Stough and Rietveld, 1997). This leads, among other things, to differences in current policy practices, such as between top-down and bottom-up approaches, with different degrees of participation by stakeholders. Aside from different policy traditions, there are also differences in how countries try to solve transport problems, depending on cultural and value differences. Research into the nature of the latter differences would give new insights into cross-country diversity in transport policy. However, it needs to be stressed that countries are losing power in transport policy to supranational structures such as the European Union. This calls for attention to problems of harmonization and standards, particularly those that hamper the introduction of sustainable transport policies. An interesting question concerns the impacts of harmonizing the European eco-tax on transport (including fuel in aviation).

An increase in the number of stakeholders leads to questions about the division of roles between the public and private sector, with pressure to define the role of markets and privatization as an alternative to the dominance of public provision and management of transportation infrastructure. Early attempts at privatization and/or deregulation of road, rail, bridge, and tunnel infrastructure, and so forth, need to be evaluated in order to identify the optimal balance of public and private roles in both North America and Europe.

As far as policy content is concerned, various new measures aimed at sustainable transport deserve attention.

We can identify three types of policy impact serving sustainable transport. First, there are policies that aim to reduce travel demand, such as combined land use and transport planning, and the greening of logistic chains through a shortening (relocation) of chains. Second, there are policies that try to enhance the replacement of non-sustainable forms of transport by more sustainable forms. This includes a range of measures to make public transport attractive and car use less attractive, common in many European cities. Finally, there are policies to make the use of existing transport systems more sustainable, such as measures that favor carpoolers, and high parking fees in inner-city areas. A more general question concerns the pricing of mobility, user charges, and public acceptance of such charges. An interesting question would be how a property-rights approach can underpin pricing policies.

A theme covering all three types of impact is strategic policy design for large seaports. Seaports suffer from increased road congestion on inland connections and various other negative externalities. To develop policy strategies to let mainports (based on volumes) move toward brainports (based on value added and intelligent chain management) would be a challenge. Evolutionary notions of regional development tell us, however, that such major policy changes are far from self-evident and require solid research if they are to support policy changes and process management (Morgan, 1997).

Technology

A number of emerging technologies may significantly contribute to sustainable solutions in transport. As with policy solutions, we can identify technologies that potentially reduce travel demand, such as the use of information and communication technology (ICT) in electronic commerce and teleworking, and technologies that may lead to a substitution of environmentally non-sustainable forms of transport, such as automated guided vehicles and MAGLEV trains. In addition, there are technologies that aim to increase the sustainability of existing transport systems, such as multimodal nodes (terminals) in freight networks, and electric and hybrid cars. There are two types of research questions relevant here: (1) Which factors influence the development of new technology solutions? (2) Which factors influence the adoption of these solutions?

Mechanisms behind progress in R&D clearly have an

Table 1.3 Technology Forces in Transport

Driving forces

- Factors influencing technology adoption such as technology complexity, actor complexity, and competition with existing technologies
- Widespread application of information and communication technology

Other forces

- Progress in R&D related to the specific nature of the technology, organizational structure of R&D, and uncertainty in costs and outcomes
- Mechanisms that promote R&D, such as funding and pooling of resources

autonomous component, dependent on the peculiarities of the technology and the organizational format involved (horizontal or vertical learning networks), and various types of uncertainty in outcomes. In general, basic research and R&D are strongly influenced by national systems of innovation. National systems of innovation include types of relationships between companies and research institutes, the system of funding of research, systems of education, and the role of governments, for example, in setting quality standards, but also as initiators of research. There is also a specific policy component involved (to be discussed in the next part).

The two strongest forces in technology are a set of factors that influence technology adoption in general and one specific technology on its own, i.e., information and communication technology (Table 1.3). Factors that influence adoption may rest on performance characteristics of the technology itself and on marketability, but also on reluctance among customers (due to price differences) and the nature of the introduction projects involved (actors' complexity, amount of investment). The embeddedness of existing (old) technologies is also important. Old technologies that are firmly embedded in hard infrastructure and in organizational structures reduce the potential for adoption of new, competing technologies. There is a need to improve methodologies that serve to identify the influence of such factors in early stages. One methodology might be based on learning from historic examples of adoption failures, both the spectacular (e.g., the recent French Aramis, an urban automated guided rail system; Latour, 1996) and the less spectacular. To develop this requires a coherent theoretical framework of adoption (failure), monitoring, and evaluation. It also requires the development of a database on complex transport projects, in which major technological attributes and critical events are registered. Technology assessment may be further improved by including the participation of stakeholders involved in the adoption of the technology.

Information and communication technology are already widely applied in transport and communication, and there seems no end to further, comprehensive applications. This technology occupies the peculiar position of contributing to transport that is increasingly unsustainable (such as in enabling global outsourcing) while offering opportunities for sustainable solutions. Important questions deal with the extent to which physical transport can be replaced by ICT, such as in creating virtual reality in leisure, in telework and teleservices, and related issues of footlooseness and the need for face-to-face contacts.

Under the heading of technology, we can also identify research and design of new technology applications. Good examples are new types of subterranean transport, advanced systems of (re)loading at nodes (ports), dynamic automatic vehicle guidance, advanced systems of goods delivery in cities, combined transport of persons and freight, and tracking, tracing, and identification systems in order to create seamless freight flows. Most of these technological solutions are based on the application of advanced information and communication technology.

Themes at the Interfaces

Behavior and Policy

At the interface of Behavior and Policy, we find various themes related to how transport policy intends to change, and actually does change, the behavior of travelers, suppliers of infrastructure, and so forth, in view of sustainability gains. There is a need to assess the extent to which policies succeed or fail, and cause unwanted side effects. An interesting new field is empirical research on traveler behavior to circumvent policies such as road pricing. There is also an ongoing need to assess the acceptability of various types of measures (fiscal, financial) and packages, as well as related organizational requirements. The approach in such research preferably includes economic and social-psychological components. Furthermore, there is the issue of coherence between usually separate sustainability policies, such as reducing congestion and air pollution, and preventing road accidents. There is a need to investigate relationships between such different policies in order to identify conflicting aims and impacts on behavior.

Pricing and financing of sustainable transport is a theme about which a great deal remains unknown. This holds, for example, for measuring external costs, practical ways to effectively implement externality taxes, and the implications of full cost pricing in terms of efficiency and equity. A lot remains to be learned about the public acceptability of fundamental shifts in pricing and financing transport, in both Europe and North America. Equally urgent is research into the types of policy that may yield the largest gains in changing travel behavior, such as changing attitudes through education and growing environmental awareness or through an active participation of travelers in the design of policy procedures. Of a more fundamental nature is the question of whether policies directed toward travel behavior are more successful than policies directed toward travel demand, such as the creation of easily accessible working and living places (Salomon and Mokhtarian, 1998), and whether the outcomes differ between Europe and the U.S.

A much-neglected research theme is how important actors influence policy-making and implementation. A good example is the role of producers of vehicles, ships, aircraft, and so forth, and the producers of fuel (energy). Sustainability changes (such as downsizing passenger cars, and low-emission aircraft) seem to rest to an important extent on decisions by these actors. On the other hand, governments may influence their behavior by using regulatory instruments or negotiated arrangements. The question would be, What institutions in Europe and North America are necessary to make such government influence possible?

Policy and Technology

Under this heading one can identify the theme of institutions and policy attitudes toward new transport technology. Institutions may advance or hamper the use of particular technologies. In the specific case of technologies that contribute to increasing the capacity of existing transport infrastructure, a hampering influence can be observed. For example, the introduction of electronic payment systems for mobility and multimedia computer assistance for travelers may suffer from societal constraints such as those based on legal and privacy issues.

Another important issue is government policy to enhance the development and adoption of new technology. National culture and the institutional environment influence how policy-makers tend to cope with these issues. This means that policy measures to enhance new technology differ between countries. R&D on sustainable transport may be encouraged by different mechanisms, such as incentives (tax) in the private sector. Otherwise, R&D may be sponsored by public sources or conducted in the public sector. The role and importance of these mechanisms are not clear in Europe and North America (Greene and Wegener, 1997). Measures that enhance technology adoption can also take many forms, varying from direct prescription of technology use to a careful stimulation of use in selected market niches. An interesting research question is which policy measures best serve the adoption of new transport technology, given different institutional environments.

Technology and Behavior

Much of the discussion under this heading is concerned with the influence of information and communication technology (ICT) on travel behavior (Hodge and Koski, 1997). With respect to households, there is still a shortage of knowledge on how ICT affects individual travel behavior. User response to real-time information systems in traveling seems to depend on context and market penetration of the technology, but many questions remain unanswered about the influence of technology on travel behavior in dynamic traffic management. Particularly, the impact of real-time information—about congestion and alternative routing, including the best connection in public transport—on actual travel behavior remains largely unknown. Clearly, further empirical research on traveler behavior is needed to gain new insights. The same holds for adoption behavior and choices in trade-off situations between using ICT and physical travel. A new specific area of research is care work, and how the use of ICT may reduce travel by care workers.

For electronic commerce, the question remains whether it is a complement of or a substitute for conventional shopping. Similar questions can be posed for the workplace and the adoption of telecommuting. A crucial ques-

tion is the extent to which ICT and faster travel speeds make housing footloose with an overall larger consumption of miles compared with previous situations. Equally important is whether there is a limit to the use of ICT due to the need for face-to-face interaction. Again, similar questions can be posed for business trips and videoconferencing. Research in these areas can benefit from differences between North America and Europe in land use patterns and cultures surrounding new technology.

The use of ICT has greatly contributed to the globalization of production. There are now longer and more customized linkages, sensitive to timing. The question here is how ICT can contribute to mitigate the negative impacts of these developments, such as by using multimodal networks and nodes (terminals), and by bundling flows.

At the interface of technology and behavior, we can also identify a cluster of questions concerning the adoption of new technology. For example, why do particular technologies fail and others succeed in gaining the favor of consumers? In addition to technology assessment, there is a clear need for a behavioral approach to adoption issues, including social-psychological factors. To date it remains largely unknown to what extent technology solutions need to match driving forces such as the need for self-realization and the need for flexibility, as well as other basic values such as privacy, in order to be accepted.

INTEGRATIVE THEMES

Our third category of research themes (Level 3) is the most ambitious one; it is the level at which behavior, policy, and technology interact in transport systems at various geographical scales. At this level we find the following classes of issues that call for attention: (1) integrative concepts, such as synergy in transport networks and efficient network use; (2) conceptual issues referring to the transport system at large, including mobility and sustainability; (3) questions dealing with generic aspects of transport systems, such as land use and transport and financing of transport; and (4) methodological questions in researching all previously indicated themes.

An important integrative concept in relation to sustainable transport is networks. The awareness of complexity in transport networks (and partly chaotic developments) has opened the door to dynamic modeling based on notions from evolutionary economics, network-niche, and chaos models (Nijkamp and Reggiani, 1998). The challenge here is in empirical testing based on solid data. In addition, the concept of networks evokes questions on the side of user appreciation. Interconnectivity is an important aim in the context of improving users' appreciation of transport networks and increasing efficiency in network use. Synergy of transport networks is a further interesting research theme in view of sustainable transport.

An equally interesting concept is chains. Chains refer to the actual use of networks and indicate flows from a particular starting point to an end point. Chains can be identified in production, i.e., starting with raw materials and ending with consumption, eventually including recycling. In logistics chains, emphasis is increasingly placed on saving time and inventory, and on customer services. In personal mobility, mainly in metropolitan areas, the focus is on door-to-door transport, and how this can be organized more efficiently. A particularly interesting common issue is how the principle of time saving influences non-sustainable transport in the design of chains, and how this can be prevented by using ICT. This touches upon questions about the shortening and repositioning of transport chains.

An integrative theme that has received attention for years is land use (urban form) and transport. Here we find considerable research on the influence of decentralization, segregation, edge cities, and so forth. Nevertheless, the influence of land use and land use policy instruments such as zoning, jobs balance strategies, and the design of compact cities remains largely untested and disputed. There is a need for solid empirical research on land use changes and response in transport behavior, preferably based on a paired-comparison design of different cities. Such research would also include patterns of air quality and noise intrusion. The latter integrative approach of land use, transport, and environmental impacts is also relevant in modeling exercises. Integrated travel demand models based on land use zones (including edge cities) preferably incorporate resulting travel patterns, emission levels, and economic and social welfare, as well as the impact of various packages of measures, such as demand-responsive transit and various systems of road tolls and separate lanes. Furthermore, there is a need to develop visions that break with current trends, such as concerning the location of workplaces and concomitant patterns of commuting.

The financing of transport and mobility is a compre-hensive theme that increasingly attracts attention. A major issue here is what type of travel costs are at stake that are now (partly) covered by non-transport sectors, such as accident costs, capital costs of infrastructure, land-related costs, and pollution. Further, it needs to be considered which of these costs can realistically be included in the price of travel, what the impact of such measures would be on travel behavior, and what mechanisms need to be developed in order to distribute the revenues. There may be an interesting institutional (cultural) differentiation here between European countries and North America, because mobility and the extent of (in)direct subsidization are appreciated in different ways. The theme of financing and (full) paying for traveling also touches upon the need for a basic reconsideration of various transport-related concepts.

A key concept that calls for reconsideration from a societal or ethical point of view is mobility. There seems to be a need to move from a merely physical (mathematical) interpretation to an interpretation that includes social concerns. One way is to include the traveler's responsibility in causing negative impacts. In this context, equity concerns are an emerging issue. Equity may refer to the environment as well as to access. With regard to environmental impacts of transport, one can distinguish between intergenerational, social, and global equity issues (Greene and Wegener, 1997). By definition, intergenerational equity is a core element of sustainability. Social equity issues stem from the fact that the people who cause environmental impacts are not usually the ones most affected by them, a difference that runs parallel with income levels. There is a need to investigate to what extent such injustices occur systematically and how these are connected with metropolitan development patterns and planning principles. The global dimension of equity rests on the fact that most negative impacts—particularly those on global air quality—originate in the developed world. However, one needs to be aware of the rapid increase in motorization in large cities of the underdeveloped world. Research is needed on how regions in the developed world can provide leadership in responding to environmental pressure from transport and mobility, and thereby provide a positive role model for the developing world.

Although it is a subject that has been around for a long time, sustainability is still a theme that needs attention. There is a need for testing sustainability indicators, including valid methodologies for evaluation and comparison (Black, 1998). In addition, particularly interesting in

Table 1.4   Key Words of Research Themes per SCAST Cluster and Position in the SCAST Research Triangle

SCAST Clusters	Level in Research Triangle		
	1	2 Interfaces	3 Integration
Sustainability	Elderly in traveling Women in traveling Leisure traveling	Policy success/failure Policy acceptability Full cost pricing Coherence in policy ICT and sustainability gains/losses Car and fuel producers Adoption behavior of customers	Sustainability measuring/comparing Delinking criterion Networks Chains Land use–transport Future images (scenarios) Integrated travel demand models
Social change	Lifestyles Residential choice Demographic trends Self-realization Care work Flexible work practice Car culture New consumer demand	Policies with largest behavioral gains Social constraints on new technology	Trend-breaking visions New interpretation of mobility Equity concerns
Globalization	Flexible production Global carriers/shippers	Enhancing role of ICT Impact on transport demand Multi-modality	Repositioning of chains
Information technology	ICT and traveling Technology assessment	Role of face-to-face contact Footloose activity Substitution of transport	ICT and networks ICT and chains Efficient network use
Institutional considerations	Flexible policy Actor participation Integrative policy Cost-benefit analysis Monitoring Decision support tools Culture and values Harmonization Public-private roles	Negotiated arrangements Barriers to adoption Adoption policy	Financing infrastructure Paying for mobility

cross-comparative research would be the influence of different physical environments and local circumstances on the sustainability impacts of transport. As an alternative approach to sustainability, the delinking criterion needs attention, particularly in connection with the question of how transport and economic growth might be delinked.

Methods of researching transport issues in both North America and Europe seem to be dominated by an engineering-based paradigm of quantitative modeling and by a narrow range of perspectives derived mainly from neo-classical economics. There is a need to incorporate a rich variety of social science methodologies, including solid qualitative methods of inquiry and more research of a sociological and social-psychological nature. At the same time, the development of separate streams of methodologies needs to be avoided, because major challenges (breakthroughs) may occur at the intersection (interplay) of different methodologies.

The research themes of this conference were organized around five different clusters, set out in previous documents: Sustainability, Social Change, Globalization, Information Technology, and Institutional Considerations (Leinbach and Smith, 1997). Table 1.4 summarizes for each of these five clusters the previously indicated research themes organized per level in the SCAST Research Triangle.

Virtues of Collaboration

Social change is not an unambiguous force occurring at a constant pace, but rather a multifaceted portfolio of modifications and drivers to prevailing trends that lead to a new constellation of society with equal or increasing complexity. Mobility, lifestyle, demographic evolution, new modes of production, and policy changes mirror this multidimensional force field. Transport is not just a passive follower of these mega-tendencies, but may influence them through ICT, logistics, new networks, and so forth.

The intricate linkage between social change and the need for environmentally benign transport behavior is a fascinating and challenging research area positioned at the interface of many scientific disciplines. The area is so vast and complex, and so deeply rooted in human behavior, that it will take an enormous and collaborative research effort to probe all the available knowledge in this field. This will also assist us in offering answers to such basic questions as: Is there a need to reverse trends and move to an eco-society in which principles of less travel demand and eco-principles are leading in the (re)design of urban structure, housing, manufacturing processes, and sourcing of energy and raw materials? Or, is it possible to move to a world in which Europeans and Americans are still relatively mobile with telecommunication as a substitute where possible, coupled with increased energy efficiency and smaller environmental and equity impacts of transport?

There are four reasons that favor transatlantic collaboration in research on social change and sustainable transport. First, the problems are common but may differ in degree and strength of driving forces. Such differences create a research landscape with a potential for experimental design otherwise absent in transport research. Second, it enhances common understanding of problems and an exchange of ideas. Joint research efforts, as opposed to independent action, have a higher chance of producing "new combinations" or breakthroughs in analysis, such as is necessary in perpetual problems (e.g., urban traffic congestion, land use/transport questions). A third benefit would follow from the pooling of knowledge. Some regions are ahead of others in particular research activities and fields. Research effort can be saved by dissemination and appreciation of results, and by using the most advanced work as a kind of benchmark. In addition, we can learn lessons from each other, as Europe did from North America with respect to long-distance transport of freight over land. A final point in favor of transatlantic collaboration is the pooling of resources. This may be helpful in situations where a critical mass of research effort is needed to obtain particular results.

However, joint research (both coordinated work and comparative analysis) requires a high compatibility in methodology and data: as compatible and up to date as possible and covering the key variables. It also requires a careful design of convincing research plans. This conference offers an excellent breeding ground for innovative ideas and plans for collaboration.

References

Black, W. R. 1997. "North American Transportation: Perspectives on Research Needs and Sustainable Transportation." *Journal of Transport Geography* 5, no. 3: 12–19.

Black, W. R. 1998. "Sustainable Transport." In B. Hoyle and R. Knowles, eds., *Modern Transport Geography*. New York: John Wiley and Sons.

Button, K. 1997. "Some Thoughts on the NSF and ESF Papers." *Journal of Transport Geography* 5, no. 3: 50–51.

ECMT. 1997. *Trends in the Transport Sector*. Paris: European Conference of Ministers of Transport.

Geenhuizen, M. van, and P. Nijkamp. 1998. "Improving the Knowledge Capability of Cities: The Case of Mainport Rotterdam." *International Journal of Technology Management* 15, no. 6/7: 691–709.

Geenhuizen, M. van, H. van Zuylen, and P. Nijkamp. 1998. "Limits to Predictability." In *Proceedings of the PTRC European Transport Conference 1998*, 291–302. London: PTRC.

Giuliano, G., and A. Gillespie. 1997. "Research Issues Regarding Societal Change and Transport." *Journal of Transport Geography* 5, no. 3: 165–176.

Greene, D. L., and M. Wegener. 1997. "Sustainable Transport." *Journal of Transport Geography* 5, no. 3: 177–190.

Hodge, D., and H. Koski. 1997. "Information and Communication Technologies and Transportation: European US Collaborative and Comparative Research Possibilities." *Journal of Transport Geography* 5, no. 3: 191–197.

Janelle, D. G., and M. Beuthe. 1997. "Globalization and Research Issues in Transportation." *Journal of Transport Geography* 5 (3): 199–206.

Latour, B. 1996. *Aramis, or the Love of Technology*. Cambridge, Mass.: Harvard University Press.

Leinbach, T. R., and J. H. Smith. 1997. "Development of a Cooperative International Interdisciplinary Program on Social Change and Sustainable Transport." *Journal of Transport Geography* 5, no. 1: 1–3.

Morgan, K. 1997. "The Learning Region: Institutions, Innovation and Regional Renewal." *Regional Studies* 13, no. 5: 491–503.

Nijkamp, P., and M. van Geenhuizen. 1997. "European Transport: Challenges and Opportunities for Future Research and Policies." *Journal of Transport Geography* 5, no. 1: 4–11.

Nijkamp, P., and A. Reggiani. 1998. *The Economics of Complex Systems*. Berlin: Springer.

Salomon, I., and P. Mokhtarian. 1998. "What Happens When Mobility-Inclined Market Segments Face Accessibility Enhancing Policies?" *Transportation Research D* 3, no. 3: 129–140.

Stough, R., and P. Rietveld. 1997. "Institutional Issues in Transport Systems." *Journal of Transport Geography* 5: 207–221.

CHAPTER TWO

Social Trends and Research Needs in Transport and Environmental Planning

Martin Wachs

TRANSPORTATION AND INFORMATION ARE BECOMING EVER MORE COMPLEMENTARY

The social trend that is coming to have the greatest influence on transportation is the growing role of information processing and telecommunications in modern society. During the first decades of the new century, the impacts of this relationship will be as influential as was the invention of the automobile and the telephone in the early part of the last century. The development of a telecommunications-transportation linkage will probably be even more influential over the next few decades than was the construction of national highway networks at mid-century. At the very least, our ability to expand mobility will increasingly depend on our ability to use telecommunications and information processing in concert with the transportation system. While fully automated highways are probably decades away, on-vehicle collision-avoidance systems, the provision of "real-time" information regarding the arrival of transit vehicles, widespread use of electronic toll collection to finance highways, the capability to navigate around traffic congestion, and the ability to reserve in advance a time slot to cross a congested bridge are nearer at hand. Larger shares of transportation budgets will undoubtedly be spent on telecommunications enhancements to expand and manage the capacity of existing facilities than will be spent on the construction of extensive new facilities. We must develop planning methods that include the capability to evaluate telecommunications enhancements to current facilities in programs for congestion relief as easily as they presently include evaluations of new transportation facilities. Regional plans for transportation usually include streets, highways, transit routes, and projects such as street widenings and extensions of transit routes. Rarely do they include the upgrading of communications capabilities, the provision to travelers of improved traffic information, or the use of electronic toll collection to reduce delays at bridges. New planning methods are needed that will incorporate technological and informational improvements as well as facilities expansions. In addition, research is needed that will help transportation agencies develop the capability to understand and forecast the economic, social, and environmental consequences of intelligent transportation systems (ITS) improvements on existing and new facilities.

The use of computers and other information-processing devices is also changing the hours and the places at which we work, and consequently changing the spatial and temporal patterns of travel and the spatial patterns of cities. The pressure for continued decentralization will be hard to minimize given the ready availability of information-exchange devices. While relatively few people are literally telecommuting by working whole days at home or at neighborhood telework centers, more are working at multiple locations in the course of a day and at unusual times of day because of information-processing opportunities at home and at night. E-mail and the Internet are changing travel patterns dramatically. We are already experiencing a great increase in non-work travel as a proportion of all travel, in part because of this and other social changes. For the same reason, we are already seeing heavier peaks of traffic at midday and on weekends at many locations than at the traditional morning and evening weekday rush hours. We are less certain of the environmental consequences of these changes than of the travel consequences, but they will be significant, and they must be addressed in the development of transportation planning and environmental regulations and procedures if those procedures are to truly accommodate emerging societal needs. While we expend great amounts of money forecasting travel and its environmental consequences at the metropolitan level, we should be developing similar capacities to forecast information transfers from one locale to another, to incorporate information flows as significant, causal determinants of regional travel and land use patterns, and to estimate the environmental consequences of these changes in telecommunications patterns and of the changes in urban form and travel patterns that they will engender. If we fail to incorporate considerations of information processing into transportation planning for the coming two or three decades, we will be planning transportation systems to meet yesterday's needs.

ENVIRONMENTAL QUALITY WITH, NOT AGAINST, MOBILITY

When the environmental movement took the transportation community by storm in the late 1970s, the United States was in the midst of building a vast national highway system. Some of us consider that system to be a great force for mobility, national unification, and economic growth. Others, in comparison, view the postwar interstate era as an overindulgence that is a monument to greed and pork barrel politics. It could well be both of these, but the magnitude and extent of the highway program of the fifties, sixties, and seventies was enormous, and the institutional machinery built to support it was equally impressive.

Not surprisingly, then, the environmental movement was at first largely an opponent of the highway program rather than a component of it. The National Environmental Policy Act, which introduced systematic environmental review and the requirement for the preparation of Environmental Impact Reports, and the Clean Air Act Amendments, which required transportation planning in pursuit of air quality goals, were in a sense reactions more than they were initiatives. Their proponents were in tension with pro-highway forces and were attempting to put a brake on what many in the transportation business thought of as progress. I have heard many transportation officials refer to the Clean Air Act requirements as "the tail that wagged the transportation dog." Interestingly—and appropriately—that perspective was being voiced with decreasing frequency as we approached the new century.

Today the situation is rather different. While of course we still have many in the transportation community who feel besieged by environmentalists, and some environmentalists continue to regard transportation officials as their enemies, we have for the most part forged a successful working relationship aimed at providing mobility in combination with environmental responsibility. A broad cross-section of the public is committed to congestion relief *and* environmental responsibility. The Surface Transportation Policy Project (STPP), considered a "progressive" transportation and environmental advocacy coalition, and the American Association of State Highway and Transportation Officials (AASHTO), the traditional coalition of road interests, actually do talk with one another and find grounds for compromise.

Given this evolution of feelings and understandings, it is possible today to urge the adoption of regulations and procedures based upon the principle that mobility and environmental quality are not mutually incompatible, but that it is our mission to serve both of these masters. In fact, to go further, many of us would even assert that the principal purpose of transportation investments is to respond to society's environmental goals, where the environment is perceived broadly as a combination of the social, economic, and natural contexts within which we live. In other words, over time, we have all become environmentalists to some extent, and the planning of transportation systems and facilities is seen to be a component of shaping the environment. The environment is no longer an afterthought—a checklist of factors and questions asked of otherwise completed transportation plans; it is becoming a fundamental determinant of and ingredient in the way we think about the environment.

ENVIRONMENTAL CONSEQUENCES OF TRANSPORTATION ARE DETERMINED MORE BY TECHNOLOGY THAN BY PHYSICAL PLANS

To the extent that our society has progressed in reducing the harmful impacts of transportation systems on the natural environment, the last thirty years have shown us that technological changes have been responsible for far more of this progress than have regional plans or facility changes. Air pollution has decreased, primarily as a result of more demanding tailpipe emission standards and longer periods during which new cars are required to meet those standards, and inspection and maintenance programs to ensure that they do so. Thus, air pollution has declined substantially in cities having the most severe problems, including even Los Angeles, despite increased driving, increased suburbanization, worsening traffic congestion, and failed efforts to encourage more environmentally responsible travel behavior.

It is difficult to attribute any recently measured improvements in air quality to transportation control measures or to behavioral changes by travelers, such as a shift to the use of public transport, walking, or cycling. Because of their failure to be used to even a significant proportion of their capacities, some states are now attempting to reconvert High Occupancy Vehicle (HOV) lanes to mixed flow, while transit use continues to decline nationally as a proportion of all travel and ride sharing is at a twenty-year low. Efforts to induce transit-oriented development have met with some limited success, but the trend toward lower density for most people in most places remains dominant even as some central-city urban residential communities grow and prosper.

During the coming decades, the most cost-effective ways to reduce pollutants from the air, water, and land that are attributable to transportation systems will continue to be through technological changes in vehicles, engines, fuels, lubricants, and telecommunications capacities linked with transport rather than through transportation control measures and other efforts to induce behavioral changes, such as major shifts from driving to public transit, cycling, or walking. Goods-movement vehicles and off-road mobile sources are not yet as tightly regulated for environmental pollutants as light-duty passenger vehicles, and I expect that they will come under closer scrutiny for regulation and technological change in the first decade of the new century.

THE FOCUS OF ENVIRONMENTAL ANALYSIS OF TRANSPORTATION IMPACTS IS SHIFTING

From ROG and NOx to Particulates

For the last thirty years, the most pressing environmental concern affecting regional transportation institutions in the United States has been air quality at the local and regional levels. And within the realm of air quality, most emphasis has been placed on the reduction of lead, oxides of nitrogen (NOx), reactive organic gases (ROG), and carbon monoxide (CO). For several different but complementary reasons, I would predict that in this new century, in the U.S. as well as in other nations, there will and should be increasing attention to other environmental consequences of transportation systems, both within the realm of air quality and beyond it. In part this is the result of the substantial progress that has already been made in addressing the environmental hazards of lead, ROG, NOx, and CO. Even with increasingly stringent ozone standards, the control of these pollutants will be accomplished to a greater and greater extent largely through national emissions standards for vehicles and through inspection and maintenance programs and the retirement of grossly polluting vehicles rather than through regional transportation plans, land use initiatives, or transportation control measures. But this progress will surely not solve the environmental problems associated with modern urban transportation systems. It is time for research on the relationships between transport and the environment to examine a number of other issues as well.

There is growing awareness that the measures employed to reduce pollutants derived from mobile sources have been far less effective at controlling particulates, which are now a recognized health hazard. Environmental requirements related to the reduction and filtering of fine particles are quickly becoming a serious problem for regional air quality and transportation planners. Because heavy-duty diesel trucks account for about three-fourths of highway-related emissions of particulate matter, and diesel engines associated with off-road activities are another major source (Sawyer and Johnson, 1995), it would appear that technological controls will continue to be an important strategy by which to meet newly revised particulate standards. This will involve more stringent control of both on-road and off-road vehicles and will place a much heavier burden of regulation and compliance on the goods-movement industry. It should also result in increased attention to the efficiency of goods movement within regional transportation plans and is one of the motivations, for example, for the inclusion of trucks-only lanes and even trucks-only highways in the latest regional transportation planning effort in Los Angeles. However, a substantial proportion of fine particles, such as entrained road dust, are caused by wind and water erosion rather than by engine emissions. Attention to the reduction of fine particles will become a more dominant part of the process of addressing the environmental impacts of the transportation system. We are not yet sufficiently well equipped in terms of scientific understanding of the phenomena to address these problems effectively in plan making, and a great deal of research is needed before particulate pollution can be more fully understood and properly managed.

The Growing Importance of Greenhouse Gases

Similarly, we are just beginning to understand the risks of producing greenhouse gases, and global warming is gaining prominence as a transportation planning and policy problem. It has been estimated that transportation is responsible for about 20 percent of worldwide CO_2, and that motor vehicles in the United States account for 20 to 25 percent of worldwide transportation emissions (or about 5 percent of the total of worldwide greenhouse gases produced by people as opposed to natural sources; Transportation Research Board, 1997, pp. 210–211). The long-term environmental consequences of the greenhouse gas buildup remain uncertain, and a great deal of current research is aimed at reducing that uncertainty. Nevertheless, with public awareness rising and the risks substantial, transportation will continue to be the focus of research on this topic, and transportation strategies are certain to be included in policies to reduce greenhouse gases. Most strategies are aimed at either reducing the amount of motor vehicle travel or substantially changing the amount and type of fuel needed to produce it (Transportation Research Board, 1997, p. 212). Once again, because there are so many other trends tending to increase rather than reduce travel, I would expect technological changes in fuels and vehicle propulsion systems to play the larger role in addressing this emerging problem, and changes in travel behavior to play a limited role. Yet it is worth noting that while regional long-range transportation planning in the United States today is a rather unimportant contributor to efforts to control greenhouse gas emissions, there are major disagreements between sectors of the professional community as to the role that it could play. There is a need to research the contributions that technological improvements and that regional transportation planning and investment strategies can make to the control of greenhouse gases, and to develop a more conscious research strategy by which to address the reduction of CO_2 emissions even as mobility continues to increase and as travel in private vehicles continues to increase worldwide.

Water Quality

Transportation facilities can dramatically change the nature of water systems. Highways and transit routes often alter the course and volume of flows in waterways and can affect natural drainage patterns. The paving of large areas of ground surface in airport and highway projects also affects runoff patterns and can result in flooding or in major changes in drainage patterns. Vehicles, highways, and transit routes are also sources of substantial amounts of liquid, solid, and gaseous pollutants that can settle on water surfaces or be carried in runoff into water courses. Over time we have come to understand that an indeterminate but large proportion of surface and ground water pollution originates in or is modified by the transportation system. The construction process is itself a source of water pollution, and the continuing operation of transportation facilities produces water pollution over many years. The U.S. Army Corps of Engineers has jurisdiction over navigable waterways in the United States, and must review and provide permits for transportation projects that will affect the character and content of flows on those waterways. Also, provisions of the Clean Water Act and regulations of the U.S. Fish and Wildlife Service can and often do limit the routing and design of transportation facilities.

In recent years it has become more common for transportation agencies to have to mitigate the impacts of their projects and programs on wetlands and waterways. When irrevocable intrusions into wetlands and waterways are necessary in order to complete transportation projects, the mitigation measures may take the form of replacement or rejuvenation of damaged wetlands or waterways located away from the project itself. Right now, for example, consideration is being given to expanding the runways at San Francisco International Airport by fill-ing in several hundred acres of the San Francisco Bay. To mitigate the effects of this proposed project, some are proposing that several thousand acres of commercial salt ponds located elsewhere on the Bay be acquired and returned to their more natural historical character as marshlands providing habitats for a large number of local species of animals, fish, and birds, and stopping points for migrating species as well. Some environmentalists portray this as a win-win proposition for the Bay Area, but the transportation agency is reluctant to accept responsibility for major wetlands restoration projects away from its own facilities, and some environmentalists continue to oppose intrusion into the Bay by the transportation agency even if the marshlands would be restored in a compensatory project. These situations are becoming ever more typical in transportation planning. Regional transportation planning methods must be improved so that we more effectively integrate concerns for water quality into the siting and design of transportation projects. This requires basic and applied research on the relationships between transportation systems and water quality, and it also requires planning processes that recognize the environmental significance of the impacts of transportation systems on water quality.

Biodiversity

The impact of transportation investments on biodiversity is emerging as a major concern of environmental organizations that monitor transportation programs and participate in public debates over transportation planning and programming. Highways, ports, airports, and rail transit lines can impact biodiversity by, for example, fragmenting habitats, placing barriers between sheltered habitats and sources of food and water, placing barriers in the way of normal animal or insect migration routes, or polluting local water courses. In the United States, there is currently no formal statutory or regulatory requirement to address biodiversity in the regional transportation planning process, but the issue of species habitats is addressed at the level of project planning because it is one of the critical components of an Environmental Impact Statement (EIS). The decision to address biodiversity at the project level can vary greatly with the scale and location of the project and with knowledge of local conditions.

A survey of state highway and transportation departments revealed that in twenty-one of the thirty-two responding states, the issue of biodiversity was raised during highway development processes. While the issue

was raised in a general sense because of the concerns of environmental groups and citizens' associations, in a few instances it resulted in contention over specific species at specific locations. Only four states reported in this survey that they had conducted scientific studies of the impacts on biodiversity of particular transportation projects, and three others described decisions made about highway location or transportation agency investments in planting or grading specifically to support biodiversity (Herbstritt and Marble, 1996). Progress has been made in the development of tools and techniques for assessing the potential impacts of transportation facilities on biodiversity. In particular, West Virginia, Pennsylvania, and Maine have all developed approaches, which vary considerably from qualitative assessments to more quantitative data collection tools (Bardman, 1997).

What role should considerations of biodiversity play in transportation planning at the regional level? While evaluations of alternative routes or project designs do take place as part of the Environmental Impact Review of specific projects, it would seem that in an environmentally responsible regional transportation planning process, the protection of areas of special ecological significance and habitats of endangered or highly valued species should be among the key considerations entering into the earliest stages of regional network analysis and into the formulation of basic alternative transportation system designs. I would project that considerations of biodiversity and habitat protection will become increasingly important in the regional transportation planning process. Government requirements and planning regulations should require the protection of threatened species and recognition of the significance of biodiversity in the development of metropolitan transportation plans. State and regional transportation planning agencies and major international transport research institutes should take the lead in developing methods and procedures for the inclusion of biodiversity considerations in regional transportation planning.

THE DEVELOPMENT OF APPROPRIATE TECHNICAL CAPACITY

The development of metropolitan transportation plans is a data-intensive activity that employs relatively standardized models to estimate traffic flows and their environmental consequences under alternative growth scenarios and for alternative proposed mixes of transportation improvements. Analytical requirements placed on the planning should be reflective of reasonable expectations regarding the ability of standard methods to provide an accurate picture of the travel and environmental consequences of alternative future urban development and transportation strategies. The capabilities of some of the most widely used mathematical modeling packages are disappointingly shallow. A major lawsuit, for example, was brought by a consortium of environmental groups in the San Francisco Bay area, challenging the adequacy of the regional transportation plan and suggesting that the plan should not be found to conform to the requirements of air quality laws because the quality of the Metropolitan Transportation Commission's estimates of the pollution reductions of alternative transportation control measures did not enable the agency to confidently implement some measures in its own plan (Garrett and Wachs, 1996). A committee of the Transportation Research Board examined the capability of current models based on existing databases to estimate the effects on air quality—and specifically on air quality conformity analyses—of transportation control measures and of new highways that are proposed to accommodate projected growth in population and travel. The committee's pessimistic conclusions stated:

> After examining the considerable literature on the relationships among transportation investment, travel demand, and land use as well as the current state of the art in modeling emissions, travel demand, and land use, the committee finds that the analytical methods in use are inadequate for addressing the regulatory requirements. The accuracy implied by the interim conformity regulations issued by the EPA, in particular, exceeds current modeling capabilities. The net differences in emission levels between the build and no-build scenarios are typically smaller than the error terms of the models. Modeled estimates are imprecise and limited in their account of changes in traffic flow characteristics, trip making, and land use attributable to transportation investments. The current regulatory requirements demand a level of analytic precision beyond the current state of the art in modeling. (Transportation Research Board, 1995, p. 5)

In part, the limitations of the models currently in use can be traced to the inability of data collection methods and theories to determine causal relationships between land use patterns, transportation facilities, travel volumes, and the production of pollutants. Beyond this, many mod-

els in widespread use have not been updated for years and have often been employed inappropriately by inexperienced staff members. The committee expressed the judgment that in most instances adding highway capacity to alleviate congestion would have beneficial effects on air quality; it acknowledged, however, that there were significant differences of opinion with respect to this question, and that results could differ from case to case, depending upon geographic conditions and particular contexts. Nevertheless, the committee's judgment was tentative, and it acknowledged that the models currently in widespread use are often inadequate to make this determination with confidence (Transportation Research Board, 1997, p. 8).

Since that report was issued, there have been a number of efforts to strengthen relevant modeling capabilities, and Howett (1999) recently stated that the models in use have shown substantial improvement over the past couple of years. A new "emissions factor" model is coming into use, and on a much broader scale the U.S. Department of Transportation has initiated a "Travel Model Improvement Program" (TMIP) to upgrade over five to seven years the capabilities of models generally used at MPOs for integrated land use/travel demand/air quality analyses. Still, there continues to be enormous variability among metropolitan areas and among the consulting firms that they retain in land use, transportation, and air quality modeling capabilities. Many smaller regional planning agencies lack the capability to conduct the sophisticated analyses that are increasingly being required as the basis of conformity determinations. Because critical estimates of the travel outcomes and conformity implications of alternative land use and transportation plans require rather sophisticated mathematical modeling, and regional planning organizations are extremely uneven in their ability to perform such analysis, it is appropriate to develop, package, and disseminate advanced software packages that would permit planning agencies to conduct appropriate and accurate forecasting as part of the regional transport and environmental planning process.

THE RELATIONSHIP BETWEEN TRANSPORTATION AND URBAN FORM

Until 1835, when public transport was introduced in many cities, virtually everyone resided within walking distance of his or her workplace. By the beginning of the twentieth century, transportation had evolved rapidly from horse-carts to omnibuses to street railways, which allowed cities to expand dramatically. Still, cities were crowded, dirty, dense, congested places. The first national conference on City Planning and the Problems of Congestion, held in Washington in 1909, featured many speeches in which leading thinkers of the day insisted that the disease, poverty, darkness, and vice of the industrial city were caused by the scourge of high-density living, and that it was the job of urban transportation planners to build public transit routes to outlying areas for the explicit purpose of lowering density.

Mary Kingsbury Simkhovich, the only woman to address this conference, urged that new immigrants to New York City be whisked to low-density suburbs before they had a chance to be destroyed by the urban densities and their accompanying vices and diseases. Subways to new outlying communities were urged, combined with low flat fares, so that low-income people could afford to live at low density at the edge in order to avoid the pitfalls of inner-city living.

The long-term trend has been toward increased motorization and steadily lower densities, and today there is enormous disagreement over the consequences of that trend and whether policymakers should attempt to reverse it. Scholars who examine trends in travel, congestion, and urban form are sharply divided over the consequences of increased motorization and decentralization.

Despite the fact that it was conventional wisdom early in this century that subways and streetcars would lead to lower density and encourage suburbanization, and that was seen as a good thing, it has now become conventional wisdom (Calthorpe, 1993; Newman and Kenworthy, 1989) that increasing decentralization, the steady lowering of densities of both residential and commercial activities, and the continued increase in reliance on automobiles for travel for all purposes are inherently unhealthful, and that they constitute a major problem for transportation policy-makers and political leaders. Adherents of this view argue that lower-density automobile-oriented communities are causing increased congestion, slower travel times, poorer air quality, and greater consumption of energy resources. It is of particular concern that decentralization is interpreted to be the cause of spatial mismatches in employment. The urban poor, primarily members of racial and ethnic minority groups who have relatively low levels of technical skill and own automobiles at lower rates than richer and whiter components of the popula-

tion, are believed by many to have decreasing access to employment opportunities, which increasingly occur at low densities at the urban fringe, away from public transit, and far from where they live (Kain, 1968).

These scholars and policy-makers believe that the solutions to such urban ills require intervention in order to change these trends. They urge more vigorous use of land use controls to consciously increase residential and commercial densities in the vicinity of transit routes, and more investment in public transportation for the purpose of expanding rail and bus networks to reach a larger proportion of the suburban population. Also part of the solution to members of this camp are increased restrictions on automobiles in the form of higher taxes and parking charges and greater introduction of traffic calming and automobile-free areas (Newman and Kenworthy, 1989).

Another school of thought, however, vigorously disagrees with this increasingly conventional liberal argument and prescription for improvement. Members of this school argue that decentralization is itself the most obvious solution to urban congestion and not a part of the problem. They counter claims of increasing congestion by showing that peak hour travel times among North American commuters are remaining roughly constant, in some cities decreasing over time, and in others increasing slightly but nowhere dramatically (Gordon, Richardson, and Jun, 1991). This occurs because people leave congested central cities and commute from suburban homes to suburban jobs at much higher speeds on relatively less congested suburban roads. It also occurs because increasingly flexible work hours and greater use of computers and telecommuting enable more and more workers to gradually adjust to spreading urban areas by traveling at a wider variety of times and places that avoid congestion and disperse travel volumes. Proponents of this position argue that attempting to concentrate populations near transit would be futile, that it would fail for lack of an adequate market of commuters seeking such environments, and that to the extent that it might succeed, it would probably worsen traffic congestion by increasingly concentrating trip ends in time and space. They point to technological changes in vehicles that have dramatically reduced air pollution and increased fuel efficiency, and argue that we need not change urban form to eliminate these unpleasant byproducts of increasing motorization. In fact, they argue that changing conditions in the labor market and increasing reliance on telecommunications technology systematically weaken the connection between urban form and transportation (Giuliano, 1995).

Research is needed to clarify our collective understanding of the consequences of changing urban densities and of alternative distributions of activities in space. The automobile, telephone, radio, computer, and other forms of information processing have all facilitated suburbanization, and densities have been lowered to levels well below those that were envisioned by the planners in the early twentieth century. Neotraditionalists would like to increase densities to the point that public transit might again be viable and mixed-use communities might again be sustainable, though certainly not to the overbearing levels typical of the central city of 1850 to 1900. In fact, the lower densities sought by planners in 1910 were actually higher than the higher densities sought by planners today, as we continue to seek some golden mean consisting of sufficient density to create a stimulating and diverse urban environment in which public transit is a viable transportation option, while not so dense as to cause crowding, traffic congestion, and various forms of contagion. We don't really know what this golden mean is; nor do we fully understand the travel and environmental consequences of developments of different types and densities.

Empirically, it would appear that by increasing the density of residential and commercial activities in an urban area, we do indeed reduce the number of daily automobile trips per household, as people rely more upon transit and walking and other modes. Over a reasonable range of densities, a doubling of residential density can yield something like a 15 percent reduction in daily trip generation per household. But while doubling the number of households reduces the number of trips per household, it increases the number of households per square kilometer, so that total travel increases. Downtown New York produces far more vehicle trips per unit of area than does any low-density suburb. Yet many planners and urban theorists urge us to densify our communities in order to have lower travel rates per household, while tolerating higher congestion levels per square kilometer because of the larger number of households.

On the other hand, some other analysts argue that the best way to reduce traffic congestion in our communities is to reduce density. If a community has only six or eight dwelling units per acre, it obviously will produce fewer trips per acre than one that has twenty or thirty dwelling units per acre. So to improve the quality of community life, it could be argued that we should build at lower densities. It is argued that people don't want to live at New York densities, and we should build many more low- and moderate-density suburbs in order to allow larger numbers of people to live in less traffic-impacted communities, even though the consequence of this is to cover a larger proportion of the land area with lower-density communities, and thus to undoubtedly encourage more travel in total, though less per unit of area.

Which approach is better? While the neotraditionalists argue for higher-density clusters of transit-oriented development, their critics insist that most people like less congested communities and prefer low-density suburbs, which in any case do not really increase the generation of traffic. While a spirited debate takes place over these issues, I foresee a future with more variety—in fact, more of each of these choices, and many others—as both inevitable and desirable. Efforts are under way in some communities to reduce densities in order to reduce traffic congestion, while other communities, most notably Portland, Oregon, are constructing urban limit lines to force higher densities within certain boundaries in order to reduce traffic congestion. A critically important contribution to urban research would be the monitoring, modeling, and evaluation of a wide variety of such experiments for the purpose of learning more systematically about the relationships between urban densities, travel, and resource consumption.

While these debates take place, North America has more registered cars per licensed driver than any other society in the world, and we also spend more public money on transit per rider served than any country in the world. And while we are probably the most mobile society that has ever existed, our communities include many people who lack health care or employment or educational opportunities because of a lack of access. The inability of some elderly people to get to health care, the inability of many people to search for work beyond their neighborhoods because of the cost of time and travel, and the frustration that parents face because they have to drive their children everywhere may well be more important social issues than the physical forms of our cities or the levels of traffic congestion on particular streets. While these issues are not entirely independent of urban form, they are not exclusively the result of urban form, either, and solutions to them can be found in many approaches and strategies that reach beyond urban form.

Suppose it is now 2050, and we are looking back from that vantage point on the year 2000, asking what changes occurred between 2000 and 2050 in the relationship be-tween travel and urban form. I believe that in the year 2050, land use and transportation planners will not con-sider the relationship between urban form and travel to be as significant as we do today. Over time those issues will have become increasingly uncoupled from one an-other. The debates we are having now might be an inter-esting footnote in a history book, but looking back on these current debates and on the communities that we are creating from the perspective of fifty years in the future, I believe that we will hardly remember that this debate ever took place.

Because the population will have continued to grow between 2000 and 2050, metropolitan areas in the future will be much larger than they are today. Much of Califor-nia, for example, will be significantly more urban than it is today. The differentiation between urban, suburban, and rural, however, will be far less pronounced than it is today. In general we will have larger urban regions, but they will be less intensely developed than they are today —except for nodes of dense development that exist for cultural reasons to satisfy the demands of people who choose to live and work at higher densities. But the qual-ity of life, the nature of daily living, and the travel pat-terns of families will be more varied from household to household than they are today, and less associated with population density or land use density. Because we will communicate with one another in so many ways over so many parts of the world, we will find ourselves work-ing at different hours, and the work different people do will be fundamentally different in time and location; we will work at home and in offices and in factories, and we will work in the morning or afternoon or evening. We will travel at a wider variety of times, and our travel will be more broadly distributed in space and time, and that dispersion of travel in both space and time will be one of the major factors that will allow us to manage an enor-mous increase in travel volumes without an enormous in-crease in congestion.

Some today believe that we cannot sustain increased motorization without choking ourselves on congestion and air pollution, and others believe that urban decen-tralization is quite sustainable because we will travel at a wider variety of times and places and, even though we will travel more, we will not all be competing for limited transportation capacity at the same hours of the day. Greater transportation capacity through automation of transport facilities and the use of communications tech-

nology will also contribute to broader ranges of choices in how we communicate with one another and how we travel to and interact with one another. Less air pollution and greater energy efficiency may well continue to be more a result of changes in technology than a result of changes in urban form, and in the future people may not even associate those issues with urban form; nor will they remember that anyone ever did. Urban form may well be less of a determinant of travel and human interaction than ever. If this proves to be the case, it will allow for a greater variety of urban forms as a reflection of tastes and historical differences among cities and differences in climate and in industrial mixes rather than transporta-tion technologies. Whether compact or dispersed urban form, or many urban forms, can provide environmentally sustainable futures is one of the most interesting and one of the most researchable questions for analysis by mem-bers of our intellectual community.

REFERENCES

Bardman, C. A. 1997. "Applicability of Biodiversity Impact Assessment Methodologies to Transportation Proj-ects." *Transportation Research Record,* no. 1601: 35–41.

Calthorpe, P. 1993. *The Next American Metropolis: Ecology, Community, and the American Dream.* New York: Princeton Architectural Press.

Frazier, J. A., and J. L. Henneman. 1996. "Project-Level Air Quality Assessment Actions: Interrelating Con-formity with National Environmental Policy Act Proc-ess." *Transportation Research Record,* no. 1520: 3–10.

Garrett, M., and M. Wachs. 1996. *Transportation Planning on Trial: The Clean Air Act and Travel Forecasting.* Thousand Oaks, Calif.: SAGE Publications.

Giuliano, G. 1995. "The Weakening Transportation–Land Use Connection." *Access,* no. 6: 3–11.

Gordon, P., H. Richardson, and J. J. Jun. 1991. "The Com-muting Paradox: Evidence from the Top Twenty." *Journal of the American Planning Association* 57: 416–420.

Herbstritt, R. L., and A. D. Marble. 1996. "Current State of Biodiversity Impact Analysis in State Transportation Agencies." *Transportation Research Record,* no. 1559: 51–63.

Howett, A. M. 1999. "Implementing the Clean Air Act: Implications for Governance, Presentation to the Ex-ecutive Committee of the Transportation Research Board." Washington, D.C., January 12.

Kain, J. F. 1968. "Housing Segregation, Negro Employment, and Metropolitan Decentralization." *Quarterly Jour-nal of Economics* 82: 175–197.

Newman, P., and J. Kenworthy. 1989. *Cities and Automobile Dependence: An International Sourcebook.* Aldershot: Gower.

Sawyer, R. F., and J. H. Johnson. 1995. "Diesel Emissions and Control Technology." In *Diesel Exhaust: A Critical Analysis of Emissions, Exposure, and Health Effects,* 67–81. Cambridge, Mass.: Health Effects Institute.

Transportation Research Board. 1995. *Expanding Metropolitan Highways: Implications for Air Quality and Energy Use.* Special Report 245.

Transportation Research Board. 1997. *Toward A Sustainable Future: Addressing the Long-Term Effects of Motor Vehicle Transportation on Climate and Ecology.* Special Report 251.

CHAPTER THREE

Research Issues Regarding Societal Change and Transport

An Update

Genevieve Giuliano
and Andy Gillespie

In "Research Issues Regarding Societal Change and Transport" (Giuliano and Gillespie, 1997), we acknowledged that "societal change" is a very broad term, and hence we would focus on selected issues that we felt were common to the U.S. and Europe and held significant promise for research. We further argued that societal change must be viewed in the context of observed changes in urban spatial patterns. We noted that decentralization and dispersion of both population and employment had been occurring in the U.S. throughout the twentieth century, and that similar trends were now apparent in Europe. Coincident with this shift in spatial form is the rise in car ownership and use, an increase in distance traveled, greater dispersion of travel patterns, and a decline in the use of public transport and non-motorized modes.

We identified two sets of issues that were promising for international cooperative research. Household- or population-related issues included growth of the elderly population, foreign immigration, decline of the nuclear family, income disparities, and changes related to information and telecommunications technology (ICT). Workplace-related issues focused on changes associated with ICT. These included growth of the contingent workforce, location patterns and spatial organization of firms, and telecommuting and other forms of flexible work. We identified ICT-related changes in the workplace as the most

promising area of research, because of the fundamental nature of these changes and their expected long-term effects on travel, spatial form, and lifestyle.

Our task here is to revisit our earlier findings and conclusions based on our own research and on the papers we heard at the SCAST conference. We follow a similar format: we begin with trends in urban form and travel patterns, and then discuss our set of issues in the context of conference discussions.

URBAN SPATIAL AND TRAVEL TRENDS

Research on changing spatial patterns shows that the trends we identified continue to be clear. The 2000 U.S. Census suggests that decentralization is continuing. There are some cities (e.g., New York and Chicago) that have seen a positive change in population, but this appears to be due to large increases in immigration or to job growth in the hi-tech sector. Annual employment data show that decentralization of employment continues. The U.S. Bureau of Economic Analysis Regional Economic Information System (REIS) provides county-level annual employment data.[1] The series begins in 1969. Figure 3.1 gives annual private-sector employment growth rates for counties located in metropolitan areas. Large metropolitan core coun-

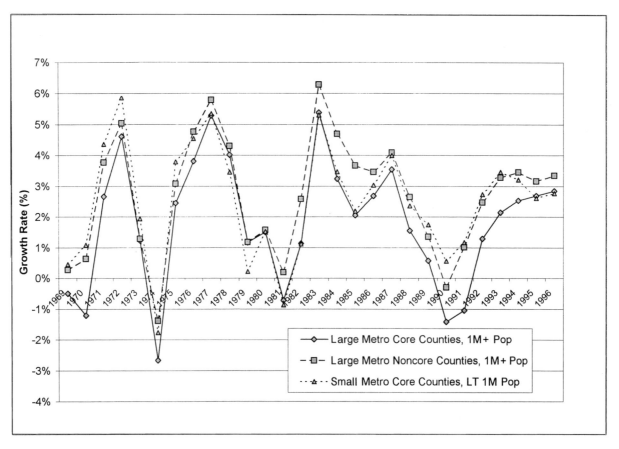

Figure 3.1 Average Annual Private Sector Job Growth

ties are those located in a metropolitan area of 1 million or more population (CMSA) and containing the central city. Large metropolitan non-core counties are the remaining counties making up the CMSA. Small metropolitan core counties are those with less than 1 million population. Typically these core counties include the central city, as smaller metropolitan areas are usually made up of just one county. Spatial boundaries are constant throughout the series. Several observations may be drawn from Figure 3.1. First, the large metropolitan core counties have the lowest growth rates throughout the series. The peaks occur in 1972, 1976, 1982, and 1987. Only in 1982 is the growth rate for large metropolitan core counties about the same as that for small metropolitan core counties. The troughs (1973, 1980, 1990) show the same pattern. Second, the small metro area counties grew fastest from 1969 through 1974, but after that year the large metro area non-core counties "catch up" and have the highest growth rate until 1986. The positions of non-core large and small core metro areas are similar for the remainder of the series. Third, the large metro core counties have consistently lower growth rates through the most recent period (1986–1996), with particularly large differences in the early 1990s. Figure 3.1 suggests that employment decentralization is continuing, with growth shifting to non-core areas of the largest metropolitan areas, as well as to the smaller metropolitan areas.

Using the same county-level private employment data, Gordon, Richardson, and Yu (1998) compared growth rates of metropolitan areas with non-metropolitan areas.

Table 3.1   Employment Change by Type of Local Authority District, 1984–91, 1991–96, in FTEs

	1984–1991	1991–1996
Greater London		
Inner London	–8.9%	1.7%
Outer London	–4.0%	–1.2%
Metropolitan districts		
Principal metropolitan cities	–2.9%	–5.5%
Other metropolitan districts	–0.7%	0.5%
Non-metropolitan districts		
Large non-metropolitan cities	–2.4%	–2.5%
Small non-metropolitan cities	–0.1%	–1.2%
Industrial districts	1.9%	–0.9%
New towns	9.8%	7.4%
Resort, port, retirement districts	6.5%	0.2%
Urban and mixed urban-rural districts	6.1%	8.8%
Remoter mainly rural districts	8.4%	6.9%

Source: 1984–91, Atkins et al., 1996; 1991–96, NOMIS.

They found higher rates for non-metro areas for 1969–1977 and 1988–1994, but not for 1977–1988. The authors conclude that while the trend away from core counties is clear, whether job growth will shift more to smaller metro areas or to non-metro areas remains to be determined.

Gillespie's summary of employment trends in Britain between 1984 and 1996 tells a similar story (Gillespie, 1999). Using annual total employment data adjusted to FTEs, Gillespie observes a net redistribution of employment in the southern half of the country from London to its neighboring regions. The northern regions of the country are continuing to lose employment. Employment growth patterns at the local district level permit investigation of urban-rural shifts. The classification scheme includes eleven types of district, ranging from the Inner London Boroughs grouping at one extreme to remote, mainly rural districts at the other. Results are given for 1984–1991 and 1991–1996 in Table 3.1.

For the 1984–1991 period, employment declines are most severe in Greater London, the principal metropolitan cities, and the large non-metropolitan cities. Employment growth is concentrated at the opposite end of the urban spectrum, in new towns and less urbanized districts. In 1991–1996 these patterns persist, with the notable exception of Inner London. Contrary to the expectations of some recent "urban renaissance" celebrants (see Amin and Graham, 1997), there has been no generalized reversal in the economic performance of cities, and the urban-rural gap continues to widen, as illustrated in Figure 3.2

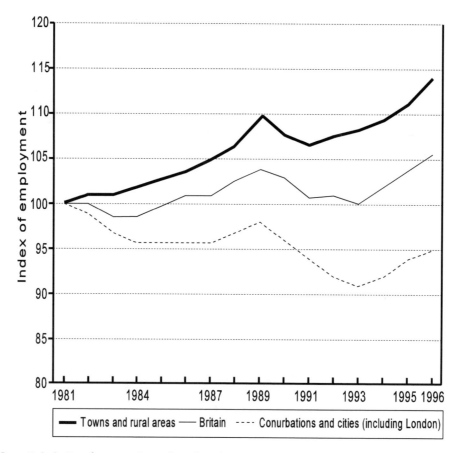

Figure 3.2   Great Britain Employment Growth, Indexed

(Turok and Edge, 1999). Most observers view the recent increase in London's employment as a short-term interruption of the longer-run trend of decline.

A continuation of travel trends documented in our 1997 paper is also evident. In the U.S., the 1995 Nationwide Personal Transportation Survey data show that car ownership and use continue to increase, although there are indications that car ownership is at last reaching saturation. The ratios of household vehicles to workers and vehicles to drivers have remained stable at about one to one. The average distance for the journey to work has increased from 10.6 miles in 1990 to 11.6 miles in 1995. Average travel time has increased less than distance, suggesting that dispersion of commute patterns is continuing. The transit mode share continues to decline, with just 1.8 percent of all person trips using public transit—only slightly less than the share for bicycles.

The interplay of spatial form and commuting patterns may be illustrated with the 1995 journey-to-work data for Greater London shown in Table 3.2 (Giuliano, 1998). Three-quarters of those who work in Central London use transit, but three-quarters of those who work in the outlying areas use private vehicles. As employment continues to decentralize, the shift away from public transit will continue.

Decentralization and the related increase in private vehicle use was well recognized by conference presenters. The vast majority of papers saw these trends as the fundamental sustainability problem. In addition to the now well-known critiques of urban sprawl on the basis of en-

Table 3.2   Journey to Work Mode Choice by Job Location, Greater London, 1995

Job location	Mode Share (%)				Number of workers
	priv. veh.	bus/rail	walk/bike	other	
Central London	17	75	5	2	972,000
Rest of inner London	40	41	16	2	738,000
Outer London	67	18	13	1	1,315,000
Rest of region	76	7	17	1	4,030,000

vironmental degradation and inefficient use of resources (examples include the papers by Adams and by Gudmunsson), other papers identified additional concerns. Henderson interprets the explosive growth of Atlanta as an effort by the "growth coalition" to suppress racial conflict. Frank sees sprawl and auto dependence as a public health problem, while the papers by O'Brien and Engwicht and by Sandqvist express concern that auto dependence reduces the freedom of children and their opportunity to experience the outdoors. A different point of view was expressed by Webber, who argues that the benefits of mobility are enormous; hence the sustainability problem is how to reduce externalities while maintaining mobility.

There was little disagreement on overall trends; however, there was disagreement on the meaning of these trends, whether they have slowed in Europe as a result of policy efforts, and to what extent it may be possible to reverse them. Tillberg questioned whether living in the countryside in fact leads to more travel; as non-work travel becomes a larger share of total travel, locating closer to non-work activities may economize on travel. Spence conducted an analysis of wasteful commuting in British cities, and his results were consistent with previous U.S. work: spatial structure explains only a small part of the journey to work. Gertz reported that the average commute distance increased while the jobs-housing balance increased in Stuttgart.

One of the classic examples of trend reversal is Freiberg. Throgmorton and Ryan reported that the city's commitment to public transit and strict land use planning has resulted in a decline in the auto mode share from 60 percent in 1976 to 43 percent in 1996. However, Freiberg's economic conditions have apparently suffered. High land costs and tax rates have discouraged economic growth, and the city has one of the highest unemployment rates in the country. Maat's discussion of problems encountered in the new towns of the Netherlands illustrates the difficulties of trying to increase development densities and maintain public transit use when market demand is moving in the other direction.

SOCIETAL CHANGE

Our earlier paper discussed several aspects of societal change meriting comparative research. We identified ICT-related changes in the workplace as the most promising area of research, because of the fundamental nature of these changes and their expected long-term effects on travel, spatial form, and lifestyle. The conference papers, our continuing research, and industry trends reinforce this conclusion. Castells discussed the broad trends associated with ICT and emphasized the fundamental nature of changes being generated, including changes in the nature of work (in his terms from "generic labor" to "self-programmable labor"), the growing importance of information transport, the increasingly rapid pace of economic activity, and the seemingly incompatible growth of supranational organizations but simultaneous decentralization and fragmentation of institutions.

Hojer's paper presents a conceptual model for how ICT might be used to reduce physical transport. Gertz identified similar strategies. The critical question, however, is, what is the potential for such strategies? Gould and Golob suggest that e-commerce may make it possible to utilize local neighborhood shops as goods-pickup locations. This would free the traveler from making multiple stops for everyday consumption (hence reducing person travel), but would likely generate more delivery traffic (thereby increasing goods movement).

Our observation of economic trends in the 1990s indicates that economic restructuring continues, as the service sector expands and restructures in response to changing technology. In previous decades, ICT allowed the relocation of back office activities to suburban and rural areas. Now the relocation process spans the globe, as ICT becomes better, faster, and cheaper. The 1990s saw the emergence of telemediated services and more forms of mobile working. Telemediation (through telephone call centers) has permitted the physical link between production and consumption of many services (e.g., banking, insurance, mortgage loans) to be severed, which in turn results in the spatial reorganization of such activities to sites where labor is available and costs are low.[2] Trends toward the "mobile office" are evident, as larger numbers of workers are either in the field or traveling between offices. In Britain, the practice of "hot-desking"[3] is increasing; in the U.S., home-based and car-based work is increasing. As we write this chapter, the new hybrid cell phone/Internet communicator/organizer is coming to market, making these mobile forms of work even more possible and convenient.

Although we could document little change in the overall patterns of population and employment growth since our 1997 paper, the one area where change was very large was in the ICT industry itself. Gould and Golob note that revenues from consumer e-commerce increased from $4 billion in 1997 to an estimated $20 billion in 1999. Growth of the Internet is simply astounding. According to Golob (2000), the World Wide Web was established in 1991, and by 1992 there were 1 million Internet host sites. The number of sites increased to 5.8 million in 1995 and jumped to 56 million by 1999. With the growth of the Internet has come a rapid expansion of Web-based activities. One of the fastest-growing activities is business-to-business e-commerce, with transactions estimated at $92 billion in 1998. Clearly these shifts in the way business is conducted will have significant impacts.

Our interest in the workplace-related impacts of ICT brings us back to spatial form. The implications of ICT for travel and urban form are difficult to exaggerate. ICT is an enabling technology that reduces location and transport constraints. It allows firms to seek comparative advantage on a global scale, while at the same time it reduces the benefits of agglomeration. ICT also permits flexible work patterns. To the extent that flexible work allows for a greater separation of home and work (or allows home and work to be coincident with one another), the link between home and work, a major constraint in household location choice, is weakened. If preferences for the amenities of small towns or the countryside dominate, population will shift in that direction. Trends of the past few decades are clear: population and employment have decentralized not only in the U.S. and Europe, but throughout the world.

It bears noting that the networked economy that has emerged is critically dependent upon low-cost, high-quality transport. The rapid increase in air travel is indicative. Figure 3.3 shows annual passenger miles for private vehicles and domestic commercial air carrier service for the U.S.[4] Note that the rate of increase is much greater for air travel from 1975 through 1990. Hesse documented the increase in freight traffic in Europe and the increasing share of surface freight moved by truck. He explains these changes as a consequence of economic restructuring. In the U.S., the substitution of person trips for package trips resulting from the rise in e-commerce is an increasingly important issue in urban transport. If efficient transport is indeed critical to the new information-based economy, efforts to restrict travel, or to substantially increase its cost, will be politically difficult to accomplish.

CONCLUSIONS

We concluded our earlier paper by stating that the most promising area for joint research is that of workplace related changes. Our reasons were as follows:

- Little is known about the nature of these changes or how they are affecting location and travel patterns.
- As ICT continues to grow and evolve, these changes are likely to increase in intensity.
- Effects of ICT are fundamental; they affect many dimensions of the work experience.
- The nature and outcomes of these changes will be mediated by local context, hence making joint, comparative study particularly fruitful.

Our own continued research on workplace-related changes, as well as much of the research presented at the SCAST conference, confirms our earlier conclusion. In the past few years, the effects of ICT have become increasingly evident. Access to the Internet has increased

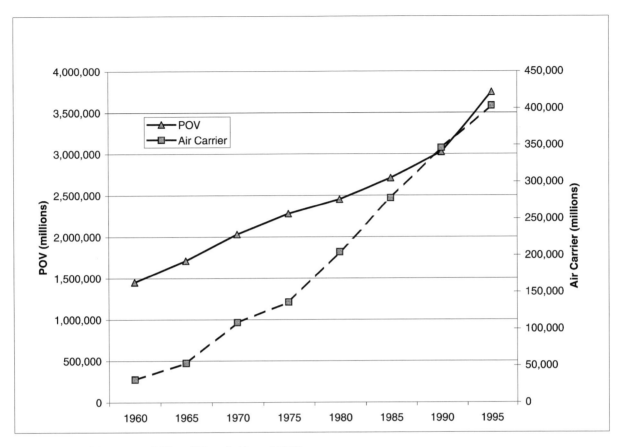

Figure 3.3   U.S. Passenger Miles of Travel, Air and POV

many-fold. Restructuring of major industry sectors continues unabated, and the interconnectedness of the global space economy continues to increase. This new world provides great spatial and temporal flexibility, which is redefining the nature of work and workplace. The friction of space is so attenuated that Couclelis and others are conceptualizing accessibility in new ways. This is a rich area for comparative research.

NOTES

1. The 1997 REIS data files were provided by Peter Gordon and Harry Richardson.

2. Giuliano's personal experience is illustrative. Her mortgage was refinanced in 1998 without a single visit to an office. The entire transaction was conducted via telephone, express mail, and e-mail. Although the mortgage loan company had an address, the loan processor worked mainly from his house. The property appraiser worked under contract and operated her business from her home.

3. In "hot-desking," one is not allocated a specific desk, but uses any desk that is available.

4. Bureau of Transportation Statistics, 1996. Air travel includes commercial air carrier service only. Private vehicle includes cars, taxi, motorcycle, and other two-axle, four-tire vehicles, and therefore includes some for-hire travel.

REFERENCES

Amin, A., and S. Graham. 1997. "The Ordinary City." *Transactions of the Institute of British Geographers* 22: 411–429.

Atkins, D., T. Champion, M. Coombes, D. Dorling, and R. Woodward. 1996. "Urban Trends in England: Latest Evidence from the 1991 Census." Urban Research Report, DOE. London: HMSO.

Bureau of Transportation Statistics. 1996. "National Transportation Statistics 1997." Report DOT-VNTSC-BTS-96-4. Washington, D.C.: U.S. Department of Transportation, Bureau of Transportation Statistics, Table 1-7.

Gillespie, A. 1999. "The Changing Employment Geography of Britain." In M Breheny, ed., *The People: Where Will They Work?* London: Town and Country Planning Association.

Giuliano, G. 1998. "Urban Travel Patterns." In B. Hoyle and R. Knowles, eds., *Modern Transport Geography*, 2nd ed. Chichester: John Wiley & Sons.

Giuliano, G., and A. Gillespie. 1997. "Research Issues Regarding Societal Change and Transport." *Journal of Transport Geography* 5, no. 3: 165–176.

Golob, T. 2000. "TravelBehavior.Com: Activity Approaches to Model the Effects of Information Technology on Personal Travel Behavior." Resource Paper for IATBR 2000. Irvine, Calif.: Institute of Transportation Studies, University of California, Irvine.

Gordon, P., H. Richardson, and G. Yu. 1998. "Metropolitan and Non-Metropolitan Employment Trends in the U.S.: Recent Evidence and Implications." *Urban Studies* 35, no. 7: 1037–1057.

Turok, I., and N. Edge. 1999. *The Jobs Gap in Britain's Cities: Employment Loss and Labour Market Consequences.* Bristol: Policy Press, for the Joseph Rowntree Foundation.

CHAPTER FOUR

Sustainable Transport

Michael Wegener
and David L. Greene

INTRODUCTION

Since the beginning of human history, transport has been an engine of growth. Without transport there would have been neither trade nor cities. The Roman Empire was built on efficient highways, the wealth of Venice on Mediterranean trade routes. Without high-seas navigation, there would not have been a British Empire, and America would have remained undiscovered. Without railways, the American West would not have been settled, and Pittsburgh and Manchester would have remained country towns. Modern economies could not work without the goods and services provided by cars, trucks, high-speed trains, and airplanes. Transport has determined the location of industries and cities and the prosperity of regions, and around this there has developed a body of theory in the spatial sciences that equates accessibility and mobility with economic and social progress.

Near the end of the twentieth century, however, the belief in the desirability of perpetual growth in mobility and transport started to fade. In many countries, highway accessibility is so ubiquitous that transport cost has almost disappeared as a location factor for industry. In metropolitan areas, the myth that rising travel demand will ever be satisfied by more highways has been shattered by reappearing congestion. People have realized

that the car has brought not only freedom of movement but also declining city centers, urban sprawl, air pollution, traffic noise, and accidents. It has become obvious that in the face of finite fossil fuel resources and the need to reduce greenhouse gas emissions, the use of gasoline cannot increase forever. There is now broad agreement that present trends in transport are not sustainable.

This experience is common to both North America and Europe, even though their geographical and institutional contexts and policy approaches differ. North American cities are more spread out and have population densities about half as high as those in European cities. Car ownership and mileage per vehicle are much higher there than in Europe, and North Americans use twice as much energy per capita for transport than Europeans. For intercity travel, air transport is much more important in North America than in Europe, whereas intercity passenger rail flourishes in Europe and is almost nonexistent in North America. Urban public transport in Europe is vastly superior to that in North America, except in the largest U.S. and Canadian cities. On the other hand, North America is more advanced than most European countries with respect to clean air legislation.

SUSTAINABILITY AND TRANSPORT

According to the World Commission on Environment and Development (1987), sustainable development is development that meets the needs of the present without compromising the ability of future generations to meet their own needs. Daly (1991) defines sustainable development as satisfying three basic conditions: (1) its rates of use of renewable resources do not exceed their rates of regeneration; (2) its rates of use of non-renewable resources do not exceed the rate at which sustainable renewable substitutes are developed; and (3) its rates of pollution emission do not exceed the assimilative capacity of the environment.

However, there is agreement that a merely environmental definition of sustainability is not sufficient. Pearce and Warford (1993) define sustainability in economic terms, as holding the sum of capital stocks of manufactured, human, and environmental assets at least constant to ensure that future generations have the same capability to develop as current generations. In addition, equity among today's nations and individuals is regarded as integral to the definition of sustainability. The Charter of European Cities and Towns Towards Sustainability (the "Aalborg Charter") (1994) states that the objective of sustainable development is "to achieve social justice, sustainable economies, and environmental sustainability."

Environmental Impacts, Resource Consumption, and Institutional Failures

The continued growth of motorized transport poses three threats to sustainability: (1) degradation of the local and global environment (excessive rates of consumption of renewable resources), (2) consumption of non-renewable resources that appear to be essential to the quality of life of future generations, and (3) other institutional failures that exacerbate the previous two problems (e.g., traffic congestion, which increases pollution and fuel consumption but also generates demand for more infrastructure and its consequences, such as further urbanization of land and still more vehicle travel). The idea that all resources must become renewable may seem impossible, but perhaps it is not. Resources are defined by human systems, especially by technology. Thus it is possible to conceive of a balance between technological advancement and changes in institutions, on the one hand, and con-

sumption of resources, on the other. Resources that are exhaustible if technology and institutions are held constant may become renewable if the necessary changes are made at the appropriate rates. This view incorporates the third category of threats by requiring human institutions, such as markets and governments, to reinforce rather than oppose sustainability.

Many, though not all, of transport's environmental impacts are the result of its prodigious use of energy in the form of fossil fuels. Incomplete combustion of petroleum fuels in internal combustion engines produces a variety of pollutants, including carbon monoxide, volatile organic compounds, various oxides of nitrogen (precursors to ozone pollution), and fine particulates. Transport, especially road vehicles, is a major source of all of these pollutants. In Europe, 47 percent of oxides of nitrogen, 39 percent of volatile organic compounds, and 66 percent of carbon monoxide emissions are produced by motor vehicles (Walsh, 1993); corresponding percentages for the U.S. are 45 percent, 37 percent, and 78 percent. Volatile organic compounds from transport also include a variety of toxic air pollutants, including benzene, formaldehyde, cyanide, and dioxin. In the U.S., road dust alone accounts for more than 40 percent of fine particulate emissions. In many countries, fine particulate emissions from motor vehicles include lead from octane-enhancing gasoline additives.

In addition to local and regional pollution, transport emissions contribute to international environmental problems. Oxides of nitrogen and sulfur contribute to acid rain, harming both terrestrial and aquatic ecosystems. Complete combustion of fossil fuels produces carbon dioxide and water vapor. Carbon dioxide is a greenhouse gas that has been accumulating in the atmosphere since the beginning of the industrial revolution. Transport produces about one-sixth of the world's anthropogenic carbon dioxide emissions. The Intergovernmental Panel on Climate Change (IPCC, 1995) estimates that carbon dioxide concentrations in the atmosphere have increased by 30 percent since 1750, due to fossil fuel use, land use changes, and agricultural activities, and that this has caused an increase in global mean temperature of 0.3° to 0.6°C since the late nineteenth century. Continued use of fossil fuels could easily double atmospheric carbon dioxide concentrations over pre-industrial levels by the end of the twenty-first century, producing an average warming of several degrees and as yet still poorly understood but potentially serious environmental impacts (IPCC, 1996).

Transport is also a major consumer of two critical "exhaustible" resources: oil and land. Transport is both the predominant and the fastest-growing consumer of oil; indeed, it is the only sector in which oil demand has been growing over the past twenty years (World Energy Council, 1995). At present, transport is highly dependent on petroleum. In the United States, 95 percent of the energy requirements for transport are supplied by fuels derived from petroleum; for the entire OECD, the corresponding figure is 99 percent (IEA, 1993). At the current rate of world oil use (25 billion barrels per year), the world's proven oil reserves of 1 trillion barrels would be exhausted after 40 years. But the U.S. Geological Survey (Masters et al., 1994) estimates that another 0.7 trillion barrels have yet to be discovered, raising the ratio of reserves to production to 70 years. At present, however, only 34 percent of oil in the ground is extracted. If this could be raised to 50 percent, and recovery rates have risen historically at 0.2 percent per year (Porter, 1995), then 2.8 trillion barrels could be recovered, enough for 110 years. If technology could be advanced to refine heavy and extra heavy oils, there would be 3.4 trillion barrels of "petroleum," lasting for 140 years. And this says nothing of the more than 14 trillion barrels of oil equivalent of shale oil and bitumen that are known to exist.

However, oil demand will not remain constant at present rates of consumption. The U.S. Department of Energy expects world oil demand to grow at about 2 percent per year over the next two decades. At that rate, the 1 trillion barrels of proven reserve would last only 30 rather than 40 years, and the speculative 3.4 trillion barrels of oil and "oil-like" resources only 65 years. However, as oil becomes increasingly difficult to find, produce, and refine, its cost will increase, and this will slow down or even reverse the growth of demand. So the threat to sustainability is not so much "running out" of oil, but the increasing costs, environmental and economic, of its continued use.

Equity Issues

Intergenerational equity is a central element of sustainability: if there were no future generations, climate change and finite resources would not be issues. However, most environmental impacts of transport also have a strong social or distributional dimension with respect to the current generation. The people who cause environmental effects are usually not those most affected. High-income households typically own more cars and make more and longer trips, and so use more energy and generate more greenhouse gas emissions than low-income households. But they also tend to live in quiet suburbs with clean air, whereas low-income households frequently live along noisy and polluted thoroughfares, yet without compensation from the suburban commuters who use these highways. The members of NIMBY groups established to keep new highways away from neighborhoods usually are among the heaviest users of urban highways elsewhere. The majority of victims of intraurban road accidents in Europe are pedestrians or cyclists, especially children, the most defenseless participants in urban transport. But some of the policies to mitigate negative environmental effects of transport may also have undesirable distributional effects, in particular transport demand management policies involving pricing, as they may restrict certain forms of mobility (even more than today) to affluent people.

Another equity dimension of environmental impacts of transport is global. Around the world, motorized transport, its appetite for fossil fuels, and the ensuing environmental impacts are growing rapidly. In 1950, 90 percent of the world's 50 million cars and trucks could be found in North America and Europe (Davis and McFarlin, 1996). Today the world motor vehicle fleet exceeds 670 million, and it is expected to rise to 813 million by 2010 (World Resources Institute, 1996). Globally expanding motorized transport has made urban air pollution a worldwide problem (Faiz, 1993); it generates one-sixth of the world's greenhouse gas emissions, is transforming landscapes from Indonesia to Brazil, and is placing increasing pressure on the world's oil supplies.

Most of these impacts originate in the developed countries (Whitelegg, 1993). Vehicles from developed countries still make up 65 percent of the world total (though motorization in developing countries is growing rapidly, at 5.7 percent per year, more than twice as fast as in the U.S., at 2.5 percent per year). If one accepts that the poorer countries of the world have a right to demand an increase in transport and mobility to develop their economy, and if at the same time there is agreement that total consumption of fossil fuels and emissions of greenhouse gases by transport must be reduced, the reductions must be largest in the richer countries of the Northern Hemisphere, who today are the heaviest users of transport energy. It is therefore urgent that the most developed regions of the world take the leadership in responding to transport's environmental and energy problems.

GEOGRAPHICAL AND INSTITUTIONAL CONTEXTS AND PUBLIC POLICIES

There are significant differences between the transport systems in North America and Europe and the perceptions of transport sustainability and the policies applied to achieve it. These differences can be explained by different geographical and institutional contexts.

North America

The primary factors distinguishing North American from European transport systems are the far lower density of development in North America, which favors a high level of mobility and disadvantages fixed-route modes, and the absolute supremacy of highway transport, which is reflected by the predominance of highway infrastructure. These factors appear to be self-reinforcing. In U.S. cities, where population densities are generally less than twenty-five persons per hectare, vehicle usage and fuel consumption rates per capita range from double to quadruple those of European cities, with densities of twenty-five to seventy-five persons per hectare (Newman and Kenworthy, 1989). This has led to the absence of significant alternatives to highway travel and the perception of highway travel as an economic necessity. The latter, in turn, is partly responsible for the unwillingness to heavily tax motor fuel.

The North American response to growing travel demand and its associated environmental problems, especially in the United States, has been to expand highway capacity and regulate environmental impacts. The strong dependence of environmental impacts on the technologies of engines, vehicles, and fuels has reinforced the predominantly regulatory approach. Regulatory policies not only have been more politically palatable, they have also worked reasonably well.

In the United States, motor vehicle emissions were first regulated by federal standards in the late 1960s. Since then, allowable emissions rates have been periodically lowered as significant numbers of metropolitan areas continued to fail national ambient air quality standards established by the Clean Air Act of 1970. The Clean Air Act Amendments of 1990 not only tightened emissions standards for motor vehicles, but required new standards for locomotives and expanded the standards for aircraft. The

1990 law also broke new ground in demanding cleaner fuels as well as cleaner vehicles (U.S. DOT/BTS, 1996). Reformulated gasoline, designed to reduce both conventional and toxic pollutant emissions for old as well as new cars, was introduced in December 1994.

Noise pollution has been addressed via regulations setting noise limits for vehicles, mitigation measures such as noise barriers to separate residential areas from major arterials, and land use controls. The Noise Control Act of 1972 gave the Environmental Protection Agency the authority to regulate emissions from major sources of noise, including transport. The federal government generally has no authority to regulate land use to control noise pollution. Land use controls are at the discretion of state and local governments, and a wide variety of approaches have been used. Noise barriers are widely used to reduce the impacts of road noise.

U.S. transportation produces 1.6 trillion metric tons of carbon dioxide each year, about one-third of the U.S. total. Because the transport sector is nearly totally dependent on fossil fuels, the chief means of reducing greenhouse gas emissions from transport in the past has been improving energy efficiency. The federal Automotive Fuel Economy Standards, also known as the CAFE standards, have resulted in a doubling of new vehicle fuel efficiency over 1974 levels. These improvements have been achieved by a combination of technological improvements and operating efficiency gains (Greene, 1996). Fuel taxes have not been used as a policy instrument to reduce fuel consumption in the U.S., although they have in Canada. In general, efficiency improvements have translated effectively into reduced fuel consumption and lower carbon dioxide emissions. The "take-back" or "rebound effect," in which efficiency improvements lead to lower fuel costs, lower transport costs, and hence increased transportation activity, appears to be small in magnitude (e.g., Greene, 1992). This partially explains the emphasis of U.S. policy on technology-based solutions to reduce greenhouse gas emissions.

Though less than a perfect solution, the predominantly regulatory approaches taken in North America have been effective in reducing emissions, constraining energy use, and improving environmental quality. But this does not mean that market-based policies have no future in North America. Under the provisions of the 1990 Clean Air Act Amendments, market-based strategies for emissions reduction have been applied successfully in the utility sector, creating renewed interest in possible applications in transport. Moreover, there is a growing understanding that the problems of congestion and land use impacts cannot be indefinitely solved by expanding capacity (NRC, 1994). At the same time, advancing electronic and information technologies are removing the technical barriers to externality pricing of transport. The key question for the future will be whether the public will accept major changes in transport pricing.

Europe

Europe has one-sixth the area of North America (3.2 million square kilometers) but one-third more population (370 million). This results in an average population density four times as high as that of the U.S. Average population density in European cities is three or four times as high as in their North American counterparts.

These numbers already explain many of the differences in the development of the transport system in Europe. Europeans have only 30 percent of the highway kilometers per capita that North Americans have and travel only 40 percent of the total distance per capita per year that North Americans do (Orfeuil and Bovy, 1993). For intercity travel in Europe, medium distances prevail, with the effect that railways were not squeezed to death by the competition between the car and the plane as in North America. European cities have always been compact enough to support efficient public transport systems, with the result that Europeans buy 40 percent fewer cars per capita than North Americans and use public transport and walking and cycling for one out of two urban trips (Orfeuil and Bovy, 1993).

The second explanatory factor is a difference in political tradition and culture between Europe and North America (cf. Barde and Button, 1990). The European countries would probably not have the efficient long-distance rail and urban public transport systems they have today if there had not been a common understanding that the provision of collective transport is a responsibility of the government and requires and deserves to be publicly subsidized.

Despite the differences in levels, the trends are similar on both sides of the Atlantic. Between 1970 and 1993, Europeans nearly doubled their daily mobility, from 16.5 km per capita per day to 31.5 km, and all of the extra mobility occurred by car, which grew by 120 percent, compared with 24 percent by rail. And there seems to be no end to the growth in mobility. It is estimated that car ownership in Germany will rise to 570 cars per 1,000 population by 2020.

The relationship of Europeans with their cars is similar to that of North Americans, but perhaps they take them less for granted. There are pro-automobile coalitions of regional lobbyists, the car and construction industries, and powerful automobile clubs, but there are now equally influential anti-car alliances of environmentalists, critical transport planners, and concerned citizen groups. Moreover, environmental damage is far more visible in a high-density spatial setting. The aesthetic devastation of century-old city structures by elevated highways, as in Rome, Stockholm, or Cologne, now generally seen as irrecoverable losses of cultural heritage, would probably have gone unnoticed in younger, nondescript urban environments. The deaths of forests in central Europe, attributed to air pollution, might not have caused the same impassioned debate in North America, with its abundance of forests. Traffic noise is more of a problem in densely built-up old towns with narrow streets than in dispersed metropolitan areas built for the automobile.

These differences in context paved the way for the adoption of environment-oriented transport policies in most European countries. The achievements of the Netherlands in introducing programs that limit cars in residential areas, extensive networks of cycling lanes, and pedestrianized neighborhood shopping centers are well known. Germany has introduced area-wide speed limits of 30 km/h in many residential neighborhoods. All European countries have fuel prices between three and four times as high as those in the United States or Canada. There is also a long tradition of public transport–oriented land use planning (Greiving and Kemper, 1999). The Netherlands, Britain, and the Nordic countries pioneered public transport–oriented new towns centered around commuter rail stations. In general, countries with the strongest interventionist planning systems have been the most successful in containing dispersal.

Compared with these largely successful policies at the local level, regulatory policies at the national and European levels have lagged behind those of North America. Emission-control legislation and technical innovations such as catalytic converters and unleaded gasoline were introduced in Europe decades later than in the U.S., and even then half-heartedly, with many exemptions in favor of the car industry and owners of existing cars. Environmental legislation in the European Union is governed by the principle of the lowest common denominator, which means that more advanced countries have been forced to accept lower standards for the sake of "coherence" and "harmonization" between member states. Despite the Union's proclaimed environmental policy, environmental concerns regularly have to take a back seat if they conflict with the primary goals of economic growth and competitiveness (cf. Whitelegg, 1993). Several European governments have pledged to substantially reduce emissions of carbon dioxide, but to date not even a stabilization of present emission levels seems realistic.

The policy context of sustainable transport in Europe, therefore, is in contrast to the U.S. and Canada, characterized by successful policies at the local level and retarded response by governments at the national and European levels.

Opportunities for Joint Research

The need for global responses to environmental and resource problems increases the value of sharing insights and understanding, and in some cases (such as greenhouse gas emissions) requires coordinating policy measures. Joint European–North American research therefore has special value. First, it contributes to a common understanding of the sustainability problem by increasing awareness of research being conducted and best practice being applied on the other side of the Atlantic, as well as through the exchange of ideas that is the essence of collaborative research. Second, the differences in geography and culture create an excellent experimental design from which to learn about transport systems and public policies.

The archetypical project type of cross-cultural research is the comparative case study. Comparative case studies steer a middle course between individual case studies and cross-sectional statistical analyses. Individual case studies offer the possibility of in-depth analysis of one particular city, region, state, or country in which both qualitative and quantitative information can be processed. The weakness of individual case studies is that their results can rarely be generalized or be transferred to another study area. Cross-sectional statistical analyses are representative for their sampled domain, but because they have to rely on available "hard" data, almost never offer the same level of insight and detail as case studies, in particular where "soft" information such as attitudinal or policy information is important.

Comparative case studies, however, if well designed, can take advantage of the benefits of either research method without suffering from their weaknesses. Comparative case studies typically involve a mix of "hard" information that can be compared and is collected uniformly in all case study areas, and "soft" information that takes into account the special situation in each case study region. To be successful, however, comparative case studies require a large amount of preparation and coordination with respect to selection of case study areas and guidelines for data collection and interviews. In the case of transnational comparative case studies, these difficulties are even greater.

Besides comparative case studies, other types of cross-cultural research projects are possible. One type of project might bring together people who complement each other by their particular specialization, either in substantive knowledge or in methodological expertise. The latter is particularly true for modeling studies, in which state-of-the-art skills are typically developed only over a long time period.

Pooling of resources may be a third reason for transatlantic cooperation where a critical mass of research effort may be required to achieve a particular result. This may require a change in policy in cases where national funding agencies in the past have been restricted to awarding research funds exclusively to research teams from their own country.

Previous contacts in the SCAST initiative have already led to a number of transatlantic research collaborations, some of which are reflected in this volume. The Berkeley SCAST conference has produced further promising ideas for future transatlantic research. It is hoped that it will be possible to implement them in the not too distant future.

References

Barde, J.-P., and K. Button, eds. 1990. *Transport and the Environment: Six Case Studies.* London: Earthscan Publications.

Charter of European Cities and Towns Towards Sustainability ("Aalborg Charter"). 1994. Signed by 80 cities and towns, 27 May 1994 in Aalborg, Denmark.

Daly, H. E. 1991. *Steady State Economics.* Washington, D.C.: Island Press.

Davis, S. C., and D. McFarlin. 1996. *Transportation Energy*

Data Book, Edition 16. ORNL-6898, Oak Ridge National Laboratory, Oak Ridge, Tenn.

Faiz, A. 1993. "Automotive Emissions in Developing Countries: Relative Implications for Global Warming, Acidification and Urban Air Quality." *Transportation Research A* 27, no. 3: 167–186.

Greene, D. 1992. "Vehicle Use and Fuel Economy: How Big Is the 'Rebound' Effect?" *The Energy Journal* 13, no. 1: 117–143.

Greene, D. 1996. *Transportation and Energy.* Lansdowne, Va.: Eno Transportation Foundation.

Greiving, S., and R. Kemper. 1999. *Integration of Transport and Land Use Policies: State of the Art.* Deliverable 2b of EU project TRANSLAND. Berichte aus dem Institut für Raumplanung 46. Institute of Spatial Planning, University of Dortmund.

Intergovernmental Panel on Climate Change (IPCC). 1995. *Climate Change 1995: The Science of Climate Change.* Second Assessment Report of the IPCC. Cambridge: Cambridge University Press.

Intergovernmental Panel on Climate Change (IPCC). 1996. *Climate Change 1995: Impacts, Adaptations and Mitigation of Climate Change.* Second Assessment Report of the IPCC. Cambridge: Cambridge University Press.

International Energy Agency (IEA). 1993. *Cars and Climate Change.* Paris: Organisation for Economic Co-operation and Development.

Masters, C. D., E. D. Attanasi, and D. H. Root. 1994. *World Petroleum Assessment and Analysis.* Reston, Va.: U.S. Geological Survey, National Center.

National Research Council (NRC). 1994. *Curbing Gridlock.* Special Report 242. Washington, D.C.: Transportation Research Board, National Academy Press.

Newman, P. W. G., and J. R. Kenworthy. 1989. *Cities and Automobile Dependence.* Aldershot: Gower Technical.

Orfeuil, J.-P., and P. Bovy. 1993. "European Mobility Is Different: A Global Perspective." In *A Billion Trips a Day: Tradition and Transition in European Travel Patterns,* ed. I. Salomon, P. Bovy, and J.-P. Orfeuil, 13–19. Dordrecht: Kluwer Academic Publishers.

Pearce, D. W., and J. J. Warford. 1993. *World Without End: Economics, Environment, and Sustainable Development.* Washington, D.C.: The International Bank for Reconstruction and Development.

Porter, E. 1995. "Are We Running Out of Oil?" Discussion Paper #081. American Petroleum Institute, Washington, D.C., December.

U.S. Department of Transportation, Bureau of Transportation Statistics (U.S. DOT/BTS). 1996. *Transportation Statistics Annual Report 1996.* Washington, D.C.

Walsh, M. 1993. "Motor Vehicle Trends and Their Implications for Global Warming." In *Transport Policy and Global Warming,* 69–93. Paris: European Conference of Ministers of Transport.

Whitelegg, J. 1993. *Transport for a Sustainable Future: The Case of Europe.* London: Belhaven Press.

World Commission on Environment and Development. 1987. *Our Common Future.* Brundtland Report. Oxford: Oxford University Press.

World Energy Council. 1995. "Global Transport Sector Energy Demand towards 2020." Statoil Energy Studies Program, Project 3, Working Group D, presented at the World Energy Council Congress, Tokyo, October 8–13.

World Resources Institute. 1996. *World Resources: A Guide to the Global Environment.* Oxford: Oxford University Press.

CHAPTER FIVE

Information and Communication Technologies and Transport

Heli A. Koski

INTRODUCTION

Information and communications technology (ICT) plays a prominent role in transport.[1] The ICT market continually launches new applications that provide not only support to traffic monitoring and control, transport logistics, and transport infrastructure management,[2] but also a means of transporting information instead of people. These ICT applications have the potential to increase the efficiency of transport networks, and therefore reduce negative externalities in transportation—for instance pollution and congestion—and increase the quality of transport networks and services. However, their actual impacts on the transport sector and the sustainable use of transportation networks are unknown. Some research has been undertaken along these lines (see, e.g., Pendyala et al., 1991; Nijkamp et al., 1996; Emmerink et al., 1998), but there are still many unresolved questions that need further investigation. This chapter will highlight some important research topics that future European-American research collaboration might address (see also Hodge and Koski, 1997).

IMPACT OF ICT ON TRAVEL BEHAVIOR

Whether or not ICT enhances sustainable transport is basically a question of whether ICT and transport are substitutes for or complements of each other, or whether the use of ICT decreases or increases industrial transport (transport of goods), commercial transport (business transport of people), and residential transport (work/leisure trips).

Industrial Transport

The order of magnitude of industrial travel essentially depends on the degree of globalization of international trade. Therefore, a critical question deserving further attention is the degree of globalization that will be due to the use of ICT. In particular, increasing commercial use of the Internet worldwide raises a question about the potential impacts of electronic commerce on the transport of goods. Now that any firm can use the Internet to extend its market area beyond its national boundaries with low marketing costs, an increasing number of firms may begin supplying products to wider geographical areas, transporting smaller sales batches, and conducting more trips for transporting products to customers, thus creating additional capacity burdens for cross-border traffic and for local, national, and international transportation networks. It will be important to carefully assess the likelihood of the realization of different industrial transport scenarios (e.g., the demand for international and national transport networks) and to evaluate appropriate incentives that will help motivate individual actors to strive for sustainability and maximum global welfare instead of national or individual goals.

Commercial Transport

Another important question is whether ICT will replace or complement commercial transport. ICT applications such as e-mail and videoconferencing technologies may take the place of face-to-face meetings and therefore reduce the length of individual business trips. On the other hand, the literature provides some evidence that even though videoconferencing may decrease the length of individual business trips, it may increase the total length of conference trips, as a higher number of people attend meetings when videoconference facilities are used (see, e.g., Mokhtarian, 1988). Moreover, ICT markets provide fancy new portable ICT applications, such as mobile phones and laptops, which may increase commercial mobility. Also, some researchers have pointed out that individuals' enjoyment of travel (or the status value of business trips) and their need for face-to-face interaction with other people may further hinder the use of ICT in place of business-related trips.

Perhaps one of the most important questions here is, what kinds of incentives will motivate firms to trade their business trips for ICT, and how reasonable is it from the global or sustainable point of view to provide these incentives to firms? It would be useful to collaboratively and comparatively evaluate such issues from both the European and the American perspective.

Residential Transport

ICT may affect more than the transport behavior of firms. It may also influence work and leisure trips or residential transport.[3] A number of topics have not yet been sufficiently covered by previous research (see, e.g., Salomon, 1986; Mokhtarian, 1997). What, for instance, will be the impact on residential transport of widespread use of mobile technologies? Who adopts new ICT applications, and how does ICT change their commuting patterns? Does the adoption of ICT in public transport affect individuals' choice of transport mode?

In addition to its direct impacts, there are various indirect ways that ICT may further affect transport behavior. First, ICT has various impacts on industrial organization (see, e.g., Gillespie, 1993). For instance, it provides more organizational flexibility, and it may facilitate decentralization of business units and enhance collaboration between firms. Second, the widespread use of ICT can change spatial form, for instance, in terms of distribution of activities. Third, ICT may have impacts on transport networks, their organization and management in urban areas, as well as on the national and international networks. All of these changes may further influence residential, commercial, and industrial transportation behavior, and thus have substantial impact on the aggregate transport demand.

The previous empirical explorations and case studies have provided controversial conclusions about whether ICT will replace or complement transport in its different modes. A brief overview of the statistical trends in the ICT markets and in the transport sectors of the industrial countries shows that that aggregate demand for ICT has increased tremendously during the past decade (see, e.g., OECD, 1999). Similarly, transport volumes—both passenger transport and freight transport—have risen steadily during the past twenty-five years (European Conference of Ministers of Transport, 1998). Moreover, there has been a clear upward trend in the number of kilometers traveled by private cars, whereas the increase in the number of passenger-kilometers traveled by buses and trains has not been as marked. These aggregate trends suggest that ICT use may not promote sustainable transport. However, these two increasing trends may also be occurring, for instance, as a result of an increase in the (world) population. More micro-level evidence about the influence of ICT use on individual and firm-level transport behavior is necessary.

INNOVATION AND DIFFUSION OF ICT SUPPORTING SUSTAINABLE TRANSPORT

Both the development and the widespread adoption of ICT technologies that promote sustainable transport behavior are necessary for the benefits in terms of sustainability to be realized. Therefore, it is essential to understand the dynamics of the ICT markets. In particular, it would be of utmost importance to explore questions such as: What incentives are needed for firms to do research and develop ICT applications that support sustainable transport? Are individuals, firms, and public organizations willing to adopt such innovations, and what is their willingness to pay for them?

Some previous theoretical and empirical studies sug-

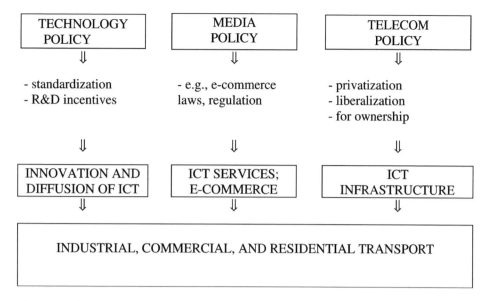

Figure 5.1   The Role of Communication Policy

gest that a coincident presence of network externalities and uncertainties may create inefficiencies in the ICT market and have clear implications for the diffusion speed of ICT (see, e.g., Economides and Himmelberg, 1995; Koski, 1999). These factors stress the importance of standards and the compatibility of new ICT applications (see, e.g., Farrell and Saloner, 1985).[4] It would be important to evaluate the kinds of problems that incompatibility of ICT applications between countries—especially between the U.S. and Europe—may create in the use of national and international transport and communications infrastructures.

The previous literature also suggests that the diffusion patterns of information technology between different regions are highly uneven (see, e.g., Hägerstrand, 1967; Antonelli, 1990; Kamann and Nijkamp, 1990). Another set of problems may then be created by the divergent diffusion rates of ICT within and among countries. This gives rise to a question about the impacts on the transport sector of such difference.

THE ROLE OF COMMUNICATIONS POLICY

Government investments have played a crucial role in the development of information infrastructure, and thus in the diffusion of ICT. Even though it has been widely

agreed that the private sector should assume the main responsibility for developing and maintaining information and communications infrastructures, network markets exhibit various inefficiencies that stress the importance of government intervention.[5] We distinguish here three critical interrelated types of ICT policy that may influence sustainable transport behavior: media policy, technology policy, and telecommunications policy (see Figure 5.1).

Technology policy exercised by the government ultimately creates the rules and legal framework for innovative behavior (see, e.g., Mowery, 1995). It also determines the degree of standardization of ICT products and gives incentives (or disincentives) to firms to do research and development. It may thus significantly influence firms' and individuals' incentives to generate and adopt ICT applications that promote sustainable transport. Media policy—for instance, laws and regulations concerning electronic commerce and the Internet—affects primarily the provision of ICT services and the development of electronic commerce. Telecommunications policy determines factors such as the degree of privatization and liberalization of the telecommunications markets and the allowance of foreign ownership, which have further implications for information infrastructure development and ICT use. Media and telecommunications policy may thus have a substantial impact on the degree of globalization of the trade, and therefore on industrial and commercial transport.

It is not clear how efficient the different types of communications policy are and how their efficiency varies with divergent techno-economic conditions. Important questions that could be collaboratively investigated by U.S. and European researchers include the following: What are the best policy approaches for supporting the development, supply, and diffusion of ICT that promotes sustainable transport? In what market areas and under what conditions is there a need for international policy, and when is a national policy approach the most suitable? A strategic assessment of the impacts and efficiency of different types of policy is needed.

Notes

1. E-mail and mobile communications systems make telecommuting possible, and videoconferencing allows business meetings to be held that do not require the transportation of people. Maybe one of the most important ICT applications that will affect both business and residential commuters in the near future is third-generation mobile communications, which enable efficient transmission of data, picture, and voice independently of users' locations.

2. For instance, telemonitoring is used for speed control, and route guidance systems give information on traffic flows and congestion delays on the roads. ICT applications such as intelligent transport systems tracking or tracing vehicles and EDI coordinating production and logistics are used to improve transport logistics. ICT is used in transport infrastructure management to ease customs clearance and in such tasks as maintaining and developing the transport infrastructure by information and decision support systems.

3. For example, people may telecommute, or they may work at home at least part of the week. They may shop via the Internet. ICT may be used in public transportation in ways that will provide more reliability, safety, and ease of use and thus increase individuals' use of public transportation. ICT used in traffic monitoring and control may result in changes in transport behavior.

4. The development of mobile phones provides an example of incompatibility of ICT between the United States and Europe: European GSM telephones cannot be used in the United States and vice versa.

5. Inefficiencies in network markets arise, for instance, from the presence of network externalities and monopolistic powers. Some other forms of market imperfections that may emerge on the ICT market are asymmetric information and multiple sources of uncertainties.

References

Antonelli, C. 1990. "Induced Adoption and Externalities in the Regional Diffusion of Information Technology." *Regional Studies* 24: 31–40.

Economides, N., and C. Himmelberg. 1995. "Critical Mass and Network Evolution in Telecommunications." In Gerard Brock, ed., *Toward a Competitive Telecommunications Industry: Selected Papers from the 1994 Telecommunications Research Conference.* Hillsdale, N.J.: Lawrence Erlbaum Associates.

Emmerink, R. H. M., E. T. Verhoef, P. Nijkamp, and P. Rietveld. 1998. "Information Policy in Road Transport with Elastic Demand: Some Welfare Economic Considerations." *European Economic Review* 42: 71–95.

European Conference of Ministers of Transport. 1998. *Trends in the Transport Sector 1970–1996.* Paris: OECD Publications.

Farrell, J., and G. Saloner. 1985. "Standardisation, Compatibility and Innovation." *Rand Journal of Economics* 16: 70–83.

Gillespie, A. 1993. "Telematic and Its Implications for Industrial and Spatial Organization." *Regional Development Dialogue* 14: 138–150.

Hägerstrand, T. 1967. *Innovation Diffusion as a Spatial Process.* Chicago: University of Chicago Press.

Hodge, D., and H. Koski. 1997. "Information and Communication Technologies and Transportation: European-US Collaborative and Comparative Research Possibilities." *Journal of Transport Geography* 5: 191–197.

Kamann, D.-J. F., and P. Nijkamp. 1990. "Technogenesis: Origins and Diffusion in a Turbulent Environment." In N. Nakicenovic and A. Grübler, eds., *Diffusion of Technologies and Social Behavior.* Berlin: Springer-Verlag.

Koski, H. 1999. "The Installed Base Effect: Some Empirical Evidence from the Microcomputer Market." *The Economics of Innovation and New Technology* 8: 273–310.

Mokhtarian, P. 1988. "An Empirical Evaluation of the Travel Impacts of Teleconferencing." *Transportation Research* 22A: 283–289.

Mokhtarian, P. 1997. "The Transportation Impacts of Telecommuting: Recent Empirical Findings." In P. Stopher and M. Lee-Gosselin, eds., *Understanding Travel Behaviour in an Era of Change.* Oxford: Pergamon.

Mowery, D. 1995. "The Practice of Technology Policy." In P. Stoneman, ed., *Handbook of the Economics of Innovation and Technological Change,* 513–557. Oxford: Blackwell.

Nijkamp, P., G. Pepping, and D. Banister, eds. 1996. *Telematics and Transport Behavior.* Berlin: Springer-Verlag.

OECD. 1999. *Communications Outlook 1999.* Paris: OECD.

Pendyala, R. M., K. G. Goulias, and R. Kitamura. 1991. "Impact of Telecommuting on Spatial and Temporal Patterns of Household Travel." *Transportation* 1991: 383–409.

Salomon, I. 1986. "Telecommunications and Travel Relationships: A Review." *Transportation Research* 20A: 223–238.

CHAPTER SIX

Globalization and Transportation

Contradictions and Challenges

Donald G. Janelle
and Michel Beuthe

This chapter summarizes a previous statement (Janelle and Beuthe, 1997) on the role and significance of transportation as an agent of globalization. Transportation is largely ignored in research statements on globalization and the changing world economy. Much of that literature concentrates on the globalization of financial markets and of the information and communication sectors (e.g., Estabrooks, 1995; Castells, 1996). Even discussions of world trade, which address changing production and consumption patterns, mysteriously make only passing reference to transportation's importance (e.g., O'Brien, 1992; Ohmae, 1995).

Yet there is a mutual vulnerability of dependence that underlies both globalization and transportation. This vulnerability alone underscores the need for explicit study of these dependencies. At stake are issues of regional inequality in accessibility, political and technical problems in standardization for flexible and timely multimodal transport, the environmental consequences of integrating networked production and consumption systems, and territorial jurisdiction over governance of the transportation economy. Current patterns of globalization have drawn on vast improvements in information transfer. However, the temporal and spatial fragmentation of production processes under globalization are dependent on access to a broad range of multiple transport options, a situation that may be linked inextricably and dangerously to a market environment of cheap petroleum.

Manuel Castells describes a global economy as "an economy with the capacity to work as a unit in real time on a planetary scale" (Castells, 1996, 92). Clearly, transportation does not meet this precondition in a direct sense. Nonetheless, parallels between recent innovations in the supply of transport resources and some of the principal features of globalized economies make current transport resources acceptably adequate to the economic agents of globalization. At issue, however, is whether these transport practices are acceptable to broader expressions of public interests, such as regional and social equity, economic efficiency, and environmental quality.

Table 6.1 provides a summary of some of the most significant features of globalization and attempts to match them with the attributes of modern transport systems. This matching of transportation practices with the needs of globalization appears to be a mutually supportive alliance. However, attention is directed to related contradictions, both to the happiness of this alliance and to the broader objectives of achieving environmental sustainability in the transport sector. For each of these contradictions, there is a related challenge.

Table 6.1 Linkages between Economic Globalization and the Supply of Transportation Resources

Globalization	Transportation
• Reliance on out-sourcing, seeking favorable labor and resource advantages • Flexibility in resource access (regardless of distance)	• Longer and more customized transport linkages, often achieved through alliances across modes and across jurisdictions
• Need for secure and efficient transactions	• Standardized equipment and procedures that allow quick and secure transactions
• Just-in-time management of production and distribution processes • Zero inventory	• Greater sensitivity to the timing of connections, arrivals, and departures, and to the capacities of vehicles or carriage units • Speed of transactions, achieved largely through reductions in terminal transfer times
• Real-time information access and exchange	• Expanded reliance on communication and computer networks for scheduling and tracking
• The need to arrange for face-to-face meetings, often on short notice	• Increased frequency of public transport services and intensified use of private fleets of vehicles and executive aircraft
• Opportunities for economies of scope • Customized production runs	• Flexibility in modal choice and timing

Source: Adapted from Janelle and Beuthe, 1997.

CONTRADICTIONS AND CHALLENGES

Spatial Concentration

Globalization depends on diverse transportation and communication capabilities of significant scale and technical complexity. Correspondingly, the expense of implementing such systems limits their availability to very few places—mostly along high-density transport corridors linking major urban agglomerations. Dispersal to less central locations either does not occur or follows much later, after major centers have secured most of the development benefits. Thus, this focus on scale economies limits the distribution of flexible production to a narrow range of world cities and regions.

Yet, if we believe that globalization is a worthy enterprise, then the challenge is to broaden its geographical base and to dampen its geographical peaks.

Regional Inequalities

Transportation and communication hubs are traditionally the major beneficiaries of economic development. However, the enhancement of this favored position through contemporary processes of globalization magnifies concerns for equity in the distribution of opportunities elsewhere, particularly in smaller places and in regions that are peripheral to the main national and global centers. Globalization offers linkages to more remote places through its international division of labor. In some cases, however, this leads to a greater homogenization of local and regional economies, to vulnerabilities associated with economic dependence on distant locations, and to the economic insecurities of abandonment owing to rapid changes in demand or in competition from other locations.

Therefore, the challenge is to determine how a globalized political economy can ensure sufficient economic diversity within regions for them to hold even a minimally essential level of local control and security over their economic futures. Existing research fails to address the extent to which global-scale outsourcing exploits the economic disparities of the First and Third Worlds or to question the dependence of globalization on the perpetuation of such disparities.

Dispossession of Transport Options

In his classic essay *Energy and Equity,* Ivan Illich (1974) observed in the context of developing countries that energy-intensive and expensive new transport systems inevitably marginalized older but functional systems. In this sense, new transport options may pose barriers to accessibility for those who cannot afford to make use of the new system or who lack the technical skill or physical health to function in a new transport environment. Examples include the displacement of safe walking and cycling environments with the space-disruptive intrusions of automobiles, making walking and cycling unsafe. In many instances, the displacement of public bus and rail transport with private automobiles has followed quickly in the wake of automobilization.

The challenge in this case is to preserve functional transport options that are accessible to everyone.

Creating Distance

Globalization is often equated with bringing the world together, yet a principal outcome is the creation of distance. In essence, globalization intensifies the demand for transport by extending supply lines to support a more spatially extensive production and distribution system. As a consequence, goods and people move over greater distances. In addition, the customization of production and transport often requires more trips and the use of

smaller carriers, all of which intensify infrastructure and energy needs.

The challenge is to make sure that these practices do not increase the risks and cost of environmental degradation, and that they do not create barriers that thwart attempts to achieve equitable and environmentally sustainable transport practices.

The depth of these contradictions and the difficulty of the challenges are illustrated by three examples:

Example 1: Just-in-time (JIT). Just-in-time production and distribution systems are designed to minimize transshipment costs and delays, reduce warehousing, and allow more flexible routing and more spatially expansive regional access than bulk inland water and rail transport. As a consequence, however, JIT increases the accumulation of distance per unit of transport.

This poses the challenge of documenting the implications and possible externalities of JIT on traffic congestion, CO_2 emissions, and accident rates for commercial vehicles and automobiles.

Example 2: The geographical dispersal of transport demand. Much of the current growth in high-technology sectors is not limited to locations along bodies of water. Thus, interior locations in Europe and North America have benefited with job growth.

However, the accompanying logistical challenge is to find ways of meeting more geographically dispersed demands and the need for face-to-face communication while minimizing the elongation of low-density routings.

Example 3: Direct transport linkage. The increasing tendency of manufacturers to serve consumers directly negates many of the transportation benefits of more traditional hierarchically structured production and distribution systems. Replacing rail and barge systems with motor freight transport reflects the increasing demands for greater route flexibility and temporal responsiveness. The advent of electronic commerce is likely to magnify these demands and place additional pressures on transport systems.

These developments challenge us with contradictions of road congestion and less optimal use of extant bulk transport systems.

Control (Regulations, Standards, and Governance)

The dominant private-sector component of transportation and the dominant ethic of capitalist transport agents do not give priority to issues of equity, balanced use of all transport opportunities, or environmental impacts. Rather, issues of market share, market penetration, and return on investment are the more likely guiding principles. The issue of state intervention in the transportation sector is one of mixed signals. The environmental and equity implications of transport investment pressure governments toward greater regulation; however, dependence on private-sector transport and interest in international trade favors less state intervention. Yet Eric Sheppard (1996) observes "an extensive history of accepted state regulation, because of the extensive fixed capital infrastructure that most transportation and communications systems require . . . and because of the public-goods characteristic of their product (accessibility)."

The declining significance of state enterprises, laws, standards, and regulations as a means toward distributive justice is noted by Gary Teeple (1995) in his book *Globalization and the Decline of Social Reform*. Privatization and deregulation hold sway in the current round of globalization. So too in transportation, it seems, they have lessened state control over the space of flows that define the emerging globalized economy. Technologies, new organizational forms, and the fluidity of commerce (particularly electronic commerce) have simultaneously opened markets and reduced the significance of national borders for screening information and resource flows.

Acceptance of this reality poses the challenge of how best to design and implement regulatory regimes and governance practices to protect society from the downside effects of competition within the transport sector and to acknowledge critical public needs for safe environments and for equity across regions and transport modes.

One illustration of these difficulties is the issue of standards for multimodal transport. There are technical complexities in implementing multimodal standards. There are conflicts in the regulatory interests of diverse stakeholders over issues of licensing, subsidies, pricing, rebates, container sizes, and other practices. The reduced sovereignty of states transfers the task of finding solutions to these issues to broader regional alliances (such as NAFTA and the European Union).

The challenge will be for these and even broader alliances to achieve legal and institutional frameworks for creating cohesive networks that are sufficient for handling integrated global and regional transport requirements.

CONCLUSION

The *ultimate contradiction* is that the contradictions identified in this statement are themselves, at least in part, the product of transport agents. Transport agents play a leading role in pressuring governments for relaxation of trade barriers, encouraging policies that favor international investment, and discouraging regulatory controls regarding the social and environmental costs of transportation practices.

The ultimate challenge for any model of a sustainable transportation future is to recognize that global mobility impinges on both social and ecological domains. The model and its implementation plan must acknowledge the requirements of large regional and global economies, give priority to diminishing the unacceptable risks of environmental degradation and social inequity, and move toward a decoupling of development from transportation.

REFERENCES

Castells, Manuel. 1996. *The Information Age: Economy, Society and Culture.* Vol. 1: *The Rise of the Network Society.* Oxford: Blackwell.

Estabrooks, M. 1995. *Electronic Technology, Corporate Strategy and World Transformation.* Westport, Conn.: Qurom Books.

Illich, I. D. 1974. *Energy and Equity.* London: Calder & Boyars.

Janelle, D. G., and M. Beuthe. 1997. "Globalization and Research Issues in Transportation." *Journal of Transport Geography* 5: 199–206.

O'Brien, R. 1992. *Global Financial Integration: The End of*

Geography? New York: Council on Foreign Relations Press.

Ohmae, K. 1995. *The End of the Nation State: The Rise of Regional Economies.* New York: The Free Press.

Sheppard, E. 1996. From Comments at the National Science Foundation—European Science Foundation Workshop on Transportation Research, Strasbourg, France, 7 October.

Teeple, G. 1995. *Globalization and the Decline of Social Reform.* Toronto: Garamond Press.

CHAPTER SEVEN

Institutional Dimensions of Sustainable Transport

Piet Rietveld

INTRODUCTION

Countries differ substantially in the procedures they use to deal with transport problems. These differences in approach may be related to factors such as differences in natural geographical conditions (e.g., low-density countries tend to have different transport problems than do high-density countries) and economic development (e.g., high-income countries usually place greater emphasis on environmental aspects of transport than do low-income countries). Another basic reason for differences among countries is that their institutional arrangements may be different. Some differences observed between Europe and the United States are listed in Table 7.1.

The roles assumed by the public and the private sector appear to vary considerably between countries in general, and between Europe and the U.S. in particular. In this chapter we will analyze these differences in more detail. We will further elaborate a theme already addressed in Stough and Rietveld 1997.

INSTITUTIONS AND TRANSACTION COSTS

Institutions can be defined as humanly devised constraints that shape human interaction (cf. North, 1990).

A related definition describes institutions as social rule structures. These rule structures can be both formal and informal. An obvious example of a formal institution is a property right specified by legislation. In addition, there are many informal institutions, both within organizations and between organizations, such as management practices, governance, and rules about who takes the initiative in large projects such as infrastructure provision. The essence of institutions is that they structure incentives in human exchange.

It should be emphasized that institutions as defined here are not identical to organizations. Organizations are groups of actors with a common interest or goal; institutions structure the relationships between actors and organizations. Sometimes organizations and institutions are closely linked. For example, "higher education" is the institution corresponding to the university organization. A similar pair is "governance" and "government."

The link between institutions and organizations can be illustrated as in Figure 7.1. On the one hand, institutions lead to the emergence of organizations. For example, international agreements between governments of countries are often a necessary condition for the existence of international firms. On the other hand, the behavior of

Table 7.1 Differences in Institutional Arrangements between Europe and the USA

	Europe	USA
emphasis on regulation transport markets	taxation	regulation
stimulation of public transport	high	low
role of rail for passenger transport	high	low
deregulation of transport markets	late	early
land use policies	strong	limited

organizations may result in changes in institutions. For example, pressure groups may have the objective of reinforcing the place of environmental property rights in laws or constitutions.

What is the basic reason for the existence of institutions? An important reason for their necessity is that they provide a basic level of justice and equity in societies. Issues of justice are not their only raison d'être, however. Coase (1937) and North (1990) have called attention to the economic importance of institutions. The key term is "transaction costs." Transactions in an economy lead to costs such as the costs of measuring valuable attributes of what is exchanged, and the costs of enforcing agreement. An example of the first type of costs concerns the determination of product quality, an issue relevant in every transport-related decision made by an individual (safety standards of roads used, quality of car bought, guaranteed service of public transport, etc.). The second type of transaction cost is equally obvious: in each transaction there is a possibility of cheating. Suppliers may not supply what was agreed upon once the customer has paid, and the customer may refuse to pay after consuming the transport service. A high level of transaction costs may imply that many potentially beneficial transactions in the transport field will never occur.

The importance of institutions is that they provide the structure for exchange that determines the cost of trans-action and the cost of transformation. For example, laws defining property rights will reduce the risks of transaction and production. The level of transaction costs will also have a strong impact on the formation of organizations. For instance, large, vertically integrated firms can be interpreted as a response to high levels of transaction costs between firms. As indicated by Coase (1937), when it is costly to transact, institutions matter.

INSTITUTIONS AND SUSTAINABLE TRANSPORT

Economic historians have called attention to the fact that the economic success of a country is critically dependent on its institutions (cf. North, 1990). Political rules, including checks and balances, well-defined property rights, and an emphasis on impersonal (as opposed to personal) links, are usually considered important factors explaining the economic success of a country. Thus, institutions matter in the explanation of economic growth.

An important question is whether institutions also matter in the achievement of sustainability, particularly sustainability in transport. Movements toward sustainable transport are in many ways influenced by institutional conditions. In some cases these conditions appear to be beneficial; in other cases, however, they appear to hamper favorable development in this direction:

- The Kyoto agreements imply the recognition of property rights to emit CO_2 in the future. This is an important new institution that may have far-reaching effects in the long run. However, international transport is not fully covered, thus leaving a gap in the agreement.
- Many countries are undergoing a process of regulatory reform in transport, implying a more limited involvement of governments in public transport activities and a larger emphasis on competition. This is expected to lead to greater efficiency of public transport firms. The implications for environmental issues are less clear, however.
- Technological change has the potential to contribute substantially to sustainable transport in the future. However, institutions may hamper such development. An example is legislation concerning underground transport. When property rights pertaining to land below surface are not well defined, investments in underground transport infrastructure are risky.
- International agreements on taxation may hamper the introduction of tax instruments, leading to undesirable

Figure 7.1   Mutal Relationship between Institutions and Organizations

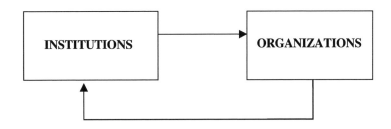

fiscal treatment of certain transport modes. An obvious example is aviation, where there are no fuel taxes for international flights, which is surprising given the local and global environmental effects involved.

- Mobility rights can be considered non-formal rights in most countries, in the sense that citizens can travel as much as they like. Efforts by governments to restrict this right to some extent by imposing limits on the right to park at certain places, limiting access to certain zones, or putting very high prices on the use of certain infrastructures at particular times of the day appear difficult to realize because citizens may consider them a violation of their fundamental mobility rights.

Below we discuss a number of these issues in more detail. Particular attention will be paid to the themes of institutions and technological change, institutions and the organization of production, territorial aspects of institutions and changes in governance.

Institutions and Technological Change

There is a reciprocal relationship between institutions and technological change. On the one hand, institutions may have an impact on the direction of technological development; on the other, technology may have an impact on institutions.

Technological change is often regarded as having high potential to contribute to the development of a sustainable transportation system. However, technology does not fall like manna from heaven. Large investments are needed in R&D to bring about technological change. Institutions such as the granting of patents for new inventions are instrumental to further technological development. There is no guarantee, however, that technological change will take place in the direction of sustainability. The major driving force in innovation and R&D is the profit-seeking motive of entrepreneurs in response to a potential market demand. When market signals are not

sustainability-oriented, technological change will have a sustainability orientation only by coincidence. Therefore, rule structures are needed to give a favorable direction to technological change. As indicated by Geerlings (1999), this may call for an active government, not only as an actor correcting for environmental effects via taxation policies, but also as a partner in public-private collaboration to facilitate the desired technological change, for example in its role as a supplier of the accompanying infrastructure.

It is interesting to note that there is also a reverse link between technology and institutions: technological change may induce change in institutions. Consider, for example, the technology-related property of non-excludability of various types of infrastructure. This property of transport infrastructure implies institutional arrangements of infrastructure supply in which public sector initiatives are dominant (Rietveld and Bruinsma, 1998). Smart cards and electronic tolling have a strong impact on the transaction costs of infrastructure when one wants to let users pay. Technology leads to a reduction in transaction costs, implying that private suppliers may also become active in the field of infrastructure operations. Information technology will probably also have profound effects on public transport operations. Smart card technology may considerably enlarge possibilities for customers to pay for transport options in a flexible way, implying new possibilities and roles for public transport operators.

Production Processes, Transaction Costs, and Institutions

The emergence of the vertically integrated firm is a response to high transaction costs, which are a consequence of numerous transactions between a variety of firms producing inputs and intermediate products. In the past, the growth of these firms was limited by the costs of command and control of large and complex organizations. Two developments can be observed in this respect. Technological change in the information and communication sector makes it easier and cheaper to control these complex organizations. This has stimulated the emergence of global players in many markets. On the other hand, the disadvantages of large conglomerations have also become evident. Lack of explicit market signals easily leads to inefficiencies in these large firms. Therefore, outsourcing has become a major strategy during the last decades. As indicated by Fukuyama (1995), in economies where market partners trust each other and institutions are favorable, transaction costs may be low, thus implying another way of organizing production processes. For transport this means, for example, that a growing number of firms contract out their transport and distribution activities. This obviously is a relevant development in view of the sustainability of transport: specialized transport companies are better equipped to achieve an efficient transport performance. They are in a much more flexible position in terms of combining shipments, finding demand for return freight, and choosing transport modes than are production-oriented firms that carry out their own transport.

Another development in this field is the emergence of just-in-time production processes, which has led to new arrangements between subcontractors and outcontractors, and a spatial reorientation of production activities. The introduction of just-in-time production has led to smaller stocks and more frequent deliveries. This may easily increase the environmental burden of freight transport. As indicated by Rovers (1999), however, the expectation that the introduction of just-in-time will make production much more transport-intensive is not necessarily true. He supplies evidence for the Netherlands indicating that by combining shipments, transport firms are able to supply at higher frequencies with only a limited increase in truck mileage.

TERRITORIES, INSTITUTIONS, AND TRANSPORT

Formal institutions are an important part of institutional systems. Since governments of nation-states have been major actors in formulating formal institutions, countries have been rather homogeneous from an institutional point of view. Two trends can be observed in this respect. On the one hand, in many countries regions have become more independent, which gives them more scope to follow their own policies and formulate their own regulations. On the other hand, supranational organizations are gaining power. In Europe, for example, this has led to a shift of emphasis in legislation away from national governments to the European Union.

The institutional and cultural differences between countries are still pervasive. This leads to higher transaction costs for international than for domestic transactions (see Van Houtum, 1998). Thus, national borders appear to have a strong negative impact on the intensity of spatial interaction, implying a bias toward domestic partners in transport networks. This obviously favors short-distance transport patterns, which are preferable in terms of environmental effects. The increasing importance of the EU may be expected to lead to lower border effects, and thus to an increase in the international orientation of spatial interaction patterns (Rietveld, 1999). This negative effect on the environment may be offset, however, by a counter-effect. A stronger supranational organization will be better equipped to impose environmentally friendly transport policies. An example would be the introduction of a fuel tax for international aviation.

CHANGES IN GOVERNANCE

The way governments operate has changed considerably during the past decades. Planning infrastructure, imposing taxes, and granting subsidies to public transport firms have become activities in which more and more actors try to determine the outcome. This has led to a decrease in the power of governments and a change in styles of governance. It has become standard in many countries for actors who will be affected by the policies to participate in the policy preparation process. The range of stakeholders involved has widened. Public-private partnerships have become common, and regulation has been partly replaced by contract-type agreements between the government and sectorial organizations.

The much more modest position of governments in transport and physical planning has been a reaction to a period of strong public sector involvement after the major economic crisis of the 1930s. Governments were assigned a large role in the development of national economies. The great failures of extreme government involvement in Communist countries were not yet generally known. But the notion of the welfare state, with its strong role of the government, collapsed after the economic crisis of the 1970s and was replaced by an institutional setting in which governments assumed a more modest role. This change has no doubt had a positive impact on efficiency in many economies, but it is less clear whether this also holds true for sustainability issues. The importance of the long-run aspects of environmental problems is evident, and it seems that a strong government cannot be missed when one wants to safeguard the interests of the coming generations.

Who Pays Transport Costs?

Even in market-oriented economies, the world is full of transactions in which the costs of activities are not borne by the consumer of the goods or services provided. For example, the guest of a family expects that a free parking place is part of the host's hospitality, just as she expects not to have to pay for the dinner to which she has been invited. On the other hand, her host would be surprised if his guest were to ask him to pay for her travel costs. A similar distribution of roles with respect to who is expected to pay travel costs takes place with shops and business services: guests usually expect the shopkeeper or service provider to provide free parking facilities, whereas the guests pay the transport costs.

With commuting, however, the distribution may be different: in some countries, commuters may have to pay for a parking place provided by the employer; in other countries, employers may compensate commuters for their commuting costs.

The above examples make clear that the question of who pays which transport costs may be answered in different ways. With respect to work-related traffic, in particular, employers may define their roles quite differently. The sustainability consequences are evident. When employers compensate workers for commuting costs, there is no incentive for workers to consider such costs when they make a decision about whether to move to a new residence. The effectiveness of road pricing alternatives would also be reduced if employers automatically paid the extra costs. The same holds true for the company car.

Fiscal authorities may have an impact on these informal institutions. By defining free parking places and compensation for commuting costs as part of income, they stimulate an open discussion that could lead to changing views on these transport costs. Such discussions make it clear that free parking places and subsidized commuting are forms of redistributing scarce resources and money between groups of commuters (defined in terms of travel mode used and distance traveled), with probably unattractive effects on sustainability and equity.

Conclusion

Institutions are an important determinant of opportunities to realize sustainable transport. A difficulty is that institutions remain implicit in transportation research. It is important to note, for example, that institutions are usually not explicit in transport models. Explicit variables in these models relate to transport volumes between locations, activities at locations, prices, travel times, infrastructure capacities, etc. The institutions appear to be implicit in the parameters of the models.

The latter observation underlines the importance of cross-national comparisons of transport phenomena in general and transport models in particular: they may shed light on the importance of the role of institutions as determinant of developments in the field of transport. The role of institutions becomes visible only when we compare different institutional settings.

References

Coase, R. H. 1937. "The Nature of the Firm." *Economica*, 386–405.

Fukuyama, F. 1995. *Trust.* London: Hamish Hamilton.

Geerlings, H. 1999. *Meeting the Challenge of Sustainable Mobility.* Berlin: Springer.

Houtum, H. van. 1998. *The Development of Cross-Border Economic Relations.* Tilburg: Tilburg University.

North, D. C. 1990. *Institutions, Institutional Change and Economic Performance.* Cambridge: Cambridge University Press.

Rietveld P. 1999. *On Barrier Effects of Borders.* Amsterdam: Vrije Universiteit.

Rietveld, P., and F. R. Bruinsma. 1998. *Is Transport Infrastructure Effective?* Berlin: Springer.

Rovers, J. 1999. *The Impact of Order-Driven Production on Freight Transport.* Amsterdam: Vrije Universiteit.

Stough, R., and P. Rietveld. 1997. "Institutional Issues in Transport Systems." *Journal of Transport Geography* 5: 207–214.

PART II

Social Change and Sustainability of Transport

CHAPTER EIGHT

Social Implications of Sustainable Transport

Richard Gilbert

BACKGROUND TO THE EST PROJECT

The Environment Directorate of the Organisation for Economic Co-operation and Development (OECD) initiated the project on Environmentally Sustainable Transport (EST) at the end of 1995 in response to several considerations:

- growing concerns about the environmental unsustainability of trends in human activity;
- particular concerns about transport's adverse environmental impacts and about the contribution of trends in transport activity to the overall unsustainability of human development;
- concern that transport activity in many places may have increased to a level at which the various costs of further increases would outweigh the economic and social advantages of the increased activity;
- awareness that conventional approaches to reducing the environmental impacts of transport, reliant primarily on improved technology, were in many important respects doing little more than offsetting the growth in transport activity; and
- awareness that an alternative to conventional approaches was available, involving the setting of ambitious but appropriate and achievable long-term

goals, on the one hand, and the application of packages of instruments designed to secure attainment of the goals, on the other.

These considerations led to the development of a plan for what became known as the EST project. The overall purposes of the project are to characterize EST and establish guidelines for policies whose implementation could lead to attainment of EST. At the core of the design of the project is a method for policy development known as backcasting, a process analogous to the forecasting methods that are more frequently used.

Policy development can be shaped in the light of present circumstances or future goals. In the former case, forecasting based on current trends provides the basis for determining what may be required to accommodate or counteract those trends. In the latter case, goals are set, and there is a process of working backward (backcasting) from the goals to determine what must be done to reach them. Policy development based on forecasting results in doing what is possible to avoid an unwanted future. Policy development based on backcasting results in doing what is necessary to achieve a wanted future.

Policy development often involves both approaches,

Box 8.1. Common EST Criteria

CO$_2$
Climate change is prevented by stabilizing atmospheric concentrations of radiative gases. Emissions of CO_2 from transport in OECD countries should accordingly not exceed 20 percent of the total of such emissions in 1990.

NO$_x$
Damage from ambient nirogen dioxide and ozone levels and from nitrogen deposition are greatly reduced, meeting WHO Air Quality Guidelines from human health and ecosystem health. Emissions of nitrogen oxides from transport should accordingly not exceed 10 percent of the total of such emissions in 1990.

VOXs
Damage from carcinogenic volatile organic compounds and ozone is greatly reduced, meeting WHO Air Quality Guidelines for human health and ecosystem health. Emissions of transport-related VOCs should accordingy not exceed 10 percent of the total of such emissions in 1990 (much less for extremely toxic VOCs).

---

although usually with more emphasis on present circumstances than on goals for the future. Engaging in forecasting rather than backcasting is especially appealing when setting goals may be controversial or when desired goals are not known or are considered unattainable. Moreover, an approach based on forecasting is likely to be incrementalist and responsibly cognizant of current realities. By contrast, an approach based on backcasting may involve large and even disruptive changes, and may appear quixotically idealistic.

A backcasting approach may nevertheless be preferable if it is necessary to develop policies capable of achieving major departures from current trends. Transportation is a sector for which such an approach could be especially valuable. Current policies and measures—many based on forecasting—have not significantly reduced the overall environmental impacts of transport, even though such reductions have been the objective of the policies. Much reliance has been placed on technology. However, the environmental benefits of technological improvement have in many respects been offset by the environmental costs of increased activity. More to the point, achieving and maintaining EST would involve dramatic overall reductions in several atmospheric emissions from transport of a scale not previously contemplated, dramatic reductions in the amount of noise from transport, and dramatic changes in how land is used.

OVERVIEW OF PHASES 1 AND 2

The initial challenge in a backcasting exercise is determining the goals to be used. In the EST project, this challenge was met during Phases 1 and 2 of the four-phase project.[1] Phase 1 primarily concerned the establishment of a definition of EST and the selection of criteria for its attainment; it also included a review of activities of OECD member country governments relevant to EST. The following definition of EST was developed during Phase 1:

> An environmentally sustainable transport system is one that does not endanger public health or ecosystems and meets needs for access consistent with (a) use of renewable resources at below their rates of regeneration, and (b) use of non-renewable resources at below the rates of development of renewable substitutes.

Six criteria for EST were selected during Phase 1. For three of the criteria—carbon dioxide, nitrogen oxides, and volatile organic compounds—both the topics and the criteria values were common to the six project teams. These are summarized in Box 8.1. For the other three—particulate matter, noise, and land use—only the topics were in common; each team was free to specify the actual criteria. These criteria are summarized in Box 8.2. The rationale for the criteria and the criteria themselves were set out in the reports on Phase 1 and 2 of the EST project.[2]

For Phase 2 (and also Phase 3), the eight participating member countries worked in six project teams, each concerned with the respective study area shown in Box 8.3.

Phase 2 involved the construction of three visions or scenarios of EST (known as EST1, EST2, and EST3) and a vision or scenario of what might be the case if current trends in activity, technology, and policy adoption were continued (the business-as-usual or BAU scenario).[3] In each of the four cases, 2030 was used as the target year and 1990 as the reference or baseline year.

The first task in Phase 2 was development of the BAU scenarios or visions for transport in 2030. The working principle for their development was that current trends will continue throughout the period 1990–2030, including trends in transport activity, in technological change, and in the implementation of relevant policies. The BAU scenarios were characterized in terms of transport activities, the environmental performance of the transport activities, and the resulting extent of conformity with the six EST criteria.

Box 8.2. Other EST Criteria

Particulates

Harmful ambient air levels are avoided by reduced emissions of fine particles, especially those less than 10 microns in diameter. Depending on local and regional conditions, this entails a reduction of 55–95 percent in the total production of fine particles (PM_{10}) from transport compared with 1990 levels.

Noise

Transport-related noise no longer results in noise levels that present a health concern or serious nuisance. Depending on local and regional conditions, this entails a reduction in transport noise outdoors to no more than 55–70 decibels during the day and 45 decibels at night, and indoors to no more than 45 decibels at all times.

Land use

Infrastructure for the movement, maintenance, and storage of vehicles is developed in such a way that local and regional objectives for air, water, and ecosystem protection are met. This will likely entail reductions in land devoted tor transport compared with 1990 levels.

The three EST scenarios represented different ways of meeting the EST criteria. They were defined in relation to the respective BAU scenarios, as shown in Box 8.4.

EST1 and EST2 were extreme scenarios. In EST1, the EST criteria were met entirely through improvements in the technology of vehicles, fuels, and infrastructure. In EST2, the criteria were met entirely through changes in transport activity (reductions in overall activity, the use of less harmful transport modes, and the more efficient use of vehicles).

The EST3 scenario for each study reflected the respective project team's assessment of the best balance of technology improvement and activity change for the study area.

The scenarios and their construction are described fully in the report on Phase 2 of the EST project.[4] In brief, the teams were able to develop BAU scenarios and then to construct EST1, EST2, and EST3 scenarios for 2030 that met the EST criteria. The EST1 and EST2 scenarios appeared to be too extreme, even though versions of them have been espoused at one time or another by various interests. The EST1 scenarios seemed as though they could

Box 8.3. Study Areas and Transport Modes Considered

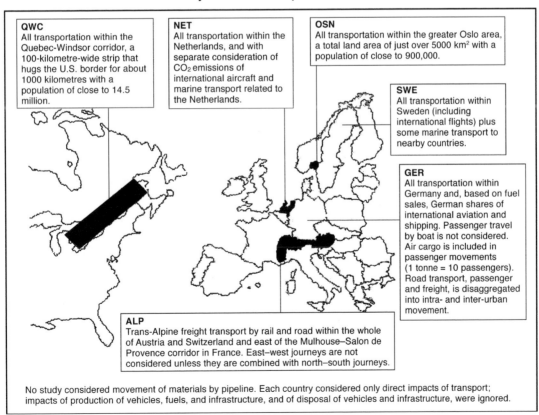

QWC
All transportation within the Quebec-Windsor corridor, a 100-kilometre-wide strip that hugs the U.S. border for about 1000 kilometres with a population of close to 14.5 million.

NET
All transportation within the Netherlands, and with separate consideration of CO_2 emissions of international aircraft and marine transport related to the Netherlands.

OSN
All transportation within the greater Oslo area, a total land area of just over 5000 km^2 with a population of close to 900,000.

SWE
All transportation within Sweden (including international flights) plus some marine transport to nearby countries.

GER
All transportation within Germany and, based on fuel sales, German shares of international aviation and shipping. Passenger travel by boat is not considered. Air cargo is included in passenger movements (1 tonne = 10 passengers). Road transport, passenger and freight, is disaggregated into intra- and inter-urban movement.

ALP
Trans-Alpine freight transport by rail and road within the whole of Austria and Switzerland and east of the Mulhouse–Salon de Provence corridor in France. East–west journeys are not considered unless they are combined with north–south journeys.

No study considered movement of materials by pipeline. Each country considered only direct impacts of transport; impacts of production of vehicles, fuels, and infrastructure, and of disposal of vehicles and infrastructure, were ignored.

Box 8.4. How the Three EST Scenarios Differed from the BAU Scenario			
	EST1	EST2	EST3
Technological progress	much greater than BAU	equal to BAU	greater than BAU
Transport activity	equal to BAU	much less than BAU	less than BAU

involve unacceptable economic costs. The EST2 scenarios gave the impression of incurring unacceptable social costs. Accordingly, the teams decided that further work should be confined to assessment of how the EST3 scenarios might be attained, and to comparisons of the EST3 and the BAU scenarios.

PHASE 3: THE SOCIAL IMPLICATIONS OF EST

Setting goals is one of the two essential components of a backcasting exercise. The other is identifying ways to meet those goals. Identifying packages of instruments for the attainment of the EST3 scenarios was the prime activity of the project teams during Phase 3 of the EST project.

A subsidiary part of the work done by the study teams during Phase 3 of the EST project concerned preliminary assessment of the economic and social implications of moving toward and maintaining EST. During Phase 3, a workshop on the economic and social implications of EST was held in Ottawa, Canada. More substantial accounts of the work on economic and social implications appear in connection with the separately published report on that workshop.[5]

The assessments of economic and social implications conducted during the EST project were preliminary and cursory. They were conducted because it was unthinkable that there should be no consideration of these matters. More substantial analyses were not conducted at this time for several reasons, including the following:

- Within the EST project, they would have distracted from the focus on environmentally sustainable transport by competing for limited resources. It is useful to consider sustainability as having environmental, economic, and social components. Ultimately, however, the environmental component must prevail, because the environment provides the limiting conditions for other activity.
- There are no accepted methods for social and economic assessment of distant scenarios. Indeed, there is some reluctance among economists and social scientists to engage in this kind of work because of the methodological perils. Commitment to full-scale assessments of EST's economic and social implications would have been premature.

With these cautions in mind, it was nevertheless considered important for several reasons to have some assessment at this time. The primary reason was that such assessment would address questions such as those raised frequently during Phase 2, when the scenarios were being constructed. The EST1 scenarios were not developed further because they would be too expensive; the EST2 scenarios were not developed further because they would involve too much coercion. The EST3 scenarios were seen as less expensive and coercive, but how much less? And what of the BAU scenarios? Were they expensive and coercive?

Two important outcomes were expected of the assessments of economic and social implications. One was that they would inform the identification of instrument packages in constructive ways. The other was that they would help with the presentation of the results of the EST project by rounding out the characterizations of EST and the strategies required to reach it.

As well, it was expected that the assessments would provide useful preliminary results of independent value. More important, they would help with the design of more substantial assessments of the implications of changing historic transport trends and moving toward EST.

The assessment of social implications addressed the following questions:

- In what ways would the social fabric be different if the EST3 scenario were attained rather than the BAU scenario, both from an individual and from a societal perspective?

- What would be the relative social costs and benefits of the two scenarios for individuals and households, for businesses of all sizes, and for local, regional, and national governments? Among factors that might be considered are family cohesion, democratic activity, social polarization, alienation, criminal activity, and what is loosely known as "lifestyle."
- In general, would people experience more freedom (or have more freedom) under the BAU scenario or the EST3 scenario?

A consultant[6] developed a set of eighteen pairs of propositions with supporting data drawn mostly from experience in the UK. The eight participating countries engaged expert advice to provide indications of agreement or disagreement with the propositions from their national perspectives. The pairs of propositions (in abbreviated form) and the responses to them are provided in Box 8.5.

There was considered to be overall agreement with a proposition if at least six of the eight countries responded and at least four of those were in agreement. Likewise, there was considered to be disagreement if at least six of the eight countries responded and no more than two of those were in agreement.

By these criteria, there were eight instances of agreement with each of the BAU and EST3 propositions. These are lightly shaded in Box 8.5. Where there is agreement with both members of a pair, the topic cell is also shaded. There was one instance of disagreement with a proposition, and it happened that there was agreement with the other member of the pair. This case is darkly shaded in Box 8.5.

The five instances of agreement with both propositions of a pair can be summarized as concurrence with the following:

- *Land use:* With BAU, sprawl will continue, increasing society's dependence on the car, and increasing the disadvantage of those without cars. With EST3, land use patterns will be more "disciplined," and transport policies will promote equity of access for those with and without cars.
- *Street life:* The greater amount of traffic associated with BAU will undermine street life, whereas the lesser amount associated with EST3 will promote street life.
- *Communities:* Society will become more anonymous with BAU; fewer people will know their neighbors.

With EST3, more time will be spent in neighborhoods, thereby promoting conviviality.

- *Children:* The main losers with BAU will be children; their independent mobility will be much constrained. Children will be the principal winners with EST. The safer environment will permit them greater independence.
- *Health:* With BAU, the health of individuals will deteriorate from lack of exercise, whereas with EST3 life will become healthier as exercise is incorporated into the daily routine.

The one instance of disagreement with one member of a pair and agreement with the other member can be summarized as follows:

- *Safety:* For pedestrians and cyclists, especially children and the elderly, life will be safer with EST3 than it is now, but not less safe with BAU than it is now.

The conclusion from this assessment of social implications is that continuation of BAU could result in growing social disparity and alienation, unhealthfulness, and loss of independent mobility among the elderly and, particularly, children. With movement toward EST3, on the other hand, life could become more egalitarian, convivial, healthful, and child-friendly, at least in comparison with BAU.

Not much weight should be attached to these conclusions, except to note that in general the teams collectively consider that social conditions will worsen with BAU, and that they will be more benign with EST3, certainly more benign than with BAU, and perhaps more benign than now.

This first attempt at exploring the social implications indicates topics for further consideration and suggests methods for addressing potential social implications of future scenarios with more rigor. Many of the thirty-six propositions in Box 8.5 could individually be the subjects of large research agendas.

NOTES

1. Phases 1 and 2 of the EST project are described in *Environmental Criteria for Sustainable Transport* (OECD, 1996) and *Scenarios for Environmentally Sustainable Transport* (OECD, 1998), respectively, both written for the most part by the author of this chapter.

2. See the sources in note 1.

3. The term *scenario* has been used in the EST proj-

Box 8.5. Summary of Responses to the Questionannaire Concerning Social Implications of BAU and EST

TOPIC	BAU PROPOSITION	A/R*	EST3 PROPOSITION	A/R*
Material wealth	GDP will continue to grow.	4/5	The economy will grow at about the same rate as for BAU.	2/3
Economy and transport activity	The close correlation between GDP and tonne-kilometers of freight and passenger-kilometers will maintained.	?	The correlation between economic activity and transport activity will be weakened compared with BAU.	?
Social polarization	Disparities between the rich and poor in terms of access to social and economic opportunities will grow larger.	7/8	Disparities between the rich and poor in terms of access to social and economic opportunities will diminish.	4/4
Car dependence	The rate of increase of car dependence will be greatest in the poorest countries.	4/4	If OECD leads by example, the prospect of dissuading poor countries from following OECD's unsustainable example is much improved.	6/6
Land use	Land use sprawl will continue, increasing society's dependence on the car, and increasing the disadvantage of those without cars.	6/6	Land use patterns will be more "disciplined," and transport policies will promote equity of access for those with and without cars.	7/7
Street life	More traffic undermines street life.	8/8	Less traffic promotes street life.	8/8
Communities	Society becomes more anonymous; fewer people know their neighbors.	8/8	More time spent in neighborhood promotes conviviality.	8/8
Children	Children are the principal loser under BAU, their independent mobility being much constrained.	8/8	Children are the principal winners under EST, the safer environment permitting greater independence.	6/8
Telecommunications	Increasing electronic mobility will promote further dispersal and encourage more travel.	4/4	Increasing electronic mobility is a two-edged sword; it has the potential to promote or destroy community life.	5/5
Uniformity	The world becomes everywhere more the same culturally—the Hilton-McCulture effect.	7/8	Cultural diversity is preserved by restraints on cross-cultural contact.	1/5
Safety	Life becomes more dangerous for pedestrians and cyclists, especially children and the elderly.	2/6	Life becomes safer for pedestrians and cyclist, especially children and the elderly.	7/7
Health	Health deteriorates from lack of exercise.	4/6	Life becomes healthier as exercise is incorporated into the daily regime.	7/7
Nutrition	Those without cards find access to healthy food increasingly difficult.	5/6	The poor gain better access to healthy food.	1/5
Crime	The threat of crime increases.	4/5	The threat of crime decreases.	2/3
Law enforcement	Numbers of strangers increase, society becomes more paranoid, and law enforcement becomes Orwellian.	1/4	Societies in which people know their neighbors are mostly self-policing.	5/6
Equality	Access will be rationed by fiat and price, increasingly discriminating against the poor.	4/5	Equitable demand management is assumed; detail of how it will be achieved remains unclear.	2/3
Participation	The scale of government will increase, diminishing the significance of the individual voter.	4/4	Community politics will be revived.	2/2
Democracy	Democracy under threat.	0/3	Democracy under threat.	0/1

*A/R indicates Agreement Ratio (number of Member country responses in agreement with the proposition/total number of responses to the proposition.

ect as a synonym for *scene*—i.e., scenario construction involved the painting of scenes of what transportation might be like in 2030. *Scenario* is more often used to describe a possible unfolding of events, as in "Let's imagine the scenario of unilateral action by the Netherlands with respect to vehicle emissions standards." In this sense, *scenario* refers to the whole sequence of events that might occur if there were unilateral action by the Netherlands. The backcasting literature is confusing as to which is the more appropriate use of *scenario*. John Robinson, who introduced the term *backcasting,* uses *scenario* in both ways. Chapter 5 of his latest book, *Life in 2030: Exploring a Sustainable Future for Canada* (Vancouver: University of British Columbia Press, 1996), is entitled "Life in 2030:

The Sustainability Scenario." It includes such phrases as "an integrated scenario of a sustainable society in 2030 was produced." Here *scenario* is being used in the way we have used it in the EST study—as a picture of a desirable future. But, elsewhere in the book *scenario* is used for an unfolding of events. What is meant by *scenario* in the EST project corresponds closely to the term *image of the future* as used by Karl H. Dreborg, "Essence of Backcasting," *Futures* 28, no. 29 (1996): 813–828.

4. See the sources in note 1.

5. Report on the Workshop on Economic and Social Implications of Sustainable Transport (Report ENV/EPOC/PPC/T(99)3, OECD, 1999).

6. John Adams of College London.

CHAPTER NINE

EU Policy Scenario Building for Sustainable Mobility

David Banister
and Peter Steen

INTRODUCTION

Travel patterns in most developed countries are increasingly dependent on the car. Levels of mobility and car ownership have risen substantially in recent years, and that increase seems likely to continue. In the EU 15,[1] there has been an increase of more than 34 percent in the numbers of vehicles owned (1985–1995), and it is expected that by 2020 that number will increase by a further 50 percent (OECD/ECMT, 1995). This will bring vehicle ownership levels in many European countries to more than 600 cars per 1,000 population. Road capacity has not increased by a similar amount (+10 percent 1985–1995), so congestion has increased, particularly in cities where little new infrastructure has been built. The growth in congestion is now officially estimated to cost about 2 percent of EU GDP (EUROSTAT, 1997).

Space is at a premium in the EU 15, as population density there is four times that in the United States (Table 9.1). This has advantages, as distances between cities are shorter, but much of the undeveloped land is safeguarded as open space, green belt, or recreational areas that cannot be used for city expansion. The role of public transport has remained important, with the car having a lower level of dominance.

Yet there is continuing concern over the relentless growth in travel, particularly by car and more recently by air. Action is needed to move toward the targets set at the Kyoto Protocol for greenhouse gas reductions (including CO_2). In addition, there is probably even greater concern about the potential impacts of local pollutants (CO, NO_x, PM_{10}, and VOC) on air quality, health, and the attractiveness of cities.

In this chapter, we report on the recently completed POSSUM[2] project, in which a new approach to scenario building has been developed. Clear targets have been set for Europe to cover the environmental, economic efficiency, and regional development objectives of the Common Transport Policy (CEC, 1998). These targets have been used as a framework within which to construct three Images of the Future (2020), which in turn depend on certain contextual elements that are taken as given—whether Europe will move toward greater polarization with strong regions or greater cooperation with a strong center and new members of the EU—and strategic elements that are subject to policy interventions.

SCENARIO CONSTRUCTION AND LITERATURE REVIEW

A scenario is a tool that describes pictures of the future world within a specific framework and under specified

Table 9.1 USA and EU15 Comparisons

1994	USA	EU15	
Population	260.7	372.1	millions
Area	9,363	3,237	1,000 sq km
Density	27.8	114.9	persons/sq km
GDP	6,650	7,344	$ billion
	25,512	19,737	$ per head
Roads	671	1,188	km per 1,000 sq km
Rail	19	48	km per 1,000 sq km
Vehicles	208	192	millions
Cars	134	158	millions
Vehicle ownership	0.80	0.52	vehicles/1,000 inhabitants
Car ownership	0.51	0.42	cars/1,000 inhabitants
Distance per car	19,000	12,500	kilometers per year
Fuel prices	$1 per gallon	$1 per liter	3.85 liters = 1 U.S. gallon
Car	85.1%	79.9%	} passenger kilometers
Air	12.4%	6.1%	
Rail and bus	2.5%	14.0%	

Source: EUROSTAT, 1997.

assumptions. The scenario approach includes a description of two or more scenarios, designed to compare and examine alternative futures (CEC, 1994). There are different traditions in scenario construction (Becker, 1997), one based in the U.S. (the American approach), and the other in the EU (the French approach).

In the American approach, a distinction is made between context and strategy, with the scenarios first being presented as the context within which the system operates and policy-making takes place. Various actors are then asked to choose between differing strategies and to adapt these—so that a "least regret" strategy can be selected by the user of the scenarios.

In the French approach, a comprehensive picture of the future is presented in terms of the current situation, a description of some future alternatives, and a description of a number of events that may connect the present situation with future ones. This is the approach that has been adopted here, but in a particular version that might be termed the Swedish approach (Rienstra, 1998; Banister et al. 2000b).

The Swedish approach has certain clearly distinctive characteristics, which have been used mainly for policy analysis (Dreborg, 1996). They are normative in their structure and are based on desirable futures or choices. They also use a backcasting (rather than forecasting) approach, in which an image of the future is constructed without taking account of current trends. A path is then constructed to show how one might move from where one is at present to this desirable future position. The scenarios, the images, and the policy paths are all validated at various stages by experts, so that feedback can be given and modification in all stages can take place. The intention is not prescriptive, but illustrative of possible future paths, as well as an indication of the nature and scale of actions (together with a timetable) of the changes necessary to achieve the scenario targets.

In this research, the basic backcasting methodology has been developed further. The same procedures have been followed in terms of identifying the images of the future for sustainable mobility (2020) and the constraints (contextual and strategic) under which policy paths can be constructed, but a new approach to policy packaging has been developed. A comprehensive range of policy measures have been investigated, and these have then been packaged in imaginative groupings so that implementation can take place through combinations of policies (Section 3), rather than the more traditional analysis based on individual actions. In addition, the policy paths are not just single measures but mixtures of packages and complementary strategies; only in this way can the targets for sustainable mobility be achieved (Banister et al., 2000b).

In the scenario-building process, targets have initially been set to give substance to the images of the future (Table 9.2). These targets relate to the desire for sustainable mobility, defined as using substantially lower amounts of non-renewable resources in 2020 than are currently being used in 1995. The images themselves are constrained by contextual elements that do not change, and strategic elements that do change over time (Figure 9.1). The contextual elements relate to the level of political intervention, with one image assuming strong local action and the other assuming strong central action; the strategic elements relate to the relative importance given to technological solutions and decoupling policies. Decoupling is a key concept, defined as maintaining levels of economic growth, but with lower levels of transport intensity—breaking the historic link between GDP growth (desirable) and traffic growth (undesirable).

Once these contextual and strategic elements have been set, the Images of the Sustainable Transport Future 2020 can be conceptualized, in figures at the EU level (Table 9.3). This table attempts to summarize in broad terms the changes necessary to achieve the three sets of targets relating to environment, regional equity, and efficiency (Table 9.2). There is a difference of emphasis between the three images, with one having slightly lower levels of po-

litical involvement in the process of change—people are expected to adopt green attitudes and values, with the catalyst for change coming from the "bottom up." The other suggests that political intervention takes place from above ("top down"), and that clear action comes from national (and supranational) politicians.

The key objective of the Common Transport Policy (CTP) CEC, 1992 and 1998) is that we should seek to achieve sustainable mobility. The images of the future have distinguished between three alternatives (for the contextual elements), but in all cases cooperation at the EU level is assumed. This assumption is consistent with the basic rationale behind the CTP. For the strategic elements, different levels of technological solutions and degrees of decoupling have been combined in the different images:

- Image 1   -with local, regional, and EU cooperation: *EU Coordination of Active Citizens;* Technology + and Decoupling +++
- Image 2   -with global and EU cooperation: *Global Cooperation for Sustainable Transport;* Technology +++ and Decoupling +
- Image 3   -with both local and global cooperation: *Accord on Sustainability.* Technology ++ and Decoupling ++

The importance of the contextual dimension must be emphasized, particularly when the implementation of different policy measures is being evaluated. It is often neglected in policy discussions.

The outcome of the scenario-building process is estimates of changes needed, and consequently recommendations about what policy decisions need to be made now in order to change the development toward sustainable mobility. It is recognized that the sustainability target for 2020 is not the definitive end-goal. Hence the targets used here (Table 9.2) are intermediate ones. The methodology puts near-time decisions in a longer time perspective and is based on today's best knowledge. New knowledge and more or less unexpected developments will result in revision of the images of the future and alternative paths to the images. This calls for flexibility and adaptability in the proposed policy recommendations. Different policy measures have been combined into policy packages in order to create synergies. This also permits the advantages and disadvantages of each measure (individually and as part of a package) to be discussed so that compensatory

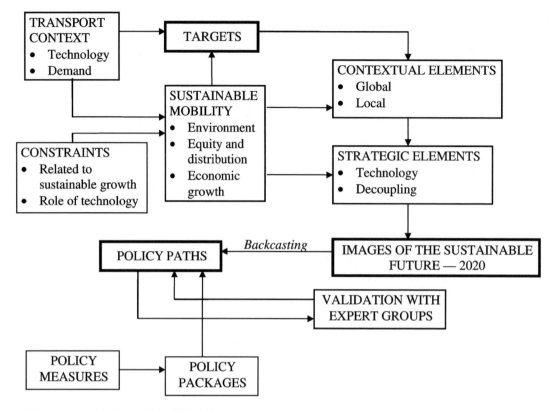

Figure 9.1 The Scenario-Building Process

actions can be taken. When packages of measures are introduced, policies are less likely to be seen as restrictive or permissive, but instead as related to achievement of particular objectives (such as sustainable mobility).

POLICY CONCLUSIONS

The full results from the scenario-building exercise are available (Banister et al. 2000a and 2000b). Here we highlight some of the more interesting policy conclusions.

Decoupling

If transport is to become more sustainable, then positive policy action is required along both dimensions—technology and decoupling (Figure 9.1). Even if the strongest priority is given to technology, this is not sufficient on its own to achieve the targets or images. As transport volumes are expected to continue to grow, strong decoupling in both the passenger and the freight sectors is essential in order to achieve sustainable mobility. This means that a decrease in transport intensity of the economy is needed.

A wide variety of policies are available for decoupling both passenger and freight transport from economic growth (see Banister et al., 2000b), without limiting economic growth. As decoupling means a shift in the transport paradigm, such changes may result in opposition from those who perceive that they may lose from these changes. Accelerated decoupling strategies will bring benefits to the overall economy, but may temporarily increase political conflicts.

To reduce these political conflicts, two important further actions are required. The nature of decoupling and its pivotal role in achieving sustainable mobility need to be presented to, and discussed among, decision-makers at all levels—an information activity. Secondly, the implications of decoupling have to be discussed with the public and business/industry in order to think through the necessary actions in terms of travel and activity patterns —a public acceptance activity.

Technology

Technology has a key role to play in moving policy in the direction of sustainable mobility, particularly in the longer term. In the shorter term, firm action and direction are required at the EU level to promote best practice and to further particular technological paths (including off-cycle performance, long-term responsibility, and automatic monitoring of emissions). For example, what should be the role of diesel fuel in urban areas? How can cleaner technology and fuels be introduced in cities, together with the necessary infrastructure? Should research and development be directed at new technology (hydrogen) or at an intermediate technology (methanol)? It may be necessary to protect the market in some areas so that the appropriate conditions for technological innovation are encouraged. In the longer term there should be an open market, with pricing and regulation determining which technologies are consistent with sustainable mobility.

Table 9.2   Policy Targets for 2020

Environmental Targets
- 25% reduction of CO_2 emissions from 1995–2020
- 80% reduction of NO_x emissions from 1995–2020
- no degradation of specially protected areas
- minor (5%) increase of net infrastructure surface in Europe

Regional Development Targets
- improve relative accessibility of peripheral regions (both internal and external); this general target includes cost and time, and allows for the replacement of physical accessibility by telecommunications

Efficiency Targets
- full cost coverage (including external costs) of transport under market or equivalent conditions
- reduce public subsidies to all forms of transport to zero, except where there are particular social equity objectives.

Table 9.3   The Three Images as Compared with the Reference Case for Growth in Travel (1995–2020)

Billion passenger km	Volume 1995	Volume 2020 Reference Case	Volume 2020 Image 1	Volume 2020 Image 2	Volume 2020 Image 3	Growth 1970-1995
Car (fossil)	3,590	5,380 (+50%)	2,260	3,550	2,470	+125%
(methanol)			0	300	0	
(electric)			560	0	620	
Aircraft	400	1,200 (+200%)	720	960	800	+250%
Bus	370	480 (+30%)	700	550	700	+50%
Rail	290	350 (+20%)	660	700	660	+40%
Total	4,650	7,410 (+60%)	4,900	6,060	5,250	+113%

Notes: These figures are national ones for all 15 EU countries plus Norway, Switzerland, and Turkey. Volumes for 1995 and trends 1970–1995 are based on ECMT, 1997. The Reference Case is a relatively cautious estimate compared to most forecasts and the historic development between 1970 and 1995.

Source: ECMT, 1997 and Banister et al., 2000a.

Actions Needed from Outside the Common Transport Policy

Some non-transport policy actions are related to structural changes in society (e.g., the consequences of IT or increased interest in local-regional markets). Other actions are a matter of more general macro economic policy intervention (e.g., a tax shift from labor to resource use—with CO_2 tax, fuel, vehicle, and car ownership tax reform). But some developments will be driven without policy interventions (e.g., the rapid growth in the use of information technology). Here actions may be needed to cope with drawbacks, such as increased urban sprawl or distributional consequences.

The Time Element

The time horizon established for the scenario-building process is 2020, but this is only an intermediate stage toward sustainability. Many decoupling measures have a long lead time, so it is important that they start now. For technology, clear guidance is required now on standards (e.g., on fuel consumption and emissions), and on whether investment should take place in intermediate technology (e.g., methanol) or whether encouragement should be given to "jump" to the eco-technology (e.g., hydrogen fuel cells). The uncertainty about changes over time should be recognized so that flexibility permits modifications in measures and targets. Failure to act now means that there is no chance of achieving the sustainability targets by 2020.

The Regional Dimension

Much of the discussion here and at the validation sessions (Figure 9.1) has concentrated on the EU level. Different problems exist in rural areas and in the peripheral regions of Europe (including the CEEC and CIS countries).[3] Uniform policies concerning regulations and taxes do not produce optimal results and can create unnecessary conflicts. Ways must be found to adapt measures to local conditions while maintaining overall EU targets and consistency of policies (e.g., differentiated [road] pricing), as much of the EU budget is invested in disadvantaged locations.

The Trans-European Networks

The Trans-European Networks (TENs) form an important component in the achievement of cohesion within Europe, but in terms of sustainable mobility their role may be more limited. The main purpose of the TENs in the context of sustainable mobility is to achieve a significant modal shift from road (and air) to rail. If the TENs only increase the supply of transport and encourage more travel overall, then sustainable mobility targets will not be achieved. This means that the TENs must form part of an integrated transport strategy that packages increases in supply of rail with reductions in supply of other modes.

Air Travel

The dramatic increase in passenger and freight travel by air (about 6 percent growth per annum, doubling every twelve years) is a major constraint on the achievement of sustainable mobility targets, as it is both long-distance and energy-intensive. The development of new technology with larger aircraft and hydrogen-powered engines may help to reduce energy use and emissions per passenger kilometer. But the effects of H_2O and NO_x emissions at high altitudes are still not clear (IPCC, 1999). The volume growth also has to be addressed. The air industry is currently benefiting from an advantageous tax situation, as there is no tax on kerosene. Equal tax treatment would help raise costs and prices in the air sector, but the low cost of air travel on shorter European routes might also affect the potential for high-speed rail. Even if rail takes over from shorter air routes, it may only release more air space for long-distance air travel, making the achievement of sustainable mobility objectives very difficult (Banister, 1999).

Support for Sustainable Mobility

Questions have been raised about the nature and scale of change required to achieve sustainable mobility. It is essential to achieve support both for the principles and for the practice of sustainable mobility. Many people are constrained by current value systems and conventions. In the validation process it has been found that there is strong support for the principles of sustainable mobility, but there are equally strong barriers to real change, with a wide range of views and no clear commonality. One prerequisite for the implementation of the proposed policy packages is a gradual shift in attitude toward the increasing importance of values in line with sustainable development.

Over the next twenty years, the amount of time available for leisure activities will dramatically increase, particularly within the demographic context of an aging population. Much of this new leisure time may involve long-distance, energy-intensive travel as people set out to see the world. The question here is whether there is anything that can (or should) be done to reduce this expected growth, which will have a severe impact on sustainable mobility. For much of the year people may be "sustainable," with local travel being undertaken on low-energy modes, but once or twice a year they may travel around the world, thus negating any overall notion of sustainability. This means that changes in lifestyle are essential to meet sustainable mobility objectives, and that actions in the passenger sector may be harder to achieve than those in the freight sector. The potential for substantial increases in unsustainable travel must be addressed.

Image 1 was characterized by cooperation on the local and regional levels (mainly bottom-up politics). Image 2, on the other hand, was characterized by a good climate for global cooperation (mainly top-down politics). If both these frame conditions materialize, then Image 3 is a feasible option. Originally it was argued that it might not be possible to combine strong decoupling with strong technological development, because the costs would be too high. However, under certain conditions a "win-win" situation may be possible—that is, a focus on both strong decoupling and technology (a new image, Image 4). Image 4 provides a good base for achieving more challenging sustainability goals. To reach such an image requires a high level of commitment and intervention of decision-makers across all sectors. The capacity for preparing decisions and implementing them is likely to be a limitation in realizing this image, as transport policy at the EU level is only one of many competing areas of action.

Transport is at a turning point, and it is clear that transport interventions alone will not move policy in the direction of sustainability. The role of transport policy among other policies must be given stronger emphasis, and more emphasis has to be placed on influencing economic, structural, agriculture, tourism, and other policies to find the means to decouple transport growth from economic development.

Notes

1. The EU is the European Union, consisting of fifteen European countries—Austria, Belgium, Denmark, Finland, France, Germany, Greece, Ireland, Italy, Luxembourg, the Netherlands, Portugal, Spain, Sweden, and the UK.

2. The POSSUM Consortium includes members from University College London, the Free University of Amsterdam, the National Technical University of Athens, the Environmental Strategies Research Group/FOA in Stockholm, EURES (the Institute for Regional Studies in Europe in Freiburg), VTT (the Technical Research Center of Finland in Helsinki), the Warsaw University of Technology, and the Scientific Center for Complex Transport Problems in Moscow. It was funded as part of the 4th Framework Strategic Research Programme of The EU DGVII Transport.

3. The CEEC countries include those in the "old" East Europe, and the CIS countries are those that make up the Commonwealth of Independent States (part of the former USSR).

References

Banister, D. 1999. "Some Thoughts on a Walk in the Woods." *Built Environment* 25, no. 2: 162–167.

Banister, D., K. Dreborg, L. Hedberg, S. Hunhammar, P. Steen, and J. Åkerman. 2000a. "Transport Policy Scenarios for the EU: 2020 Images of the Future." *Innovation* 13, no. 1: 27–45.

Banister, D., D. Stead, P. Steen, K. Dreborg, J. Åkerman, P. Nijkamp, and R. Schleicher-Tappeser. 2000b. *European Transport Policy and Sustainable Mobility.* London: E + FN Spon.

Becker, H. 1997. *Social Impact Assessment.* London: UCL Press.

Commission of the European Communities. 1992. *The Future Development of the Common Transport Policy: A Global Approach to the Construction of a Community Framework for Sustainable Mobility.* Brussels: CEC.

Commission of the European Communities. 1994. *Strategic Transport Glossary.* Brussels: CEC.

Commission of the European Communities. 1998. *The Common Transport Policy: Sustainable Mobility— Perspectives for the Future.* Communication from the Commission to the Council, the European Parliament, the Economic and Social Committee and the Committee of the Regions, Brussels, December, COM (1998) 716 Final.

Dreborg, K. H. 1996. "Essence of Backcasting." *Futures* 28, no. 9: 813–828.

ECMT. 1997. *Trends in the Transport Sector.* Paris: ECMT.

EUROSTAT. 1997. *EU Transport in Figures: Statistical Pocketbook.* Luxembourg.

IPCC. 1999. *Aviation and the Global Atmosphere.* Cambridge: Cambridge University Press.

OECD/ECMT. 1995. *Transport and Sustainable Development.* Paris: OECD.

Rienstra, S. 1998. *Options and Barriers for Sustainable Transport Policies: A Scenario Approach.* Rotterdam: Netherlands Economic Institute.

CHAPTER TEN

A Study of EU-U.S. Integrated Policies
to Address the Consequences of Social Change
for the Sustainability of Transport

Hans Kremers

INTRODUCTION

Although the European Union and the United States have similar problems with social change and the sustainability of transport, the impact of policies to tackle these problems might be totally different in each country due to variations in organization and culture. The rising incomes of people in the EU and the U.S. and social change during the post–World War II period have led to a significant increase in the demand for transport, especially by road and air. This has caused enormous congestion and environmental problems, especially around cities and airports. (See World Bank, 1996 and publications of the OECD such as OECD, 1995 for details.)

In the past decade, governments have questioned the sustainability of the existing transport system and devised policies to address the problems resulting from the increased demand for transport. Many countries in the EU, including France, Germany, and the Netherlands, are trying to revitalize their neglected railroad systems and implement policies that will allow people to choose a more environmentally friendly and less congested means of transport, as exemplified by the increasing government taxes on gasoline. But local EU governments have realized that an overall EU policy is necessary to achieve such goals. Dutch drivers living near the border soon found

out that they could obtain cheaper gas in Belgium or Germany. We refer readers to the EU Green Paper (EC, 1996) for details on policies in the EU. In contrast, the implementation of such policies in the U.S. does not cause such difficulties because of that country's large size and the greater integration of its constituent states.

Apart from the intended substitution effects, changes in EU policy designed to tackle transport problems may also impel EU-based companies to increase the prices of their products because of increased transport costs and higher environmental taxes. These indirect effects would decrease the EU's competitiveness in comparison with the U.S., which makes the EU reluctant to implement the necessary policies. Similar reasoning applies to the U.S. This calls for the EU and the U.S. to work together on policies that can be successfully applied to transport problems. Such a scientific effort will require a common analytical framework, preferably a general equilibrium approach.

Applied General Equilibrium modeling (AGE) is advocated and applied by many well-known researchers, including John Whalley of the University of Warwick (UK) and Wolfgang Wiegard of the University of Tübingen (Germany) in the EU, and John Shoven of Yale University and Thomas Rutherford of the University of Colorado in the U.S. It is viewed as an ideal framework for appraising the effects of policy changes on resource allocation and for assessing who gains and who loses. Up until now, AGE has been used mainly in public finance, international trade theory, and environmental economics. The TRENEN project in the EU has already addressed the application of AGE models in this field. The present research proposal aims to extend the use of AGE to study the impacts of the separate policies implemented to date by the U.S. and the EU and compare them with an integrated approach as it might affect people's welfare and the sustainability of transport. Such an approach would greatly benefit from the expertise and local knowledge of a research team consisting of EU and U.S. researchers working on AGE and on transport problems.

THE ARCHITECTURE OF A TRANSPORT IMPACT MODEL

Our initial framework for studying the impact of transport policies is based on the applied general equilibrium models introduced by Shoven and Whalley (1992). The advantage of a general equilibrium model is that the equilibrium is seen as the result of an adjustment process among the economic variables in the model. It therefore not only takes into account the economic factors that play an important role in a transport and environment model, but it also describes the behavior of the agents that might result in such an equilibrium.

We explicitly concentrate on modeling the transport sector as it relates to the economy and its impact on the environment. Nijkamp and van Geenhuizen (1997) describe a number of driving forces behind the current state of transition in transport in the EU. First of all, companies and regions are increasingly engaged in global trade, causing a shift away from regional competition toward global competition. This requires sourcing materials, labor use, and marketing over long distances, using often fragile networks.

Modern European society is showing a shift toward individualization. The traditional nuclear family is losing ground to alternative lifestyles, leading to a larger number of households with different consumption patterns, working schedules, and retirement plans. The emergence of new lifestyles leads to different patterns of mobility,

varying from a mobile society with more development in the direction of individual mobility, to a homebound society with more activities around the house.

There is also a tendency toward spatial separation of residential and employment sites, which is leading to an increasing need for commuting between city centers and suburbs, and for intra-suburban trips using a complex network of different transport modes. Suburbanization itself was a consequence of the development of public transport decades ago. The extent and scale of suburbanization have been unprecedented since the early 1960s, when the private car and higher income levels brought low-density housing within the reach of large groups of upper- and lower-class families. This is a good example of the interaction between transport and land use.

Economic efficiency is increasingly being replaced as a goal by eco-preservation. Under eco-preservation, the emphasis is on the long-term stability of eco-systems based on the joint interests of man and nature. Among other effects, this has led to the recycling of products and waste materials. The organization of an underlying production and distribution chain has major impacts on the demand and organization of transport.

These changes in society affect the demand for transport through the economic activities that people develop in response to such changes. Transport demand is therefore seen as a derived phenomenon resulting from the need to move and communicate in order to perform economic activities in a modern economy. In our framework model, we concentrate on transport as a derived demand, and assume that the agents in our model do not derive any direct utility or profit from transport. Figure 10.1 gives an integrative view on transport, economic activities, and the environment.

The model describes the economy of a country consisting of several regions. The country offers several modes of transport, each with its own infrastructure, which we consider as given. A transport mode might be interpreted as road transport or rail transport, but it can also be interpreted as peak-hour transport or the transport of data through a telephone network. Each region is supposed to consist of a representative consumer, and a representative producer that produces the region's composite commodity.

Figure 10.1 illustrates our model. For reasons of simplicity, we consider only one region, which we denote as region 0, with a similarly denoted consumer and producer.

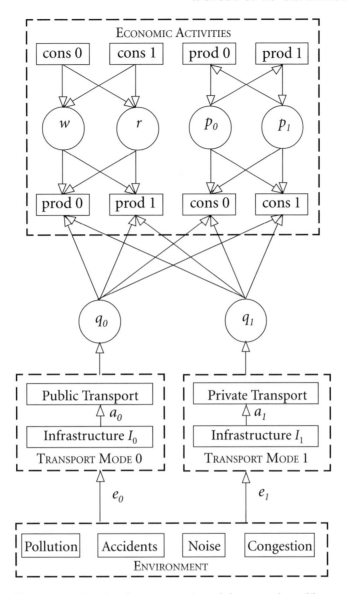

Figure 10.1   Graphical representation of the general equilibrium framework. The variables p_0, p_1, q_0, q_1, w, and r denote the prices of commodities 0 and 1, transport modes 0 and 1, the wage rate and the interest rate on the underlying markets. An arrow pointing toward a market represents a supply and an arrow pointing from a market represents a demand of the good traded on this market by the agent on the other end of the arrow. a_0 and a_1 denote the input demand for infrastructure, and e_0 and e_1 the enviromental costs of transport mode 0 and 1 respectively.

We have aggregated the other regions' consumers, producers, and commodities into one aggregate consumer 1, one aggregate producer 1, and one aggregate commodity 1. The different transport modes are aggregated into a public transport mode and a private transport mode 1.

The economic activities in the country are modeled by the two consumers and 1 that supply labor to the country's labor market and capital to the country's capital market, and two producers and 1 that produce the consumer goods, using labor and capital as primary inputs, and the commodities and 1 as intermediary inputs. Each consumer has a time endowment, which is allocated between labor, leisure, and transport. Given consumption prices p_0 and p_1, the wage rate w, and the interest rate r, each consumer spends the income obtained from labor and capital on the consumption of goods.

In order to be able to participate in these economic activities, both the consumers and the producers need transport. The consumers do not obtain direct utility from transport, while transport is only a cost to the producers. We measure transport in volume units. In the case of road transport, for example, these units might be ton kilometers, but in the case of information transfer they could be bytes. Given the per unit price q_0 of public transport and q_1 of private transport, each consumer demands a certain number of passenger units by public transport and by private transport, while each producer demands a certain number of freight units by public transport and by private transport.

Given the prices p_0 and p_1 of the consumer goods, the transport prices q_0 and q_1, the wage rate w, and the interest rate r, consumers spend their income and time endowment on consumption and leisure in such a way as to obtain a maximum amount of utility. In order to obtain this utility, it is necessary for them to spend some of their income and time endowment on transport. The units of transport that consumers need to obtain their consumption bundle and labor supply are given as a function of these entities. The transport price and the speed per unit of transport of each mode determine their optimal bundle of the available transport modes.

The producers maximize their profits by supplying as much as possible of their commodity to the market, depending on their production technology. They need to spend some of their profits on an optimal, i.e., cost-minimizing, mix of transport modes, taking into account the price and speed of each mode.

Alternatively, to cope with imperfect competition issues in applied general equilibrium models, a producer's behavior is also regularly described by a pricing rule, which provides the prices the producer considers acceptable at a production level.

Each transport mode or 1 consists of an industry or 1 and the underlying infrastructure with capacity I_0 or I_1. The transport industries, such as Dutch Railways in the Netherlands, provide transport to the public and the private transport markets. On the public transport market, the industry can obtain q_0 per unit of transport supplied, while the private transport industry can obtain q_1 per unit supplied.

We assume that each transport industry has a constant returns-to-scale production technology. In this way, their activity levels are determined by the total demand for their transport units. In addition to having a_0 or a_1 units of infrastructure as an input into its production technology, each transport industry also uses environmental quality, denoted by e_0 per unit of transport by the public transport mode and e_1 per unit of transport by the private transport mode. Environmental quality is interpreted here as an input into the transport mode's production function. Thus we can also refer to the environmental costs of each transport mode. This reduction in environmental quality may be in the form of emissions, but may also refer to noise or accidents. A fourth type of external effect of the transport industry is congestion. We call a transport mode congested if its demand for infrastructure —a_0 for transport mode and a_1 for transport mode 1 in Figure 10.1—exceeds its infrastructure's capacity, I_0 and I_1 respectively. Note that the speed of a transport mode can be determined as a function of its infrastructure demand and capacity. Transport speed can also be seen as an output of the transport industry. There is no market for transport speed. Also, the production of speed may not necessarily exhibit constant returns to scale. The behavior of a transport industry can then be described by a profit-maximization problem.

For each transport mode, the impact of its economic activities on the environment through its use of transport is given in this model by the use of environmental quality. Verhoef (1996) distinguishes four types of external effects of transport: accidents, pollution, noise, and congestion, which are caused primarily by road transport. We describe the impact of the transport industry on the environmental quality E of the country by assuming E to be a function of the use of environmental quality e_t by all transport modes t. This change in environmental quality affects the utility of the consumers and the profits of the producers, and it can therefore be interpreted as an external effect to both parties.

Since this section deals with a general equilibrium model, all important variables are determined by the model itself. The wage rate w is determined as the clearing rate of the country's labor market, and the interest rate r as the clearing rate of the capital market. The prices p_0 and p_1 of the commodities clear the underlying commodity markets. For the private transport market, the price q_1 clears the market. On the other hand, the price of the public transport mode q_0 is usually set by national or regional/local governments in the EU according to some pricing rule.

We have assumed that the transport industries apply constant returns-to-scale technology to provide transport units to their respective markets. Then the unit price of the private transport industry, q_1, is determined by the unit cost, while the activity level clears the private transport market. The activity level of the public transport industry also clears the market.

Figure 10.1 clearly shows that no market exists for environmental quality. Consequently, there is no price that regulates the use of environmental quality by the different transport modes, and these transport modes therefore do not take their impact on the environment into account; i.e., the environmental costs of their activities, e_t, equal zero. The external effects of transport, in the form of emissions, accidents, and noise, directly affect the utility of the other agents in a negative way. The consequences of congestion on other agents' utility are indirect. We have already mentioned the reduction in speed of the transport mode when demand for infrastructure or transport itself increases. In the case of congestion of a transport mode t, i.e., when the demand for infrastructure by the transport industry t exceeds its capacity, both the consumer and the producer are restricted in their demand for transport by this mode. Hence their optimization problems are subjected to an extra constraint on their demand for transport. Under these circumstances, they switch to another mode, or they forgo some of their economic activities. Due to congestion, the consumer cannot achieve all the consumption or supply all the labor he desires, and therefore he has less utility. The producer cannot sell all his output or obtain all the necessary inputs, and therefore cannot fulfill the demand for his commodity.

THE RESEARCH PROFILE

Extensive economic relations exist between the EU and the U.S. As a consequence, the separate transport policies they have adopted will have major consequences for these economic relations, which might make it difficult to get these policies implemented. Imposing extra taxes on environmentally unfriendly modes of transport in the EU might force producers there to increase their prices, thereby seriously damaging their competitiveness with respect to their counterparts in the U.S. If transport policies are to be effective in the EU as well as in North America, a common approach is called for.

In order to be able to assess the consequences of common transport policies and compare them with already well-studied individual policies, we need a framework for comparison. The general equilibrium framework we introduced earlier might play this role. We can set up a multi-country model, with the U.S. as one country with different regions, and the EU as a set of single-region countries. This model should benefit from the various types of transport impact studies that have already been performed in these countries separately. Thus the framework of the previous section can be seen as summarizing the result of a meta-analysis of these studies. (See Kremers, Nijkamp, and Rietveld, 2000 for more details on this idea.)

We should also consider the network or spatial character of transport. The framework model in the previous section currently determines whether congestion exists only by determining that there is excess demand for transport units, whether it be kilometers on the road or bytes on a computer network. But we would like to talk about urban congestion or local depreciation of environmental quality, thereby bringing in the spatial context of transport. In order to extend the framework model to include the network character of transport, so-called transportation network equilibrium models can provide a solution. These models are relatively unknown in economic theory, but an extensive literature on this field exists in mathematical programming. See Friesz, 1985 for an overview; Harker, 1987; or more recently, Kanwalroop, Nagurney, and Ramanujam, 1999.

If we are able to operationalize such a spatial general equilibrium model into an applied model—i.e., find sufficient and appropriate data to calibrate a benchmark—we can perform simulations with respect to different transport policies to assess their impact on environmental quality and congestion in the different countries. Large databases already exist for the TRENEN project in the EU, and the GTAP database in the USA may also yield a solution. These data determine the aggregation of the variables representing the economic activities. The variables in the previous section are at their most aggregate level, and should be deaggregated toward the available data. Other entities necessary for successful calibration, such as elasticities, could be obtained from a meta-analysis of the appropriate literature.

The calibrated model provides us with a benchmark equilibrium that we can use to assess various transport impact policies. Transport policies that may be considered include the previously mentioned policies, which have already been implemented and are well-studied. But we can also address policies that could be implemented cooperatively by the EU and the U.S., and compare them to the aforementioned individual policies. Thus different coalitions among the various countries in the model could be considered.

This approach could teach us a lot about the impact of transport policies on different societies. The U.S. and the EU differ significantly in their attitudes toward transportation and its consequences for economic activities. But input from both sides is necessary. Expertise on transport in the EU can best be obtained from European resources such as the aforementioned TRENEN project; the same is true for the U.S. The idea is to provide a framework in which we can productively join forces and expertise with a goal to increase our knowledge about the sustainability issues associated with transport.

REFERENCES

EC (Commission of the European Communities). 1996. *Green Paper towards Fair and Efficient Pricing in Transport: Policy Options for Internalizing the External Costs of Transport in the European Union.* Brussels: Directorate-General for Transport.

Friesz, T. 1985. "Transportation Network Equilibrium, Design and Aggregation: Key Developments and Research Opportunities." *Transportation Research-* A19A: 413–427.

Harker, P. T. 1987. *Predicting Intercity Freight Flows.* Utrecht, the Netherlands: VNU Science Press.

Kanwalroop, K. D., A. Nagurney, and P. Ramanujam. 1999. *Environmental Networks: A Framework for Economic Decision-Making and Policy Analysis.* London: Edward Elgar.

Kremers, H., P. Nijkamp, and P. Rietveld. 2001. "The Scope of Meta Analysis for Transport Impact Policy Analysis in Environmental Economics." In R. Florax, P. Nijkamp, and K. Willis, *Comparative Environmental Economic Assessment.* London: Edward Elgar.

Nijkamp, P., and M. van Geenhuizen. 1997. "European Transport: Challenges and Opportunities for Future Research and Policies." *Journal of Transport Geography* 5, no. 1: 4–11.

OECD. 1995. *Urban Travel and Sustainable Development.* Paris: OECD.

Samuelson, P. A. 1952. "Spatial Price Equilibrium and Linear Programming." *American Economic Review* 42: 283–303.

Shoven, J. B., and J. Whalley. 1992. *Applying General Equilibrium.* Cambridge: Cambridge University Press.

Verhoef, E. 1996. *Economic Efficiency and Social Feasibility in the Regulation of Road Transport Externalities.* Amsterdam: Thesis Publishers.

World Bank. 1996. *Sustainable Transport: Priorities for Policy Reform.* Development in Practice. Washington, D.C.: World Bank.

CHAPTER ELEVEN

Transport–Land Use Relations in Restructuring Metropolitan Areas

Implications for Air Quality in Chicago and Stockholm

Lars Lundqvist
and Tschangho John Kim

INTRODUCTION

Implications of U.S. Legislation for Transportation and Land Use

Recent U.S. legislation, including the Clean Air Act Amendments of 1990 (CAAA), the Intermodal Surface Transportation Efficiency Act of 1991 (ISTEA), and the Transportation Equity Act for the 21st Century (TEA-21), has highlighted the connection between transportation and air quality. Among other changes from previous versions of the Clean Air Act, the CAAA established a classification for designating geographic areas on the basis of their measurable levels of specific-criteria air pollutants. The CAAA also began to use the control of transportation, rather than just technological improvements, as a means of attaining air quality goals. It requires states to demonstrate that their transportation plans and projects conform to their plans for attaining and maintaining compliance with the National Ambient Air Quality Standards (NAAQS). Federal funds are available only for projects that demonstrate conformity.

The CAAA and ISTEA have focused attention on the connection between transportation and land use as a means of attaining air quality goals. To date, most of the reductions in air emissions have stemmed from technological advances such as more sophisticated air pollution control equipment for factories and catalytic converters in automobiles. Despite the significant air quality gains realized through technological improvements in the past and the prospects for future improvements, technological advances in transportation may not be able to compensate for the increased use of automobiles. The U.S. EPA predicts that the increased VMT (vehicle miles of travel)—even at a conservative 2 percent growth per year—will begin to outpace technological gains in air quality by the year 2005 (Kessler and Schroeer, 1995, p. 247).

The eroding ability of technological improvements to compensate for increasing VMT and perceptions of increasing traffic congestion and commuting times suggest that fundamental changes that alter the demand for transportation may be required to improve and protect air quality. Land use planning focused on reducing VMT and the quantity of vehicle trips may be an effective long-term means of improving air quality. These tactics can include a variety of strategies, such as the promotion of flexible work schedules, transit use, and growth management.

The 1990 CAAA and
Its Implications for Chicago

The 1990 CAAA imposed new and more stringent requirements for ozone non-attainment areas, in particular for the reduction of volatile organic compound (VOC) emissions from mobile sources. Ozone non-attainment areas are classified on the basis of how badly the NAAQS for ozone are exceeded. Los Angeles is classified as the worst area, and seven other non-attainment areas fall into the severe classification, including the Chicago region, consisting of the city of Chicago and its suburbs.

According to the mandates imposed by the 1990 CAAA, the non-attainment areas must be brought into compliance with the ozone standards by the year 2007. This requires in the case of Chicago a reduction of VOC emissions by 45 percent from the 1990 level. In order to comply with these mandates, many strategies of transportation control measures have been suggested for reducing emissions and VMT. Some of those suggestions are voluntary in nature, some are pricing strategies, and some are regulatory (U.S. EPA, 1990). A brief assessment of trip data for the Chicago area indicates that in the long run, a comprehensive and system-wide land use/transport strategy for environmentally efficient mobility will be necessary.

In Chicago, there were a total of 20.4 million person-trips per day in 1990, of which about 18 million person-trips, or 88 percent, were made using automobiles and 2.4 million person-trips, or 12 percent, were made using transit. In terms of VMT, a total of 103.8 million miles were traveled by 14 million automobiles per day, for an average distance of 7.4 miles per car per day. Of the total VMT, about 40 percent were from work-related trips. The average distance traveled by an automobile for work-related travel was about 10.8 miles. Among the 2.4 million persons using transit per day, 61.5 percent used it for work-related trips.

SWEDISH ENVIRONMENTAL POLICY AND
LAND USE/TRANSPORT IN STOCKHOLM

In Communication Committee, 1997, the goals related to reductions of emissions are expressed according to Table 11.1. Other goals relate to the impacts of air pollution on human health, noise, natural and cultural qualities, and natural resources. We may conclude that the intermediate objectives regarding the reductions of sulfur and VOCs

seem possible to attain, while the CO_2 and NO_x objectives look very hard to reach. The nationally determined goals for reductions of sulfur, nitrogen oxides, and carbon dioxide emissions have been adopted by municipal- and county-level authorities in the Stockholm region.

Traffic emissions play an increasing role in the environmental debate. This is due to the fact that point source emissions from industry and from power-generation and space-heating plants within the region have been (or are being) reduced drastically. Sulfur dioxide emissions from combustion were reduced by more than 50 percent in the Stockholm region during the 1980s. In this situation, dispersed emissions from transportation and consumption activities become more important. The transportation sector is the predominant source of nitrogen oxide emissions, with road traffic accounting for about 50 percent. The total emission of nitrogen oxides was marginally reduced in the late 1980s, and the reduction is expected to continue due to the growing use of catalytic converters in cars. About 50 percent of carbon dioxide emissions emanate from the transportation sector, with road traffic contributing about 25 percent. It should be concluded that transportation and road traffic are significant sectors in terms of their regional production of emissions.

The national transportation policy should provide individuals and industries in all parts of the country with a transport supply that is socioeconomically efficient and sustainable over the long term. Five subgoals have been formulated:

- *Accessibility:* The transport system should be designed to meet the basic needs of individuals and industries.
- *High transport quality:* The design and function of the transport system should provide a high quality of transport to industries.
- *Good environment:* The design and function of the transport system should be adapted to the requirement of a healthy environment for all, with the natural and cultural environment being protected against damage. Conservation of land, water, and other natural resources should be promoted.
- *Safe traffic:* The long-term goal for traffic safety is that nobody should be killed or seriously injured in traffic accidents. The design and function of the transport system should be adapted to these requirements.
- *Positive regional development:* The transport system should promote positive regional development by equalizing differences in development potential in different

Table 11.1 Operationalization of Emission Reduction Goals and Initial Developments

Substance	Base year	Intermediate objective	Result 1995	Long-term objective
Carbon dioxide	1990	–15% by 2020	+10%	–60% by 2050
Nitrogen oxides	1980	–50% by 2005	–11%	–80% by 2020
Sulfur	1980	–45% by 2005	–37%	–90% by 2020
Volatile organic compounds	1988	–70% by 2005	–26%	–85% by 2020

parts of the country and by counteracting disadvantages from long transport distances.

In comparison with earlier statements of national transportation policy objectives, the new proposal upgrades the environmental and safety subgoals and makes them more precise. Internalization of external costs for congestion, accidents, and environmental damage constitutes an important component of the present transport policy.

Conclusions

In both Chicago and Stockholm, a fundamental reduction in long-term mobile source emissions will most likely require a radical departure from conventional land use/transport planning in order to affect the level of VMT. Also, more short-term road pricing and mode-switching strategies (particularly relevant in the European discussion) will affect accessibility and land use (Wegener, 1996). Combined policy packages, including incentives and control measures in both the land use and transportation systems, have been suggested by analysts with a global perspective on urban development (see, e.g., Newman and Kenworthy, 1989), as well as from the European perspective (see, e.g., Johansson and Mattsson, 1995; OECD, 1995; and Wegener, 1996).

Aim and Scope of the Research

The purpose of our research proposal is to compare the transport/land use relationships in Chicago and Stockholm from the standpoint of air quality. Through this process we will draw policy implications with respect to how we should go about restructuring land use and transportation to achieve better air quality. We will comparatively assess the extent to which the existing land uses in Chicago and Stockholm affect VMT and the resulting mobile source emissions and air quality. An integrated land use/transport model developed by Kim (1989), as outlined below, will be used and applied to both cities in order to shed light on possible policies.

A comparative study of mobility patterns, land uses, driving forces, and incentives in the U.S. and Europe is essential in its own right. The patterns of land use and transportation are very different. We want to compare and explain location choice and transport behavior. The development of population, production activities, income, household formation, and other important background factors will be analyzed, and their relative impact on spatial behavior will be studied. Scenarios and expected developments will be collected and compared. Some of the differences in 1980 are outlined in Table 11.2.

In order to further analyze the differences and similarities between the urban systems of Chicago and Stockholm, we propose to use the land use/transport model TRANSACT (see Kim, 1989 and Lundqvist, 1998). Its main components can be summarized as follows:

Objective:
Minimize {Total cost for travel and deliveries (according to user equilibrium in the transportation networks) + handling costs for exports + opportunity cost for capital and land used for settlements}.

Constraints:
1. The *total exports* from designated export zones should attain a *stipulated level* for each commodity.
2. *Goods and services should be balanced* by zone and commodity: Deliveries from other zones (by various trans-

Table 11.2   Some Comparisons between Chicago and Stockholm Data for the Land Use/Transport Model TRANSACT (both referring to 1980)

Item	Chicago	Stockholm
Population	7.7 million	1.52 million
Employment	3.5 million	0.84 million
Number of zones	74	30
Public transit share (peak hour)	22%	56%
Number of nodes in road network	1060	397
Number of road links	2902	921
Number of volume/delay functions	1	12
Observed/estimated interzonal traffic flows:		
• car	yes	yes
• transit	yes	yes
• truck	yes	yes*
• rail	yes	no
Sectors (employment share):	manufacturing (30%)	manufacturing (22%)
	trade (20%)	private services (33%)
	services (50%)	public services (45%)

*available between 25 municipalities

port modes) + production in the zone should be no less than deliveries to other zones (by various transport modes) + intermediary and final use in the zone + exports.

3. There should be required *entropy levels* on travel, delivery, and export patterns (gives rise to transport and export patterns of the "gravity" type and modal split of the "logit" type).

4. *The land market should be balanced.* The demand for land is determined by endogenous zone- and commodity-specific land consumption coefficients (depending on settlement density) and by the endogenously computed activity levels. The supply of land for settlements in each zone is exogenously determined.

5. *Definitional linkages* should be established between route and link flows and between route flows and delivery volumes.

6. Flows, production levels, and export volumes should be *non-negative*.

The model combines several modeling traditions:

- input-output analysis;
- economic base theory;
- entropy-maximizing gravity models for trip and transportation patterns;
- logit models for mode choice;
- transportation network equilibrium modeling (including trip distribution, mode choice, and route choice);
- market equilibrium on markets for land, goods, and services; and
- cost minimization as the main economic principle.

The intention is first to apply the prototype model (TRANSACT) with as few changes as possible to the two cities. Later adaptations of the model to the individual cities may be attempted in order to improve its explanatory power.

Since the transport cost of the objective is computed in accordance with user equilibrium (the sum of integrals of all link cost functions, from zero to the actual link flow), TRANSACT will generate a market-oriented solution with equilibrium on the markets for transportation, goods, services, and land. The prices of land, goods and services are determined through these market equilibriums. The prices of land and capital also affect the density of settlements through the cost-minimizing choice of building technology by firms and households. The structure and capacity of the transportation networks are specified exogenously. The land supply, too, is exogenous, reflecting a certain land-release policy. The existence of the city relies on the exogenously determined export requirements.

TRANSACT can be seen as a generalized version of a combined transportation network equilibrium model and is solved by developing a similar type of partial linearization technique for an equivalent optimization problem. A description of the Frank-Wolfe type of algorithm is given in Lundqvist (1998). Basically, the algorithm seeks in each iteration a direction of improvement from the current solution and then determines a step size to be executed. The complicating factor is the set of land use constraints: both land consumption coefficients and activity amounts are non-linear functions of the land price, and a non-linear equation system has to be solved in each main iteration of the algorithm in order to calculate land use and transportation patterns.

COMPARATIVE LAND USE/TRANSPORT STUDIES IN THE LITERATURE

Concern for interactions between land use, transport, and the environment is not new. For many years the separation of uses to minimize nuisances has been a fundamental concern of land use planners. Evidence that air pollution represents such a nuisance has been confirmed by research demonstrating that air pollution significantly reduces land values (Knaap, 1997). Recognition of the relationship between transportation and land use is also not new. Mitchell and Rapkin (1954) demonstrated as early as 1954 that traffic is a function of land use. For decades, transportation planners have divided the process into the four steps known as trip generation, mode choice, trip distribution, and route choice. In this process, land use is taken as a given, and the transportation system is designed to accommodate transportation demands.

Land use has recently come to be viewed less as a given and more as a factor determined in part by transportation policy (Moore and Thorsness, 1994). The notion that transportation systems affect land use is not new. What is relatively new, and has been fueled by the CAAA and ISTEA, is the notion that transportation and land use planning can serve to further air quality goals. New mod-

els need to be developed that include feedback from transportation policy to land use. In Europe the interest in sustainable urban systems has led to a renewed interest in land use/transport modeling (Johansson and Mattsson, 1995; OECD, 1995; Lundqvist, 1996; Wegener, 1996). This research can aid our effort to develop models that incorporate the complex dynamic interrelationships between land use, transportation, and the environment (LTE). A recent survey of LTE models can be found in Wegener 1998, and some examples of land use/transport models are reported in Lundqvist et al., 1998.

One example of comparative approaches to urban systems evaluation is represented by the statistical analysis of Newman and Kenworthy (1989), based on data from thirty-two major world cities, including Chicago and Stockholm. Their diagram for the relation between per capita gasoline use and urban density is well known and has been the subject of much controversy. Stockholm is fairly representative of the European cities, while Chicago has low per capita gasoline use compared to many other U.S. cities. A second example is the classification of urban systems according to land use dispersion and travel behavior, as illustrated by the so called "Brotchie triangle" (see Brotchie et al., 1996). This concept has been used both for comparison of actual cities and their development over time, and for presentation of model results (see, e.g., Wegener, 1996).

COMPARATIVE EUROPEAN AND NORTH AMERICAN RESEARCH PROFILE

The research outlined above is inherently comparative, combining empirical and theoretical investigations. Stockholm and Chicago are very different and seem fairly representative of the European and U.S. urban contexts. Therefore, both a comparative empirical analysis of background factors, trends, driving forces, incentives, institutional conditions, etc., and an attempt to model the land use/transport interactions through a single unified approach seem worthwhile. The interpretation of the estimated model properties may be related to the results of the empirical analysis. The comparative approach may also include an analysis of planning ambitions, policy alternatives, model tools, and decision support systems.

The authors gained a lot of experience from long-term Swedish and North American research collaboration. Our volume *Network Infrastructure and the Urban Environ-*

ment (Lundqvist et al., 1998) was a result of that collaboration and includes contributions from studies of Chicago and Stockholm. Earlier collaborations on combined network equilibrium models for the two cities are reported in Boyce and Lundqvist, 1987; Zhang, 1995; and Abrahamsson, 1996.

EXPECTED RESEARCH RESULTS/PERSPECTIVES

We expect that the comparative analysis will shed light on the basic mechanisms behind mobility and location choice. The combination of empirical and theoretical perspectives will offer a broad picture of exogenous and endogenous factors affecting land use/transport interactions in urban systems. Since location and mobility, together with relevant socioeconomic background factors, largely determine point sources and mobile sources of emissions, the research will also lead to findings on the environmental implications of differential urban developments. The proposed model is strategic in nature and can indicate on only a rather crude geographical level the location (production and consumption activities) and mobility (VMT over modes and links) characteristics that are necessary inputs for projections of emissions. For geographically more detailed results, which may be required for assessing distribution of pollutants, concentrations, and emissions, geographical (and/or functional) disaggregation may be necessary.

Both the empirical and the theoretical investigation will handle policy alternatives that are popular in the discussion of sustainable cities and sustainable transport. They rely on various combinations of investments, regulations and pricing options. The potential effect of integrated policy packages will receive special attention. The comprehensive nature of the proposed model is well suited for a strategic evaluation of package policies.

REFERENCES

Abrahamsson, T. 1996. "Network Equilibrium Approaches to Urban Transportation Markets." Ph.D. thesis, Royal Institute of Technology, Stockholm, Department of Infrastructure and Planning, TRITA-IP FR 96-13.

Boyce, D. E., and L. Lundqvist. 1987. "Network Equilibrium Models of Urban Location and Travel Choices: Alternative Formulations for the Stockholm Region." *Papers of the Regional Science Association* 61: 93–104.

Brotchie, J. F., M. Anderson, P. G. Gibbs, and C. McNamara. 1996. "Urban Productivity and Sustainability: Impacts of Technological Change." In Y. Hayashi and J. Roy, eds., *Transport, Land-Use and the Environment.* Dordrecht: Kluwer.

Communication Committee. 1997. *New Course in Traffic Policy: Final Report of the Communication Committee.* (In Swedish.) SOU 35. Stockholm: Fritzes.

Johansson, B., and L.-G. Mattsson. 1995. "From Theory and Policy Analysis to Implementation of Road Pricing: The Stockholm Region in the 1990s." In B. Johansson and L.-G. Mattsson, eds., *Road Pricing: Theory, Empirical Assessment and Policy.* Dordrecht: Kluwer.

Kessler, J., and W. Schroeer. 1995. "Meeting Mobility and Air Quality Goals: Strategies That Work." *Transportation* 22: 241–272.

Kim, T. J. 1989. *Integrated Urban Systems Modeling: Theory and Applications.* Norwell, Mass.: Kluwer.

Knaap, G. J. 1997. "The Determinants of Metropolitan Land Values: Implications for Regional Planning." Portland, Ore.: Metro.

Lundqvist, L. 1996. "Using Combined Network Equilibrium Models for Environmnetal Assessments of Land-Use/Transportation Scenarios." In Y. Hayashi and J. Roy, eds., *Transport, Land-Use and the Environment.* Dordrecht: Kluwer.

Lundqvist, L. 1998. "A Combined Model for Analyzing Network Infrastructure and Land-Use/Transportation Interactions." In L. Lundqvist, L.-G. Mattsson, and T. J. Kim, eds., *Network Infrastructure and the Urban Environment: Advances in Spatial Systems Modelling.* Heidelberg: Springer-Verlag.

Lundqvist, L., L.-G. Mattsson, and T. J. Kim, eds. 1998. *Network Infrastructure and the Urban Environment: Advances in Spatial Systems Modelling.* Heidelberg: Springer-Verlag.

Mitchell, R. B., and C. Rapkin. 1954. *Urban Traffic: A Function of Land Use.* New York: Columbia University Press.

Moore, T., and P. Thorsness. 1994. "The Transportation/ Land Use Connection." PAS report # 448/449, Chicago: American Planning Association.

Newman, P. W. G., and J. R. Kenworthy. 1989. "Gasoline Consumption and Cities: A Comparison of US Cities with a Global Survey." *Journal of American Planning Association* 51, no. 9: 24–37.

OECD. 1995. *Urban Travel and Sustainable Development.* Paris: European Conference of Ministers of Transport, OECD.

United States Environmental Protection Agency (U.S. EPA). 1990. "Guidance for Initiating Ozone/CO SIP

Emission Inventories Pursuant to the 1990 Clean Air Act Amendments." Triangle Park, N.C.: U.S. Environmental Protection Agency, Office of Air Quality Planning and Standards.

Wegener, M. 1996. "Reduction of CO_2 Emissions of Transport by Reorganisation of Urban Activities." In Y. Hayashi and J. Roy, eds., *Transport, Land-Use and the Environment.* Dordrecht: Kluwer.

Wegener, M. 1998. "Applied Models of Urban Land Use, Transport and Environment: State of the Art and Future Developments." In L. Lundqvist, L.-G. Mattsson, and T. J. Kim, eds., *Network Infrastructure and the Urban Environment: Advances in Spatial Systems Modelling.* Heidelberg: Springer-Verlag.

Zhang, Y.-F. 1995. "Parameter Estimation for Combined Models of Urban Travel Choices Consistent with Equilibrium Travel Costs." Ph.D. thesis, Department of Civil Engineering, University of Illinois, Chicago.

CHAPTER TWELVE

Social Change and Transportation in U.S. Edge Cities

Morton E. O'Kelly
and Brian A. Mikelbank

INTRODUCTION

Metropolitan form is so strongly influenced by transportation technology that stages of historical urban morphology are often named for the prevailing transportation system (Taaffe, Gauthier, and O'Kelly, 1996, Chapter 6): the electric streetcar, the freeway, and the beltway all shaped their eras. The emergence of the traditional central business district (CBD) was a function of transportation technology, as well as a variety of other interacting social and economic spatial forces. However, as former industrial urban areas have aged, and as new urban areas have grown, the forces that created the CBD and held it together have been severely weakened. What we see now is a landscape of somewhat concentric rings, emanating from the center. Beginning at what was once a lively core, but is now, to some degree, an abandoned center, we see a ring of "first suburbs." These were the recipients of the first shift out of the city center. Beyond these are rings of newer vintage, each having had its own "day in the sun" as development sprawled outward. Each is now passed by as suburb-bound families and businesses seek out the emerging growth areas even farther from the center.

Sprawl

This haphazard urban-expansion growth has gained much media attention of late: we are entering a period of intense concern over the sustainability of urban sprawl. Transport impacts are some of the most widely recognized issues relating to sprawl. Christine Todd Whitman, the former governor of New Jersey, has been one of the most vocal opponents of sprawl. Speaking at a "Smart Growth" conference in 1998, she likened the intensity of the sprawl battle to the international competition during the Cold War space program, saying that we are fighting a "space race . . . not *outer* space but *open* space," and the enemy is sprawl. The explicit slant to the New Jersey anti-sprawl program is "space": better claim some of it for nature, or else it will be eclipsed by this unorganized, unplanned era of urban growth. She said, "Every state suffers when it develops haphazardly. Sprawl eats up open space . . . creates traffic jams that boggle the mind, and pollute the air. Sprawl can make one feel claustrophobic about the future our children and grandchildren will inherit." Her plan to preserve 1 million acres passed by a

2-to-1 margin in November 1998. The 1 million acres represent half of all New Jersey's undeveloped land: half for nature, half for "smart" growth (ideally, transit villages, pedestrian-centered towns, etc.). The hope is to change the focus from development at the fringe to *redevelopment* where infrastructure and services already exist—in the central cities—and programs are under way to make that easier for developers.

On a broader scale, the Clinton administration introduced its "Livability Agenda." Gore (1999) proposed to reverse the tide of what he claims to be decades of bad planning with several proposed programs, among them more than $700 million in tax credits to assist communities in their efforts to find alternative solutions to congestion, beyond the building of more and/or wider highways; $1.6 billion to help states reduce pollution and congestion; and $50 million to assist in finding regional solutions (an implicit recognition of the importance of the geography/scale of the problem).

While urban sprawl has certainly achieved national prominence in the policy arena, it is not a topic without debate. Tierney (1999) points to the fact that while land is being developed at a rate of fifty acres an hour, this rate is but half what it was in the 1980s, and a mere one-fourth of the rate that prevailed in the 1970s. He calls our attention to the fact that the most built-up state, New Jersey, is still two-thirds undeveloped. However, development at the fringe is arguably inefficient: low-density, land-intensive, single-use-dominated, and transit-incompatible.

Edge Cities

Closely related to sprawl, and one of its visible outcomes, is the emergence of what Garreau (1991) calls "Edge Cities." These areas have at least 5 million square feet of office space and 600,000 square feet of retail space, have populations that increase at 9 A.M. on weekdays, and are seen as their own urban entities in terms of shopping, employment, and residential activity. Edge cities are relatively new on the scene; the typical edge city was primarily a rural or residential area thirty years ago. However, rush hour traffic to and from these suburban centers now strains the beltways and outerbelt freeways. Office employment and services, traditionally considered non-basic economic activity, have become the backbone of suburban economies, and in this sense are primary "basic" employment generators. A large share of the businesses in edge cities are headquarters and offices seeking freeway-fronting

prestige locations. Edge cities are also home to small businesses; the top ten areas in terms of businesses with fewer than fifty employees are all edge cities (Garreau, 1994). A variety of businesses have found a new locational freedom, and as they continue to out-migrate to the fringe, edge cities are born and continue to prosper. As these cities grow, the value of sites for further development becomes entwined with the prestige of the surrounding residential community, and a premium is placed on visibility from major arteries. Furthermore, edge cities have retained high concentrations of service establishments. On a per-employee basis, edge cities quite often rank in the top ten in the number of drinking establishments (7), nightclubs (8), restaurants (8), and ethnic restaurants (9) (Garreau, 1994).

TRANSPORT AND EDGE CITIES

Edge cities are transforming both the residential and business landscapes of urban and suburban areas. By their very nature they have intensive levels of daily in- and out-mobility to adjacent areas. While this is an obvious remark, there have been few previous quantitative studies of the level of interaction between an edge city and the rest of the adjoining metropolitan area.

This new geography is affecting urban transportation patterns in a variety of ways: (1) edge city to/from the CBD during the A.M./P.M. peak hours; (2) inter-edge city; and (3) intra-edge city. The edge city–CBD case is perhaps, on the surface, the most mainstream. Like most suburb–CBD traffic, it is primarily unidirectional: the main flow is to the CBD in the morning and from it in the afternoon. Traffic reduction in this case is difficult. High-income suburbanites favor the drive-alone mode: except in the case of extreme congestion, it seems that car or van pools, High Occupancy Vehicle lanes, and express transit services are of limited appeal to this demographic group. In addition, traditional transit has a difficult time serving the increasingly low-density development of these new suburbs. One possible solution (currently being discussed in Columbus, Ohio) is sending smaller commuter buses into suburban communities, which would feed into transit hubs, and on to express buses to the CBD. Montgomery County, Maryland, has been doing this successfully for more than twenty years to get its dispersed suburbanites into Washington, D.C. (Goldberg, 1997). Ironically, traffic volume in the opposite direction (responding to the spatial mismatch hypothesis) should actually face relatively low congestion: daily access from the CBD to suburban job growth could, at least in theory, be provided if transit is routed against the mainstream flow, and some jurisdictions are finding this against-the-flow commute to be on a steady increase. The volume of the commute from Long Island to New York City has become relatively stable, while the reverse commute continues to grow (Lutz, 1995). Chicago's reverse-commute corridors were experiencing the early stages of congestion nearly ten years ago (Jordan, 1994). More recently, Chicago reverse-commuters are the largest growth market for the Chicago Transit Authority's bus system, at over 20 percent of all riders (Worthington, 1997). Philadelphia identified several employment clusters outside of the city, and initiated, in partnership with business owners, feeder bus systems to take employees from that city's metro system to suburban work locations (Wade, 1994).

At the inter-edge city scale, edge cities are creating a tremendous demand for transportation services at peak commuting hours, as workers commute between suburban homes and suburban office parks. Evenings and weekends provide little congestion relief, as leisure-time activities are often no longer centered in the downtown area. Many of the outerbelt roads and highways that were originally designed as circumference routes around major cities have become major connecting arteries between these suburban cities. In some areas, the demand for transportation along these corridors has become so intense that there are expensive and disruptive road-widening projects, and new outer-outerbelts are envisaged far beyond what just ten years ago would have been regarded as the edge of the city. However, new construction obviously is not a sustainable solution. When the time horizon is expanded, the costs and disruption of installing enough infrastructure to keep options open beyond the next few decades are simply overwhelming. It is not clear whether new construction and/or outerbelt widening can keep up with travel demand growth.

Across the country, tensions are mounting between cities and suburbs, as highway dollars are channeled toward suburban construction while existing, and aging, downtown infrastructure is neglected. In addition, some evidence is beginning to show that the non-transport user benefits of incremental highway construction may be limited. Again, transit seems unlikely to be a savior. When

the issue was reducing congestion into a relatively compact CBD, transit was, at least on paper, a workable solution. Radial bus or rail lines ran from dispersed suburbs and converged like spokes on the economic focal point, or hub, of the region. Patterns of residence and employment are certainly different in the edge city case; transit lines would have to run from one low-density sprawling suburb to another.

On the whole, few seem willing to bring up the topic of transit at the edge city scale. In Atlanta, before losing federal construction money, northern county commissioners were adamantly opposed ("The people in this county absolutely do not want MARTA"; "I would do everything I could to fight that [the northern extension of MARTA services]"), going so far as to say it would be a "waste of time" (Goldberg, 1998). The tone has changed considerably since the area lost federal highway construction funds, and discussion of linking the northern suburbs is under way. In general, though, we hear immediate objections in the form of "no new taxes," affordability issues, objections to user fees, and an argument from the "who congests—who pays" perspective. Many who live in the suburbs fight any kind of parking, transit, or transfer station facility, using a not-in-my-backyard (NIMBY) argument.

When the problem of intra-edge city congestion is considered, there is the temptation to apply the same lessons learned from intra-CBD congestion, but again, this is difficult because the differences are many. The first is that hub-and-spoke, grid-based, or otherwise compact CBDs were well served by transit, but not so these expansive, land-intensive edge cities. Next, low density, high incomes, high auto-ownership rates, and ample parking make intra-edge city transit an even less likely solution.

NUMERICAL EXAMPLES FROM DUBLIN, OHIO

These conflicts between sprawl, edge cities, downtowns, suburbs, congestion, and planning are playing out in obvious ways in the nation's larger cities. It is important to note, though, that the same forces are at work at a lower level of the urban hierarchy. We present as an example the case of Dublin, Ohio, a suburb of Columbus that is facing many, if not all, of these fringe transportation problems. Dublin is a rapidly growing suburban community located on the I-270 outerbelt, to the northwest of the Columbus Metropolitan Statistical Area (MSA). The morning and evening peak traffic flows clog the roads. The rates of commercial and residential development have been staggering. Local community surveys continue to list transportation-related problems (and improvements thereof) as the most important citizen concern. Because one of the authors of this chapter served on the Steering Committee for the City of Dublin's Community Plan, we were able to obtain a full range of data on land use, network conditions, journey to work, A.M. peak origin to destination (OD) flow, and all future planned network upgrades. These data were discussed as part of the community plan and were analyzed extensively by an engineering consulting firm (Barton Aschman).

Dublin has experienced recent rapid population growth, from 16,366 persons (5,533 households) in 1990 to an estimated 29,000 persons (10,783 households) in 1998. What makes these data remarkable is that the 1980 census showed Dublin with just 1,230 households! In 1990, only 19 percent of workers who resided in Dublin actually worked in Dublin. The rest commuted to jobs in Columbus, or to other parts of the metropolitan area. Dublin, in turn, attracts large numbers of workers into its cluster of typical edge city employment opportunities, including office employment, retail, and light industry. The overwhelming majority of trips are made by automobile (90 percent reported "drive alone" as their journey-to-work mode in the 1990 Census). The only other significant mode is a small fraction by carpool. This intense in- and out-commuting is at the heart of the traffic problems inherent in an edge city, and the most recent data show that the pattern has intensified.

The case studied here reflects assumptions that were gradually revised during the planning process. The political realities of community plan development involved an iterative readjustment of density scenarios. Initial density estimates would have allowed such intense levels of development that the city could have expected intolerable levels of traffic congestion. Thus, the planning scenarios were adjusted to a lower-density growth, in an effort to alleviate projected bottlenecks, and the traffic planning was carried out on the basis of those data. The projected interaction matrix is based on this lower-growth scenario, and shows predicted interzonal traffic. The edge city is an open system, with flows into and out from this jurisdiction to the surrounding suburban and urban communities. The authors started with the OD flow matrix, and divided the origins and destinations into *internal*

and *external* nodes. (There are 213 internal traffic analysis zones [TAZ], and there is a related data set that shows the land use in each TAZ.) The external nodes link Dublin to surrounding cities.

Define $T_{ij}(k,m)$ to be the traffic flow from i to j, where i is in area k, and j is in area m. k and m take the values of 1 or 2:1 for the *internal* nodes, and 2 for the *external* nodes. The following are key calculations and summations that synthesize by origin and by destination the volumes of interactions beginning and ending in various categories of origins and destinations respectively:

- $\sum_j T_{ij}(1,1) = O_i(1,1)$ origin and destination in Dublin; reported by origin
- $\sum_j T_{ij}(1,2) = O_i(1,2)$ origin in Dublin, external destination; reported by origin
- $\sum_j T_{ij}(2,1) = O_i(2,1)$ external origin, destination in Dublin; reported by origin
- $\sum_j T_{ij}(2,2) = O_i(2,2)$ external origin and destination; reported by origin
- $\sum_i T_{ij}(1,1) = D_j(1,1)$ origin and destination in Dublin; reported by destination
- $\sum_i T_{ij}(1,2) = D_j(1,2)$ origin in Dublin, external destination; reported by destination
- $\sum_i T_{ij}(2,1) = D_j(2,1)$ external origin, destination in Dublin; reported by destination
- $\sum_i T_{ij}(2,2) = D_j(2,2)$ external origin and destination; reported by destination

The position of these various quantities in a two-region interaction system is shown in Table 12.1. One of the most useful products of an analysis of this type is a quantified measurement of the number of traffic flows into and out of the edge city, together with a breakdown of these according to whether they are locally or externally "driven."

The data show that a large number of trips come into Dublin from outside the city. Further, of those externally originating trips along I-270, about 25 percent pass through the study area. Thus, the open nature of the edge city makes it susceptible to through traffic flows, which dominate local traffic. Another interesting observation is that the trips that originate from external zones outside to the northwest of Dublin pass predominantly through the city (i.e., the majority of those trips do not have internal zones as their destination). The accounting method can be used to quantify the share of traffic bound for various destinations at the entry and exit "gateways" of the city—the northern and southern edges of I-270 as it

Table 12.1   Accounting Scheme for the Dublin Traffic Flows

		Destination					
		Inside study area		*summary by origin*	Outside study area		*summary by origin*
Origin	**Inside study area**	Tij(1,1)		*work locally*	Tij(1,2)		*work in other city*
				Oi(1,1)			Oi(1,2)
Summary by destination		Came to work from inside	Dj(1,1)	*OD = 25,961 VMT = 93,135*	*exit from study area from local source*	Dj(1,2)	*OD = 24077 VMT = 123,535*
	Outside study area	Tij(2,1)		*commute in*	Tij(2,2)		*pass through*
				Oi(2,1)			Oi(2,2)
Summary by destination		Came to work from outside	Dj(2,1)	*OD = 29,681 VMT = 148,853*	*exit from study area passing through*	Dj(2,2)	*OD = 14,150 VMT = 125,205*

Table 12.2   Summary of In and Out Flow Characteristics at Two Gateways to the City

	Symbol	South/Westbound lanes	%	Symbol	North/Eastbound lanes	%
Northern gateway	Oi(2,1)	8,891	*77%*	Dj(1,2)	5,630	*66%*
	Oi(2,2)	2,670	*23%*	Dj(2,2)	2,876	*34%*
Southern gateway	Dj(1,2)	5,140	*62%*	Oi(2,1)	6,263	*73%*
	Dj(2,2)	3,177	*38%*	Oi(2,2)	2,267	*27%*

crosses into and out of the city. As Table 12.2 shows, there is a huge exchange of population into and out of the city: at the morning peak, roughly 15,200 vehicles (8,891 in the north and 6,263 in the south) come into the region from external zones, and have their destination in Dublin. At the same time, roughly 10,700 (5,140 in the south and 5,630 in the north) leave the region from the gateways.

From the destination point of view, the intense clustering of trip ends around the freeway is evident. The fact is that more than half of the trips to most employment destinations come from external origins (displaying a magnet or trip attraction effect). This shows that there is an intensive level of in-commuting to jobs in the Dublin area from external zones. The obvious solution of having more employees live close to these workplaces in Dublin is unfortunately not a practical one, as the high cost of housing in the city makes affordability a major issue. Other solutions, involving transit and light rail commuting, are under discussion and consideration by the regional transit agency.

Conclusions

This study has highlighted some of the issues facing edge cities, and has illustrated the growing concern with sprawl and growth in a variety of cities in North America, specifically Dublin, Ohio. It was seen that the planning of traffic capacity for a suburban municipality may progress with a view to local "isolated" conditions, despite the obvious and very real openness of the system in which this traffic is situated. Larger social issues involving the mobility of the young and the elderly are not discussed here, but it is clear that the edge city automobile-oriented system is not serving the needs of these groups. In terms of the broader themes of the conference, we can only echo the sentiment expressed by discussants: that this is a "stressed" traffic system. The case study does serve to highlight the contrasting view of sustainability in North American market economies, where the prevailing solution is to attempt to build one's way out of a traffic jam. I-270 is currently being widened to four lanes in both directions all across the northern edge of Columbus, and the city's capital budget contains many major road-widening and bridge projects.

REFERENCES

Garreau, J. 1991. *Edge City: Life on the New Frontier.* New York: Doubleday.

Garreau, J. 1994. "Edge Cities in Profile." *American Demographics,* February, 24–33.

Goldberg, D. 1997. "Drawing on Experience with an Innovative Bus System, Montgomery County, MD. Is Working Hard on Suburb-to-Suburb Transit Solutions." *The Atlanta Journal Constitution,* November 3.

Goldberg, D. 1998. "Can't Get There from Here: First in a Two Part Series—Northside's East-West Nightmare." *The Atlanta Journal Constitution,* May 10.

Gore, A. 1999. "Vice President Gore's Livability Announcement." Monday, January 11, 1999.

Jordan, J. 1994. "Reverse Commuting on the Rise." *New York Times Current Events Edition,* August 7.

Kamin, B. 1990. "Reverse Commuters Feel Rush-Hour Crunch." *Chicago Tribune,* June 8.

Lutz, P. 1995. "Reverse Commuting Is Making Some Gains." *New York Times Current Events Edition,* April 30.

Taaffe, E. J., H. Gauthier, and M. E. O'Kelly. 1996. *Geography of Transportation.* 2nd ed. Saddle River, N.J.: Prentice Hall.

Tierney, J. 1999. "Despite Scare, There Is Plenty of Room for the Suburbs to Keep Sprawling." *New York Times,* February 22, A18.

Wade, B. 1994. "Reverse Commuting: Transit Takes a Turn." *American City and County,* August, 37–44.

Whitman, C. T. 1998. Remarks of New Jersey Governor Christine Todd Whitman at the Partners for Smart Growth Conference, Austin, Texas, Tuesday, December 15.

Worthington, R. 1997. "Pace Gains from Reverse Commuters City-to-Suburb Riders Increasingly Use Bus." *Chicago Tribune,* July 3.

PART III

Dependence on the Automobile

CHAPTER THIRTEEN

Keeping the Holy Grail

The "Mobility View" of the Danish Automobile Club FDM

Jörg Beckmann

INTRODUCTION

Modern societies have given rise to a number of technical artifacts that have become paradigmatic. One of late modernity's most recognized (and contested) objects is certainly the automobile. In its current technical formation, the automobile has become the prime means of transportation in most of the industrialized countries. It signifies a distinct way of moving in space and time, and it has led to a particular mobility paradigm. *Automobilization as a modern mobility paradigm* is woven into the fabric of contemporary society. For many of us it provides "normal spatial mobility"—the type of routine spatial mobility that is exercised on a daily basis. This paradigm, however, has produced a number of anomalies that are often seen as a threat to automobilization's further existence. In other words, automobilization has produced risks that have a disruptive cultural and ecological effect, which in turn threaten the very foundations of this mobility paradigm. The growth of such risks has caused some to claim that we are now witnessing the end of the car as we know it. Environmental degradation of all kinds will limit the further expansion of the automobile—or such is the argument that is often put forward (Bode et al., 1986; Wolf, 1986). This, however, has proven to be wishful thinking (Canzler 1999). Automobilization, I will

argue in this chapter, is not necessarily in danger of extinction. It is, rather, in a state of constant change, reacting to and reacting upon other social processes in a dialectic process.

These changes in the fabric of automobilization have not led to a paradigm shift in the sense that the paradigm has produced anomalies that can no longer be resolved from within. The changes I am speaking of have modified the type of automobilization rather than replaced the paradigm as such. In the past, the mobility paradigm of automobilization was traditional and growth-oriented. These changes, however, lead me to claim that automobilization—just like modern societies themselves (Beck, 1992) —has since become *reflexive*.

For quite some time now, transport "experts" as well as "non-experts" have been concerned with the risks of automobilization. They acknowledge that traditional automobilization has created circumstances under which it cannot continue, and they are now engaged with the distribution and redistribution of such risks. Despite these increasing concerns, reflexive automobilization is anything but a homogeneous formation. Even under reflexive automobilization, "experts" and "non-experts" may well facilitate a traditional approach toward the automobile and its risks. Hence, the notion of reflexive auto-mobilization reflects the fact that the car culture is now imposing its dangers, threats, and risks on its own fabric. It also pays tribute to the fact that an increasing number of actors—ranging from local road protestors to international environmental agencies, from Golf GTI clubs to multinational car manufacturers—are taking part in the distribution and redistribution of these risks. The notion does not suggest that all auto actors nowadays are car-critical. There are many individuals and organizations who participate in a driving culture without being reflexive themselves. Nevertheless, these non-reflexive actors may very well recognize and respond to auto-related risks. But they do so in their own way. Their risk response often merely serves the purpose of modernizing the traditional trajectory of automobilization, thus shifting its risks in time and space.

Some of these agents—often stigmatized as traditional rather than reflexive modernizers—are the national automobile clubs (Krämer-Badoni et al., 1971). As self-declared consumer organizations, the AAA in the United States, the RAC in Britain, the ADAC in Germany, and FDM in Denmark share at least the possibility of being reflexive toward a traditional type of automobilization. I will focus here on Denmark's FDM (Forenede Danske Motorejere) in order to show how one automobile club has defined and responded to the risks of automobilization. In order to get a grip on the risk rationality of FDM and relate it to the three dimensions of automobility, I will explore the "mobility view" of the club. I understand a "mobility view" as something of a cultural filter employed by the different subjects of automobilization. Through this filter, individuals and organizations perceive auto-related risks. By means of their mobility view, they define and act upon both traffic accidents and the environmental threats posed by the car.

In order to disclose the content of FDM's mobility view, I looked—in the literal sense of the word—at the covers of the club's monthly magazine, *Motor,* employing quantitative methods of picture analysis. My content analysis of 780 consecutive issues from January 1961 to December 1996[1] is based on the three-dimensional model of automobility. It attempts to capture the transformation in the representation of three pictorial elements: the subjects of automobility, its vehicles, and its spatio-temporalities as they are seen through the eyes of FDM. In the limited space given here, I will present and explain only the most significant findings of my analysis. Hence, the purpose of this chapter is to reveal the content of FDM's mobility view, rather than to show how this view acts as a cultural filter in the club's definition of and response to the risks associated with cars.

DISEMBODIED AUTOMOBILIZATION

My analysis of *Motor*'s covers reveals a significant decline in the frequency of representations of human subjects over the approximately thirty-seven-year period. At the same time, the number of covers that picture automobiles and/or show a spatio-temporal context remains fairly constant. The human being is gradually bracketed out of the representations of automobilization. While the 1960s and 1970s are characterized largely by a linkage between the three dimensions, the following two decades are marked by a sharp decline in "classical representations" of human beings. In the 1960s and 1970s, humans and automobiles somehow merge together to form an "automotive unit," inseparable from its surrounding spatio-temporalities. There are strong ties between the three dimensions of mobility. Automobilization entails a human being using an automobile to explore space. Thus, in many representations the human being is placed in or next to an automobile, united in such a way that they are embedded in a rural or urban space. During these years, the *Motor* covers suggest that automobilization is about "what one can do with the automobile as a vehicle," i.e., "where one is able to go, and what one is able to do when one gets there." Figures 13.1 and 13.2 serve as meaningful examples and help to herald the change in *Motor*'s cover.

The cover from September 1962 (Fig. 13.1) clearly shows the integral part the automobile plays in the everyday life of those who are fortunate enough to possess such a commodity. A young woman has apparently taken a trip to the countryside and is enjoying a letter from her beloved. The beautiful scenery and the fantastic weather contribute to her well-being—and so does the "friendly Volkswagen," which comes across as something of a good companion that is guarding its owner.

On the cover from November 1989 (Fig. 13.2), the human being has been dismissed and the car has moved into the center of the picture. Now it is the automobile itself that is of interest. The added text emphasizes the importance of the vehicle's outer appearance. The earlier illustration of the automobile's practical value has now been replaced by an aesthetic statement. The new Mazda 323 is a "Japanese vehicle with round features" rather than merely an automobile that can take its user wherever she wants to go (. . . in order to read a recently received letter). Additionally, the surrounding space serves to highlight this aesthetic statement: it is round, just like the shape of the automobile. Rather than providing "a nice setting" for a particular activity, the space is there solely to illuminate the uniqueness of this particular automobile.

After the humans have left the scene, the automobile remains at center stage as the focus of our attention. It is not part of the staging anymore, but rather the main actor. Consequently, its use-value is supplemented by, and to a degree replaced by, its sign-value. The traditional use-value of the automobile, to facilitate trips, is no longer what the makers of *Motor* are concerned with. The automobile has changed character. Instead of being a vehicle for making trips, it has become an object for a variety of other ends—and, not least, an end in itself.

Figure 13.1   Cover from September 1962

THE CAR'S SPATIO-TEMPORAL ABSTRACTIONS

Although there are no significant changes in the absolute number of "spatio-temporal representations" over the thirty-seven years, the generic characteristics of the pictured times and spaces change dramatically. These changes can be summarized as the car's escape from its "traditional environment," as reflected in the increasing abstraction in the representation of the car's spatio-temporalities. The automobile's traditional environment consists of urban and non-urban spaces, in which the vehicle is used for traveling over geographical distance. Abstract spaces, by contrast, are spaces that are not part of this traditional environment. An exhibition hall, for instance, would be such an abstract space. Furthermore, abstract spaces are also spaces of a "de-familiarized traditional environment." If the urban or non-urban space is altered in a way that alienates it from its original role of providing a traditional environment for the automobile, then it has turned into an abstract space. These spatial abstractions are often undermined by abstract temporalities. Examples include photographs of costumed veterans standing beside or driving an old jalopy. Whereas the spatiality is not necessarily an abstraction of the car's normal environment in these images of the past, the temporality is that

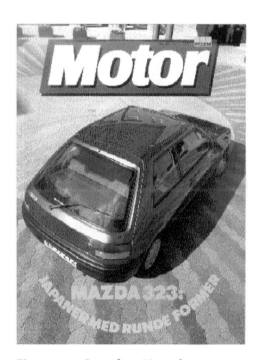

Figure 13.2   Cover from November 1989

of abstract nostalgia. Both types of abstractions enable a displacement of car usage from its present concrete context. The round area on the cover from November 1989 (Fig. 13.2), for instance, mirrors one way of abstracting space from the car's traditional environment. First of all, it appears to be an area that is usually reserved for non-motorized traffic. Hence it is not part of the car's traditional environment. Second, the setting has been chosen deliberately, because of the emphasis it puts on the generic, i.e., "round," design of the automobile. It is an abstract car-space.

The negation of spatio-temporal boundaries is a key theme of the mobility paradigm of automobilization, most visible in the continual abstraction of the spatio-temporalities represented on the journal covers. Lifting the car out of its natural environment and placing it in another, artificial reality disconnects automobility from some of its self-produced problems. No traffic jams, no accidents, and no summer smog limit the expansion of automobilization in such an artificially produced environment. The automobile then reveals its true meaning: it is a vehicle for escape from the here and now—a getaway car. This abstraction of the car's spatio-temporalities must be seen in conjunction with the disappearance of the human being from the cover. Both developments affect the communicative message and alter the meaning of the automobile itself. In this context, I take the vanishing of the subject as another indicator of the "disembedding" of the car from its "real" social surroundings. Without a subject and disconnected from its own spatio-temporalities, the car can now be re-embedded into any artificial context. Once freed from both its user and its spatio-temporalities, the car is finally in line with its representations on the covers of *Motor*. It has become the universal vehicle—a handy means for any sort of end.

CARS AS UNIVERSAL OBJECTS

To recapitulate, over the years from 1961 to 1996, the context in which the automobile was placed on the covers of *Motor* changed substantially. Analysis reveals that a strong abstraction from the automobile's traditional environment took place. While many of the early issues show the automobile in an urban, suburban, or rural context, the later issues place it within abstractions of such traditional environments. The car is thereby removed

from one context and subsequently placed in another. This de- and recontextualization can be viewed as a consequence of the increasing difficulties that automobilization has had to cope with. In its traditional environment, the threats produced by automobilization have now become visible: mass motorization, congested urban and suburban roads, degradation of landscapes due to road infrastructure extensions, and overcrowded parking areas. Thus, to sustain a positive image of the automobile, it is moved into ever more abstract contexts. These abstractions of space focus attention on the single automobile, with the result that space and time become subordinated to the vehicle.

In addition to the disappearance of the traditional setting, *Motor*'s covers are marked by the vanishing of the "subject as user." These two processes coincide and alienate the first dimension of mobility, the vehicle, from the two other dimensions. The automobile is now alone, disembodied. It is no longer simply a vehicle; it is now a metal container that can be filled with any number of social and cultural meanings. There is no longer a limit to the meanings that can be ascribed to the automobile. Both spatio-temporal and subject-related restrictions are gone: former spatial limitations have been rendered abstract; it is now possible to drive *anywhere*. And former subjects of automobilization have been removed from the cover; it is now possible for anyone to drive anywhere or to fill the vehicle with any sort of meaning.

This development becomes even clearer if one focuses on yet another transformation of *Motor*'s cover illustrations. The above-mentioned disembodiment and decontextualization in the representations of automobility is supplemented by a shift in the representation of the vehicle itself. While the early issues do not identify the featured automobiles or show the manufacturer's symbol, later issues, after the early 1980s, are increasingly defined by a specified automobile or type of automobile. The covers now feature a particular automobile, shown in different contexts, or a particular type of automobile, such as the cars that are often selected for testing by FDM's experts. This specification is accompanied by a more direct presentation of the vehicle itself. Instead of being only one element in the picture, the automobile is placed up on a stage of some sort, where everyone can see (or read) exactly what kind of car is being presented here. Hence, the communicative message is more or less that mobility cannot be exercised properly with just any old car. Mobility can be adequately realized only with the featured automobile. Here again one dimension of mobility, the vehicle, receives central importance.

The transformation of the automobile as reflected in the covers of *Motor* can best be described as a process in which the dynamic vehicle moves away from its earlier role as "a companion" in our everyday activities (see Fig. 13.1). Instead of being shown with the subject, the car is now separated from its user. It stands for itself and has moved from a peripheral position toward the center of automobility. Thus, the automobile has become less a vehicle for traversing space and more a pivotal object for all sorts of other vehicle-related activities—as echoed, for instance, by the rise of "do-it-yourself" sections.

The covers reveal that FDM's mobility view is clearly vehicle-oriented. It tends to ignore the other dimensions of mobility. Both the subject and time/space are subordinated to the needs of the car. Thus, as a result of the content analysis, I now claim that the mobility view of FDM is determined by the gradual disappearance of the human being (particularly as a user of cars); an increasing abstraction of the spatial context over time; and the growing importance of the technical and aesthetic formation of the automobile itself.

The figurative expression of this mobility view is "the car as universal vehicle." Over the years, the status of the automobile has been successfully transformed from niche product to mass vehicle. The car has become normalized, gradually transcending from a special machine for well-defined tasks to a ubiquitous tool—a vehicle used by many and for many purposes. It is no longer only a machine for traveling through space, but a vehicle that is "constructed" to overcome a variety of other everyday problems. In FDM's mobility view, the automobile represents security and safety in a world that is increasingly characterized by a lack of these qualities. It is the mediator that bridges the "ontological uncertainty" of the risk society and the individual's search for certainty. And this is precisely what provides for the stabilization of such a one-dimensional, vehicle-determined mobility view. This view of FDM, with the car at its center, finds fruitful ground in a society where sociality between humans is increasingly supplemented by a "sociality with objects," following Karin Knorr-Cetina (1997). Such "objectualization" implies that "objects displace human beings as relationship partners and embedding environments, or that they increasingly mediate human relationships, mak-

ing the latter dependent on the former" (Knorr-Cetina, 1997: 1).

CONCLUSION

The one-dimensional vehicle-oriented mobility view of FDM offers us further insight into automobilization. As the subject vanishes and the vehicle moves to center stage, the relationship between the traditional object (the car) and the subject (the user) is altered. During the 1960s and 1970s, the driver relates to the automobile as a means through which to fulfill his or her wants, needs, and wishes. This can be achieved either practically, through the overcoming of geographical distance, or symbolically, through signification in which the car serves as a signifier for whatever the user wants, needs, or wishes to signify. The motorist as a subject thereby imposes his or her wants on the object and, thus, defines the car's uses according to his or her own needs. Simultaneously, however, the object foists its wants upon the subject. Here the automobile expresses its wants through its users. Hence, the user is defined by the car's particular way of responding to the user's wants (see also Knorr-Cetina, 1997: 16). Under the current mobility view of FDM, the objects and subjects of mobility move together. But they do so without a transposition of status. It is not that the subject becomes the object and vice versa; both user and vehicle remain what they are. They simply tighten their mutual dependency in a circular process. Although I regard this particular feature of FDM's view as embedded in reflexive automobilization, I do not regard it as reflexive in itself. The fact that FDM's view is part of a process in which automobility has turned against itself does not qualify it as a mirror of a reflexive stance toward (auto)mobility. This becomes clear once we return to the notion of the mobility view as a cultural filter.

The above sketch of FDM's mobility view is intended to depict the cultural filter through which the risks of automobilization are perceived and acted upon. Both the publishers and the readers of *Motor* share a particular view of mobility. Their common mobility view shapes their definition of and response to risk. The above analysis, based on the interpretation of cover illustrations, suggests a crucial hypothesis to be tested in a subsequent investigation. If the mobility view of FDM is vehicle-determined, then the risk responses favored by the club must also emphasize one-dimensional, vehicle-oriented interventions. At the core of FDM's definition of and response to the risks of automobilization, then, lies the car itself. If so, the meaning of the car would be transformed and more or less turned upside down. The mobility view would enable a shift in the car's meaning from "the problem" to "the solution," in that it becomes fitted with additional technology. "Reflexivity," in this case, is not questioning the basis on which automobilization unfolds. It is not self-critical. The responsive behavior of FDM would then contribute to the reproduction of a traditional, growth-oriented type of automobilization. It makes possible the self-modernization of the "car culture," in that it turns the risks of automobilization into mere technological challenges.

Note

1. Some issues, however, were missing. These were issues 1962/11, 1972/25, and 1980/03. Issues 1981/07 through 1981/11 were not published because of a strike in the Danish printing industry.

References

Beck, U. 1992. *Risk Society: Towards a New Modernity.* London: Sage.

Bode, P. M., W. Hamber, and W. Zängel. 1986. *Alptraum Auto. Ein hundertjährige Erfindung und ihre Folgen.* München: Raben.

Canzler, W. 1999. "Der anhaltende Erfolg des Automobils. Zu den Modernisierungsleistungen eines aussergewöhnlichen technischen Artefaktes." In G. Bechmann, W. Rammert, and G. Schmidt, eds., *Technik und Gesellschaft, Jahrbuch 10.* Frankfurt: Campus.

Knorr-Cetina, K. 1997. "Sociality with Objects: Social Relations in Postsocial Knowledge Societies." In M. Featherstone, ed., *Theory, Culture and Society: Explorations in Critical Social Science.* London: Sage.

Krämer-Badoni, D., H. Grymer, and M. Rodenstein. 1971. *Zur sozio-ökonomischen Bedeutung des Automobils.* Frankfurt am Main: Suhrkamp.

Wolf, W. 1986. *Eisenbahn und Autowahn. Personen -und Gütertransport auf Schiene und Strasse. Geschichte Bilanz, Perspektiven.* Hamburg: Rasch und Röhring.

CHAPTER FOURTEEN

Car Dependence as a Social Problem

A Critical Essay on the Existing Literature and Future Needs

Roger Gorham

INTRODUCTION

In the past ten years or so, a conceptual understanding of how urban development has occurred in North America has gained prominence among environmentalists, activists, and some members of the planning community. The extreme view of that paradigm can be paraphrased as follows: Inappropriate land use, poorly designed suburban development patterns, and the absence of transportation alternatives render individuals and households slaves to their cars. A coalition of forces—including car manufacturers, road-building lobbies, suburban tract-housing developers, land speculators, and unscrupulous politicians —have been imposing these inappropriate land uses on the rest of society, who are then forced into choices they would rather not make, locking them into a dependence on their cars. This dependence, in turn, results in excessive vehicular travel, ever-escalating traffic congestion, poor air quality, and very high transportation energy consumption per capita. In this view, households are victims of constraining land use choices made by powerful interests.

The counter-argument to this paradigm often appears as follows: Land use or urban form as it has developed in the outlying areas of metropolitan regions over the past several decades has simply been the result of market mechanisms, the collective output of many individual choices about where and how to live or locate by households and firms seeking to maximize their private utility. The same "coalition of forces" noted in the above paradigm —car manufacturers, road-building lobbies, suburban tract-housing developers, land speculators, etc.—merely represent the supply side of the equation, seeking to provide households and firms with their demanded product. The resulting "sprawl," therefore, is the result of a well-functioning market mechanism of supply and demand, although the effects are at certain times and places exacerbated by constraints imposed by planners. Land development patterns are determined solely by the preferences of land consumers: households, firms, and shoppers.

Neither paradigm adequately addresses the question of car dependence. Focusing on cities and urban form as the sole or even primary source of car dependence (e.g., Newman and Kenworthy, 1989; Litman, 1998) is inadequate. Yet to suggest that car dependence is simply a lifestyle choice made by free-willed economic units maximizing their utility (e.g., Gordon and Richardson, 1996) is equally unsatisfying, since it does not adequately recognize the impacts of the constraints on choices. Consequently, while the term "car dependence" is frequently invoked in the literature, the phenomenon itself is rarely properly addressed in research or policy debates.

Litman and Newman and Kenworthy are right to focus on car dependence as a real and widespread phenomenon in western civilization, with potentially destructive impacts on a personal, societal, and global level. I argue, however, that the way the concept has been conceived in the literature does little to advance an understanding of what car dependence is, what causes it, how it can be measured, and how it can be avoided or reversed. This essay will critique the way the term "car dependence" has been used in the North American and Australian literature. It will suggest an alternative characterization of car dependence, and propose three distinct but interrelated components of car dependence. Finally, it will discuss briefly how these components are interrelated.

CRITIQUE OF AUTOMOBILE "DEPENDENCE" AS USED IN THE LITERATURE

Automobile dependency consists of transportation and land use patterns that increase automobile ownership and use, reduce travel choices, and disadvantage non-drivers relative to drivers.

—Litman, 1998

Litman's understanding of car dependence demonstrates two erroneous assumptions about car dependence prevalent in the literature that hinder the development of a useful theory. The first is that the phenomenon of car dependence is associated only with the built, or physical, environment. The second is that car dependence is akin to car ownership or car use; that is, high levels of car ownership or use necessarily imply a relationship of dependence.

The first of these assumptions is implied more by assertion than by theoretical rigor. Newman and Kenworthy's works, for example, abound with assertions that car dependence stems from a physical condition related to patterns of urban development, without offering any satisfactory definition or characterization of "automobile dependence," a term taken to be self-evident. The closest they come is a listing of attributes that they ascribe to cities they have a priori labeled as automobile-dependent (Newman and Kenworthy, 1999). These attributes are grouped under the headings "Transportation Priorities in Auto Cities," "Residential Development Priorities in Auto Cities," and

"Cultural Priorities in Terms of Urban Space in Auto Cities." In other words, all of the attributes of the car-dependent city relate in one way or another to the physical development of the city. They are careful to couch these categories in terms of attitudes ("priorities"), but the implication by assertion is that the results of these "priorities"—the actual built environment—determine behavior. The built form seems to be the only decision input of any importance into households' day-to-day lifestyle choices, and in particular their reliance on the car for access to goods, services, activities, and human interaction.

Like Litman, Newman and Kenworthy equate car dependence with car use and ownership, even though they do not elaborate on the nature of the relationship among these phenomena. High levels of car use and ownership are assumed to be indicative of a dependent relationship; without an explanation of the relationship between use and dependency, the equation amounts to a mere tautology (i.e., "People use cars because they are dependent; they are dependent because they use cars"). In fact, high levels of car ownership and use do not automatically imply car dependence. Households may change their driving habits in response to a change in shopping location choices, for example. An increase in car use associated with such a change may or may not reflect a change in underlying car "dependence"; it may simply reflect a preference for one shopping location over another.

One of the few studies to look at car dependence as a phenomenon divorced from physical-determinist overtones, and also as distinct from car use or ownership, was a 1995 study for the Royal Automobile Club, titled simply "Car Dependence" (RAC 1995). This work provides an important early contribution to the literature on car dependence. The authors find that people do not purchase cars in order to fulfill a given "level" of car dependence. Rather, their level of car dependence evolves through ownership as their activity patterns adjust to increased car access. In other words, car dependence is a process, rather than an end-state.

Similarly, this dynamic and interdependent process can by extension be associated with processes of urban form and land use change, although the RAC report is somewhat weak in its consideration of the physical aspects of car dependence. Both car dependence and urban form are processes, evolving over time. No doubt they interact, each influencing and being influenced by the other. In this sense, households can be said to be participants in the dynamic of land use change, rather than passive victims of land use imposed on them by conspiratorial forces. They actively engage in the construction of their built space, and the more they do so, the more bound they are to the very tool of that construction, the car. The cycle of dependence is so hard to break precisely because of the active role that households have in building it up in the first place. In the loop of car dependence, households are active victims, or passive victimizers, depending on one's perspective.

Characterizing Car Dependence

The RAC report distinguishes between car-dependent trips and car-dependent lifestyles. Certain trips by nature require the use of a car; a car-dependent lifestyle, however, is a structural and long-term phenomenon. Even a household whose lifestyle cannot be characterized as "car-dependent" may engage in trips that are car-dependent. Car-dependent trips—those for which alternatives are not viable because of the location of the trip ends in both time and space—are a relatively straightforward phenomenon to identify, but defining lifestyles that are "car-dependent" is particularly problematic, since doing so implies value judgments that transport analysts are frequently reluctant to make.

In spite of definitional difficulties with respect to the concept of lifestyle car dependence, the RAC report identifies several distinct manifestations of car dependence that are useful to draw on here to try to characterize car dependence. First, members of car-dependent households tend to misperceive the actual costs of driving, often by discounting or minimizing fixed costs. Second, car-dependent households have incomplete knowledge or misperceptions about available travel alternatives (such as public transport availability or cycling journey times). Third, car-dependent households may withdraw from active engagement in transportation decisions, using the car in an automatic and routine way "without active consideration of alternatives."

These manifestations suggest a potentially useful way to characterize a household with a car-dependent lifestyle. Such a household perceives that sustained abstinence from regular car use would create a social or economic burden so great that such abstinence either is considered intolerable or is inconceivable in the first place. An important implication for research of such a characterization is that an understanding of car dependence requires disaggregate research, at least at the household level, if not below. In addition, the basis of this characterization is perception; the household perceives a condition following on from abstinence from car use, whether such a condition obtains in fact. Clearly, understood as a perception of burden in the absence of car use, car dependence is not the same as car use or car ownership.

These considerations suggest that to the three manifestations of car dependence suggested by the RAC report, a fourth can be added: Car-dependent households would demonstrate an unwillingness or inability to change their behavior in response to an input change, such as cost. The levels of car usage would be relatively unresponsive to changes in the cost of driving in a car-dependent household. This last manifestation can be measured quantitatively, via the price elasticity of demand for car use, so it may be researchers' best proxy to quickly gauge the levels of car dependence in a society.

Formally, the price elasticity of car use would be understood as the percentage change in use observed from a 1 percent change in the costs, although "costs" here must be understood more broadly than simply out-of-pocket costs. Price elasticity itself is a composite of two different effects. The substitution effect represents a change in demand caused by consumers' substituting different goods vis-à-vis their previous consumption patterns after a price change; if the cost of gasoline goes up, for example, some consumers may choose to use public transport instead. The income effect represents a change in demand because, in real terms, consumers have a different amount of money to spend; if the cost of gasoline goes up, some consumers may simply reduce the amount of driving they do, because to maintain their previous levels would exceed their budget constraint.

The Components of Car Dependence

Both the income and the substitution effect are linked to car dependence, but in different ways. Car dependence can be shown to have several distinct components; the income and substitution effects impact these components differently.

1. *Physical/Environmental dependence:* The built environment, including urban form, regional structure, the distribution of activities within those structures, and the nature or status of collective transportation modes,

causes an individual or household without a car to feel cut off from social activities, friends, family, businesses, shops, and work. This component relates specifically to the substitution effect noted above. In the event of a change in the costs of owning and operating a car, substitutes are not available.

2. *Psycho-social dependence:* Emotional and behavioral associations with the car render the individual reluctant to alter his or her association with it, even after a cost change. This type of dependence, often the target of manufacturers' marketing efforts, is particularly associated with the income effect discussed above.

3. *Circumstantial dependence:* The nature of the activities in which a household regularly engages renders it dependent on the car. In this type of dependence, the household adopts its lifestyle to the technological capacity of the car. The car is perceived as a necessary input to "production."

Talking about these "components" of car dependence in isolation from each other is somewhat artificial; the links and interdependencies among them are many, and they are strong. Dividing the sources of car dependence into these three categories merely provides a point of access.

Physical/Environmental Car Dependence

That land use has an impact on travel behavior is a basic and long-standing tenet of transport planning. Land use is a, if not the, principal exogenous component in classical metropolitan transport planning models, providing the key input to the heuristic variable of trip-generation rate, on which the remainder of the transport forecasting system is based. Land use—particularly net residential density—has also been a key component in public transport planning and ridership assessment (Pushkarev and Zupan, 1977). Empirical studies show clearly the importance of urban and regional form in influencing travel choices. In the San Francisco Bay Area, the mode shares of trips to and within the Central Business District (CBD) of San Francisco proper have been shown to resemble those of European cities—about 30 percent by car (Gorham, 1997), which is in the same range as figures reported for German and Italian cities (Monheim, 1996) and Stockholm (Gorham, 1997). However, only about 4 percent of all trips in the region actually go to or are within the CBD, compared with 28 percent for the Stockholm region. In

other words, people in the San Francisco region use their cars substantially less when they go downtown—but they rarely go downtown.

Most of the research to date (see Handy et al., 1998 for a good summary) has focused on impact assessment of hypothetical land use changes; that is, how would an increase in residential densities, changes in land use mix, or the prevalence of transit-oriented development influence observed travel behavior? Such questions are necessary but not sufficient to understand physical car dependence in metropolitan areas. What is needed is a further fleshing out of the issues of land use adoption, feedback, and cost-effectiveness.

Land use adoption. Some researchers are beginning to focus on the behavioral aspects of land use adoption and the transport implications. Who lives in dense, centrally located parts of metropolitan areas? Who lives downtown? If they live there by choice, is their decision motivated by transport or environmental concerns? Who lives in more remote, suburban locations, and what underlies their lifestyle decision to locate there? The answers to these questions will probably suggest that there is much more at play in the production of car dependence than simply environmental or physical factors.

The question is particularly intriguing for European metropolitan areas, which have been more heavily centralized than those in North America, but which have steadily seen an increased pace of decentralization in the last several decades. One intriguing phenomenon is the conversion of formerly agricultural villages on the fringes of moderate-sized cities in Britain, France, and Switzerland into bedroom communities. These conversions occur without any outward change in appearance; the farmers simply move out, and the urban professionals move in. Compact in form, these villages often do not have enough population to support even basic services, which makes it necessary to use a car, with trip distances often quite large by European standards. In essence, Europeans who live in these kinds of villages behave much like their North American counterparts who live in exurban subdivisions.

Feedback effects. Questions about feedback effects have been largely ignored in the argument that compact urban form will reduce car use. In particular, there are probably two important feedback effects that need to be considered. First, if compact urban form reduces the demand for car travel, as its proponents claim, will there be a reduction in the amount of road space demanded? If so, will this result in excess capacity? Absent a price change, what would keep present non-users from converging onto this excess capacity? Following this feedback effect to its logical endpoint, the necessary corollary to a program of compact urban form is the decommissioning of road space allocated to cars. A second feedback effect involves the system of land use itself. Compact urban form means creating nodes of relatively higher value, but also higher cost, at certain places relative to others. What will keep these value differentials from fraying at the edge? What will keep areas of high land cost from bleeding into areas of low land cost? Specifically, why should households and firms choose to spend the money to locate in a compact urban center when they can locate in a less intense area for significantly less money?

Cost-effectiveness. This set of questions touches on the costs of different types of development. Considerable research has gone, and continues to go, into this subject (RERC, 1974; Frank, 1989; USEPA, 1993; Sorensen and Esseks, 1998), although nearly all of it seems to be North American- or Australian-based. As a research question, the focus for our purposes should be, How expensive is it to change land uses of present or potential future urban settlement, and how cost-effective is such a policy? In short, what is the long-run cost per vehicle mile of travel avoided?

Psycho-social Car Dependence

Psychological and sociological car dependence, arguably two very different types of car dependence, are tentatively grouped together here. It is not clear whether they are manifestly distinct, or rather different academic approaches to the same phenomenon. In this discussion, however, we will consider the psychological apart from the sociological literature.

Psychological Car Dependence

The psychology literature has surprisingly little to say about car dependence. This silence may be related to the fact that psychology as a research discipline tends to focus on behaviors considered aberrant. Since excessive lifestyle dependence on the car is not considered a deviant form of behavior, the psychological literature has not addressed the phenomenon; instead, to the extent that psychology has anything to say about transportation, it is mostly limited to the field of ergonomics—how the human brain processes new information and reacts in dangerous driving situations.

Nevertheless, there are numerous anecdotal accounts of various psychological phenomena associated with car use and car ownership, many of these from the transportation literature or advocacy group arguments. These include:

- sexual fetishism of the car (by both men and women);
- cocooning behavior on the part of car users, i.e., using the car as a withdrawal space from the world and, frequently, even one's own family; and
- displacement of aggression, frustration, and feelings of personal or sexual inadequacy into the car and/or into the act of driving

While stories about each of the above types of behaviors abound, most of them comic or tongue-in-cheek, there is virtually no serious psychological literature that looks at them. I have been unable to locate any efforts to either quantify the extent of such phenomena or explain them in a theoretically consistent way. One potentially promising approach might stem from the observation that in each of these situations, the car seems to be substituting for an emotional need that is lacking. That is, it acts as a proxy for a human attachment or bond that does not exist or is weak.

Within the transportation field, however, there is a small body of literature, for the most part European-based, beginning to emerge that looks at the psychological aspects of car dependence. Most of this literature focuses on the perceptions and attitudes of car users facing the prospect of behavioral change for environmental reasons (for example, Tertoolen et al., 1998; Forward, 1997; Steg and Vlek, 1997). This literature focuses on the gap between attitudes (e.g., about social needs) and behavior (car use). Tertoolen et al (1998), for example, note that the gap between environmental attitudes and day-to-day behavioral patterns often results not in changes in behavior, but rather in changes in the rationalization processes of such behavior. In sum, while some literature does speculate on the underlying psychological nature of car "dependence," it is interesting to note that it is researchers in transport, rather than psychology, who have paid more attention to this issue (Goodwin, 1997; Hart and Spivak, 1993).

Goodwin (1997) notes that "dependence" in the psychology literature has two connotations that might be relevant for a psychological approach to automobile dependence. One of these understands dependence as an addictive or habitual reliance on something. Goodwin elaborates on the possible "narcotic" effects of speed—the adrenaline rush—on human pleasure centers, or the resulting performance enhancement for a number of human endeavors. This "narcotic" effect, however, need not be limited to the speed aspects of car use. The mere movement of the car (whether at high or low speeds), the cocooning environment created by the car's inner environment, and the habitual use of the car in a sequence of daily activity patterns all might be said to produce addictive or narcotic qualities for the user.

The other interpretive connotation of "dependence" is related to child development, in particular the dependent nature of the mother-child relationship. Dependence in this sense is related in a literal way to survival; the child's dependence on the mother is a question of life and death. Car dependence as expressed in western culture does indeed carry overtones of death. In many regions and for many socioeconomic subcultures, contemplating the prospect of losing automobility is like contemplating death itself. The car becomes an extension of one's corporeal self. The vociferous argument against GIS-based road-pricing systems using smart cards is a concrete example. Systems that can identify where my car is are a violation of my civil liberties, because the authorities could use them to track my movements. In this argument, the car and the person are indistinguishable; civil liberties applied to the individual are automatically applied to the car, because it is a material extension of the self.

Goodwin (1997) calls both types of dependencies "metaphors" in relationship to their use for transportation analysis. It is not clear, however, why notions of dependence, as drawn from the psychology literature, should be understood merely as metaphors when applied to transportation. After all, if the relationship of the car owner or driver to the car is perceived psychologically as death avoidance, then that relationship should really, not just metaphorically, be characterized as a dependence. It is not surprising, then, that as a matter of pure self-preservation, car owners and drivers vociferously oppose planners' attempts to wean them off their cars.

Social Car Dependence

A washing machine serves as equipment and plays as an element of comfort, or of prestige, etc. It is the field of play that is specifically the field of consumption.

—Jean Baudrillard, *Consumer Society*

Social car dependence has been the subject of a small body of literature (Hagman and Tengstrom, 1991; Teng-

strom, 1995; Lewis and Goldstein, 1984; Popenoe, 1977), but this literature remains tangential to the mainstream of transport planning research. Much of it focuses on car ownership and the role of the meaning of the car in consumer culture. Indeed, this literature understands the car as the quintessential consumer item. It considers the car to be a symbol of both freedom and social (economic) status, even while noting the irony that the freedom may be more of a slavery to technology and consumerism. Mainstream planners and researchers are probably not unaware of this literature, yet it figures minimally in their work. Why is this so? The answer is probably related to two phenomena: the esoteric nature of this literature, and the overwhelming magnitude of the problem it conjures up. How can we, as planners, researchers, or transportation professionals, hope to change the very meanings embedded in the car?

As understandable as this reaction is, I want to argue that it is unfortunate, because the meaning of the car, the "signs" the car embodies, are not fixed by forces untouchable by policy; they can be influenced by clear, well-thought-out and well-executed strategies, provided that the underlying forces are well understood. To make this argument, I will rely on Baudrillard, as esoteric a thinker on this subject (from the planner's point of view) as can be imagined.

Baudrillard rejects the Galbraithian view—and a view implicit in much of the sociology of the car literature—that demand for specific consumer products is itself a necessary output of the production process. That view holds that car manufacturers produce not only the car, but also the demand for the car, or perhaps, in the eyes of conspiracy theorists, all of the supportive institutional and infrastructural mechanisms that create or facilitate that demand. Baudrillard suggests that such an argument is too simplistic and reductionist—that to match the production of specific demands to specific consumer items is to misapprehend the nature of demand and desire as created by what he calls the system of signs, which is consumerism. Rather, he argues, a system of demands is created by a system of production, in which the one constant is desire, pure and simple. Desire is not, indeed cannot be, created for particular products over the long run, because the desire is based on the sign-value (power, prestige, comfort, attitude), not the use-value, of the consumer item. The consumption of consumer goods is the consumption of signs, and those signs can easily be substituted one for the other. This has important implications for planners and researchers. Baudrillard's concept suggests that there is no inherent sociological dependence on the automobile per se, but rather a dependence on the signage underlying it. From this, it would follow that a possible research agenda would be to identify those signs, to understand how they were created, how they came to be so tightly identified with the industrial artifact "the car," and what that artifact—and car consumption patterns as a whole—might look like with different sets of signs associated with it.

Circumstantial Car Dependence

The third major component of car dependence is called here circumstantial car dependence, although in a sense it might also be called economic or technological car dependence. If, as shown above, Baudrillard argues that it is the sign-value of the car that produces its status as a consumer item, there is nevertheless an element of its use-value that is critical in the creation of car dependence, at least in certain segments of the population. Circumstantial car dependence describes a relationship between the technological capacities of the car and particular aspects/requirements of an individual's lifestyle. It is associated with evolutive changes in economic activity with the development of widespread car availability.

An extreme example is the car-dependent lifestyle of the freelance string bassist. As a professional musician, the bassist is tied to her instrument as a matter of economics: she must have it with her when she engages in professional activity. The instrument itself is large, bulky, and expensive, so transport solutions that require it to be physically carried over long distances or expose it to the elements are not practicable. Since she works freelance, she cannot leave the instrument at her place of work, because she has no single place of work. In short, she is car-dependent. This car dependence is independent of urban development patterns and psychological or social projections of meanings onto the car. It is not, however, independent of the level of economic activity in the metropolitan region, and of the demand for freelance bass services.

Several points are worth noting about circumstantial car dependence. First, the industries in which circumstantially car-dependent people engage may themselves have undergone—or continue to undergo—large organizational or structural shifts in response to the widespread adoption of the car. These changes might include temporal or spatial changes (changes in where and when ac-

tivities are carried out) or simple expansion—there are simply more opportunities to engage in the activity, and these are, therefore, more spread out. Second, the car itself is an artifact of technological production, and is influenced by lifestyle demands. It is a composite of a number of technological systems; its current form is the result of interplay among the technologies involved—what constitutes the range of possibilities—and the needs and demands of society, filtered by the profit-seeking behavior of car producers. In other words, the car creates circumstance, but circumstance also creates the car. Car and society change together. Consequently, it would be simplistic to suggest that circumstantial car dependence is a reaction by households (or firms) to the technological capacity of the car. The rapid growth in popularity of the sport utility vehicle in North America in the last ten years is an example of this process.

The key for researchers and policy-makers addressing circumstantial car dependence is to focus on strategies isolating the dependence-inducing activities from other activities in which the household engages. The focus should be to keep that car dependence from "bleeding" into other activities and transport choices. Pricing may play an important role. By shifting a greater proportion of car-related cost burdens to use, as opposed to ownership (for example, through road-pricing, pay-as-you-go-insurance, strict limitations on free-parking provisions, etc.), policy can help ensure that circumstantially car-dependent people tie that dependence only to those activities for which circumstances require a car.

Conclusion: Interactions among Types of Car Dependence

The three types of car dependencies outlined in this chapter interact significantly, and it is probably difficult in practice to identify particular behaviors with any one of them. The perceived need of a parent to have access to a car in case of emergency, for example, is not clearly a question either of physical/environmental dependence or of social/psychological dependence. Both undoubtedly play a role. In addition, the way psychological or social dependence on the car manifests itself in the real world is likely to involve the perception or assertion of physical or circumstantial dependence. This social addiction might be expressed as the sense that there are no alternatives available because of bad planning, or that the car is the only viable means of transport for a particular set of activities, when, in fact, such perceptions are false. In these cases, the underlying condition of car dependence is no less real.

In this essay I have tried to argue that the term "car dependence" as it is predominantly used in the literature has hindered the development of a theory of car dependence, and thus has not served the research or policy-making communities particularly well. It has tried to offer an alternative conception of car dependence, based on individual perceptions of the non-viability of alternatives, in the hope of aiding the development of such a theory. It has also tried to identify the basic components of those perceptions, and to offer suggestions about how research might approach them. What it has not attempted to do, however, is to discuss the potentially harmful effects of car dependence on a host of social issues, from local and global environmental degradation, social isolation of large segments of society, and degradation of inner-city social fabrics, to the potential economic costs of wholesale abandonment and reconstruction of urban and exurban areas, which car dependency would seem to facilitate, if not actually cause. The strength of the connection between these issues and car dependence remains to be shown, but such an effort would require the development of a truly complete theory of car dependence.

REFERENCES

Cervero, Robert, and Roger Gorham. 1995. "Commuting in Transit versus Automobile Neighborhoods." *Journal of the American Planning Association* 61, no. 2 (Spring).

Forward, Sonja. 1997. "Behavioural Factors Affecting Modal Choice." Paper presented at 8th Meeting of the International Association of Travel Behavior Research, Austin, Texas, September.

Fouchier, Vincent. 1997. *Les Densités Urbaines et le Développement Durable: Le Cas de l'Île-de-France et des Villes Nouvelles*. Paris: Secretariat Général du Groupe Central des Villes Nouvelles.

Frank, James. 1989. *The Costs of Alternative Development Patterns: A Review of the Literature*. Washington, D.C.: Urban Land Institute.

Frank, Lawrence. 1994. "An Analysis of Relationships between Urban Form (Density, Mix, and Jobs: Housing Balance) and Travel Behavior (Mode Choice, Trip Generation, Trip Length, and Travel Time)." Washington State Transportation Center in cooperation with the Federal Highway Administration and the Washington State Transportation Commission,

Research project T9233, task 34. Washington State Department of Transportation, Olympia.

Goodwin, Phil B. 1997. "Mobility and Car Dependence." In Talib Rothengatter and Enrique Carbonell Vaya, eds., *Traffic and Transport Psychology: Theory and Application*. New York: Pergamon Press.

Gordon, Peter, and Harry W. Richardson. 1989. "Gasoline Consumption and Cities: A Reply." *Journal of the American Planning Association* 55, no. 3 (Summer).

Gordon, Peter, and Harry W. Richardson. 1996. *The Case for Suburban Development*. San Ramon: Building Industry Association of Northern California.

Gorham, Roger. 1996. "Regional Planning and Travel Behavior: A Comparative Study of the San Francisco and Stockholm Metropolitan Regions." Master's thesis, Department of City and Regional Planning, University of California at Berkeley.

Gorham, Roger. 1997. "Comparative Neighborhood Travel Analysis: An Approach to Understanding the Relationship between Planning and Travel Behavior." Paper presented at 8th Meeting of the International Association of Travel Behavior Research, Austin, Texas, September.

Hagman, Olle, and Emin Tengstrom. 1991. *The Meaning of the Automobile*. Publications in Human Technology, no. 3. Goteborg: University of Goteborg.

Handy, Susan. 1996. "Urban Form and Pedestrian Choices: A Study of Austin Neighborhoods." *Transportation Research Record*, no. 1552 (November).

Handy, Susan L., Kelly Clifton, and Janice Fisher. 1998. *The Effectiveness of Land Use Policies as a Strategy for Reducing Automobile Dependence: A Study of Austin Neighborhoods*. Report No. SWUTC/98/465650-1 (Southwest Region University Transportation Center, Center for Transportation Research, University of Texas at Austin). Springfield, Va.: National Technical Information Service.

Hart, Stanley, and Alvin Spivak. 1993. *Automobile Dependence and Denial: The Elephant in the Bedroom— Impacts on the Economy and Environment*. Pasadena: New Paradigm.

Kockelman, Kara M. 1997. *Travel Behavior as a Function of Accessibility, Land Use Mixing and Land Use Balance: Evidence from the San Francisco Bay Area*. Paper no. 970048, prepared for presentation at the 76th annual meeting of the Transportation Research Board. Washington, D.C.: Transportation Research Board.

Lewis, David, and Laurence Goldstein, eds. 1983. *The Automobile and American Culture*. Ann Arbor: University of Michigan Press.

Litman, Todd. 1998. World Wide Web page of the Victoria Transport Policy Institute.

Monheim, Rolf. 1996. "Parking Management and Pedestrianisation as Strategies for Successful City Centres." In *Sustainable Transport in Central and Eastern European Cities: Proceedings of the Workshop on Transport and Environment in Central and Eastern European Cities, 28th–30th June 1995, Bucharest.* Paris: OECD Publications.

Newman, Peter, and Jeffrey Kenworthy. 1989. *Cities and Automobile Dependence: An International Sourcebook.* Aldershot, UK: Gower Publishing Company.

Newman, Peter, and Jeffrey Kenworthy. 1999. *Sustainability and Cities: Overcoming Automobile Dependence.* Washington, D.C.: Island Press.

Popenoe, David. 1977. *The Suburban Environment: Sweden and the United States.* Chicago: University of Chicago Press.

Pushkarev, Boris, and Jeffrey Zupan. 1977. *Public Transportation and Land Use Policy.* Bloomington: Indiana University Press.

Real Estate Research Corporation (RERC). 1974. *The Costs of Sprawl: Environmental and Economic Costs of Alternative Residential Development Patterns at the Urban Fringe.* Washington, D.C.: The Council on Environmental Quality, the Office of Policy Development and Research, Department of Housing and Urban Development, and the Office of Planning and Management, Environmental Protection Agency.

Royal Automobile Club (RAC). 1995. *Car Dependence: A Report for the RAC Foundation for Motoring and the Environment.* Edited by Phil Goodwin. London: RAC Foundation for Motoring and the Environment.

Sorensen, A. A., and J. D. Esseks. 1998. *Living on the Edge: The Costs and Risks of Scatter Development.* Dekalb, Ill.: The American Farmland Trust.

Steg, Linda, and Charles Vlek. 1997. "The Role of Problem Awareness in Willingness-to-Change Car Use and in Evaluating Relevant Policy Measures." In Talib Rothengatter and Enrique Carbonell Vaya, eds., *Traffic and Transport Psychology: Theory and Application.* New York: Pergamon Press.

Tengstrom, Emin. 1995. *Sustainable Mobility in Europe and the Role of the Automobile: A Critical Inquiry.* Stockholm: Swedish Transport and Communication Research Board.

Tertoolen, Gerard, Dik Van Dreveld, and Ben Verstraten. 1998. "Psychological Resistance against Attempts to Reduce Private Car Use." *Transportation Research Part A,* no. 3 (April): 171–182.

CHAPTER FIFTEEN

Growing Up With and Without a Family Car

Karin Sandqvist

Introduction: Three Stages of Automobility

In industrialized countries, the twentieth century was characterized by growth in the number of automobiles, with the most rapid increase in the United States. As automobiles have become more ordinary, their meaning has changed. Elsewhere (Sandqvist, 1997), I have discussed three successive stages of automobility: the romantic stage, the transitional stage, and the totally car-dominated stage. In the romantic stage, very few people actually can afford an automobile, but many harbor romantic dreams of future car ownership. In this stage, everyday mobility is based on walking, bicycling, and public transport (or horses), and distances between home, work, and shopping are adapted to this fact. In Western Europe, with Sweden as my specific example, the romantic stage lasted until the 1960s. In the transitional stage, so named because it seems to be simply an in-between stage, most families own a car. Although car availability is the norm, there is still enough public transport and neighborhood services to make it possible to lead a normal life without owning a car. This is the stage in which most of Western Europe finds itself today. The third stage is primarily represented by the U.S., but also includes most of Canada and Australia. In this stage, distances between everyday destinations are adapted to cars, and most households find that they need more than one car. Car ownership is far from a dream: it is regarded as an everyday necessity.

Quite obviously, the progression from one stage to the next depends on increasing car ownership, and this in turn rests on the fact that many people are drawn to automobiles and are willing to spend a great deal of money to buy and maintain a car. Although cars are transport vehicles, their appeal goes beyond strictly utilitarian transport; they are a means to display dominance and power, to experience a sensation of speed and adventurous freedom, to escape from social controls, and to express status and identity. Several of these characteristics are particularly suggestive of a masculine identity.

With the progressive stages of automobility, there are also changes in the appeal of automobiles. In the romantic stage, driving a car automatically makes one the fastest and strongest traveler on the road, as "other traffic" consists of pedestrians, bicycles, and horse-drawn carts. In the stage of total car dominance, an ordinary sedan is not enough, so one may need a van to keep from feeling small and vulnerable among the many trucks. The sensation of adventure is lost when driving is part of everyday life, and the exciting sensation of speed can rarely be indulged when there are congested roads and strict speed limits even on superhighways. Even when the objective speed is fast, the subjective sensation is less than on a winding country road. Thus, some of the non-utilitarian appeal of automobiles decreases with the more advanced stages. On the other hand, the role of the car as a means of utilitarian transport increases when the infrastructure is built for automobile mobility, as it is in the later stages.

Apart from stage-related changes in the individual experiences of owning and driving a car, which can affect the appeal of automobiles, the social construction of driving and owning cars also changes with the times. In Sweden, increased car ownership was construed as "democratic equality" in the 1950s and 1960s (Tengström, 1991), a highly positively charged concept that overlooked the fact that many people were concerned about the increased traffic. Today, although the social construction of meanings around automobiles still includes "freedom," "democracy," "good living conditions," and "equality," there is the additional meaning of "environmental problems" and "unsustainability."

The Rise and Fall (?) of the Appeal of Automobiles

In Sweden, women initially showed much less interest in cars than men. If women had had equal power over the infrastructure in the early stages of automobility, perhaps the course of history would have been different in relation to car dependency. Not until the car became integral to everyday household activities, including the chauffeuring of children, did women's rate of driving begin to approach men's. Today, women still seem to view cars less favorably than men do. Recently, there also seems to be a growing generation gap, with young people appearing somewhat disenchanted by automobiles.

In the following, I will present some data bearing on the changing appeal of automobiles in Sweden over most of the twentieth century, taking into account the difference between men and women.

To have a car of one's own. "How important is it for you to have a car that you can call your own?" was one of fifty questions in a nationwide survey conducted in 1997 by a reputable survey institute (SIFO, 1997). The study was done on behalf of the Swedish Petroleum Institute, whose business it is to promote the interests of the petroleum sector. The response categories to the question above were "very important," "rather important," "not particularly important," and "not at all important." The answer "very important" is particularly interesting from the perspective of trying to measure the appeal of the automobile as private vehicle. We can assume that people who consider it "very important" to have their own car will make a considerable effort to buy and keep a private vehicle.

If we also make the assumption, supported by empirical research (Jansson et al. 1986), that a person's attitude toward owning a car is formed at a young age and remains fairly stable thereafter, we can view the difference between generations as indicative of the changing meaning of cars over time. In Table 15.1, the respondents in the oldest age group were young during World War II and the 1950s, when cars were rare in Sweden. In the 1950s and 1960s, the rate of car ownership rose quickly (Statistics Sweden, 1987). Among the respondents in this age group, 60 percent of the men, but only 24 percent of the women, viewed having their own car as "very important."

Among the men, there is a decreasing trend from older to younger age groups, while for women we find an inverted U-shaped pattern, although it never quite reaches the male level. The response of the youngest age group is markedly different from that of their elders, as they much less often find it "very important" to have their own car. This age group, 15–29 years, is not precisely comparable with the rest, as it contains some people who are too young to have a driver's license. However, even allowing for the fact that some of the youngest respondents perhaps should not have been included, there is still an evident decline in the appeal of having a car of one's own.[1]

Driver's licenses. Verbally admitting to wanting a car of one's own is one thing, but actual behavior is another.

Table 15.1 "How important is it for you to have a car that you can call your own?" Percentage answering "Very important." (Swedish: "Hur viktigt är det för dig att ha en bil du kan kalla din egen?" Svar: "Mycket viktigt.")

Age	Year of birth	Men %	Women %
65–	prior to 1932	60	24
50–64	1933–1947	51	39
30–49	1948–1967	48	37
15–29	1968–1982	26	18

Source: SIFO, 1997.

Obtaining a driver's license is an act that indicates some sort of commitment to the world of motor vehicles. Obviously, this commitment can be motivated by strictly utilitarian transport needs as well by as less utilitarian, more emotional motives.

In Sweden, 18 is the youngest age at which one can obtain a driver's license, although driving practice is allowed some time before that. In comparison with the U.S., it is expensive and difficult to obtain a driver's license in Sweden, with many requirements and time-consuming tests of theoretical knowledge and driving in traffic. Once obtained, however, licenses are not often withdrawn. They are updated only every ten years, with the simple requirement of providing a recent photograph. Thus, Swedes view obtaining a driver's license as a life-time investment.

Tables 15.2 and 15.3 show the statistics on the percentages obtaining a driver's license by birth cohort. Table 15.2 is compiled from three large surveys conducted from 1978 to 1990 by the national institute Statistics Sweden. The respondents were classified into four age intervals: 18–24, 25–44, 45–64, and 65–75. In Table 15.2, the age class 18–24 is left out, as a substantial number of young adults can be assumed to have not yet obtained a driver's license. However, after the age of 25, this situation becomes rare.

For an easy comparison of the rates of obtaining a driver's license over the age cohorts, we can take the middle year of the birth-year intervals as the comparison point, as shown in Table 15.2.

The data in Table 15.2 show an initial marked difference between men and women. Among the earliest cohort, who reached driving age before World War II, 68 percent of the men were license holders, as compared with 15 percent of the women. Among both genders, the percentage of license holders increases quite consistently thereafter, although the rise is steepest among the women. For the latest (youngest) cohort, the gap has narrowed to 94 percent for the men and 86 percent for the women.

For a comparison with the earliest cohort responding to the survey question "How important is it for you to have a car that you can call your own?" the age group born in 1928 should be the most relevant. The difference between male and female license holders, 88 percent and 57 percent, respectively, is about as large as the gender difference in responses to the importance of having one's own car.

For data on the young adults, I consulted two types of sources. The first was the above-mentioned surveys by Statistics Sweden. The second was data that had recently

Table 15.2   Percentage of License Holders among Mature Adults (>24 yrs), by Year of Birth

Year of birth	Median year of birth	Men	Women	Age at survey and survey year
		%	%	
1904–1913	1909	68	15	65–74 yrs, in 1978
1908–1917	1913	73	24	65–74 yrs, in 1982
1916–1924	1920	85	43	65–74 yrs, in 1990
1914–1933	1924	84	45	45–64 yrs, in 1978
1918–1937	1928	88	57	45–64 yrs, in 1982
1926–1945	1936	93	77	45–64 yrs, in 1990
1934–1953	1944	92	78	25–44 yrs, in 1978
1938–1957	1948	93	81	25–44 yrs, in 1982
1946–1965	1956	94	86	25–44 yrs, in 1990

Source: Adapted from Statistics Sweden, 1993.

Table 15.3   Percentage of License Holders among Young Adults (18–24 yrs), by Year of Birth

Year of birth	Median year of birth	Men	Women	Data source
		%	%	
1954–1960	1957	75	61	Stat. Swed, survey 1978
1958–1964	1961	77	63	Stat. Swed, survey 1982
1965–1971	1968	81	71	Nat. Road Adm. 1999
1966–1972	1969	73	66	Stat. Swed, survey 1990
1966–1972	1969	77	68	Nat. Road Adm. 1999
1969–1975	1972	72	63	Nat. Road Adm. 1999
1973–1979	1976	65	56	Nat. Road Adm. 1999

Source: Adapted from Statistics Sweden, 1993, and unpublished statistics from the National Road Administration.

Table 15.4. Percentage of License Holders by Birth Year and Age

Year of birth	Percentage of license holders at age			
	18 yrs	19 yrs	21 yrs	24 yrs
Males	%	%	%	%
1965	—	—	—	87
1968	—	—	85	86
1971	57	74	80	83
1973	44	69	76	80
1975	42	64	73	78
1977	36	59	69	—
1979	30	54	—	—
1982	30	—	—	—
Females				
1965	—	—	—	81
1968	—	—	77	79
1971	42	61	70	74
1973	30	55	67	72
1975	31	53	64	69
1977	26	47	60	—
1979	22	43	—	—
1982	21	—	—	—

Source: Unpublished statistics from National Road Administration.

Table 15.5 "What drawbacks do you see with cars?" Percentage answering "The environment," by age and gender. (Swedish: "Vilka nackdelar ser du med bilen?" Svar: "Miljön.")

Age	Year of birth	Men	Women
		%	%
65–	prior to 1932	23	43
50–64	1933–1947	34	54
30–49	1948–1967	48	60
15–29	1968–1982	54	69

Source: SIFO, 1997.

been calculated by the National Road Administration. It was based not on surveys, but on the actual number of driver's licenses issued by this administration to young adults of various ages, and the actual number of Swedish inhabitants in the age class. Table 15.3 shows the data from both sources. For the age cohort born 1966–1972, we have two sets of data, with a discrepancy of 2–4 percentage points. This difference still allows us to conclude that the younger cohorts, born after the late 1960s or early 1970s, obtain licenses at a lower rate than their somewhat older counterparts.

The data from the National Road Administration are more detailed than the survey, and actually gives the proportion of licenses holders of each age (from 18 years up to 24 years) for several calendar years. In Table 15.4, the percentage of license holders is displayed by actual birth year and age, as far as data are available for each combination of birth year and age. Naturally, if we follow each birth cohort horizontally, from 18 to 24, we find a steadily increasing number of license holders. If we instead compare vertically, over the corresponding age levels, we find a steadily decreasing number of license holders in recent years. The same trend is evident for both genders. Whether this is just a temporary decrease, perhaps due to hard economic times, or whether it is a real change indicating a growing disenchantment with automobiles will be shown in the future.

Environmental concerns. The same survey that asked about the importance of having a car of one's own also asked many other questions about cars. One of these was "What drawbacks do you see with cars?" The respondents were not provided with answers to choose from. Instead, they had to volunteer their responses. The most common answer in all groups was "the expense." However, the second most common answer was "the environment." ("Accidents," "noise," and "they make cities ugly" were some other answers, which were not counted as "environment" in the survey.) In Table 15.5, the percentages responding "the environment" are displayed by gender and age. In this question we find a consistent pattern, with younger respondents more often mentioning the environment as a drawback with cars, and women more often than men.

To conclude, the data presented in this section indicate a generation gap between Swedes who were young adults in the 1950s and those who were young adults in the 1990s. For men, the early cohorts seemed highly involved with automobiles (as measured by the motivation to have a car of one's own and the frequency of obtaining a driver's license) and are presently little concerned with the environmental problems caused by cars. The later cohorts, most of whom have grown up with a family car, seem less involved with the vehicles and more concerned with their environmental problems. For women, the generational differences are less unidirectional, but Swedish women seem consistently less attracted to automobiles than their male compatriots, i.e., less involved and more aware of their drawbacks.

FAMILY TYPES AND CAR OWNERSHIP IN SWEDEN

"Families with children need cars" is conventional wisdom in Sweden. Often this wisdom is used to argue for lower taxes on cars, as in the following excerpt from a newsletter from the Swedish Road Association (a lobby organization backed by motor organizations, oil companies, and road builders). Evamarie Törnström, chairperson of the network "Women on the Road," is responding to Ingrid Segelström, spokesperson for a government transport commission (in Swedish: KomKom) that recommended higher taxation on road traffic. Segelström also argued that this would not hit women unduly, since they use cars less than men. Törnström, of course, was of a different opinion:

> Those who, at their own expense and on their own time, perform the major transport work for the family (shopping, caring for elderly relatives, social contacts, community work, driving their own and others' children to activities, school, and daycare, etc.) should therefore not be punished economically and by taxation, but should rather be encouraged in the socially useful work they perform. (*Sverige i rörelse*, no. 12 [November 1996]: 4)

How many families with children really own a car?[2] Certainly, most of them do, as do most Swedish households in general. In Sweden, with 8.8 million inhabitants, the total number of families with children (under the age of 18) is 1,135,000. The large survey of living conditions conducted in 1995 (Statistics Sweden, 1997) tells us that 916,000 of these are two-parent families (married or cohabiting parents). One-parent families number 218,000, most of them headed by a single mother rather than a single father. The rate of car ownership differs consider-

ably between one- and two-parent families. Whereas about 95 percent of two-parent families have a car (and 30 percent have two cars), only 60 percent of one-parent families have a car. In total numbers, this corresponds to 873,000 two-parent families with at least one car, and 43,000 two-parent families without, as well as 132,000 one-parent families with a car, and 86,000 such families without a car.

As we can conclude from the above, carless families are a minority, and they are usually fatherless as well. In Sweden, households with children rarely contain grandparents, and this is also true for one-parent families, making it almost certain that there is only one possible driver in these families (although occasionally there may be an older sibling, over age 18).

Car maintenance and women. Time-use studies show that car maintenance in Sweden is a male task in which women rarely engage (Statistics Sweden, 1992). Whether the low rate of car ownership in single-parent families is due entirely to economics or whether women's limited interest in cars and car maintenance plays an important role has apparently not been investigated. Instead, in studies of single mothers, not to have a car seems to be a non-issue in Sweden, as it is simply not discussed (Ensamma mammor, 1994; SOU, 1983: 51; Lassbo, 1988; Modig, 1990).

Car ownership as a personal characteristic. According to the 1995 follow-up on Swedish living conditions, the proportion of households with cars peaked around 1990 (Statistics Sweden, 1997). Since that time there has been a decrease, but mainly among the younger segments of the population. The middle-aged (45–64 years, born 1931–1950) and, particularly, the elderly (65–84 years, born 1911–1930) have increased their rate of car ownership greatly since 1975 (when the respondents in the same age categories, of course, had been born twenty years earlier). In the category "married persons 45–64 years without children," 96 percent have at least one car, while in the category "married persons 65–74 years," 89 percent have a car or cars. These categories were born 1931–1950 and 1921–1930, respectively.

The increase among the middle-aged and elderly is most likely related to the strong cohort effect of car ownership in Sweden. Unlike the elderly in earlier decades, most of today's elderly have owned cars since their youth, and the same is even more true of the middle-aged. In fact, owning a car seems to be a stable personal characteristic, especially for men ages 40 to 70. In a given year, less than

2 percent of car-owning men in this age group give up car ownership. (Changing to another car does not count.) Women have a somewhat higher propensity to give up car ownership (Jansson et al., 1986).

The study by Jansson et al. (1986) also showed that economic factors were important only in the young adult years. The high cost of car ownership might be a deterrent for the young adults, but after a person had settled into either car ownership or a car-free lifestyle, economic changes seemed to make little difference either way. The car owners continued to be car owners; the car-free remained car-free. At least, this was the situation during the studied period, 1950–1984. Although it seems likely that the same will hold in the future, there is, of course, no certainty. However, the fact that car ownership is as high among childless couples as among two-parent families casts doubt on the conventional wisdom that children are a decisive factor in car ownership, particularly since single mothers so often seem to manage without a car.

What Difference Does a Car Make for Children?

While the conventional wisdom holds that "families with children need at least one car," there has so far been little effort to find out to what extent a car really makes a difference for children. However, an investigation to find out how car access shapes experiences and mobility for children ages 12 to 16 is now in the planning stage.

Children's developmental experiences. With increasing numbers of cars in neighborhoods and increasing numbers of cars in families, children's opportunities for developing independence have been curtailed. Instead of walking to school on their own, they are increasingly chauffeured by their parents (Whitelegg, 1993). In Sweden, it has also been demonstrated that neighborhood traffic characteristics make a difference with respect to how much freedom children are granted to move around at ages 8–11 (Heurlin-Norinder, 1997). Between the ages of 12 and 16, children are in a developmental stage at which peers and independence from adult supervision become increasingly salient. Although their parents and other relatives of course remain important, children of this age must learn to act on their own and make their own decisions, for example, regarding leisure activities.

So while on the one hand being driven in a car may re-strict children's experiences, on the other hand car availability may enlarge their experiences. The car is likely to allow a wider variety of leisure activities, as well as to facilitate visits to widely dispersed relatives. For families with children, relatives are almost always an important part of the social network (Gunnarsson, 1990).

Apart from the objective difference that car ownership might make in children's lives, for 12-to-16-year-olds, who are beginning to develop their own value system, the subjective meaning of car ownership is an important subject to study. How do the parents and their children view not owning a car and owning one or two cars? Is not owning a car something to be ashamed of, or can it be a source of pride in view of the rising concern with the environment? Do the car-owning families, who are the norm today, feel that they have achieved "the good life," or do they feel that their car is "a necessary evil," a phrase that has been used in relation to cars in the U.S.? (Sandqvist, 1997).

Sample. As we have seen, car ownership varies with family type; furthermore, there is an understandable variation according to urbanity. In Stockholm, particularly in its central section, the rate of car ownership is much lower than in the suburbs or in the countryside. In contrast to the U.S., the central parts of Stockholm are inhabited predominantly by the middle class and the wealthy. The "problem categories," immigrants and the unemployed, live primarily in certain types of suburbs with apartment buildings. Thus, the lower rate of car ownership in the central areas is due not to limited resources per se, but rather to parking problems and good public transport.

These considerations add up to the necessity of a stratified sample. About 200 families with children ages 12 to 16 will be interviewed, in three neighborhood types: central Stockholm, suburb, and smaller city. In each, families will be stratified according to family type (single-parent and two-parent families) and car ownership (none, one, and two cars). Therefore, certain rare combinations, such as two-parent families living in the suburbs without a car, will be over-sampled in order to make comparisons possible.

Data collection. The children's travels and activities will be followed for a year, which will allow the charting of activities on schooldays, weekends, and seasonal holidays. Christmas, winter holidays, and summer vacations all have their special characteristics and meaning for growing children. Parents and children will be interviewed in order to obtain qualitative and quantitative information so that comparisons in the following areas can be made in relation to car availability:

Contacts with relatives, the "extended family," are basic for children's identity. In broken families, contact with the absent parent is crucial; otherwise grandparents, uncles, aunts, and cousins are very special people.

Organized leisure activities, such as scouting, sports, and playing music, are important in helping children to develop their interests. Are children without a car more restricted in their opportunities?

Children's relationships with their peers are important at this age. Does car availability make a difference?

Summer holidays provide an opportunity for families to spend time together with the extended family or to create new experiences. Camps where children can practice scouting, horsemanship, or sailing are also common.

Traveling abroad is a popular activity among Swedes, and trips to exciting places are frequently a source of status in children's peer groups.

Swedish schools close for a week each year for winter sports. Some families have the means to go to a resort, but many children stay home. How does this differ between families with and without a car?

Parents' attitudes toward their children's independent mobility is important. When parents have the means to chauffeur their children, do they do so to such an extent that their young teenagers never learn to practice independent mobility: walking, bicycling, and using public transport? Are some parents afraid to let their children use public transport?

Conclusion

According to the presented data, the current high rate of car ownership among the middle-aged and older segments of the Swedish population had its origins much earlier in the last century, when these people were young and highly drawn to the idea of having their own car. This was especially true for men. In the late twentieth century, young adults (who usually have grown up with a family car) seem less attracted to the idea of car ownership; they are more concerned with the environmental drawbacks of cars and less eager to obtain a driver's license, even though the infrastructure now makes a car less dispensable in everyday life. Taking this generation

gap seriously, is seems possible that transport history in Sweden (and Western Europe) might take a different course from that in the U.S. Total car dominance may not be inevitable.

If it is true that attitudes toward cars that are formed early in life have long-lasting effects, it is important to investigate the experiences of today's children, particularly how these are related to a family car.

Notes

1. It is not entirely unreasonable to ask youngsters under legal driving age how important it is for them to have a car of their own. We can easily imagine a survey asking unemployed people "How important is it for you to have a job?" In fact, 6 percent of the respondents *without* a car in their household found it "very important" to have a car of their own.

2. In Sweden, the term "car availability" is often used instead of "car ownership," because a significant number of people use a company car, which is technically owned by their employer. I will use "availability" and "ownership" interchangeably.

References

Ensamma mammor. 1994. *En rapport om ensamståendes mödrars hälsa och livsvillkor* [Single Mothers: A Report on Single Mothers' Health and Living Conditions]. Folkhälsoinstitutet, 24.

Gunnarsson, L. 1990. "Släkt och vänner" [Relatives and Friends]. In B.-E. Andersson and L. Gunnarsson, eds., *Svenska småbarnsfamiljer*. Lund: Studentlitteratur.

Heurlin-Norinder, M. 1997. "Hur kom du till skolan idag?" En enkätstudie kring barns rörelsefrihet i fyra bostadsområden ["How Did You Get to School Today?" A Study of Children's Mobility in Four Neighborhoods]. Stockholm: Stockholm Institute of Education.

Jansson, J. O, P. Carlebring, and O. Junghard. 1986. *Personbilsinnehavet i Sverige 1950–2010* [Car Ownership in Sweden 1950–2010]. Linköping, VTI: rapport 301.

Lassbo, G. 1988. *Mamma-(pappa)-barn* [Mother-(Father)-Children]. Göteborg Studies in Educational Sciences 68, Göteborg: Göteborgs universitet.

Modig, C. 1990. *Ensam förälder är många* [The Single Parent Is Many]. Stockholm: SESAM.

Sandqvist, K. 1997. *The Appeal of Automobiles: Human Desires and the Proliferation of Cars*. Stockholm: The Swedish Transport and Communications Research Board.

SIFO. 1997. *Svenskarna om bilen i samhället.* Dokument #3271910. Stockholm: Sifo Research and Consulting AB.

SOU. 1983. *Ensamföräldrarna och deras barn* [Single Parents and Their Children]. Report from the Governmental Commission on Single Parents and Their Children. Stockholm: Ministry of Social Affairs.

Statistics Sweden. 1987. *Inequality in Sweden: Changes and the Present.* Living Conditions, Report #51.

Statistics Sweden. 1992. I tid och otid. En undersökning om kvinnors och mäns tidsanvänding 1990–1991 [At All Times of Day: An Investigation of Women's and Men's Use of Time]. Living Conditions, Report #79.

Statistics Sweden. 1993. Våra dagliga resor 1982–1991. Levnadsförhållanden, rapport 82, Statistics Sweden (1997) 1. Välfärd och ojämlikhet i 20–årsperspektiv 1975–1995 [Living Conditions and Inequality in Sweden: A 20-Year Perspective, 1975–1995]. Living Conditions, Report #91.

Tengström, E. 1991. *Bilismen—i kris?* [Automobility—In Crisis?]. Stockholm: Rabén & Sjögren.

Whitelegg, J. 1993. *Transport for a Sustainable Future: The Case for Europe.* London: Belhaven.

CHAPTER SIXTEEN

Sustainable Lifestyles?

Microsimulation of Household Formation, Housing Choice, and Travel Behavior

Ilan Salomon,
Paul Waddell,
and Michael Wegener

INTRODUCTION: LIFESTYLES AND SUSTAINABILITY

There is growing awareness that the way of life practiced in the most affluent countries of the world is not sustainable. People in the richest countries consume significantly more energy and other resources per capita than people in the poorest regions, and by the same margin they generate more noxious emissions and waste. And this imbalance is increasing due to the faster growth in income in the already richer regions and the subsequent changes in lifestyles and consumption and travel patterns. In more general terms, there is a close relationship between income development and fundamental lifestyle decisions, which in turn determine housing choice and travel behavior. The hypothesis is that, irrespective of advances in resource efficiency and pollution control, continued growth in income will lead to less and less sustainable lifestyles unless policies make resource consumption, pollution, and car mobility less attractive.

This chapter discusses an approach to examining this relationship by combined modeling of household formation, housing choice, and travel behavior in urban regions. The basic rationale of the approach is that fundamental lifestyle decisions linked to phase of life and income strongly influence spatial behavior with respect to choice of residence and job location as well as mobility patterns.

The combined model under development proceeds in a nested fashion from modeling basic lifestyle decisions of individuals as a function of demographic development, career dynamics, and household formation, to modeling intra-urban location and housing choice of households, and from there to modeling daily activities and travel decisions of household members. By using event-based microsimulation with random-utility-based choice functions, short-term learning within the nested model structure becomes feasible. Medium-term and long-term adjustment of behavior is made possible by a model structure with short simulation periods of one year's duration. The model is spatially disaggregate by modeling choice behavior at the high-resolution raster or parcel level. The integrated model is to be used to model the impacts of policy packages in the fields of land use planning, transport infrastructure, transport regulation, and transport taxation designed to give incentives for more sustainable lifestyles.

The modeling concepts presented in this chapter are based on previous work by the three authors. Salomon (1983) pioneered the lifestyle approach in activity-based transport modeling. Waddell (2000a; 2000b) has developed UrbanSim, an urban economics–based model of metropolitan land development and firm and household location. Wegener (1985, 1998) has applied microsimulation techniques to modeling household location choice in a model of the regional housing market of Dortmund, Germany, the IRPUD model. Salomon and Wegener are currently developing a microsimulation model of urban travel behavior for the city of Netanya in Israel.

MICROSIMULATION IN URBAN MODELING: STATE OF THE ART

Microsimulation was first used in social-science applications by Orcutt et al. (1961), yet applications in a spatial context remained occasional experiments without deeper impact, though covering a wide range of phenomena such as spatial diffusion (Hägerstrand, 1968), urban development (Chapin and Weiss, 1968), transport behavior (Kreibich, 1979), demographic and household dynamics (Clarke et al., 1980; Clarke, 1981; Clarke and Holm, 1987; Holm et al., 2000) and housing choice (Kain and Apgar, 1985; Wegener, 1985). In recent years microsimulation has attracted new interest because of its flexibility to model processes that cannot be modeled in the aggregate (Clarke, 1996). Today there are several microsimulation models of urban land use and transport under development (Hayashi and Tomita, 1989; Mackett, 1990a; 1990b; Landis, 1994; Landis and Zhang, 1998a; 1998b; Waddell, 2000a; 2000b; Wegener and Spiekermann, 1996).

A different approach emerged from the theory of cellular dynamics. Cellular automata (CA) are objects associated with areal units or cells. CA follow simple stimulus-response rules, changing or not changing their state on the basis of the state of adjacent or nearby cells. When random noise is added to the rules, surprisingly complex patterns that closely resemble real cities can be generated (White and Engelen, 1994; Batty and Xie, 1994; Batty, 1997). More complex stimulus-response behavior is given to CA models in multi-reactive agents models. Multi-reactive agents are complex automata with the ability to control their interaction pattern. They can change their environment as well as their own behavior; i.e., they are able to learn (Ferrand, 2000). The distinction between the behavior of multi-reactive agents and the choice behavior generated in microsimulation models is becoming smaller.

Probably the most advanced area of application of microsimulation in urban models is travel modeling. Aggregate travel models are unable to reproduce the complex spatial behavior of individuals and to respond to sophisticated measures for managing travel demand. As a reaction, disaggregate travel models aim at a one-to-one reproduction of spatial behavior by which individuals choose between mobility options in their pursuit of activities during a day (Axhausen and Gärling, 1992; Ben Akiva et al., 1996). Activity-based travel models start from interdependent "activity programs" of household members and translate these into home-based "tours" consisting of one or more trips. This way interdependencies between the mobility behavior of household members and between the trips of a tour can be modeled, as can intermodal trips that cannot be handled in aggregate multimodal travel models. Activity-based travel models do not model peak-hour or all-day travel but disaggregate travel behavior by time of day, which permits the modeling of choice of departure time. There are also disaggregate traffic assignment models based on queuing or CA approaches, such as in the TRANSIMS project (Nagel et al., 1998; Barrett et al., 1999), which reproduce the movement of vehicles in the road network with a new level of detail.

THE THREE MICROSIMULATION MODULES

The model under development will go beyond the approaches reviewed in the previous section, bringing together approaches that have been developed in different streams of research in urban and transport modeling: microsimulation of household formation, housing choice, and travel behavior. In doing so it will stay below the level of disaggregation of vehicle movements in TRANSIMS, but in its spatial and temporal resolution it will exceed current aggregate land use transport models.

Household Formation

The household formation microsimulation module models the evolution of household attributes associating each household with a particular lifestyle.

"Lifestyle" is an empirical concept that attempts to capture human spatio-temporal behavior. It can be viewed as the sum of activities, distributed in time, space, and interpersonal and intrapersonal dimensions. It is a physical expression of the pattern of activities in which the individuals aspire to engage subject to constraints (Salomon, 1983, 1997). For the purpose of forecasting behavior, the concept of lifestyle seems to be richer in information than the conventional classification of market segments along sociodemographic and economic (SDE) variables.

As lifestyle expresses one's aspiration with regard to one's way of life (i.e., activities in time and space), people's revealed behavior is either consistent with their aspirations or a deviation therefrom in the presence of constraints. Thus, identifying a person's lifestyle is expected to be instrumental in predicting her behavioral response to new situations.

In the social sciences, lifestyles usually are represented as free-form narratives or "stories." The story format, though open and potentially rich in content, is not suitable for mathematical modeling. Therefore lifestyles need to be translated into some kind of quantitative representation, which, however, should preserve as much of the variation in lifestyles found in reality as possible. Such a representation is the representation of lifestyles as fuzzy objects. In the proposed model, a "lifestyle" therefore is a fuzzy object defined by a set of probabilistic membership functions. A probabilistic membership function is a vector of probabilities specifying the likelihood that individuals with a particular lifestyle belong in a particular category of a set of classified attributes.

The probabilities of the membership functions can be found as observed frequencies in empirical investigations, such as household surveys. In the absence of such surveys, they are determined by expert judgment and calibrated against observed aggregate distributions. The calibration is performed by microsimulation, by which a fictitious spatially disaggregated population of individuals and households is generated that conforms as far as possible to the membership functions defining each lifestyle, aggregate observed distributions such as population by age and sex, and the observed spatial distribution of land use and activities by zone.

In the household formation module, the following household events are modeled simultaneously for households and household members (see Fig. 16.1a): birth, aging, death; new household, dissolution of household; marriage/divorce, cohabitation/separation, separation of child, person joins household; new job, retirement, unemployment; change of income. Even though household formation events in reality are the outcome of more or less rational decisions, most of them will be modeled not as decisions, but simply as a result of the passage of time, i.e., as transitions (Wegener, 1985). Typical transitions are changes in the state of a household with respect to age or size conditional on the relevant probabilities for events such as aging/death, birth of a child, and relative joins or leaves household. Also, clearly choice-based events such as marriage or divorce are modeled as transitions because the

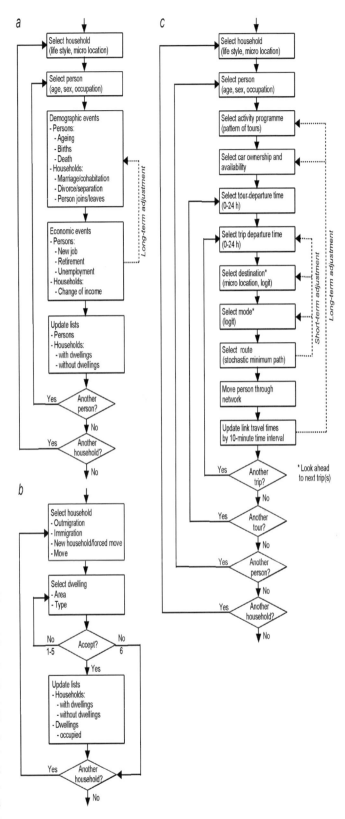

Figure 16.1 Microsimulation of Household Formation (a), Housing Choice (b), and Travel (c)

causal chain behind them is not represented in the model. Some events result in the dissolution of households or the creation of new households. Others, such as a new job or unemployment, are triggered by external events, such as hiring or firing in the labor market represented in another part of the model not described here. Change of income is a consequence of employment-related events.

Beyond these straightforward relationships, there is wide scope in the model for introducing more complex interdependencies between household and economic events. For instance, the increase in dual worker households may be in part a lifestyle choice and in part a necessity dictated by rising housing costs and stagnant real incomes. Children may delay new household formation or marriage. Childbearing may be postponed on the basis of some combination of lifestyle preferences and response to housing cost and income expectations. The role of labor market expectations in shaping these choices is an area of considerable policy implication.

Housing Choice

The housing choice microsimulation module models location and housing choice decisions of households who move into the region (immigration), move out of the region (out-migration), move into a dwelling for the first time (starter households), or move out of one dwelling into another (moves). Dwellings are affected by aging and by decisions on new construction, upgrading, and demolition modeled in other submodels not described here.

The housing choice model is a Monte Carlo microsimulation of transactions in the housing market. A market transaction is any successfully completed operation by which a household moves into or out of a dwelling or both. There are two types of actors in the housing market: households looking for a dwelling ("dwelling wanted") and landlords looking for tenants or buyers ("dwelling for rent or sale"). The household looking for a dwelling behaves as a satisficer; i.e., it accepts a dwelling if this will improve its housing situation by a considerable margin. Otherwise it enters another search phase, but after a number of unsuccessful attempts it abandons the idea of a move (Fig. 16.1b). The amount of improvement necessary to make a household move is assumed to depend on its prior search experience, i.e., to go up with each successful search and down with each unsuccessful search. In other words, households adapt their aspiration levels to supply conditions on the market. The attractiveness of a dwelling for a household is a weighted aggregate of the attractiveness of its location, its quality, and its rent or price in relation to the household's housing budget. The attractiveness of the location and the quality of the dwelling are themselves multi-attribute-encompassing relevant attributes of the neighborhood and of the dwelling.

Travel Behavior

The travel behavior microsimulation models for each member of each household the selection of an activity program (defined as a schedule of tours), car availability, and, subject to that, for each trip departure time, destination, mode, and route (see Fig. 16.1c): Each household is defined by its household attributes, its lifestyle, and its residential location, and by the personal attributes of its members. A location in the model is a micro location, i.e., a street address, geographical coordinates, or a raster cell. The destination of a trip is selected by logit choice, where locations of destinations are also micro locations. Generalized costs of travel to the destinations are calculated as the logsum of minimum paths of relevant modes: walking, cycling, public transport, and car (if available), with a random disturbance term added to each link impedance and waiting/transfer time in the public transport network (stochastic minimum paths). For work, school, and university trips, the destinations are already known. Mode choice is performed by logit choice based on the generalized costs of stochastic minimum paths; the selected route is the stochastic minimum path. After each trip, the travel times of all transversed road links are updated to account for congestion. If congestion is encountered during a trip, short-term adjustment resulting in a postponement of the trip or a change of mode or route may occur. In order to facilitate long-term learning, information on the generalized costs of the congested network by time of day of the current simulation period is used in the next period.

One important objective of this approach to traffic microsimulation will be to accomplish realistic assignment of travelers to modes and routes without extensive iteration, as computing requirements of iterative assignment in large urban road networks has proved to be a serious problem in TRANSIMS (Nagel et al., 1998; Barrett et al., 1999).

PLANNED WORK

The development of the model is based on previous work by the authors. The lifestyle concept is implemented for the first time in the activity-based transport model for

Netanya. All three microsimulation modules are planned to be integrated in both UrbanSim and the IRPUD model.

Lifestyles in Netanya

The city of Netanya (population 150,000) is situated at the northern rim of the metropolitan area of Tel Aviv. It was founded in 1928 as an independent resort town, which over the years, with the sprawl of the metro region, has become part of it. Given this history, Netanya is clearly not the typical suburban community. It consists of a mix of lifestyles, which to a great extent represents the Israeli urban scene.

To identify the lifestyle-based market segments in Netanya and the proxy variables that indicate membership, a small survey was conducted in which individuals had to identify four lifestyle groups in Netanya, and to provide a short narrative description of the group. Then they were requested to provide a quantitative assessment for one of the lifestyle groups. This pilot study was performed with the cooperation of Israeli students of geography at the Hebrew University.

Some twenty-four students filled out the questionnaire. In total they provided fifty-eight responses to the question requesting four lifestyle labels, but these referred to forty-one different lifestyles. This large number indicates either that the respondents had not internalized the concept of lifestyle and actually provided simple SDE variables as the relevant classification basis, or that there are many diverse lifestyle segments in the Israeli (or Netanya) population.

An analysis of the responses suggests, based on an acquaintance with Israeli society, that in some cases a single variable is sufficiently powerful to discriminate a group out of the population as a lifestyle segment. For example, being labeled ultra-orthodox provides sufficient information to reveal the lifestyle of the person being described. This group was mentioned in eight out of fifty-eight responses. However, being labeled a member of the middle class conveys very little information about the person's or household's lifestyle. Further analysis of the classification provided in this experiment is under way.

Integration of Microsimulation into UrbanSim

The design and implementation of the UrbanSim model is highly disaggregate, and applies a behavioral and dynamic disequilibrium approach using annual time steps. The initial beta version contained a microsimulation of land development at the parcel level, and modeled location choice of households at the level of household groups

of similar sociodemographic and economic type. Location choice was simulated with a logit model of housing type and zone (Waddell, 2000a). In the current implementation, the residential and employment location components have been fully converted to microsimulation of lists of individual households and jobs. Location choice, land development, and price adjustment are now simulated at the level of raster cells of 150 by 150 m, though the resolution is arbitrary and can be changed in accordance with data and computing resources (Waddell, 2000b).

Further changes to the UrbanSim model will require implementing model components to simulate household formation and travel, since the current model implementation takes both as exogenous and links to external models for these attributes. The current housing choice model component is already close to the proposed specifications, simulating housing choice with a logit model of development type and micro-location at the grid cell level. The major difference in the data structure required to implement the proposed specifications is the incorporation of individual persons, since only households are now modeled. The current model design is being applied in four metropolitan areas in the United States: Eugene-Springfield, Oregon; Honolulu, Hawaii; Salt Lake City, Utah; and Seattle, Washington.

In addition, a new software architecture for urban simulation has now been completed that greatly facilitates the creation, evolution, and coordination of model components (Noth et al., 2000). The model system is implemented in Java and is available as open source software (like Linux) to facilitate extension and collaboration without proprietary restrictions (Waddell, 2000b).

Integration of Microsimulation into the IRPUD Model

Because of its modular structure, the IRPUD model (Wegener, 1998) is well suited for the integration of microsimulation modules. The present aggregate submodels of household formation and travel behavior are currently being replaced by microsimulation modules. The microsimulation of housing choice will replace the present hybrid microsimulation, which is disaggregate in its modeling of behavior but aggregate in its data.

Certain complications arise with respect to the spatiotemporal database underlying the model. In the present model, all simulation results of each simulation period are written into the database on a zonal basis for use in the next simulation period. After the simulation, all results are retained in the database for ex-post analysis and the production of diagrams and maps. This implies that the microsimulation modules of household formation and housing choice have to maintain their own disaggregate database consisting of the lists of households, household members, and dwellings, but that the microsimulation data are also stored in aggregate form in the present database.

The micro locations used in the microsimulation modules are implemented in the IRPUD model by raster cells, where a micro location is a pair of coordinates indicating the row and column in a matrix of raster cells. The size of the raster cells is 100 m by 100 m. As no household and workplace data at this level of spatial disaggregation are available for the Dortmund urban region, aggregate data for statistical districts and subdistricts are disaggregated using Monte-Carlo simulation with GIS-based land use polygon data as ancillary information. The method is described in Wegener and Spiekermann (1996) and Spiekermann and Wegener (2000).

The integration of the three microsimulation modules into the IRPUD model is a step toward making the whole model disaggregate (Wegener and Spiekermann, 1996). For the future it is planned to apply the same principles to the existing aggregate submodels of industrial and services location and industrial, commercial, and residential construction.

CONCLUSIONS

This chapter has outlined a modeling framework in which household formation, housing choice, and daily mobility are modeled in three microsimulation modules interlinked by a common disaggregate database.

The modeling framework permits the application of the principle of microscopic activity-based transport modeling to changes in the life cycle of households and individuals and to decisions on residential location. This opens the way for modeling the links between long-term lifestyle decisions and medium- and short-term residential and daily mobility.

Microsimulation will make urban models richer in behavioral content and more responsive to land use and travel demand management policies. The higher spatial and temporal resolution will also make them suitable to model micro-scale environmental phenomena such as traffic noise and air pollution. This will be an important prerequisite for using the models for the identification of more sustainable lifestyles.

NOTE

The research reported here has in part been supported by the German-Israeli Foundation for Scientific Research and Development in the project "Sustainable Mobility in Cities," and National Science Foundation (U.S.) grant CMS-9818378: "Reusable Modeling Components for Land Use, Transportation and Land Cover."

REFERENCES

Axhausen, K. W., and T. Gärling. 1992. "Activity-Based Approaches to Travel Analysis: Conceptual Frameworks, Models and Research Problems." *Transport Reviews* 12: 324–341.

Barrett, C. L., et al. 1999. *TRansportation ANalysis SIMulation System (TRANSIMS). Version TRANSIMS-LANL-1.0.* Vol. 0: *Overview.* LA-UR 99-1658. Los Alamos, N.Mex.: Los Alamos National Laboratory. http://transims.tsasa.lanl.gov/documents.html

Batty, M. 1997. "Cellular Automata and Urban Form: A Primer." *Journal of the American Planning Association* 63: 264–274.

Batty, M., and Y. Xie. 1994. "From Cells to Cities." *Environment and Planning B: Planning and Design* 21: S31–S48.

Ben-Akiva, M. E., J. L. Bowman, and D. Gopinath. 1996. "Travel Demand Model System for the Information Era." *Transportation* 23: 241–266.

Chapin, F. S., and S. F. Weiss. 1968. "A Probabilistic Model for Residential Growth." *Transportation Research* 2: 375–390.

Clarke, G. P., ed. 1996. *Microsimulation for Urban and Regional Policy Analysis.* European Research in Regional Science 6. London: Pion.

Clarke, M. 1981. "A First-Principle Approach to Modelling Socio-economic Interdependence Using Microsimulation." *Computers, Environment and Urban Systems* 6: 211–227.

Clarke, M., and E. Holm. 1987. "Microsimulation Methods in Spatial Analysis and Planning." *Geografiska Annaler* 69B: 145–164.

Clarke, M., P. Keys, and H. C. W. L. Williams. 1980. *Micro-Analysis and Simulation of Socio-economic Systems: Progress and Prospects.* Leeds: School of Geography, University of Leeds.

Ferrand, N. 2000. "Multi-reactive Agents Paradigm for Spatial Modelling." In A. S. Fotheringham and M. Wegener, eds., *Spatial Models and GIS: New Potential and New Models,* 167–184. London: Taylor & Francis.

Hägerstrand T. 1968. *Innovation Diffusion as Spatial Process.* Chicago: University of Chicago Press.

Hayashi, Y., and Y. Tomita. 1989. "A Micro-analytic Residential Mobility Model for Assessing the Effects of Transport Improvement." In *Transport Policy, Management and Technology: Towards 2001—Selected Proceedings of the Fifth World Conference on Transport Research, Yokohama*, 91–105. Ventura, Calif.: Western Periodicals.

Holm, E., U. Lindgren, and G. Malmberg. 2000. "Dynamic Microsimulation." In A. S. Fotheringham and M. Wegener, eds., *Spatial Models and GIS: New Potential and New Models*, 143–165. London: Taylor & Francis.

Kain, J. F., and W. C. Apgar, Jr. 1985. *Housing and Neighborhood Dynamics: A Simulation Study*. Cambridge, Mass.: Harvard University Press.

Kreibich, V. 1979. "Modelling Car Availability, Modal Split, and Trip Distribution by Monte Carlo Simulation: A Short Way to Integrated Models." *Transportation* 8: 153–166.

Landis, J. D. 1994. "The California Urban Futures Model: A New Generation of Metropolitan Simulation Models." *Environment and Planning B: Planning and Design* 21: 99–422.

Landis, J. D., and M. Zhang. 1998a. "The Second Generation of the California Urban Futures Model. Part 1: Model Logic and Theory." *Environment and Planning B: Planning and Design* 25: 657–666.

Landis, J. D., and M. Zhang. 1998b. "The Second Generation of the California Urban Futures Model. Part 2: Specification and Calibration Results of the Land-Use Change Submodel." *Environment and Planning B: Planning and Design* 25: 795–824.

Mackett, R. L. 1990a. *MASTER Model (Micro-Analytical Simulation of Transport, Employment and Residence)*. Report SR 237. Crowthorne: Transport and Road Research Laboratory.

Mackett, R. L. 1990b. "Comparative Analysis of Modelling Land-Use Transport Interaction at the Micro and Macro Levels." *Environment and Planning A* 22: 459–475.

Nagel, K., R. J. Beckman, and C. L. Barrett. 1998. *TRANSIMS for Transportation Planning*. LA-UR 98-4389. Los Alamos, N.Mex.: Los Alamos National Laboratory. http://transims.tsasa.lanl.gov/documents.html

Noth, M., P. Waddell, and A. Borning. 2000. "A Software Architecture for UrbanSim, an Urban Land Use Modeling System." In progress. Current version available at http://www.urbansim.org

Orcutt, G., M. Greenberger, A. Rivlin, and J. Korbel. 1961. *Microanalysis of Socioeconomic Systems: A Simulation Study*. New York: Harper and Row.

Salomon, I. 1983. "The Use of the Life-Style Concept on Travel Demand Models." *Environment and Planning A* 15: 623–638.

Salomon, I. 1997. "Incorporating Newly Emerging Travel and Activity Patterns in Microsimulation Approaches." Working Paper, Department of Geography, Hebrew University, Jerusalem.

Spiekermann, K., and M. Wegener. 2000. "Freedom from the Tyranny of Zones: Towards New GIS-Based Spatial Models." In A. S. Fotheringham and M. Wegener, eds., *Spatial Models and GIS: New Potential and New Models*, 45–61. London: Taylor & Francis.

Waddell, P. 2000a. "A Behavioural Simulation Model for Metropolitan Policy Analysis and Planning: Residential Location and Housing Market Components of UrbanSim." *Environment and Planning B: Planning and Design* 27: 247–263.

Waddell, P. 2000b. UrbanSim. http://urbansim.org

Wegener M. 1985. "The Dortmund Housing Market Model: A Monte Carlo Simulation of a Regional Housing Market." In K. Stahl, ed., *Microeconomic Models of Housing Markets*, 144–191. Lecture Notes in Economics and Mathematical Systems 239. Berlin/Heidelberg/New York: Springer-Verlag.

Wegener, M. 1998. "The IRPUD Model: Overview." http://irpud.raumplanung.uni-dortmund.de/irpud/pro/mod/mod.htm

Wegener, M., and K. Spiekermann. 1996. "The Potential of Microsimulation for Urban Models." In G. P. Clarke, ed., *Microsimulation for Urban and Regional Policy Analysis*, 149–163. European Research in Regional Science 6. London: Pion.

White, R., and G. Engelen. 1994. "Cellular Dynamics and GIS: Modelling Spatial Complexity." *Geographical Systems* 1: 237–253.

PART IV

Quality, Equity, and Mobility

CHAPTER SEVENTEEN

Sustainable Transport and Quality of Life

A Psychological Analysis

Birgitta Gatersleben
and David Uzzell

INTRODUCTION

The ideology of uncontrolled economic growth, irrespective of its environmental or health consequences, has now been replaced by an ideology that regards sustainability as an essential part of societal development in general, and of urban life in particular. Furthermore, it is believed that only by balancing economic activity and environmental quality will we be able to ensure and sustain human well-being. In order to be able to assess whether there are any demonstrable gains in human well-being, we need to evaluate the impact of sustainability policies. Such evaluation has to go beyond economic indicators (Henderson, 1994). The identification of appropriate indicators and their relative importance is still a subject of debate. In general, three classes of indicators have been distinguished: environmental, economic, and social (see Hodge, 1997; Michalos, 1997).

This chapter describes a social-psychological field study of people's perceptions and evaluations of transport-related problems. The study was conducted in a medium-sized town in the UK in April 1999. It is suggested that a similar study in the United States might yield valuable information on the perception and evaluation of transport-related problems.

SUSTAINABLE TRANSPORT

One important goal of sustainable development can be described as sustaining or improving the quality of life of all people, now and in the long term (see, for instance, WCED, 1987). It is generally agreed that decision-making in sustainable development should include economic, environmental, and social costs and benefits in a society or community (Hodge, 1997; Michalos, 1997). Environmental indicators of sustainable development generally measure the level of environmental degradation. Economic indicators measure the level of economic prosperity. The definition of social indicators is less clear, but they generally focus on social-psychological aspects of the quality of life, such as safety, development, work, and leisure time (Andrews and Withey, 1976; Henderson, 1994).

Figure 17.1 describes a conceptual social-psychological model of sustainable transport. It is presumed that different transport systems (the availability and use of travel modes) are perceived to be more or less sustainable because of the costs and benefits they have for the environment, the economy, individuals, and the community.

The perception of negative and positive consequences of different transport systems influences the overall evalua-

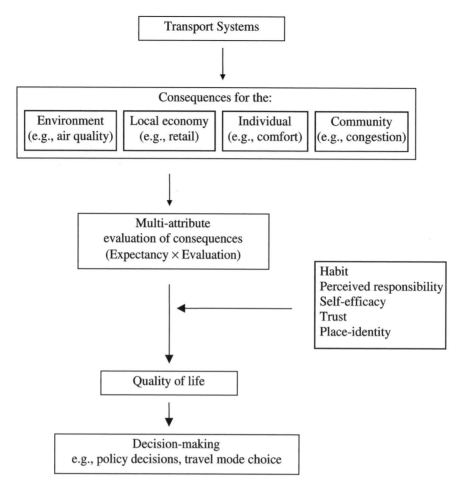

Figure 17.1   A Social-Psychological Model of Sustainable Transport

tion of these transport systems in terms of the quality of life. The extent to which people are willing to change their own behavior or to accept sustainable transport schemes depends on their perceptions and evaluation of current and possible future (sustainable) transport systems. People may be less willing to change their travel mode if they believe that current transport systems already have a positive benefit for their well-being.

The perceptions and evaluation of the consequences of different transport patterns depend not only on the actual costs and benefits of a transport system, but also on social-psychological mechanisms that may have an important influence. These mechanisms will be de-

scribed after a brief analysis of the environmental, economic, and social-psychological costs and benefits of transport.

Environmental consequences. Cars have been a liberating force in society: they have opened up choices and opportunities with respect to where people live, work, and take their leisure. However, on the negative side they cause many kinds of environmental pollution. Roads, for instance, are often built at the expense of the natural environment. The scenic beauty of streets is affected by parked cars. Vehicular transport is one of the major sources of noise pollution. Moreover, transport is a significant source of the greenhouse gases that cause global warming (Whitelegg, 1993; Godlee and Walker, 1992). Many studies are now being conducted to examine the short-, medium-, and long-term effects of air pollution on human health (Godlee and Walker, 1992). These studies show that air pollutants emitted by cars can damage the respiratory systems of people who are particularly sensitive and at risk. Moreover, scientists now believe that long-term exposure to low levels of pollutants may be a cause of leukemia (EPAQS, 1995).

Economic consequences. Transportation has a positive effect on the local and national economy, since it creates jobs and makes shopping and working areas more accessible. Steg and Vlek (1997), however, showed that a large number of Dutch car users (45 percent of the respondents in their study) agree that a reduction in car use can have a positive effect on the economy. Employment is influenced by more than the production of cars and road building. Building cycling lanes and producing bicycles and cleaner buses also create jobs (Friends of the Earth, 1990). Furthermore, bicycle facilities are cheaper than car facilities, and riding a bike is cheaper than driving a car (Seiderman and Russell, 1997).

A study in Copenhagen has demonstrated that after pedestrianization, not only did more people come into the city, but they stayed there longer (Gehl and Gemz, 1996). Examples for the United States illustrate that adding new cycle paths can attract business (U.S. Department of Transportation, 1992). Studies in Germany and the UK have shown that, although initial problems may occur in the first (one-to-three-year) transition period, well-designed pedestrianization schemes can increase the number of shoppers in the stores and improve the vitality of town centers (Hass-Klau, 1993).

Social-psychological consequences of car use. Several studies have examined why people own and use cars. Tertoolen (1994) found that car use is reinforced by such factors as reduced travel time, prestige, flexibility, privacy, route selection, the ease of taking luggage, and protection against the weather. Inhibitors include congestion, parking problems, feelings of guilt, traffic, accident risk, and commuting stress (Steg and Vlek, 1997). Slotegraaf et al. (1997) developed a method to study the emotional and affective motives of car use. The study showed that for car users, factors such as getting a thrill from speeding, taking risks, and feelings of superiority from having a bigger car may also be important dimensions in the process of evaluating their cars.

Car Use as a Commons Dilemma

Imagine that you have the choice of taking your children to school by car or letting them go by themselves, either on foot or by bicycle. Different factors will probably influence your decision, of which the safety of your children is almost certainly the most important. Over the last couple of years in Guildford, England (as in other Western European towns), the number of cars on the road has increased substantially. As a consequence, the fear of car accidents involving children has also increased. If all parents let their children go to school either on foot or by bicycle, there obviously would be far less car traffic during school hours, the streets would be much safer, and the air would be cleaner. It would therefore be best for everybody not to drive. However, for each individual it would be quicker, more convenient, and safer to use the car, especially when others have chosen not to use theirs.

This is a typical example of a commons dilemma. The defining characteristics of social dilemmas are that (1) each participant receives more benefits (or lower costs) for a self-interest choice than for a public-interest choice, and (2) all participants as a group would benefit more if they all chose to act in the public interest rather than according to self-interest (Gifford, 1997). The commons dilemma paradigm is often used in environmental psychology to describe people's choice of travel mode (see Vlek et al., 1993; Tertoolen, 1994; Van Lange et al., 1998). Studies on social dilemmas have shown that individuals and organizations will be more or less inclined to perform pro-social behavior (i.e., pro-environmental behavior) depending on the following circumstances:

Evaluation of costs and benefits: Paradoxically, if people find the common good more important, they are more inclined to make self-interested choices (Gifford, 1997). The definition of the common good is important. It can be the environment, the local economy, even the livability of a community.

Problem perception: Laboratory experiments have shown that the extent to which a common good is depleted (e.g., the environment polluted) influences people's willingness to behave in a pro-social way. For our study, this means that the extent to which people believe the roads are congested and/or the air is polluted may influence their willingness to reduce their car use. Several studies have shown that awareness of environmental problems may affect people's willingness to change their behavior (Baldassare, 1992; Steg and Vlek, 1997).

Personal responsibility: The extent to which people feel personally responsible for the problems caused by car use may have a significant effect on their willingness to change. People who believe that their actions are not harmful are less willing to change their behavior than people who believe they are part of the problem (Steg and Vlek, 1997).

Self-efficacy and trust: Steg and Vlek (1997) showed that most car users do not believe that other people will make cooperative choices, although this is necessary to solve transport problems. Van Lange, Van Vugt, Meertens, and Ruiter (1998) found that people with a pro-social value orientation and a high trust in others express higher preferences for public transport and car-pooling than do people with a pro-social value orientation and low trust or people with a pro-self orientation.

THE GUILDFORD STUDY

In April 1999, a questionnaire was sent to 1,500 randomly selected households in the borough of Guildford. A total of 439 (30 percent) completed questionnaires were returned. Fifty-three percent of the respondents were male and 47 percent female. The average age of the respondents was 43 (Gatersleben and Uzzell, 2000). The study was conducted among people living in the town center (n = 148), people living in suburban areas outside the town center (n = 103), and people living in rural areas outside the town (n = 163). The samples in each area were similar in income, age, and level of education.

The questionnaire asked about the environmental, economic, and social-psychological costs and benefits of current transport use in Guildford. It included a number of questions to determine the social-psychological variables that influence people's evaluations and perceptions. Respondents were also asked to evaluate a number of alternative strategies for addressing the transport problems in Guildford and were asked to what extent they would be willing to change their behavior. Below we provide a short summary of some of the results of the study.

The data revealed that people who live in rural areas use public transport less often and their cars more often than people who live in urban areas. This may not be sur-

prising, since public transport provision is likely to be better in urban areas than in rural areas. Moreover, people who live in rural areas will probably have to travel longer distances (e.g., to go shopping) than people in urban areas. However, we also found that for trips of less than one mile, people who live in rural areas use their car significantly more often (43 percent of the time) than do people who live either in the town center (32 percent) or in suburban areas (34 percent). Furthermore, rural dwellers walk significantly less often (48 percent of the time) than people who live in urban areas (61 percent) or suburban areas (54 percent). A similar distinction was found for travel modes for distances between one and three miles.

These results cannot be explained in terms of travel distances or differences in transport provision. To further investigate the reasons for the differences, we examined whether the perceptions of the costs and benefits of car use varied between respondent groups depending on their residential location. We found that the groups do not differ in their beliefs about the benefits (e.g., safety, price, convenience) or the costs (e.g., parking problems, environmental problems) of car use. Only one significant difference was found. People who live in rural areas perceive fewer congestion problems (mean = 3.78; 1 = no congestion, 5 = high congestion) than people in suburban areas (M = 4.18) or the town center (M = 4.26). This might suggest that people in rural areas justify their higher car use by indicating that they cause less congestion. It may also suggest that people in rural areas use their car more than people in urban areas because it is easier for them to get around by car; i.e., they experience less congestion.

The groups do not vary in the extent to which they are willing to reduce their car use. Respondents in rural areas are somewhat more likely to say that they would shop in another town if parking charges were to be increased, and somewhat less likely to change their travel mode. But they are equally likely to pay the higher parking charges, and they are more likely to use expanded park-and-ride schemes.

There is no difference between the three groups in the extent to which they feel responsible for transport problems in Guildford; nor do they feel more or less in control over the solutions. Moreover, they do not vary in the extent to which they believe that other people will cooperate to solve the problems. Residents who live in the town center are slightly more likely to believe that Guildford's transport problems are caused mainly by people who live elsewhere, while those who live outside the town are slightly less likely to believe that people outside Guildford will not cooperate to solve the problems.

Generally, we did find that people are more willing to try to reduce their own car use when they believe that driving has more negative environmental consequences (r = .30, p < .001), when they have higher self-efficacy (i.e., feel more control over the solutions; r = .31, p < .001), feel more responsible (r = .22, p < .001), and have greater trust in the cooperation of others (local authorities and other car users; r = .22, p < .001). Moreover, respondents are more likely to change their travel mode from car to public transport in response to certain car travel reduction measures when they believe that car use has more negative consequences (r = .33, p < .001) or lesser benefits (r = −.21, p < .001), when they believe that they have more control over the solutions (r = .34, p < .001), and when they have more trust in the cooperation of others (r = .17, p < .01).

Similar but weaker relationships were found for the use of various travel modes for short distances. People who use their cars more (for distances between one and three miles) believe that car use has more benefits (r = .16, p < .01) and fewer negative consequences (r = −.14, p < .05), and they feel less in control over solutions to possible problems (r = −.12, p < .01). However, they do feel more responsible for the problems (r = .23, p < .001). People who use public transport more (for trips of less than one mile as well as for trips of one to three miles), however, perceive lower benefits of car use (r = −.21, p < .001) and more negative consequences (r = .13, p < .01). They believe that they can contribute to the solutions (r = .10, p < .05), and they feel less responsible for the problems (r = −.17, p < .01).

In conclusion, it appears that the use of different travel modes cannot be explained merely by differences in travel distances and the availability of alternative transport, although these factors are undoubtedly important. This is also supported by our finding that more than half of our respondents (about 51 percent) said that they were in principle willing to reduce their car use. However, when they were asked to what extent they believed it was likely that they would use other travel modes if these were expanded, 40 percent or less admitted that they would consider or intended to use such services. Aspects such as the perceived positive and negative consequences of car use for the environment and for people themselves are also

important. Moreover, people's willingness to change their actual use of different travel modes is related to the extent to which they feel that their personal car use contributes to transport problems (responsibility), the extent to which they feel that changes in their travel mode will help solve possible problems (self-efficacy), and the extent to which they believe that others are also willing to help solve possible problems (trust). When developing policy measures that aim to change travel mode choice, it would be efficacious to accompany physical planning measures with communication strategies that focus on increasing knowledge of the costs and benefits of different travel modes, feelings of responsibility for the problems, increasing mutual trust, and control over the solutions.

A COMPARISON WITH THE UNITED STATES

There are many ways in which a medium-sized European town such as Guildford differs from towns in the United States. The urban structure of European towns, for instance, is more dense. European countries have a longer history of public transport. It is often stated that the United States is a car society. North Americans are presumed to attach more importance to their cars than Europeans. This is perhaps not surprising, as car ownership levels are higher in the United States, which, when combined with the fact that operating costs are considerably lower there and average distances traveled are greater, means that car use is higher in North America. It is thus suggested that as a consequence, North Americans lead a more car-dependent lifestyle. These differences may make a number of comparisons between North American and Europeans interesting and valuable for future research on sustainable transport. Up until now, the few of the social-psychological studies that have been conducted on transport problems have focused on the European experience. Little is known about the perceptions and evaluation of transport-related problems in the U.S. We do know, for example, that Europeans are generally more concerned with environmental problems than are Americans (Dunlap et al., 1993).

It would be interesting to study whether these differences actually exist. If so, it might be beneficial to learn how this "psychological car dependency" has evolved among Americans, and why it has not evolved in Europe.

Although Europeans and Americans may differ with respect to what they value in their lives, there will also be many similarities. An analysis of the differences and the similarities in the perceptions and evaluations of North Americans and Europeans might provide more insight into those aspects that influence decision-making related to transport. Moreover, it might provide more insight into the sensitivity of these aspects to cultural differences and social change and to the opportunities for behavioral change.

REFERENCES

Andrews, F., and S. Withey. 1976. *Social Indicators of Well-Being: Americans' Perception of Life Quality.* New York: Plenum.

Baldassare, M., and C. Katz. 1992. "The Personal Threat of Environmental Problems as Predictor of Environmental Practices." *Environment and Behavior* 24, no. 5: 602–616.

Dunlap, R. E., G. H. Gallup, Jr., and A. M. Gallup. 1993. "Of Global Concern." *Environment* 35, no. 9: 7–40.

EPAQS (Expert Panel on Air Quality Standards). 1995. *Particles.* London: HMSO.

Friends of the Earth. 1990. "Less Traffic More Jobs: The Direct Employment Impacts of Developing a Sustainable Transport System in the United Kingdom." Summary written for the LEPU seminar Less Traffic More Jobs, 10 February, 1999, South Bank University, London.

Gatersleben, B., and D. Uzzell. 2000. "Residents' Perceptions of Transport Problems and Sustainable Solutions in Guildford." GBCRS report 1. Unpublished report, University of Surrey, Guildford.

Gehl, J., and L. Gemze. 1996. *Public Spaces, Public Life.* Copenhagen: The Danish Architectural Press.

Gifford, R. 1997. *Environmental Psychology: Principles and Practice.* Boston: Allyn and Bacon.

Godlee, F., and A. Walker. 1992. *Health and the Environment.* London: British Medical Journal.

Hass-Klau, C. 1993. "Impact of Pedestrianisation and Traffic Calming on Retailing: A Review of the Evidence from Germany and the UK." *Transport Policy* 1: 1.

Henderson, H. 1994. "Paths to Sustainable Development: The Role of Social Indicators." *Futures* 26: 125–137.

Hodge, T. 1997. "Toward a Conceptual Framework for Assessing Progress toward Sustainability." *Social Indicators Research* 40: 5–98.

Michalos, A. C. 1997. "Combining Social, Economic and Environmental Indicators to Measure Sustainable Human Well-Being." *Social Indicators Research* 40, 221–258.

OECD (Organisation for Economic Cooperation and Development). 1982. *The OECD List of Social Indicators.* Paris: OECD.

Seiderman, C. B., and R. H. Russell. 1997. "How Better Bicycle Facilities Can Enhance Local Economies." Paper written for Velo-City Falco Lecture Prize. http://www.tlcnetwork.org/velocity.html

Slotegraaf, G., E. M. Steg, and C. A. J. Vlek. 1997. "Affective Motives of Car Use" [Diepere drijfveren van het autogebruik]. Unpublished report, University of Groningen, the Netherlands. (In Dutch.)

Steg, L., and Ch. Vlek. 1997. "The Role of Problem Awareness in Willingness-to-Change Car Use and in Evaluating Relevant Policy Measures." In T. Rothengatter and Vaya E. Carbonell, eds., *Traffic and Transport Psychology.* London: Pergamon.

Tertoolen, G. 1994. "Uit eigen beweging . . . ?! Een veld-experiment over beinvloedingspogingen van het autogebruik en de daardoor opgeroepen psycholo-gische weerstanden" [Psychological Reactions to Transport Policy Measures]. Doctoral dissertation, University of Utrecht, the Netherlands. (In Dutch.)

U.S. Department of Transportation, Federal Highway Administration. 1992. National Bicycling and Walking Study, Case Study no 7: "Transportation Potential and Other Benefits of Off-Road Bicycle and Pedestrian Facilities." Washington, D.C.: U.S. Department of Transportation.

Van Lange, P. A. M., M. Van Vugt, R. M. Meertens, and R. A. Ruiter. 1998. "A Social Dilemma Analysis of Commuting Preferences: The Roles of Social Value Orientations and Trust." *Journal of Applied Social Psychology* 28, no. 9: 796–820.

Vlek, Ch., L. Hendrickx, and L. Steg. 1993. "A Social Dilemmas Analysis of Motorised-Transport Problems and Six General Strategies for Social Behaviour Change." In *Transport Policy and Global Warming*, 209–225. Paris: European Conference of Ministers of Transport (ECMT).

WCED (World Commission on Environment and Development). 1987. *Our Common Future.* Oxford: Oxford University Press.

Whitelegg, J. 1993. *Transport for a Sustainable Future: The Case for Europe.* London, New York: Belhaven Press.

CHAPTER EIGHTEEN

Introducing Environmental Equity Concerns into the Discourse on Sustainable Transport

A Research Agenda

Eran Feitelson

INTRODUCTION

Transportation issues are increasingly being discussed in the context of sustainable development, most commonly under the rubric of sustainable transport (Banister and Button, 1993; Greene and Wegener, 1997; Whitelegg, 1993). Discussions of sustainable transport, however, are usually limited to the environmental impacts of transport and possible measures to address these effects. Many of the sustainable transport initiatives, and transport sections of sustainable development programs, take an even narrower view, whereby only a limited set of emission and pollution effects are addressed.

However, the notion of sustainable development is much broader than is implied by the interrelationship between growth and the environment. In addition to environmental and development dimensions, there is also an equity dimension. Thus sustainable development programs should balance three meta-goals: growth, intergenerational equity (environmental protection), and intragenerational equity. Transport affects economic growth, development patterns, the distribution of opportunities available to different population groups, and the environment. While the extent of these effects is often debated, their importance is widely acknowledged. It is not surprising, there-fore, that transport policy goals are often defined in terms similar to the three meta-goals noted above. Thus, while the sectorial implications of sustainable development are still somewhat fuzzy, it is obvious that sustainable transport policies should balance all three goals (Greene and Wegener, 1997).

Masser et al. (1992) have suggested that the focus of attention in the transport field has been shifting toward the environmental goal. However, if it is accepted that sustainable development is in essence a balance between three goals, a move toward one goal without due regard to the others may reduce sustainability, even if it is the environmental goal toward which policies are shifting. Scenario analysis conducted in the European context indicates that the three goals are not complementary (Rienstra et al., 1997). Hence, all three trade-offs between the meta-goals have to be addressed concurrently if unsustainable development is to be precluded.

In practice, most attempts to operationalize sustainable development and sustainable transport notions have focused on the growth-environment trade-off. Growth-equity trade-offs have also been the subject of extensive discussions in the social sciences. In the transport field they have been manifest in discussions of the interrelations between private and public transport, the impact of transport investments on peripheral areas, and—on a more general level—the interrelations between accessibility-enhancing policies and mobility-enhancing measures (Salomon and Mokhtarian, 1998).

In contrast to the extensive literature on the first two trade-offs, the third potential trade-off, that between environmental and intragenerational equity (abbreviated hereafter as "equity") goals, has received very limited attention. Only in recent years have questions of environmental equity received serious attention. Yet these questions have not been coupled with the discourse on sustainable transport. Indeed, equity concerns have received little more than lip service in the burgeoning sustainable transport literature.

Three types of environmental equity analyses can be formulated in the transportation context: (1) comparisons of populations exposed to environmental externalities generated by transport with populations not exposed (termed here the direct effect); (2) analyses of the distributional implications of policies advanced to address the environmental externalities of transport; and (3) identification of equity facets of the environmental aspects of transport's effects on land use, urban form, and activity patterns (termed here the indirect or secondary effects).

Direct Environmental Equity Effects of Transport

Transportation is the source of multiple environmental externalities. These include externalities resulting from the energy used to move through space (the traffic), effects of the infrastructure needed to facilitate movement (regardless of whether and to what extent it is used), and indirect effects resulting from the effects of transport on land use and development patterns. The externalities differ also in terms of the spatial scale of their effects. In Table 18.1, the different environmental externalities of transport are categorized in accordance with these two criteria, cause and spatial scale.

From an environmental equity perspective, the most obvious question to ask is, who is directly affected by the externalities noted in Table 18.1? This question is not pertinent, however, to all the externalities noted there. Specifically, it is not pertinent to global effects, as all the people are affected by such externalities regardless of who

they are, though their contributions to the problem may differ systematically. It is also less pertinent for infrastructure effects.

While the question posed above is pertinent to traffic externalities at both the local and regional levels, the analysis and implications may differ by scale. At the regional level, the effects are governed to a significant extent by climatic and synoptic variables. However, the actual occurrence at specific sites is governed by meteorological variables (Luria et al., 1996). Hence, identification of the affected parties, on a non-incidental level, and relating such effects to specific actions or inaction in the transport realm may require complex, data-hungry regional models. Local effects, by contrast, are relatively consistent over time and space, and hence can be predicted with greater confidence. Therefore, the emphasis is likely to focus, at least in the near future, on identification of those directly affected by traffic-induced externalities at the local level. Despite the seemingly restrictive delineation of this research question, it should be noted that it is unlikely that the answer would be insensitive to the type of externality. Thus, a separate analysis would have to be conducted for each issue identified as a traffic-induced local effect in Table 18.1.

Identification of the people affected by local externalities may also prove difficult, as emission levels and dispersion patterns are often unknown. In many cases emission levels are inferred from producers' data or are approximated on the basis of other places' experience. Only rarely are the actual emissions monitored. Inspections also fail to give a true picture of emissions at the source (Glazer et al., 1995). Moreover, a high percentage of emissions are often caused by a small percentage of older cars. Thus, even small changes in the composition of the vehicle fleet in a given area can have a substantial effect on emissions and local exposure. An even more difficult issue is the modeling of dispersion patterns, as these are affected by local variance in physical properties as well as urban form and development patterns (Karim et al., 1998). Dispersion patterns are also a function of the type of effect and the media through which they travel; hence there are different dispersion models for noise, pollutants, vibrations, and particles.

The purpose of an equity analysis, however, is not merely to identify who is affected by each externality, but to analyze systemic differences between those affected and those not affected. To this end it is necessary to identify those people who potentially could have been affected

Table 18.1 The Environmental Effects of Transportation

Source	Local	Regional	Global
Traffic	Noise; vibrations; CO; particles	NOx, ground-level ozone	CO_2
Infrastructure	Reduced groundwater recharge; loss of visual amenities	Flooding; ecosystem severance	
Land use effects	Changes in emission and exposure patterns; effect of development on open space	Energy use effects of changes in urban form	

but were not. Obviously, the choice of such a control group can have a substantial effect on the results of any equity analysis.

Most analyses of the environmental equity of point sources compare population attributes in the statistical areas or jurisdictions where the sources are located to those where no similar sources are located. This option is not pertinent for most land transport facilities, as these are mostly linear segments within hierarchical networks. These segments often form the edge of statistical areas or run along jurisdiction boundaries. It is also likely that network constraints require that a certain segment be aligned through a specific jurisdiction. There may, however, be latitude regarding the alignment within the jurisdiction. In such a case the micro alignment considerations would be those of interest from an environmental equity perspective, but would not be reflected in the jurisdiction-wide data.

The difficulty of identifying appropriate unaffected areas is compounded by the hierarchical nature of transport facilities, especially roads, and their ubiquity. It is likely that most jurisdictions would include roads from several levels of the hierarchy. Analysis of the distribution of exposure from a certain level of the hierarchy (such as limited-access highways) or a certain element in the networks (such as interchanges) would not necessarily correspond to the cumulative exposure.

Due to the difficulties inherent in identifying appropriate unaffected control groups, it is possible that the emphasis in the transportation case would have to be on degree of exposure. In such a case a metropolitan or regional regression analysis would have to be undertaken of the type shown below:

$$ETki = f(Ekji, Ii, Mi)$$

where $ETki$ is emissions of type k from transport in area i, $Ekji$ is emissions of type k from facility j (road segment, bus depot, etc.) in area i, Ii is the average income in area i, and Mi is the percentage of minorities in area i. The actual specification of the regression would have to be adjusted for the different facilities and externalities.

Yet, even if a statistically significant correlation is found between exposure and population attributes, the direct implications with respect to environmental equity are unclear, as exposure can be an outcome of metropolitan and market processes, and not of faulty or malicious siting processes (Been, 1994; Feitelson, forthcoming). To understand the causes for the distribution of environmental externalities from transport facilities, it is necessary, therefore, to undertake a longitudinal analysis that will take into account technological factors (what was possible at the time that siting decisions were made), institutional issues, market dynamics, and population dynamics.

Longitudinal analyses intended to shed light on the process that may lead to inequities face several methodological difficulties, too. The longevity of transport infrastructure and the fact that the time span over which large transport projects are discussed and built lasts many years (often more than a decade) makes even the identification of a starting point problematic. It is not clear whether the analysis should begin with the spatial array and options available at the time the project was initially proposed, at the time it was approved or financed, or at the time construction commenced. It is also unclear at what point in its development process a transportation project begins to affect prices in nearby areas, and subsequently land use or population shifts.

In discussing the possibility that a project was steered into a politically weak area, it is important to discern the viable alternatives that could have been chosen at the time the decision was made. Quite obviously the identification of options not chosen (and perhaps not even discussed at the time), and the determination of whether they were indeed viable alternatives involve judgment. Such judgment may well determine the study's outcome —i.e., whether the inequitable outcome was a result of a political process, technical constraints, or a market outcome.

POTENTIAL SECOND-ORDER ENVIRONMENTAL EQUITY EFFECTS

The implications of transport's land use effects on the distribution of those exposed to direct local effects is perhaps the most obvious indirect environmental equity effect of transport. However, the discussion of indirect effects may go well beyond this case.

As many analysts have shown, urban size and form and modal split are interrelated (Newman and Kenworthy, 1989; Banister, 1992). Modal choice is also affected by income, age, car availability, regularity of journeys, relative travel times and monetary costs, systems' reliability, safety and security considerations, and trip attributes, many of which are affected by urban form. From an environmental equity perspective, this complex relationship may have several implications.

Radial limited-access highways and suburban rail improve the accessibility of suburban areas, while passing through inner rings. In such cases, those living in the inner rings may suffer most from the environmental externalities of such facilities (including the loss of visual amenities and open space), while enjoying only minimal or no direct benefits from these corridors. At the same time, the nature of these facilities (whether they are oriented toward public or private transport) may affect modal choice, at least along a certain corridor, and hence total emission levels and their distribution in space. In such cases environmental equity concerns should not be limited to whether radial routes were aligned through the weakest part of the inner rings. Rather, the question can be expanded to include whether the distribution of benefits and environmental costs from such facilities is related to income, class, race, or other pertinent social variables. The answer is likely to differ according to the facility analyzed, city structure, and motorization rates.

The income, age, gender, and class distribution of users will differ, in most cases, between limited-access highways, bus lanes, and suburban rail. Use patterns will also be affected by city structure, in particular employment patterns and the demographic, socioeconomic, ethnic, and racial residential patterns. These latter patterns also determine who is likely to be adversely affected by the environmental externalities imposed by radial services on inner neighborhoods. Thus, limited-access highways serving wealthier strata and running through lower-income neighborhoods can be seen as having a regressive effect from the environmental perspective as well. At the same time, bus lanes serving the car-less (usually a function of age, gender, and income) through wealthier neighborhoods can be seen as progressive even when they are not subsidized, once the environmental equity effects are brought into consideration.

The distribution of benefits and environmental costs may well vary between societies and regions for similar cases, as a function of motorization rates. The extent to which different population groups can benefit from the different facilities noted here is a function of the availability of cars and the costs of driving. Where such costs are low, as in the U.S., the extent to which limited-access highways are regressive (according to both income and environmental criteria) may be mitigated by the high level of their use by lower-income groups.

The contribution of transport to the increasing footlooseness of various activities may also have some implications from an environmental equity perspective. Greater footlooseness of industry and LULUs,[1] combined with the increasing ability of wider sets of groups and regions to close themselves to such facilities (Feitelson, 1997), may lead to the formation of "pollution havens"—areas where such LULUs concentrate because of their economic and political marginality (Blowers and Leroy, 1994). Transport can thus indirectly affect the environmental equity distribution of different point sources (such as hazardous materials).

By increasing mobility differentially, transport may have determined the locational opportunities available to different population groups. As Fishman (1987) and others have noted, the increasing mobility of the upper middle class around the turn of the century allowed them to escape the polluted environs of the industrial city to the suburbs. As mobility improved, the difference between the mobile and immobile may have increased, especially in car-based societies and environs. This may well consign the car-less to the most accessible sites, in direct proximity to public transport. These may also be the most polluted environs, especially from transport.

THE ENVIRONMENTAL EQUITY EFFECTS OF TRANSPORT POLICIES

Transport policies often incur environmental benefits as well as costs. Thus an environmental equity analysis of such policies should include the distribution of both the benefits and the costs.

The distribution of the benefits of measures designed to mitigate the environmental effects of transport would largely be a function of the distribution of the direct environmental cost they are designed to mitigate. Bae (1997), for example, found that the progressive effects of the implementation of federal clean air standards in the Los Angeles basin are a result of the current regressive distribution of the health effects of air pollution. In other words, inequitable direct effects at the regional level result in a progressive distribution of the benefits associated with measures designed to reduce region-wide pollution levels.

The difficulty of identifying the positive effects of policy tools is directly correlated with the difficulty of identifying exposure levels. The availability of the necessary data and models differs according to scale and issue. A difficulty of particular importance from an environmental equity perspective is the lack of data on the attributes of transient populations exposed to street-level pollution. These include pedestrians, employees (differentiated by exposure to street-level air) and users of the transport system. As these groups can be substantive in some sections of cities (especially in proximity to the central business district and within it), estimates of the distribution and the magnitude of the benefits of policies geared to reduce pollution in such areas are likely to be highly inaccurate if they take into account only residents in these areas.

In order to determine the distribution of costs, it is necessary to identify the direct costs imposed by the policy tool discussed. These can be both monetary and non-monetary costs (for example, in terms of time or lost mobility opportunities). Once these have been identified, it is necessary to identify who bears these costs. Yet the implications would most likely vary between households. Thus there is room for a second-stage analysis, in which the behavioral implications of the costs should be discerned.

After the attributes of those who bear the monetary and non-monetary costs are identified (not an easy task in itself), it may be necessary to identify those households whose behavior might change as a result of such a cost increase. These households may be more difficult to identify, as often they would not be found in the same place or mode before and after the policy is enacted. Yet the total cost for such households, especially in terms of opportunities available to them, may be the most consequential. For example, these are the households that would change their modal choice or reduce the number of their trips if environmentally induced taxes on trips were imposed (whether by means of higher fuel taxes, electronic pricing, tolls, or other means). In this case it is likely that these households, which are obviously the most price-sensitive, would exhibit specific socioeconomic attributes. In other words, it is more than likely that the burden of such a policy would not be distributed evenly across classes. One way to identify such distribution consequences is to analyze the attributes of those households who indicate that they are price-sensitive in stated preference type studies analyzing the implications of such policies.

A TENTATIVE RESEARCH AGENDA

The purpose of this chapter is to advance a research agenda that would allow environmental equity aspects to be incorporated into the sustainable transport discourse in a systematic and meaningful manner. The previous sections have outlined some of the many problems and issues that have to be addressed. Clearly, secondhand effects are much more difficult to analyze than first-order effects. This is true for analyses of both the distribution of noise exposure and the distributional consequences of policies geared to mitigate such exposure. Therefore, it is suggested that the research agenda should begin with analyses of the first-order distribution effects of various transport facilities and policies.

The starting point for any research agenda must be the identification of those affected by transport externalities. Therefore, the first item on the environmental equity research agenda should be identification of the distribution implications of such externalities. Such studies would have to address the multiple methodological problems identified above. As many of these problems are aggravated when a link within a network is considered, it is suggested that the first studies would focus on terminals rather than routes. In analyzing such facilities, the particular difficulties associated with each type of externality should be identified. Specific attention should be given to the differences between analyses of local versus regional externalities.

Once the number of studies analyzing the distribution implications of various transport facilities and pollutants starts to grow, it may be possible to identify the extent to which such facilities are sited in a way that systematically affects certain population groups. While a meta-analysis may be of particular usefulness in this case, it is likely that an initial perception of whether there is a systematic bias against any population group can be formed earlier.

If a correlation is identified between class, race, religion, or any other population attribute and exposure, a longitudinal study is warranted. The purpose of such a study is to verify the extent to which the original siting decision willfully targeted a certain population group, or whether the spatial proximity was an outcome of larger economic and geo-political-demographic factors. That is, it would have to try to discern the process that led to the environmental inequity. If a series of such studies are conducted, it may be possible to discern, as a third stage of the research agenda, whether there are systemic factors that lead to the evolution of environmental inequities from transport facilities. If such systemic factors are identified, it would be possible to discuss whether they are society-specific or generic to the capitalistic mode of production in its current form, and hence to what extent they can be modified within the existing societal structure.

After the distribution implications of exposure patterns of environmental externalities of transport are discerned, a second strand of research can be developed. This strand would focus on the equity implications of policies geared to address the environmental externalities of transport. At first it would be necessary to discern the benefits and cost of specific policies designed to address specific externalities. Later it might be possible to ask why certain externalities are addressed while others are not, and what the distribution implications of such decisions are.

On the basis of these studies, from both strands, it may be possible to identify data needs that are important for such analyses, and then to initiate systemic data-collection efforts that would allow us to monitor over time whether the environmental inequities increase or decrease. If the

arguments about closing the frontier (e.g., Feitelson, 1997) are true, it can be expected that the pressures would rise to site facilities in areas of least resistance or in proximity to existing facilities, thus worsening existing inequities. Thus, the importance of such monitoring may increase, even if no current inequities are identified.

CONCLUSIONS

The basic premise of this chapter, that environmental equity should be an integral part of the discourse on sustainable transport, is likely to be widely agreed upon. However, introducing environmental equity concerns into the discourse in an analytic and meaningful way is fraught with methodological problems. Therefore, a research agenda is advanced. It argues that in the first stage we must discern the essence and scope of environmental equity issues from transportation facilities, and of policies designed to address the environmental externalities of transport. Only then can the reasons for possible inequities be addressed in a meaningful manner, and can systemic data collection efforts be undertaken.

This research agenda is admittedly ambitious, involving multiple studies that would require several years to conduct. Moreover, even when this research agenda was completed, it would encompass only the direct environmental equity effects of transportation and of the policies advanced to address transport's environmental impacts. Analyses of the secondary environmental equity effects would require further research.

This long road may seem daunting, and perhaps dispiriting for those seeking immediate answers to environmental equity concerns. However, the research agenda merely reflects the lack of work on these issues so far, and hence the length of the road that needs to be traveled before such concerns can be incorporated in an intelligent and systemic manner into the discourse on sustainable transport.

By identifying the need for a new research agenda, and the issues that this research agenda should address, this chapter sets a challenge. If this challenge is addressed, and eventually met, an important step toward incorporating the missing environmental equity trade-off in the sustainable transport discourse would be made. Moreover, unless this challenge is met, and the long road mapped here traversed, the sustainable transport discourse will continue to be lacking.

Note

1. Locally undesirable land use.

References

Bae, C.-H. C. 1997. "The Equity Impacts of Los Angeles' Air Quality Policies." *Environment and Planning A* 29: 1563–1584.

Banister, D. 1992. "Energy Use Transport and Settlement Systems." In M. J. Breheny, ed., *Sustainable Development and Urban Form*. London: Pion.

Banister, D., and K. Button, eds. 1993. *Transport: The Environment and Sustainable Development*. London: Spon.

Been, V. 1993. "What's Fairness Got to Do with It? Environmental Justice and the Siting of Locally Undesirable Land Uses." *Cornell Law Review* 78: 1001–1085.

Been, V. 1994. "Locally Undesirable Land Uses in Minority Neighborhoods: Disproportionate Siting or Market Dynamics?" *Yale Law Journal* 103: 1383–1422.

Blowers, A., and P. Leroy. 1994. "Power Politics and Environmental Inequality: A Theoretical and Empirical Analysis of the Process of 'Peripheralisation'." *Environmental Politics* 3: 197–228.

Feitelson, E. 1997. "The Second Closing of the Frontier: An End to Open-Access Regimes." *Tijdschrift voor Economische en Sociale Geografie* 88: 15–28.

Feitelson, E. 2001. "Malicious Siting or Unrecognized Processes? A Spatio-temporal Analysis of Environmental Conflicts in Tel Aviv." *Urban Studies* 38: 1143–1159.

Fishman, R. 1987. *Bourgeois Utopias: The Rise and Fall of Suburbia*. New York: Basic Books.

Glazer, A., D. B. Klein, and C. Lave. 1995. "Clean on Paper, Dirty on the Road: Troubles with California's Smog Check." *Journal of Transport Economics and Policy* 29: 85–92.

Greene, D. L., and M. Wegener. 1997. "Sustainable Transport." *Journal of Transport Geography* 5: 177–190.

Karim, M., H. Matsui, and R. Guensler. 1998. "A Mathematical Model of Wind Flow Vehicle Wake and Pollutant Concentration in Urban Road Microenvironments, Part II: Model Results." *Transportation Research D* 3: 171–191.

Luria, M., M. Peleg, S. Alper, V. Matviev, Y. Tzachi, I. Seter, and I. Lapidot. 1996. "The Formation of O_3 over Israel: A Growing Concern and a Potential International Issue." In Y. Steinberg, ed., *Preservation of Our World in the Wake of Change*, vol. 6. Jerusalem: ISEEQ.

Masser, I., O. Sviden, and M. Wegener. 1992. "From Growth to Equity and Sustainability: Paradigm Shift in Transport Planning?" *Futures* 24: 539–558.

Newman, P. W. G., and J. R. Kenworthy. 1989. *Cities and Automobile Dependency: An International Source Book*. Aldershot: Gower.

Rienstra, S. A., D. Stead, D. Banister, and P. Nijkamp. 1997. "Assessing the Complementarity of Common Transport Policy Objectives: A Scenario Approach." *Innovation* 10: 273–287.

Salomon, I., and P. Mokhtarian. 1998. "What Happens When Mobility-Inclined Market Segments Face Accessibility-Enhancing Policies?" *Transportation Research D* 3: 129–140.

Whitelegg, J. 1993. *Transport for a Sustainable Future: The Case of Europe*. London: Belhaven Press.

World Commission on Environment and Development. 1987. *Our Common Future*. Oxford: Oxford University Press.

CHAPTER NINETEEN

Women and Travel

The Sustainability Implications of Changing Roles

Amanda Root,
Laurie Schintler,
and Kenneth Button

INTRODUCTION

There has been a marked shift in the way that transportation is perceived. One element is the appreciation of the increased mobility of women. Women have traditionally tended to travel shorter distances than men. In the last twenty years, though, women's overall mobility patterns have begun to look more like men's. One reason is that the number of women in the workforce has increased, while at the same time women continue to travel as the primary caretakers of household and family obligations. Demographic change, new family structures, and concerns about personal safety are also contributing to the growing motorization of women. As a result, the detailed travel patterns of women still differ significantly from those of men.

The increasing importance of women as travelers has implications for the ways that transport policy must be reviewed in an era in which sustainability has become a key issue. At one level, there is the issue of gender equity with respect to how transportation strategies are devised. In addition, however, appreciation of the particular nature of women's travel behavior, and their designed behavior, may actually facilitate an easier path to sustainable development.

TRANSPORT AND SUSTAINABILITY

Sustainability is a global concept. It is defined by the Brundtland Commission as "ensuring that the needs of the present are met without compromising the ability of future generations to meet their needs" (World Commission on Environment and Development, 1987). This definition, however, conveys little clarity about how the needs of the present generation are to be balanced with those of future generations. In itself it also says nothing about sustainability in transportation. Indeed, it takes little imagination to develop plausible scenarios in which the expansion of transportation may be the preferred sustainable option.

Although the process of climate change is complex, there is broad agreement that anthropogenic change is taking place. The Intergovernmental Panel on Climate Change (1996) noted a "discernible human impact on the climate" in 1996. Transportation emissions are responsible for some 23 percent of carbon dioxide emissions in OECD countries, up from 19 percent in 1970. Carbon dioxide, together with other "greenhouse gases," acts like an insulator, heating up the earth.

At the meso level, transportation emissions can be damaging to forestry, with transportation producing about 65 percent of the nitrogen oxides emitted in the UK. Transportation also damages local environments, e.g., through smog, land-take or eminent domain, and physical destruction of landscapes. Locally, car fumes produce approximately 75 percent of the UK's annual carbon monoxide, which can cause stress, asthma, headaches, and fertility problems, and 40 percent of the hydrocarbons, which harm respiratory health. Exhaust fumes produce just over half of the UK's particulates, which cause respiratory and circulatory ailments, and benzene, which is carcinogenic.

Besides their immediate impact, meso and local levels of environmental intrusion are important to the sustainability of sociopolitical systems. Sustainable development, although couched largely in environmental terms, also implies a sustainable social and political system (Button and Nijkamp, 1997). Environmental spillover can lead to international and interregional tension. A degraded local or urban environment poses social problems and is a severe handicap for economic development. Thinking of sustainability only in terms of global warming is inadequate.

WOMEN AND MOBILITY

Women use transportation differently than men do. In 1975/76, women in the UK drove about 20 percent of the miles driven by men, although by 1994/96 the gap had closed, and women were driving about 40 percent of the miles that men drove (Table 19.1). In part this was because the traditional lower levels of access to cars diminished as car ownership rose; but in the past, shorter distances were also a function of the types of trip made by women. Women travel shorter distances than men in the UK by all modes, apart from buses and as passengers in private cars, and they also walk more. Even allowing for the fact that a few men travel a great deal on business, it appears that women's mobility is strongly limited by caring for children and the elderly, and by their domestic responsibilities. In this sense the pattern has changed little. In 1994/96, women under age 20 in the UK were traveling almost identical distances to men, but between the ages of 26 and 59, the prime years of domestic caring responsibilities, women's travel dropped to just over half of men's, a pattern broadly equivalent to that of twenty years earlier.

This type of situation is not unique to any country.

German women have less access to cars than men do, with the biggest differences between men and women who have a car available in the household but do not have a driver's license (Zauke and Spitzner, 1997). This suggests that as more women obtain driver's licenses, these gender differences may be reduced. Hanson and Hanson (1981) offer insights into the importance of married women's employment to travel patterns in Sweden, while Dyck (1990) looks at similar issues in Canada.

Women also tend to make more complicated trips than men. Working women run more household errands than do men on both inward and outward commutes, and irrespective of the number of persons in a household or its structure. On average 65 percent of American women (Table 19.2) make stops on their way home, and 25 percent make more than one stop. The places visited differ, with women tending more often to visit schools, daycare centers, and stores than men; the latter are twice as likely to go to a restaurant or bar. Women's multiple destinations also mean that many forms of fixed track transport are not as well suited to their travel needs. The trend for these more complex commuting patterns is upward. In the U.S., the number of intermediate stops made on the way to work has grown by about 50 percent since 1980, and the number on the way home by about 20 percent. Gordon et al. (1998) point out that the distance of trips also affects these data, as does who is making them. Women alone, for example, make more short-distance nonstop work trips.

DEMOGRAPHIC CHANGE AND WOMEN

In the U.S., between 1969 and 1995, the highest rates of population growth were in the older age cohorts, in which females form the largest group. Additionally, demographers suggest that as the entire population ages, the proportion of very elderly women who still have mobility requirements will increase further (Spain, 1997). As elderly women currently tend not to have driver's licenses (Table 19.3), they have only limited use of cars as passengers. This picture will change dramatically when the current cohorts of younger and middle-aged women begin to enter the older age categories. A far higher proportion of these women, perhaps as many as 50 percent according to German evidence, will have been car owners for the majority of their lives, and will expect to use cars for their mobility in their old age.

Table 19.1   Distance Traveled (Miles) per Person per Year in the UK, 1975/76 and 1994/96

		17–20 years		21–25 years		26–59 years		60+ yrs	17+yrs
		Male	Female	Male	Female	Male	Female		
Walk	1975/76	308	319	238	283	191	258	222	233
	1994/96	276	281	222	249	178	208	171	195
Bicycle	1975/76	97	25	95	36	69	28	29	45
	1994/96	112	31	90	13	73	22	18	40
Car/van driver	1975/76	2,086	533	4,995	1,072	6,059	1,047	899	2,569
	1994/96	2,722	1,520	6,201	2,794	8,550	3,136	1,908	4,363
Car/van passenger	1975/76	1,950	2,006	1,188	2,391	738	2,014	774	1,278
	1994/96	2,233	2,586	1,782	2,321	1,080	2,515	1,299	1,733
Motorcycle	1975/76	585	40	264	66	76	10	14	58
	1994/96	54	27	72	22	92	10	8	37
Local bus	1975/76	817	1,263	512	637	289	466	422	447
	1994/96	567	744	279	385	139	249	302	262
Rail	1975/76	773	855	481	477	649	218	177	383
	1994/96	452	636	605	744	620	408	210	441
Total distance traveled	1975/76	6,974	5,338	8,134	5,143	8,338	4,208	2,751	5,238
	1994/96	6,919	6,318	9,596	6,901	11,075	6,811	4,278	7,404

Source: UK Department of Environment, Transport and the Regions, 1997a.

In the 1980s and 1990s, the increase in the number of new women drivers exceeded that of new men drivers. This can be partly attributed to the declining quality of public transport in some countries, but it also reflects more general trends of greater population dispersion as incomes rise, higher labor force participation rates, and changes in family structure. A more geographically dispersed population requires more complex travel patterns to meet traditional household and family obligations, let alone labor force participation. There was a 90 percent increase in the proportion of women with driver's licenses in the UK between the mid-1970s and the mid-1990s, but only a 17 percent increase in the proportion of license-holding men. In 1975/76, almost twice as many men could drive as women, but by 1993/95 the differ-ence had lessened to 81 percent of men and 55 percent of women (see Table 19.1).

Over recent decades, the mobility of women in the U.S. has also steadily improved. Between 1969 and 1995, the average number of annual person-trips made by women increased by 11 percent. The rate of increase was less for men, despite the fact that the population growth rates for both men and women were about 40 percent over the same time period. Since 1969, the number of licensed female drivers in the U.S. has increased by 95 percent, in comparison with a 53 percent increase for men (Hu and Young, 1999). Despite improvements in the mobility of U.S. women, they are still not as mobile as men. Women drive on average 27.8 person-miles a day, compared with 35.2 person-miles a day for men. Women also tend to have

Table 19.2 Stopping for Errands during the Morning and Evening Commute

	One stop		Two or more stops	
	Women	Men	Women	Men
Between home and work				
1 adult, no child	11%	15%	5%	5%
2 adults, no children	13%	14%	6%	8%
1 adult, child (age 0–5*)	32%	41%	1%	23%
2 adults, child (age 0–5*)	15%	38%	6%	15%
1 adult, child (age 6–15*)	14%	32%	16%	14%
2 adults, child (age 6–15*)	17%	25%	5%	12%
Between work and home				
1 adult, no child	32%	29%	20%	31%
2 adults, no children	29%	30%	17%	25%
1 adult, child (age 0–5*)	15%	31%	32%	49%
2 adults, child (age 0–5*)	28%	42%	19%	29%
1 adult, child (age 6–15*)	29%	38%	34%	32%
2 adults, child (age 6–15*)	29%	33%	16%	29%

*Age of youngest child

Source: U.S. Nationwide Personal Transportation Survey.

shorter commutes in terms of distance and travel time. Lastly, women are passengers for about half of the traveling they do, while men are passengers only 25 percent of the time.

Women often have different reasons for traveling than men. In 1994/96, UK women made 28 percent fewer commuter journeys and 68 percent fewer trips during work than men. Evidence shows that women take on a greater share of household responsibilities, in connection with which they make 65 percent more trips to take children to and from school and approximately 30 percent more shopping trips. The same pattern appears across the previous ten years. The limited mobility of women is often explained by the socioeconomic circumstances they face. In contrast to men, women tend to have lower income levels, limited access to a private vehicle, and more domestic and household duties (Mensah, 1995; Gordon et al., 1989). Approximately 50 percent of all person-trips made by women are for family and personal business, and 65 percent of the trips women make are to take someone else someplace.

These circumstances limit the mobility of women. First, they generally encourage more reliance on mass transit (Hanson and Johnston, 1985; Hanson and Pratt, 1990). Second, the need to perform household and domestic duties such as raising children may prevent women from taking full-time employment, limiting the amount of time and money that they can spend on work- or leisure-related travel (Rutherford and Wekerle, 1988). Some would argue, though, that these special circumstances do not so much limit the mobility of women, but rather encourage more ecological travel. In fact, trip chaining is seen as an attempt to do more at the same time or to optimize efficiency.

WOMEN AND SECURITY

Women are generally physically smaller than men, and they more often travel with vulnerable children. This can evoke real fears of attack and affects perceptions of the safety of travel. In the UK in the late 1980s, it was found that between 50 percent and 70 percent of women were frightened of going out after dark in cities (Atkins, 1990). In the mid-1990s, one in eight women surveyed said they felt so unsafe on public transport that they avoided it (UK Home Office, 1996), and 11 percent of women interviewed never ventured out after dark. Traveling at night often makes women feel unsafe; for example, 10 percent of women in the UK felt "unsafe" or "very unsafe" waiting on a railway platform in the daytime, but this figure rose to 53 percent at night (Crime Concern and Transport and Travel Research, 1997). Similarly women felt more afraid waiting for underground trains, or walking to a car in a parking lot or parking garage. Women are more often attacked at home, by people they know, than by strangers outside (Hall, 1985), yet the fear of public spaces and "stranger danger" is strong among particular groups, especially middle-class and younger women (Pain, 1997).

Despite these concerns, it appears that, largely because of car ownership, women are less confined to their homes than they were a century ago (Gavron, 1968; Hamilton et al., 1991), and more women now travel later in the evening.

Table 19.3   Full Car Driving License Holders 1975/76–1993/95

	Percentage/Individuals					
	Male		Female		All adults	
	1975/6	1993/5	1975/76	1993/5	1975/76	1993/5
17–20	35	50	20	42	28	46
21–29	77	82	43	68	60	74
30–39	85	90	49	74	67	81
40–49	83	89	37	72	60	80
50–59	75	88	25	59	50	73
60–69	59	82	15	39	36	60
70 or over	33	61	4	19	15	35
All adults	69	81	29	55	48	67
Millions of license holders	13.3	17.4	6	12.7	19.3	30.1

Source: UK Department of Environment, Transport and the Regions, 1997b.

Currently, about 50 percent of all moonlighters in the U.S. are women (Spain, 1997). Furthermore, many women who work during the day must run their household and domestic errands in the evening hours. These trends raise security issues for women, particularly for those who choose to travel by public transit.

POST-FORDISM AND WOMEN

Post-Fordism represents a cluster of changes that have occurred in industrialized countries since the Second World War. Hall (1988) describes it as a shift to the new information technologies, involving more flexible, decentralized forms of work organization; the contracting out of functions and services; the targeting of consumers by lifestyle, taste, and culture rather than by social class; the rise of the service and white-collar classes; and the feminization of the workforce.

In labor market terms, post-Fordism involves a structure that is increasingly volatile and unsteady, with economic cycles being rapidly transmitted through the system, undermining the basis for stable development. With respect to employment, this can mean more temporary jobs, the polarization of highly skilled and deskilled workers, and the reduced ability of the state to meet social welfare

objectives. Post-Fordism also affects consumption, creating a maximization of individual choices through personal consumption and rendering leisure journeys ever more important as forms of consumption become arguably more commoditized. In these ways, post-Fordism is imposing new demands and constraints on women's lives and travel patterns. These constraints, however, cannot operate without resistance. They also position women, with a large degree of congruence, in the role of those categorized above as likely to value accessibility more than mobility.

The characteristics are associated with social trends labeled here post-Fordism. Those whose primary orientation is toward the "users'" set of characteristics are likely to be in a position to understand the values of traffic management and restraint better than those, such as engineers, whose professional and personal lifestyles are geared toward mobility. More abstractly, post-Fordist changes in the economy and cultural sphere are leading to qualitatively new situations or conjunctures in which women are most appropriately positioned to develop new cultural patterns and to participate in constructing new ways in what Castells (1997) calls the "space of flows." One hypothesis is that these opportunities would be correlated with regions, or nations, where post-Fordist changes are most commonly found.

PSYCHOLOGY AND WOMEN

Psychological factors influence human behavior (Caplice and Mahmassani, 1992). Research shows gender differences with respect to psychological attributes, with women tending to be more ambivalent and more risk-averse. There is some specific evidence that women are more risk-averse than men when it comes to making travel-related decisions. In a study of Los Angeles, given the hypothetical choice between a route that is relatively long but predictable in terms of travel time and another that is less predictable but potentially shorter in terms of travel time, women tended to select the former and men the latter (Abdel-Aty et al., 1996).

Psychology plays a part in many transportation choices. Feelings are never unequivocal in their linkage to behavior, but it is appropriate to discuss ambivalence in the context of transport choice. Women are, in general, considered more exposed to ambivalent feelings than men in their roles as parents. Parker (1995) claims that "we can speak of the creative outcome of manageable [maternal] ambivalence." Similarly, Giddens (1995) argues for greater recognition to be given to complex emotions, such as ambivalence, that are inscribed in private as well as public life.

It would appear that some groups of women are prone to ambivalent feelings, but that their analysis of these can prompt leaps in thought and creative solutions to problems (Parker, 1995). It would be useful to investigate whether women's ambivalence is transferred to decision-making about cars, mobility, and accessibility, and thereby gain further insights into why women currently choose to travel more ecologically than men. Perhaps this discourse would have the power to break down the falsely dichotomized notion of good (i.e., sustainable) versus bad (i.e., unsustainable) transportation choices and illuminate the complex ways in which most women want the benefits of cars, the faster lifestyles they make possible, and the conveniences they offer.

CONCLUSIONS

There is a need to take more notice of gender in transportation modeling. More important, there are causes for hope that women's influence will lead to moves toward more sustainable transport. Women's experience as marginalized workers who combine home and work responsibilities can make them more able to change their transport habits and more aware of the values that accompany the notion of sustainable development. Finally, it is suggested that recognizing the ambivalence of women toward cars—via an appreciation of their utility and a simultaneous knowledge of the environmental and social harm they cause—is perhaps the biggest methodological challenge facing those concerned with making transport more sustainable.

The findings are encouraging in one sense but problematic in another. They are based upon rather diverse and often fragmented pieces of information. The arguments are often founded on limited empirical evidence, and sometimes they are anecdotal in nature. Public policy is inevitably made on the basis of imperfect information, even though informed judgment is generally superior. There is a need to better understand the travel behavior of elderly women, for example, and to revise models of travel demand to more accurately represent this behavior. There also is a need to better understand how women's travel behavior varies by trip purpose or work schedule, together with a need to better understand the psychology of women and how it affects their travel behavior.

There is also the normative aspect of policy, involving objectives and goals. Again our understanding regarding women and travel is limited. The concept of need as a measure of social demand is well established in transport policy-making, but how this extends to women is less clear. There are issues about whether women as a group suffer more from travel poverty than do men, in the sense that they cannot travel the distances that they wish, nor to their preferred destinations. Information about subjective views on safety is also lacking, but has particular relevance if women are concerned about the well-being of their children.

REFERENCES

Abdel-Aty, M., R. Kitamura, and P. Jovanis. 1996. "Investigating Effect of Travel Time Variability on Route Choice Using Repeated-Measurement Stated Preference Data." *Transportation Research Record* 1493: 39–45.

Atkins, S. 1990. "Personal Security as a Transport Issue: A State of the Art Review." *Transport Reviews* 10: 111–126.

Button, K. J., and P. Nijkamp. 1997. "Social Change and Sustainable Transport." *Journal of Transport Geography* 5: 215–218.

Caplice, C., and H. Mahmassani. 1992. "Commuting Behavior: Preferred Arrival Time, Use of Information, and Switching Propensity." *Transportation Research A*, 26: 409–418.

Castells, M. 1997. *The Rise of the Network Society.* Oxford: Basil Blackwell.

Crime Concern and Transport and Travel Research. 1997. *Perceptions of Safety from Crime on Public Transport.* London: UK Department of Transport.

Dyck, I. 1990. "Space, Time, and Renegotiating Motherhood: An Exploration of the Domestic Workplace." *Environment and Planning A*, 22: 459–483.

Gavron, H. 1968. *The Captive Wife: Conflicts of Housebound Mothers.* London: Penguin.

Giddens, A. 1995. *The Transformation of Intimacy.* Oxford: Basil Blackwell.

Gordon, Peter, A. Kumar, and Harry W. Richardson. 1989. "Gender Differences in Metropolitan Travel Behaviour." *Regional Studies* 23: 499–510.

Gordon, Peter, Yu-chun Liao, and Harry W. Richardson. 1998. "Household Commuting: Implications of the Behavior of Two-Worker Households for Land-Use/Transportation Models." In Lars Lundqvist, Lars-Göran Matterson, and T. John Kim, eds., *Network Infrastructure and the Urban Environment.* Berlin: Springer.

Hall, R. 1985. *Ask Any Woman: A London Enquiry into Rape and Sexual Assault.* Bristol: Falling Wall Press.

Hall, S. 1988. "Brave New World." *Marxism Today* (October): 24–29.

Hamilton, K., L. Jenkins, and A. Gregory. 1991. *Women and Transport: Bus Deregulation in West Yorkshire.* Bradford: University of Bradford.

Hanson, S., and P. Hanson. 1981. "The Impact of Married Women's Employment on Household Travel Patterns: A Swedish Example." *Transportation* 10: 165–185.

Hanson, S., and I. Johnston. 1985. "Gender Differences in Work-Trip Length: Explanations and Implications." *Urban Geography* 6: 193–219.

Hanson, S., and G. Pratt. 1990. "Geographical Perspectives on Occupational Segregation of Women." *National Geographic Research* 4: 376–399.

Health Education Authority/Sports Council. 1992. Allied Dunbar National Fitness Survey. London.

Hu, P. S., and J. Young. 1999. *Summary of Travel Trends: 1995 Nationwide Personal Transportation Survey.* Washington, D.C.: Federal Highway Administration, U.S. Department of Transportation.

Intergovernmental Panel on Climate Change. 1996. *Climate Change 1995: Second Assessment Report.* Cambridge: Cambridge University Press.

Mensah, J. 1995. "Journey to Work and Job Search Characteristics of the Urban Poor: A Gender Analysis of Survey Data from Edmonton, Alberta." *Transportation* 22: 1–19.

Murkami, E., and J. Young. 1997. "Daily Travel by Persons with Low Income." Paper for NPTS Nationwide Personal Transportation Survey, Symposium, Washington, D.C.

Pain, R. 1997. "Social Geographies of Women's Fear of Crime." *Transactions of the Institute of British Geographers,* n.s. 22: 231–244. London: Royal Geographical Society.

Parker, R. 1995. *Torn in Two: The Experience of Maternal Ambivalence.* London: Virago Press.

Pickrell, D., and P. Schimek. 1998. *Trends in Personal Motor Vehicle Ownership and Use: Evidence from the NPTS.* Boston: U.S. Department of Transportation Volpe Center.

Rutherford, M. B., and R. G. Wekerle. 1988. "Captive Rider, Captive Labour: Spatial Constraints and Women's Employment." *Urban Geography* 9: 116–137.

Spain, D. 1997. *Societal Trends: The Aging Baby Boomers and Women's Increased Independence.* Washington, D.C.: Federal Highway Administration, U.S. Department of Transportation.

UK Department of Environment, Transport and the Regions. 1997a. *National Travel Survey 1994/6.* London: HMSO.

UK Department of Environment, Transport and the Regions. 1997b. *Transport Statistics Great Britain, 1997 Edition.* London: HMSO.

UK Home Office. 1996. *Anxieties about Crime: Findings from the British Crime Survey 1994.* London: HMSO.

World Commission on Environment and Development. 1987. *Our Common Future.* Oxford: Oxford University Press.

Zauke, G., and M. Spitzner. 1997. "Freedom of Movement for Women: Feminist Approaches to Traffic Reduction and a More Ecological Transport Science." *World Transport Policy and Practice* 3: 17–23.

CHAPTER TWENTY

Mobility Behavior of the Elderly

Its Impact on the Future Road Traffic System

Georg Rudinger

INTRODUCTION

Modern societies are undergoing a major demographic transition. A larger proportion of the population is reaching old age. Moreover, an increasing number of these individuals are licensed to drive, and they drive more than their age cohorts a decade ago. Mobility is viewed by the elderly as essential to their quality of life. Some important questions thus arise: How will the elderly's specific mobility behavior affect road traffic, and how will elderly people in particular cope with the changing demands of future road traffic? What can be done to enable the elderly to remain mobile? What factors contribute to the continued competence of older drivers, and what strategies can help them compensate for age-related limitations? (Ellinghaus, Schlag, and Steinbrecher, 1990; Rudinger, 1998; Tränkle, 1994).

These are among the questions posed by the research project Elderly people in road traffic (AEMEÏS), sponsored by the Federal Highway Research Institute, Germany. This study investigates the mobility behavior of elderly people empirically: In what way and how frequently do they drive in traffic? Although various older groups (e.g., pedestrians and cyclists) are of interest for their role in the traffic system, the focus is on licensed

drivers. This study is the continuation of a project that investigated the life situations, attitudes, and mobility behavior of older drivers in the mid-1980s (Hartenstein et al., 1990). A quasi-longitudinal comparison is possible as well, since our survey at least partly replicates a similar study that was conducted in 1986. The comparative analyses, however, have not yet been finished.

A short description follows of the basic parameters of the AEMEÏS project (see also Kahmann, 1998). The research started in 1996 and was to have finished with a final report in November 1999, but that report had not been published as this book went to press (summer 2001). The author of this chapter is the principal investigator. Additional expertise came from collaborating with colleagues from sociology and traffic research. The empirical study is a survey-like investigation of a sample of 2,032 representative subjects drawn from the older segment of the German population, ages 54 to 75+ (see Tables 20.1, 20.2).

The design of the study and the stratification of the sample took into account these strata: old vs. new Federal Länder, region (rural/urban), gender, and driving experience.

Table 20.1   AEMEÏS: Sample

Sample West Germany

	Men	proportion of drivers[1]		**Women**	proportion of drivers[1]	
55–64 years	273	264	(96.7%)	300	185	(61.7%)
65–74 years	183	156	(85.2%)	253	125	(49.4%)
≥ 75 years	78	52	(66.7%)	151	59	(39%)
Total	**534**	**472**	**(88.3%)**	**704**	**369**	**(52.4%)**

[1]People who have driven within the past 12 months.

Table 20.2   AEMEÏS: Sample

Sample East Germany

	Men	proportion of drivers[1]		**Women**	proportion of drivers[1]	
55–64 years	193	171	(88.6%)	218	81	(37.2%)
65–74 years	108	79	(73.1%)	169	50	(29.6%)
≥ 75 years	40	25	(62.5%)	66	16	(24.2%)
Total	**341**	**275**	**(80.6%)**	**453**	**147**	**(32.5%)**

Total sample Germany: N = 2,032

[1]People who have driven within the past 12 months.

THE AIMS AND SCOPE OF OUR RESEARCH PROJECT

In brief, the main objectives of AEMEÏS are

- to identify factors that influence elderly people's outdoor mobility, their decisions about driving, and their mobility behavior in general;
- to collect basic statistics on elderly people's use of public transport and on their driving behavior (e.g., amount of driving, frequency of driving);
- to develop target group–specific traffic-safety measures aimed at improving the elderly's outdoor mobility and reducing accidents;
- to increase quality of life by supporting an independent and mobile aging; and
- to assess how and how often elderly people will drive in the future.

OUR PROJECT IN THE CONTEXT OF RELATED RESEARCH

We propose a heuristic model of traffic behavior, which is shown in Figure 20.1. This model is based on the underlying assumption that an individual's mobility behavior is determined by a variety of individual and environmental factors (e.g., Holte, 1994). Concepts with significant impact on behavior are summarized at different levels around the center. This model serves multiple purposes. In addition to helping to structure the extensive field of important concepts that influence individual mobility behavior, it provides a theoretical framework for selecting the constructs. This was important for the development of our research instrument (a comprehensive questionnaire). The model provides a framework to use in determining which concepts should be considered in the study and which should be excluded. It describes a general structure

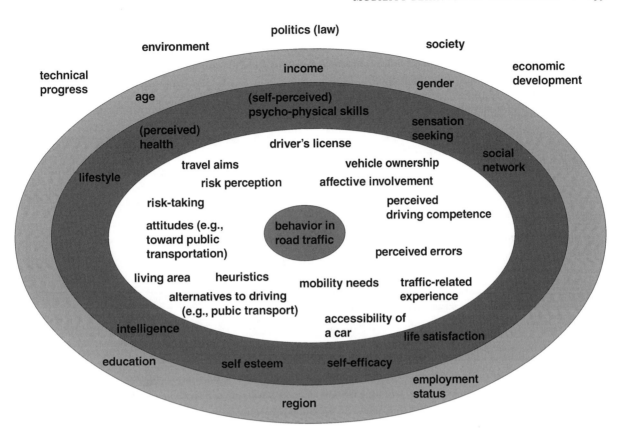

Figure 20.1   A model of behavior in road traffic

but says nothing about the causal relationships between the different levels. One of the aims of the project is to explore those causal relationships.

The different levels of the model represent constructs that have been identified in past and recent research as important in the context of outdoor mobility among the elderly, with a focus on elderly drivers (e.g., Hu, Trumble, and Lu, 1995; Hu et al., 1998). The model also implies—of course—the concepts that we are currently studying:

Sociodemographic Structure (reflected by the stratification of our sample BS)

- age, gender, marital status
- education, employment status, income
- region

Affective, Cognitive, and Behavioral Characteristics of Ss (in the questionnaire B Q)

- (self-perceived) health
- life satisfaction
- self-efficacy
- social network
- subjective age
- sensation seeking
- lifestyle
- (self-perceived) psycho-physical skills

Traffic-Related Characteristics of Ss (in S & Q)

- driver's license
- vehicle ownership, accessibility of a car

- alternatives to driving (e.g., using public transport)
- living area

Traffic-Related Affective, Cognitive, and Behavioral Characteristics of Ss (Q)

- mobility needs
- perceived driving competence
- attitudes (e.g., toward public transport)
- risk-taking (trait)
- risk perception (state)

Behavior in Road Traffic (Q)

- use of public transport and driving behavior (e.g., distances, amount, frequency of driving, crash involvement)

AEMEÏS is a multidisciplinary project, integrating (socio)demographic, traffic-related, psychological, and sociological perspectives to elucidate the overall context that influences the outdoor mobility needs and behavior of the elderly.

A number of prototypical hypotheses will be screened in AEMEÏS. They include the following:

- Self-perceived health status is a significant predictor of changes in driving habits (e.g., less frequent driving, shorter trips, avoidance of demanding traffic situations).

Apart from these monocausal relationships, the significance of this concept, as well as the others, will be examined within a network of influencing factors (using multivariate analyses).

- Subjective age accounts better for differences in self-perceived psycho-physical skills, in risk perception, and in frequency of driving than does chronological age.

In the research literature on gerontology and developmental psychology, we find much evidence of diversity in the aging process and for distinctive individual differences with respect to older people's competencies, activity levels, and cognitive and intellectual functioning (e.g., Kruse and Rudinger, 1997). Nevertheless, most research studies in the field of traffic science still use chronological age rather than alternative variables such as subjective age. Another gerontological research project of our department (which was called Images of Old Age/

Aging and Social Structure) developed a highly reliable and valid scale of subjective age. This scale is also applied in the AEMEÏS project.

- The heterogeneous group of elderly people can be divided into homogeneous groups on the basis of lifestyle differences.

These groups differ with regard to several aspects of their mobility behavior. For example, elderly people who are intellectually curious and socially active drive more frequently and more often in demanding traffic situations (such as heavy traffic, bad weather conditions, and darkness) than do those who tend to be indifferent and passive.

SELECTED EMPIRICAL RESULTS

Different perspectives can be chosen to analyze the relationships between influencing factors and elderly people's outdoor mobility and traffic behavior in general. One focuses on "causal" factors. For example, what sociodemographic and psychological characteristics are associated with the driving behavior of the elderly? This perspective is chosen frequently in traffic research studies. Another perspective might be called a segment-specific approach: Can the elderly as a group be subdivided into homogeneous subgroups? For example, are there variables that characterize those elderly people who have a positive attitude toward public transport? It is important to bear this second perspective in mind, since "the elderly" —and particularly the "very old"—are a very heterogeneous group. This helps us to identify and understand their different mobility needs, their diverse driving behavior, and the variety of their compensatory strategies. This perspective allows us to determine the size of the different homogeneous subgroups of the elderly, and identify the characteristics of these subgroups as a basis for improving traffic safety and options for outdoor mobility.

At an early stage of the AEMEÏS project, homogeneous groups of elderly persons were identified on the basis of lifestyle differences. Of course, other basic variables may also be suitable for identifying homogeneous subgroups, such as the subjects' objective life situation.

Two prototypical results of our empirical analyses follow. The first pertains to social factors and accident involvement, the second to lifestyle and mobility behavior.

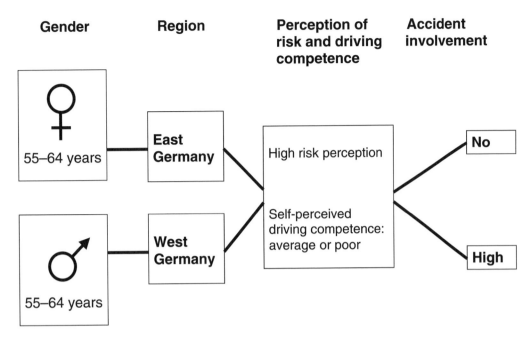

| Gender | Region | Perception of risk and driving competence | Accident involvement |

Figure 20.2   Empirical Results: Social Factors and Accident Involvement

By applying Configurational Frequency Analysis, or CFA (von Eye, Spiel, and Wood, 1996), to our data, we detected two types with respect to the association between social factors, on the one hand, and accident involvement, on the other. A type is defined as a constellation or configuration of variables that is observed much more frequently than expected by chance, given the structure, occurrence, and interdependencies of these variables.

Type 1: "young old" women (age 55 to 64) who live in East Germany, consider driving dangerous and their own driving skills average or poor, and have never been involved in an accident.

Type 2: "young old" men (age 55 to 64) who live in West Germany, consider driving dangerous and their own driving skills average or poor, and have a high rate of accidents.

The two types show a very interesting interaction between region × gender × self-perceived skills and accident involvement (see Fig. 20.2). However, this is merely a description of associations; no inference about reasons and causes can be drawn: Have these East German women never been in an accident because they do not drive in traffic? Do they not drive in traffic because they consider driving dangerous and their skills poor? Or is the converse true? Do these West German men consider driving dangerous and their own skills as average or poor be-

cause they have frequently been involved in accidents, or vice versa? Further analyses are needed.

Using factor and cluster analyses, we identified five lifestyles in our sample: stimulation-seeking, intellectually curious, indifferent, passive, and negativistic (for details see Rudinger, 1999). In connection with these lifestyles, we isolated seven types, taking mobility behavior into account (see Figure 20.3).

Each line path (in the upper part of Fig. 20.3, and in the lower part) indicates a different type. Instead of describing and interpreting each of these seven types, we have grouped them in three more comprehensive patterns:

Pattern 1: Stimulation seekers and intellectuals who are characterized by medium or low risk perception exhibit the following pattern of driving behavior: they drive often, they drive many miles, and they drive often in demanding traffic situations (e.g., bad weather conditions, complex intersections); i.e., they exhibit extensive and intensive mobility behavior (the lines in the upper part of Fig. 20.3).

Pattern 2: Stimulation seekers with low risk perception exhibit less extensive driving behavior; i.e., they still drive often, including in demanding traffic situations, but they drive a moderate number of miles.

Pattern 3: Intellectually curious, passive, and negativis-

Figure 20.3   Empirical Results:
Lifestyles and Mobility Behavior

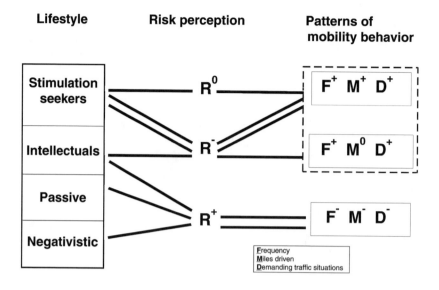

tic people who are characterized by high risk-perception rates drive seldom, drive few miles, and rarely drive in demanding traffic situations; i.e., they show low-intensity mobility behavior.

For reasons of simplicity, a further grouping could lead to two very comprehensive mobility styles: pattern 1 and pattern 2 (which differ only in the number of miles), on the one hand, and pattern 3, on the other. The fact that intellectuals are found in both macro patterns or mobility styles seems a very interesting feature of the analysis, and raises the general question of interpretation and underlying mechanisms. Special analyses (of correspondence), not presented here, yielded proximities

- between stimulation seekers and young old (55–64) males who are still employed and have a medium level of education;
- between passive people and medium old (65–74) females who are retired and live in small villages;
- between negativistic people and retired males who live in medium-sized towns and have a low level of education; and
- between intellectuals and young old people (55–64) who live in large cities and have a higher education; however, there is no relation between this lifestyle and gender or occupational status. So the splitting of the

intellectuals into two types or patterns (high and low mobility) might be due to the split in gender and/or occupational status. More detailed analyses are in progress.

Considering these relations for the interpretation of the CFA results, the question arises of the proportional impact of lifestyles vs. sociostructural conditions. First, multiple regression analyses show that the influence of lifestyle on mobility behavior is reduced when sociostructural parameters are simultaneously taken into account. This result, however, does not hold for attitudes toward mobility; the close connection between lifestyle and these attitudes remains stable in the context of sociostructural parameters as well. However, these are very preliminary results (for details, see Rudinger, 1999).

COMPARATIVE EUROPEAN AND NORTH AMERICAN RESEARCH

As our results show, lifestyle is more or less closely connected with mobility behavior. So it would be of major interest to compare European and U.S. lifestyles and their impact on mobility behavior. However, in this comparison one has to face general problems of cross-cultural research (van de Vijver and Leung, 1996), since lifestyles reflect cultural specificity (in a sense, lifestyle and culture are almost synonymous concepts). A further research challenge is closely linked to this problem: Where does mobility as a cultural value fit into the hierarchy of the national/cultural value and belief system among Europeans (Germans), on the one hand, and Americans, on the other? What is the relation between actual mobility and mobility as a cultural value and the traffic-related infrastructure of a society (e.g., the public transport system)? Last but not least, a cross-cultural comparison of individual and societal compensatory mechanisms that maintain mobility skills and behavior on a functional level would be most interesting and fruitful (Schaie and Mollenkopf, 2000).

PERSPECTIVES: SCENARIO

Finally, a scenario is planned that links together six domains (see Fig. 20.1). The scenario should forecast the future traffic and transport system as it relates to the intensified mobility behavior of the elderly. The six domains are the following:

- demographic development (see introduction);
- economic development, including the economic situation of different groups of the elderly;
- politics and law: fundamental change in the German government's policy, multimodal transport, ecological and social sustainable transport, uniting Europe;
- social development and structure: changes in social norms and belief systems and in stereotypes of aging, changes in leisure-time activities, changes in social contact patterns and working conditions, telecommunication and multimedia (communication instead of mobility);
- the traffic system: technological progress within the traffic system (e.g., telematics; Rudinger, Holte, and Espey, 1998), intelligent linkage between public and private transport; and
- individual resources: lifestyle, living conditions, attitudes toward aging, subjective age, quality of life, etc., life satisfaction, need of mobility, competencies, and compensatory strategies (e.g., Rudinger, 1998).

A workshop will be organized to specify the influencing factors of these domains. Significant facets of the factors will be discussed in terms of their extrapolated future change and their possible effects on the traffic system. As a central consequence and development of the workshop, a questioning of national and international experts is planned. These experts will assess the likelihood of change in the significant elements and the possible degree and direction of their effect on future traffic.

NOTE

I would like to thank Viola Kahmann, Hardy Holte, and Elke Jansen for their invaluable work in the research project AEMEÏS and for their invaluable assistance in preparing this paper.

REFERENCES

Ellinghaus, D., B. Schlag, and J. Steinbrecher. 1990. "Leistungsfähigkeit und Fahrverhalten älterer Kraftfahrer" [Driving Performance and Driving Behavior of Elderly Drivers]. In Bundesanstalt für Straßenwesen, ed., *Unfall- und Sicherheitsforschung Straßenverkehr,* Heft 80. [Bonn]: Bergisch Gladbach.

Hartenstein, W., J. Schulz-Heising, J. Bergmann-Gries, F. Krauß, R. Rudat, and M. Smid. 1990. "Lebenssituation, Einstellung und Verhalten älterer Autofahrer und Autofahrerinnen" [Life Conditions, Attitudes, and Behavior of Elderly Drivers]. In Bundesanstalt für Straßenwesen, ed., *Schriftenreihe der Bundesanstalt für Straßenwesen, Reihe Unfall- und Sicherheitsforschung Straßenverkehr,* Heft 79. [Bonn]: Bergisch Gladbach.

Holte, H. 1994. "Kenngrößen subjektiver Sicherheitsbewertung" [Characteristics of Subjective Risk Evaluation]. In Bundesanstalt für Straßenwesen, ed., *Berichte der Bundesanstalt für Straßenwesen, Mensch und Sicherheit,* Heft M 33. [Bonn]: Bergisch Gladbach.

Hu, P. S., D. J. Trumble, D. J. Foley, J. W. Eberhard, and R. B. Wallace. 1998. "Crash Risks of Older Drivers: A Panel Data Analysis." *Accident Analysis and Prevention* 30, no. 5: 569–581.

Hu, P. S., D. J. Trumble, and A. Lu. 1995. *Driving Decisions and Vehicle Crashes among Older Drivers.* Report prepared for the U.S. Department of Transportation. Washington, D.C.

Kahmann, V. 1998. "Elderly People in Road Traffic: A Pilot Study." Paper presented at the EuroConference "Keeping the Elderly Mobile: Outdoor Mobility of the Elderly—Problems and Solutions." Kerkrade, the Netherlands, 11 June 1998.

Kruse, A., and G. Rudinger. 1997. "Lernen und Leistung im Erwachsenenalter" [Learning and Performance in Middle Age]. In F. E. Weinert and H. Mandl, eds., *Enzyklopädie der Psychologie. Themenbereich D: Praxisgebiete.* Serie I: Pädagogische Psychologie. Band 4: *Psychologie der Erwachsenenbildung,* 46–85. Göttingen: Hogrefe.

Rudinger, G. 1998. "Restrictions, Compensations and Competencies of the Elderly in Mobility and Road Traffic Behaviour." Paper presented at the EuroConference "Keeping the Elderly Mobile: Outdoor Mobility of the Elderly—Problems and Solutions." Kerkrade, the Netherlands, 11 June 1998.

Rudinger, G. 1999. "Ältere Menschen im künftigen Sicherheitssystem Straße/Fahrzeug/Mensch" [The Elderly in the Future Safety System "Road/Vehicle/Subject"]. In Berufsverband Deutscher Psychologen, ed., *Verkehrspsychologie auf neuen Wegen: Herausforderungen von Straße, Wasser, Luft und Schiene.* Bonn: Deutscher Psychologen Verlag.

Rudinger, G., H. Holte, and J. Espey. 1998. *Evaluation of In-Vehicle Safety Devices.* Report to the German Highway Research Institution. Bonn: Bergisch Gladbach.

Schaie, K. W., and H. Mollenkopf. 2000. "Mobility in the Elderly." German American Academic Council Conference at Penn State University, 10–14 April 2000.

Tränkle, U. 1994. *Autofahren im Alter* [Driving in Old Age]. Köln/Bonn: Deutscher Psychologen Verlag.

Van der Vijver, F., and K. Leung. 1996. "Methods and Data Analysis of Comparative Research." In J. W. Berry, Y. H. Poortinga, and J. Pandey, eds., *Handbook of Cross-Cultural Psychology,* 2nd ed., vol. 1: *Theory and Method.* Boston: Allyn and Bacon.

Von Eye, A., C. Spiel, and P. K. Wood. 1996. "Configurational Frequency Analysis in Applied Psychological Research." *Applied Psychology* 45: 301–325.

CHAPTER TWENTY-ONE

Residential Location and Daily Mobility Patterns

A Swedish Case Study of Households with Children

Karin Tillberg

INTRODUCTION

Everybody sees the value of mobility but fails to see the equally great importance of stationarity.

—Hägerstrand, 1992, p. 35

Since the Second World War, the spatial structures of Western societies have been reshaped by private mass motorization. Before cars came on the scene, society was characterized by a *territorial* organization: dwellings, workplaces, and services were mixed together, and the city structure was dense. Later, improvements in transport technology and better and wider roads brought with them the ability to cover an ever-increasing distance within a certain amount of time. For the land use pattern, this meant a change to a *functional* organization: Mixed land use has now given way to a pattern of distinct functions, in which dwellings, workplaces, and shopping centers are clustered in their own separate areas, and even recreational establishments follow a centralized pattern. Greater distances between activities are in today's functionally organized society offset by "time proximity."

Improvements in transport technology have led to a reduced need for people to live geographically close to their place of work. There is thus, at least for some social groups, more room for consideration of individual preferences (for example, the desire to be close to nature) in the choice of where to live. The phenomenon of counterurbanization is well-known in Western countries.

In light of the fact that the importance of geographical distance as a constraint on human activity in a strict technical sense has steadily decreased, my interest is in whether residential location is still a factor in total distance traveled and in the content of daily mobility patterns.

I have two primary aims. The first is to study how total distances traveled by car differ between households living in the countryside and in town. This aspect is interesting from an energy standpoint, as it is often claimed that counterurbanization leads to increased car mobility. My second aim relates to the conflict between the demands for mobility and the demands for stationarity in an increasingly functionally organized society. The question here is whether residential location (urban or rural) is a factor in this conflict. The two aims have different theoretical frameworks and will therefore initially be treated separately here.

THE FIRST RESEARCH AIM:
COUNTERURBANIZATION AND TRANSPORT
GENERATION

In many Swedish regions, there has been an out-migration of households from middle-sized and larger towns to the surrounding countryside, resulting in a stagnation or even decrease in the population of urban areas in favor of small rural settlements. Between 1990 and 1995, the population of the smallest settlements (50 to 200 inhabitants) increased by 6 percent, while the Swedish population as a whole increased by only 2.9 percent (SCB, 1997). The growth in the smallest settlements took place mainly in areas close to larger towns.

This development is often questioned from an ecological point of view, as longer distances between home and work supposedly lead to an increase in car use. Few studies, however, have compared the energy expended for travel in rural areas versus towns. Most of them have focused on differences between cities, concluding that the lower the urban density, the higher the fuel consumption (for example, Newman and Kenworthy, 1989; Naess et al., 1996; see also Breheny, 1995). In the general debate, the concept of the "compact city" is put forward as the most ecologically sustainable alternative.

Work-related trips are a common focus of transport research and planning. This is surprising, because commuting accounts for only 33 percent of the total number of kilometers traveled in Sweden, whereas recreational travel accounts for 53 percent and domestic trips (to shops, hospitals, etc.) for 14 percent (Tengström, 1991). Thus, Berg's (1996) criticism of the concept of the compact city is relevant. He points out that this structure demands a lot of recreational trips out from the city. Fuhrer and Kaiser (1994) point out the paradox in the fact that those who live outside towns with access to green areas commute to work in town, and those who live in towns leave them for recreation. Their study indicates that those who live close to green areas may travel less for recreation than those who do not.

From earlier research (for example, Hanson and Hanson, 1993), it is clear that a person's daily travel pattern and modes of transport are influenced more by socioeconomic factors such as access to a car, age, sex, and income than by the geographical location of his or her dwelling. To explore whether out-migration from a town to the nearby countryside leads to an increase in car use, it is necessary to compare socioeconomically similar households. For my study, I have thus chosen only households with children ages 7 to 17 from housing areas with similar average income levels in a regional center, in an urbanized rural area, and in a small, peripheral town. All areas have access to the same labor market. Families with children were selected because they are over-represented among those moving to the countryside.

All trips made by the selected households are included, with a special focus placed on recreational trips. The questions for this first research aim are: Do households in the countryside travel less for recreational purposes than those in the regional center, taking advantage of their better access to nearby green areas? How does this affect the total number of kilometers traveled by car as compared with households living in the regional center? What is the extent of car use in a peripheral community with short distances to services, organized sport activities, and nature, but where a much higher percentage of the workforce commutes daily to larger towns?

THE SECOND RESEARCH AIM: THE CONFLICT
BETWEEN MOBILITY AND STATIONARITY

Transport ceased to be a metaphor of Progress when mobility came to characterise everyday life more than the image of "home and family." Transport became "the primary activity of everyday existence."
—Prato and Trivero, 1985

According to Hägerstrand (1973), the increase in individual mobility has eliminated the conflict between territorial and functional societal structures, or at least kept it latent. But when the transport technology has been built into the spatial structure of society, it will no longer serve as a tool of freedom but as a means of compulsion. Hägerstrand questions whether an individual's ability to cover ever-greater distances within ever-shorter time spans actually means that the possibility of shifting location within the daily activity program has also improved (Hägerstrand, 1990). In city planning, he claims, the focus too often is on the transport supply as such, not on the spatial distribution of service needs. The criterion of a good transport structure should be whether people can carry out their daily activities in an unbroken sequence.

The car's role can be related to consumer society in general. It is a society in which people experience a constant lack of time, because the availability of services and goods has steadily increased, while the amount of available time remains fixed. The car is a means by which time is compressed and space widened (Hultman, 1994). This in turn leads to greater possibilities of consumption and to a geographically wider range of contacts, leading to the need for increased mobility. Paradoxically, a Swedish study showed that individuals with access to cars more often felt that there was not enough time for them to carry out their daily activities than did those without cars. In Hägerstrand's (1970) terms, the fact that the individual is indivisible means that time becomes the principal constraint within a widening geographical range of action. He doubts that technical solutions exist to overcome this lack of time; on the contrary, it will increase as communication and transport technology continue to improve.

Modern daily life tends to be split into short time sequences spent at a number of different places. Most daily tasks are no longer carried out at home; instead, every errand requires a separate trip, often at a specific time. Daily time and spatial constraints are usually so strict that the opportunity for spontaneous activities is limited (Björk, 1997). The amount of continuous time spent at home is becoming shorter, making time-consuming domestic tasks more difficult to carry out. Instead, coordinating one's daily activities with their associated transportation demands has become a task in itself. Yet the home is still viewed by most people as a center and symbol of continuity in an increasingly fragmented life. In fact, they may attach more importance to this notion the more mobile they become.

Human geographers have introduced the concept of "time-space-compression" to describe the consequences of transport and information technology development. The literature is full of expressions like "speed-up," "global villages," and "spatial barriers" (Massey, 1994). But *who* is actually experiencing this increase in mobility? Despite all the technical possibilities for covering ever-greater distances faster, the demand for *stationarity* remains. There exists a dialectic between, and at the same time a mutual dependency of, some people's mobility and others' stationarity. In the next section, this question will be dealt with from a gender perspective. The opposition between spatial flexibility and mobility, on the one hand (to meet the demands of the production sphere), and stationarity in terms of being available at home, on the other (to meet the demands of the domestic sphere), will be discussed.

Mobility and Stationarity from a Gender Perspective

The mutual dependency of mobility and stationarity and the demand for women to compromise between them becomes obvious in the study of Hanson and Pratt (1995). It confirms earlier results showing that women in Great Britain generally travel shorter distances to work than men do. In contrast to the widespread opinion that this is because women work in low-income sectors within which jobs are spread out and can therefore usually be found close to home, however, the authors claim that women's incomes are lower *because* they have to choose jobs close to home in order to minimize work trips and maximize the time available for domestic tasks. When the geographical radius within which women can accept a job is smaller than men's, so will the number of alternatives be.

According to Forsberg (1992), the term "flexibility" used to characterize female-dominated service jobs. Now, in the information age, it has come to mean always being accessible and geographically mobile, something that is difficult for many women to live up to when they have to combine work and domestic responsibilities.

On an aggregated level, quite a lot is known from earlier research about the differences between the travel habits of men and women. Swedish men travel 34 kilometers a day by car, and women 22 (Svenskarnas resor, 1994). Independently of how long the trip to work is, a larger share of the men go there by car. Little, though, is known about the relationship between residential location and gender differences in travel habits. My interest is in whether the strategies of mothers and fathers to meet the demands for both flexibility and stationarity differ between urban and rural areas.

In an increasingly functionally organized society, children's mobility has also changed, both quantitatively and qualitatively. While the average daily travel distances per person have steadily increased, children's independent mobility has decreased since the 1960s (Vilhelmsson, 1985). As the amount of time that children spend in cars, being driven by an adult, increases, the time they spend walking or biking on their own steadily decreases. As Sandqvist (1998) points out, while children used to do some of the family's shopping, thus easing their parents' time constraints, it is now the parents who have to adapt their daily time budget to their children's leisure activities.

The questions for the second research aim are: How do

gender differences in mobility patterns vary geographically? How does the degree to which children's leisure activities act as constraints on the parents' time budget differ between the town and countryside?

CONCRETIZING METHODOLOGY AND EXPECTED RESULTS

The Choice of Study Areas

For the first research aim—to compare car mobility at three different locations with access to a single labor market—the following three study areas were chosen. They are all in Gävleborg County, which has a typically stagnating regional center and a slight population increase in the surrounding countryside:

1. Gävle (70,000 inhabitants) is a regional center that offers a variety of workplaces and services.

2. The rural coastal area approximately 20 kilometers northeast of Gävle has experienced in-migration in recent years, primarily because summer cottages have been turned into permanent residences, but to some extent also through newly built houses. From here, the majority of the workforce commutes to Gävle.

3. The small town of Ockelbo (3,000 inhabitants) is 50 kilometers northwest of Gävle; 35 percent of the work force commutes daily out of the municipality, mainly to Gävle.

Indications from a Pilot Study

In May 1998, a pilot study was carried out involving seventeen households in these three areas. Its aim was to use the travel diary as a method in a preliminary way, preparing for a major study later. Every member of these households age 7 and older filled in a travel diary from Monday to Sunday. Of course, no conclusions can be drawn from this small sample. But there were some interesting tendencies, which have helped build hypotheses for the main study:

The households in the regional center of Gävle, although having the shortest average distances to work, traveled the longest total distances during the week of investigation. This was because the Gävle households "overcompensated" for their shorter work trips by taking longer recreational trips during the weekend. This indication is interesting, not least because of the general tendency for people to work at home one or more days a week. Recreational trips can play an even larger role when work trips

are reduced, so the effect of residential location on recreational trips will be more important.

In the rural coastal area, both parents tended to drive their children to various sports activities on weekday evenings. The parents had very little time for activities of their own, or for social visits. In Gävle and the small town of Ockelbo, however, the fathers themselves apparently found time to participate in regular sport activities, such as running or shooting. There, the children generally got to their evening activities on their own, on foot, by bicycle, or on skates. The question thus arises: When the time-budget constraints of a household are eased due to children's ability to travel on their own, is the time saved offset by the fathers' recreational trips?

An often cited reason for moving from town to a rural area, such as the coastal area northeast of Gävle, is parents' desire for their children to grow up in a calm and friendly environment. Inquiries about young adults' housing preferences have shown that a residence close to nature is often equated with being a good place for children to live (Borgegård et al., 1994). This small pilot study indicates that children who grow up in the rural settlement have less freedom of movement than do those in the regional center and peripheral town, in that they depend on their parents to drive them to their activities. Furthermore, children living in the seaside settlement supposedly get relatively less daily physical exercise, as they go by bus or car to school, whereas the children in Gävle and Ockelbo go by bike, on foot, or on skates.

Expected Results

The hypotheses formulated for this research are:

- Households in the city travel more for recreational purposes than do those in the countryside.
- Children's activities pose greater constraints on their parents' time budgets in the countryside than in the city. In particular, women in the countryside have less time available for their own recreational trips.

There is an opposition between the longing for continuity in life and a peaceful environment for the children, which acts as a driving force for many families moving to the countryside, and the demands of a functionally organized society for high daily mobility, including children's traveling to organized sport activities. This opposition, to be analyzed from a gender perspective, is reflected in the daily mobility patterns of men and women.

After the categorization of households (e.g., "double income, highly mobile, rural" and "single parent, no car, urban"), one or two households from each category will be selected for an interview study. It will aim at nuancing how parents in different settings view the organization of their daily activities, especially recreational trips.

REFERENCES

Berg, Per G. 1996. *Rörlighet och rotfasthet. Ett human-biologiskt perspektiv på framtidens transporter och kommunikationer.* Malmö: Liber Hermods.

Björk, Mia. 1997. "Hemarbetets modernitet—en fråga om kön, kunskap, tid och rum." *Akademisk avhandling,* 1. Stockholm: Institutionen för Arkitektur och Stadsbyggnad, KTH.

Borgegård, Lars-Erik, et al. 1994. "Att stanna eller flytta—om hälsingeungdomars val efter grundskolan." *Gerum,* no. 24. Umeå: Geografiska institutionen vid Umeå universitet.

Breheny, Michael. 1995. "Counterurbanization and Sustainable Urban Forms." In John Brotchie et al., eds., *Cities in Competition: Productive and Sustainable Cities for the 21st Century,* 402–429. Melbourne: Longman Australia.

ECOTEC. 1993. *Reducing Transport Emissions through Planning.* London: HMSO.

Forer, P. C., and H. Kivell. 1981. "Space-Time Budgets, Public Transport, and Spatial Choice." *Environment and Planning* A 13: 497–509.

Forsberg, Gunnel. 1992. "Kvinnor och män i arbetslivet." In J. Acker et al., *Kvinnors och mäns liv och arbete.* Stockholm: SNS Förlag.

Fortuijn, Joos Droogleever, and Lia Karsten. 1989. "Daily Activity Patterns of Working Parents in the Netherlands." *Area* 21, no. 4: 365–376.

Fuhrer, Urs, and Florian G. Kaiser. 1994. *Multilokales Wohnen. Psychologische Aspekte der Freizeitmobilität.* Bern: Verlag Hans Huber.

Hägerstrand, Torsten. 1970. "Tidsanvändning och omgivningsstruktur." *Bilaga 4 i SOU* 4. Stockholm: Allmänna Förlaget.

Hägerstrand, Torsten. 1973. "Rörlighet, rike och region. Några synpunkter på hur transport-och kommunikationsutvecklingen påverkar samhällsutvecklingen." In *Ymer.* Stockholm: SSAG.

Hägerstrand, Torsten. 1990. "Social interaktion och fysisk rörlighet." *Plan* 3–4. Årg 44.

Hägerstrand, Torsten. 1992. "Mobility and Transportations: Are Economics and Technology the Only Limits?" *Facta & Futura* 2, no. 2: 35–38.

Hanson, Perry, and Susan Hanson. 1980. "Gender and Urban Activity Patterns in Uppsala, Sweden." *Geographical Review* 70: 291–299.

Hanson, Perry, and Susan Hanson. 1993. "The Geography of Everyday Life." In T. Gärling and R. G. Golledge, eds., *Behavior and Environment,* 249–269. Amsterdam: North-Holland.

Hanson, Susan, and Geraldine Pratt. 1995. *Gender, Work and Space.* International Studies of Women and Place. London: Routledge.

Hultman, J. 1994. *Social Geography and the Environment: The City and the Household in a Culture of Mobility and Consumption.* Lund: Institutionen för kulturgeografi och ekonomisk geografi vid Lunds Universitet. Rapporter och Notiser 129.

Lenntorp, Bo. 1976. *Paths in Space-Time Environments: A Time-Geographic Study of Movement Possibilities of Individuals.* Lund: Meddelanden från Lunds Universitets Geografiska Institution.

Mårtensson, Solveig. 1974. "Drag i hushållens levnadsvillkor." In *Ortsbundna levnadsvillkor. Bilagedel 1 till Orter i regional samverkan,* 233–264. *SOU:* 2. Stockholm.

Massey, Doreen. 1994. *Space, Place and Gender.* Cambridge: Polity Press.

Naess, Petter, Synnoeve L. Sandberg, and Per Gunnar Roe. 1996. "Energy Use for Transportation in 22 Nordic Towns." *Scandinavian Housing and Planning Research* 13, no. 2 (May).

National Atlas of Sweden. 1993. *Work and Leisure.* Stockholm: Almqvist & Wiksell.

Newman, P. W. G., and J. R. Kenworthy. 1989. *Cities and Automobile Dependence: A Sourcebook.* Aldershot: Gower.

Prato, Paolo, and Gianluca Trivero. 1985. "The Spectacle of Travel." *Australian Journal of Cultural Studies* 5: 25–43.

Sandqvist, Karin. 1998. "Kön, bilism och samhällsutveckling." Paper prepared for the Department of Child and Youth Studies, Stockholm Institute of Education.

Statistiska Centralbyrån (SCB). 1997. "Ny statistik för småorter." *Pressmeddelande,* 22 August.

Svenskarnas resor. 1994. *Resultatrapport. Riks-Resvaneundersökningen.* Örebro: Statistiska centralbyrån.

Tengström, Emin. 1991. *Bilismen—i kris? En bok om bilen, människan, samhället och miljön.* Kristianstad: Rabén & Sjögren.

Vilhelmsson, Bertil. 1985. *Resurser och resor—äldres aktivitet och handikapp i trafiken.* Göteborg: Kulturgeografiska institutionen vid Göteborgs universitet.

PART V

Increasing Travel and Transport

CHAPTER TWENTY-TWO

Driven to Travel

The Identification of Mobility-Inclined Market Segments

Ilan Salomon
and Patricia L. Mokhtarian

Introduction

It is a truism repeated countless times in the course of a transportation professional's career: "Travel is a derived demand"—that is, derived from the demand for spatially separated activities. Belief in this truism underlies a number of transportation policies designed to reduce motorized travel (whether to reduce congestion, improve air quality, or reduce the consumption of non-renewable energy). For example, much attention has been given to land use policies designed to bring origins (residences) closer to destinations (work, shopping, entertainment). "Neo-traditional" developments, which mix diverse land uses and maintain higher densities than the typical suburban sprawl, are often suggested as a potential scheme to reduce motorized travel.

But what if a significant segment of the population enjoys traveling and would therefore be inclined to evade policies designed to facilitate less motorized travel? In fact, there are a number of indications to support the hypothesis that some people assign positive utilities to travel, independently of the utility of performing the activity at the trip destination.

There are two forms of travel that raise some doubts about the validity and utility of the derived demand assumption. The first is the phenomenon of joyriding, in which the activity itself is the travel, and consequently, it could in principle be analyzed under the derived demand assumption (where the activity is not confined to a specific location as it is in other cases). This type of travel has received little if any attention in trip generation models, implying that its magnitude is too small to be of importance, or that we lack the ability to model it because of its complexity and variation. The second type of travel that poses a problem vis-à-vis the derived demand assumption is the excess travel that is embedded within routine trips to work, shopping, or leisure activities. Research suggests that some excess travel can be attributed to the desire to travel and the benefits of travel aside from getting to the destination.

In recent years there has been a growing quest among transportation planners and environmentalists to address transportation problems through improvements in accessibility rather than mobility. Presumably (given travel as a derived demand), if changes in the spatial distribution could significantly enhance access to activities, the amount of travel could be reduced. This quest is part of a broader debate about transportation/land use interactions in which a central theme is whether increased density should be a policy objective for achieving transportation goals (Newman and Kenworthy, 1989; Steiner, 1994; Handy, 1996).

Improvements in accessibility can be accomplished through many different policy instruments. In addition to land use policies, which take a long time to implement and may involve high capital costs, there are some other, less costly options. For example, telecommunication-based versions of various activities (telecommuting, teleconferencing, teleshopping) are promoted in the hope that they will substitute for a trip to engage in the "equivalent" activity—that is, that they will increase accessibility by offering "virtual mobility" (Mokhtarian and Salomon, forthcoming). The implicit assumption that travelers are cost-minimizers also underlies various pricing strategies (congestion pricing, higher fuel taxes, higher parking fees) designed to reduce the net attractiveness of more distant destinations by increasing the cost to get there. While pricing policies are generally geared toward reducing mobility, they may also affect accessibility. In fact, from a political perspective, pricing policies may be more attractive if they are supplemented by changes in accessibility. Pricing policies differ in their spatial effects: congestion pricing and parking fees are usually applied to a specific area, whereas increased fuel taxes do not affect a specific location. Consequently, the latter type of pricing policy only reduces mobility, whereas the former alters the relative accessibilities of affected and unaffected locations.

The context of transatlantic comparative studies is uniquely relevant for researching the relationship between mobility and accessibility. The difference in urban structure, travel patterns, culture, and policy processes offers an opportunity to view the role of some of these factors and, through the understanding of the differences, provide important input to policy-making in both the North American and European contexts.

ATTITUDES AND EXCESS TRAVEL

While we acknowledge the general truth that travel is a derived demand, our study in progress contests that conventional wisdom as an *absolute* behavioral dictum. Specifically, we suggest that some people have an intrinsic urge to travel for travel's own sake, beyond the utility of the destination itself, although this urge may be stronger in some people and for some circumstances than others. The question has important implications: If, in fact, some

people are utility-maximizers rather than cost-minimizers, and if travel has an intrinsic utility, then policies seeking to motivate travel reductions may not have as large an effect as desired or expected. Our premise is neither new nor restricted to the United States. Despite Americans' alleged "love affair with the automobile," we believe a thirst for mobility to be universal—and note that similar observations have been made for at least a quarter-century, by scholars from different countries and representing different disciplines (Reichman, 1976; Jones, 1978; Hupkes, 1982; Marchetti, 1994).

Conventional economic thought assumes that travelers weigh the disbenefit of distance or travel time against the benefit of the destination when assessing alternative destinations. For example, as Goodwin and Hensher (1978: 25) express it, the nature of travel as a derived demand implies that the decision to travel or not involves "a simple trade-off between the advantages or benefits to be derived from being at a destination and the disadvantages or costs involved in traveling to that destination." In fact, much transportation development is based on the argument that travelers seek to save travel time, and that their value of time is the justification for investments in transportation infrastructure.

But there are a number of indications that people travel more than would be expected if the fulfillment of activity demand could be satisfied only through accessibility. If true, this phenomenon has obvious implications for environmentally oriented policies intended to reduce travel. We will refer to this phenomenon as excess travel, meaning travel that exceeds what could be a minimum satisfying level. The evidence for excess travel is arising in a variety of different contexts.

The concept of excess or wasteful commuting, for example, has received much attention over the last fifteen years (e.g., Small and Song, 1992), where excess commuting is defined as the amount exceeding that predicted by standard location models. In general, some of this apparently excess travel may be due to ignorance with regard to the network structure or available services, some due to constraints on the individual (such as the need to consider two careers in choosing a residential location), some due to the omission of factors increasing the utility of more distant destinations, and some due to a utility for travel itself. In the current context we refer to the latter condition.

A 1997 study demonstrates that worldwide increases in

real income are associated with a transition from slower (transit) to faster (automobile and airplane) modes, with the consequence that per capita distances traveled are increasing (Schafer and Victor, 1997). An Australian study found that given the current urban structure, satisfaction with one's commuting time peaked at a travel time of fifteen minutes—not zero minutes, as the derived demand principle implies (Young and Morris, 1981). Some of our earlier work on the demand for telecommuting illustrates that not everyone who is able to telecommute wants or chooses to do so (Mokhtarian and Salomon, 1996).

There is a large body of literature on attitudes toward, and use of, the automobile (see, e.g., Wachs and Crawford, 1992; Webber, 1992). Automobile advertisements frequently play to the drive for mobility, as these recent examples illustrate: "It's an unrestricted round trip ticket to anywhere" (Acura Integra); it "takes me places roads don't even go" (Ford Explorer); "you should go to the amazing places on earth which are by definition *far*" (Izuzu Trooper); "a car so advanced, it might set telecommuting back a few years" (Honda Accord).

Following Jones (1978), we suggest that the utility of engaging in an activity requiring travel can be usefully decomposed into three components: the (net) utility of the activity at the destination, the *disutility* (negative aspects) of travel to the destination (generalized cost), and the *utility* (positive aspects) of travel to the destination (usually unobserved subjective factors). While destination choice models explicitly trade off the first two components, mode choice models ignore the utility of the destination (which is assumed to be fixed and constant across all mode alternatives) and compare just the observed disutilities of each mode (through measures of travel time and cost), assuming that the alternative with the least negative observed disutility has the highest probability of being chosen. The third component—the positive aspect of travel—is seldom addressed quantitatively.

This multi-component nature of the utility of an activity/trip combination illustrates the extreme that (contrary to the implication of Goodwin and Hensher's statement) a trip can be made even when the utility of the activity itself is zero or even negative, as long as the positive utility of travel outweighs the combined magnitudes of the other two components. In these cases the demand for travel (which appears to be excess travel if the third component is unmeasured) is *not* derived from the demand for the activity, as is universally assumed, but from the demand for travel per se (Reichman, 1976; Hupkes, 1982). The more common case is one in which the third component increases the total utility of a more distant destination beyond what it would otherwise seem to be, again resulting in apparently excess travel when that more distant destination is chosen.

Building on the previous work described above, we have identified a number of character traits or desires that are likely to be associated with a positive utility for travel:

- *Adventure-seeking:* The quest for novel, exciting, or unusual experiences will in some cases involve travel as part or all of the experience itself, not just as a means to the end ("getting there is half the fun").
- *Variety-seeking:* A more mundane version of the adventure-seeking trait, the desire to vary from a monotonous routine may lead one, for example, occasionally to take a longer route to work or visit a more distant grocery store.
- *Independence:* The desire to get around on one's own is a common manifestation of this trait.
- *Control:* This trait is likely to partially explain travel by car when reasonable transit service is available.
- *Status:* Traveling a lot, traveling to interesting destinations, and traveling "in style" (e.g., in a luxury car) can be symbols of a desired socioeconomic class or lifestyle.
- *Buffer:* A certain amount of travel can provide a valued transition between activities such as home and work.
- *Exposure to the environment:* "Cabin fever" is one manifestation of the desire to leave an enclosed building and "go somewhere," just to experience something of the outdoors. Microsoft's ad campaign "Where do you want to go today [on the Internet]?" elicited this response in a letter to *Newsweek*: "How about 'outside'?" When Ted Leonsis, president and CEO of AOL Studios, was asked who was the biggest competitor to AOL, he replied, "Nice weather."
- *Escape:* Related but not identical to the "exposure" desire is the need to get away from an oppressive aspect of the current environment. There may or may not be a specific destination involved, and (if there is) it may be indoors or out.
- *Scenery and other amenities:* These may lead someone, for example, to take a longer route than necessary to a destination.
- *Synergy:* The ability to conduct multiple activities at or

Table 22.1 Hypothesized Relationships among Travel Liking, Perceived Mobility, and Satisfaction

		TRAVEL LIKING	
		Dislike	Like
PERCEIVED MOBILITY	Low	Balanced	Deprived
	High	Surfeited	Balanced

on the way to a more distant destination, or the ability to be productive while traveling may result in apparently excess travel.

The premise of this research, based on Ramon (1981), is that an individual's decision about engaging in travel is moderated by a number of factors beyond the utility of reaching the destination where the ostensible purpose of the trip can be accomplished. Specifically, we identify the following factors as important to the travel and mobility choices made by individuals:

- *Travel liking (TL):* One's general affinity for travel, measured on a semantic scale from "strongly dislike" to "strongly like." In Ramon's survey of 474 adults in Jerusalem in 1977, three out of five people expressed some degree of affinity for traveling.
- *Objective mobility (OM):* The amount one travels, measured by number of trips and/or distance.
- *Perceived mobility (PM):* One's view of the amount traveled, rated on a semantic scale from "a little" to "a lot."
- *Satisfaction (S):* One's satisfaction with the amount traveled, measured by the response to the statement "I would like to travel [much more than / the same amount as / much less than] I do now." One out of

three respondents to Ramon's survey said they wanted to travel more or much more than they presently did.

Those individuals wanting to travel more than now are considered "deprived," those wanting to travel the same amount are classified as "balanced," and those wanting to travel less are considered "surfeited." Individuals who feel surfeited are likely to exploit access-enhancing policies, and their responses are in the "right" direction. However, the balanced and particularly the deprived groups are not likely to respond in the desired direction, especially if they perceive the marginal costs of travel to be very low. If these two groups are sufficiently large, it may offset the benefits accrued from the accommodation of the desire to reduce travel of the surfeited group.

As attitudes toward travel vary across individuals, so may their preference toward reducing or increasing their amount of travel. We have hypothesized, as shown in Table 22.1, that individuals who like to travel and perceive their current mobility as low would prefer alternatives requiring more travel over closer, neighborhood-based alternatives.

WHAT CAN BE LEARNED FROM A NORTH AMERICAN AND EUROPEAN COMPARISON?

The differences in urban structure, urban travel patterns, and planning procedures between Europe and North America raise some interesting issues with regard to accessibility enhancement as a policy objective. Generally, European cities are characterized by a number of dimensions that seem to better correspond to the idealized land use patterns sought by American planners and researchers. They tend to be more densely populated, with residential land uses within the central cities being occupied by the middle and upper social classes, while the share of suburban residences is smaller than in American cities. Mixed land uses are also more prevalent in European cities. All of this is also associated with a significantly higher share of public transport use in Europe.

In view of Europe's apparent achievement of the ideal sought by American planners, it would seem that the potential for land use policies as measures to reduce motorized travel may be of less interest to European policymakers. However, there are a number of reasons why both European and American planners and policy-makers should gain from comparative research along the lines suggested in this chapter.

While seemingly so different in accessibility and modal shares, some trends in Western Europe are indicating a transition toward American patterns. Increases in auto ownership, decreasing use of public transport, and increasing suburbanization reflect some preferences of contemporary Europeans. This putative imitation of the "American" dream may in fact be a manifestation of a basic desire for increased mobility by some market segments, irrespective of the urban structure.

Thus, there may be a greater need than first imagined for European planners to consider new accessibility-enhancing policies. Indeed, European planning procedures provide greater capacity to affect land use patterns than is the case in North America. On the other hand, it is relevant to assess the extent to which such policies are counter to, rather than consistent with, prevailing trends and basic human desires, and the nature of transatlantic similarities and differences in those trends and desires.

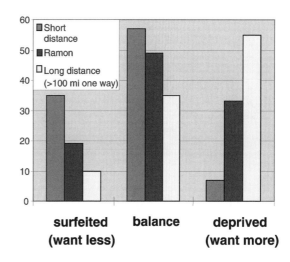

Figure 22.1   Travel Satisfaction

THE AMERICAN CONTEXT:
PRELIMINARY FINDINGS

We have designed a questionnaire that measures the above-mentioned characteristics as well as attitudes toward various aspects of travel, lifestyle and personality traits, amount of travel, and demographic information. Our purpose is first of all to measure the affinity for travel in the sample, and secondly to relate that liking to the characteristics described above. Some 8,000 questionnaires were sent to randomly selected households in three communities in the Bay Area, representing a variety of land use patterns. With an overall response rate of 25 percent, after discarding responses with too much missing data we retained about 1,900 cases for further study.

Some of the initial analyses support the hypothesis that travelers are not cost (or distance) minimizers. For example, consonant with the Australian study mentioned earlier, workers' reported ideal one-way commuting time is just over sixteen minutes. Only 3 percent desire a commute of zero to two minutes, suggesting that entirely eliminating the commute does not resonate with most people as a desirable aspect of telecommuting. Almost half of the respondents prefer a commute of twenty minutes or more. In subsequent analysis, we model the ideal

commute time as a function of objective variables such as the actual time and demographics, as well as the subjective measures described above (Redmond and Mokhtarian, 1999).

More than three-quarters of the respondents indicate that they "sometimes" or "often" divert to longer routes to observe scenery, explore new places or routes, or travel just for fun. More than a fifth sometimes or often engage in at least ten such indicators of excess travel.

To measure satisfaction, respondents were asked whether they wanted to travel less or much less (surfeited), about the same (balanced), or more or much more (deprived) than they were traveling now. A distinction was made between short-distance and long-distance (more than 100 miles one way) travel, and within each category the question was asked overall as well as by purpose and mode. Here we focus on the "overall" responses.

Figure 22.1 shows a clear difference between satisfaction with short- and long-distance travel. For short-distance travel, respondents are five times as likely to be surfeited (35%) as deprived (7%), although a majority (57%) are balanced. For long-distance travel, on the other hand, a majority (55%) are deprived, and relatively few (10%) are surfeited. It is noteworthy that Ramon's study of 474 Jerusalem residents more than twenty years ago, using a

Figure 22.2   Travel Liking

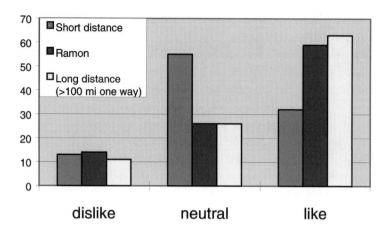

similar measure of satisfaction but not distinguishing between short-distance and long-distance travel, found a distribution of responses similar to the average of our short-distance and long-distance ratings.

Respondents were also asked to rate their travel liking on a five-point scale (strongly dislike to strongly like), with the same distinctions by distance, purpose, and mode. Again, clear differences between overall ratings for short- and long-distance travel emerge, as shown in Figure 22.2. Levels of dislike are similar for both short-distance (13%) and long-distance (11%) travel. But a majority (55%) of respondents are neutral about short-distance travel, whereas an even larger majority (63%) are positive about long-distance travel.

Thus, there is clearly a stronger affinity for long-distance travel, but even short-distance travel is not viewed negatively. This suggests that, despite the expressed desire to reduce short-distance travel shown in Figure 22.1, people may in fact not be highly motivated to do so. For this measure of travel liking, it is noteworthy that Ramon's data coincide almost exactly with our long-distance distribution, suggesting that one's perception of long-distance travel dominates the reported liking for travel generally.

Further analyses of the data will help to identify the magnitude and characteristics of those market segments who, because of being mobility-oriented, are less respon-

sive to accessibility-enhancing improvements. We believe these insights can help inform the development of more effective transportation policies.

NOTE

Parts of this article draw from Ilan Salomon and Patricia L. Mokhtarian, "What Happens When Mobility-Inclined People Face Accessibility-Enhancing Policies?" *Transportation Research D* 3, no. 3 (1998): 129–140; and Patricia L. Mokhtarian and Ilan Salomon, "How Derived Is the Demand for Travel? Some Conceptual and Measurement Considerations," forthcoming in *Transportation Research A*. The research described here is funded by the University of California Transportation Center and Daimler-Chrysler.

REFERENCES

Goodwin, P., and D. Hensher. 1978. "The Determinants of Travel Choice: An Overview." In D. Hensher and Q. Dalvi, eds., *Determinants of Travel Choice*, 1–65. New York: Praeger.

Handy, S. L. (1996) "Understanding the Link between Urban Form and Non-Work Travel Behavior." *Journal of Planning Education and Research* 15, no. 3: 183–198.

Hupkes, G. 1982. "The Law of Constant Travel Time and Trip-Rates." *Futures* 14, 38–46.

Jones, P. M. 1978. "Destination Choice and Travel Attributes." In D. Hensher and Q. Dalvi, eds., *Determinants of Travel Choice,* 266–311. New York: Praeger.

Marchetti, C. 1994. "Anthropological Invariants in Travel Behavior." *Technological Forecasting and Social Change* 47: 75–88.

Mokhtarian, P. L., and I. Salomon. 1996. "Modeling the Choice of Telecommuting 2: A Case of the Preferred Impossible Alternative." *Environment and Planning A,* 28: 1859–1876.

Mokhtarian, P. L., and I. Salomon. 2000. "Emerging Travel Patterns: Do Telecommunications Make a Difference?" Invited resource paper for the 8th meeting of the International Association for Travel Behaviour Research, Austin, Texas, September 21–25, 1997. In H. S. Mahmassani, ed., *Policy Applications of Travel Behavior Models.* Oxford: Elsevier Science.

Newman, P. W. G., and J. R. Kenworthy. 1989. *Cities and Automobile Dependence.* Aldershot: Avebury.

Ramon (Perl), C. 1981. "Sociological Aspects in the Analysis of Travel Behavior in an Urban Area: Jerusalem as a Model." Ph.D. dissertation, The Hebrew University, Jerusalem. (In Hebrew.)

Redmond, L. S., and P. L. Mokhtarian. 1999. "The Positive Utility of the Commute: Modeling Ideal Commute Time and Relative Desired Commute Amount." Submitted to *Transportation.*

Reichman, S. 1976. "Travel Adjustments and Life Styles: A Behavioral Approach." In P. R. Stopher and A. H. Meyburg, eds., *Behavioral Travel-Demand Models,* 143–152. Lexington, Mass.: D. C. Heath and Company.

Schafer, A., and D. Victor. 1997. "The Past and Future of Global Mobility." *Scientific American* (October), 58–61.

Small, K. A., and S. Song. 1992. "Wasteful Commuting: A Resolution." *Journal of Political Economy* 100, no. 4: 888–898.

Steiner, R. L. 1994. "Residential Density and Travel Patterns: Review of the Literature." *Transportation Research Record* 1466: 37–43.

Wachs, M., and M. Crawford, eds. 1992. *The Car and the City: The Automobile, the Built Environment, and Daily Urban Life.* Ann Arbor: University of Michigan Press.

Webber, M. M. 1992. "The Joys of Automobility." In M. Wachs and M. Crawford, eds., *The Car and the City: The Automobile, the Built Environment, and Daily Urban Life,* 274–284. Ann Arbor: University of Michigan Press.

Young, W., and J. Morris. 1981. "Evaluation by Individuals of Their Travel Time to Work." *Transportation Research Record* 794: 51–59.

CHAPTER TWENTY-THREE

Picnics, Pets, and Pleasant Places

The Distinguishing Characteristics of Leisure Travel Demand

Jillian Anable

INTRODUCTION

The growth in traffic of between 83 percent and 142 percent predicted to take place between 1989 and 2025 on the UK road network (DoT, 1989) caused considerable debate and marked a turning point in the definition of the problems and the framing of national and local government transport policy in the UK. Although these forecasts have been revised in the light of subsequent economic downturns, the most recent forecasts still predict a doubling of 1990 traffic levels over the next forty years (DETR, 1997a). This translates into an additional 11 million cars on the roads.

These trends, and their underlying causes of increasingly entrenched car-dependent lifestyles and longer journey lengths, are well documented and go largely undisputed. So too are the social, environmental, and economic consequences of this growth in travel and the urgent need for strategies to manage this demand. So why is a major contributing factor to these trends largely ignored by policy-makers, transport researchers, and those collecting empirical data?

The "major factor" implied here is leisure travel. In all its variety of forms, this journey purpose is responsible for 40 to 50 percent of all distance traveled in most western economies, and represents one of the only journey purposes with essentially universal participation. More poignantly, in terms of car dependency, leisure constitutes one of the fastest-growing sectors of car-based travel demand. Nevertheless, transport policy has tended to concentrate on commuting journeys within urban areas and has approached traffic problems in rural areas and off-peak leisure demand with less urgency. Sustainable rural transport and tourism is now beginning to ascend the policy agenda, without, however, any clarification of what is meant by leisure or any understanding of the particular car-dependent attitudes associated with it. Contradictory and ambivalent attitudes and cultural issues remain inadequately acknowledged in any attempt to find solutions to the specific conflicts generated by leisure travel demand.

At the same time, attempts to address problems of ever-increasing demands for road space on both sides of the Atlantic have begun to focus on a range of activities defined as *mobility management*. This broad approach is aimed at encouraging the use of alternative modes by changing behavior on behalf of organizations and individuals and is reflective of the wider change in transport policy direction from a "predict and provide" approach to one of managing demand. It involves increasing understanding of travel behavior and the reasons for individual journeys within specific contexts and organizational settings. Yet what is happening is a move toward such demand-management policies without a full understanding of "car-dependent" attitudes and the ability and willingness of people to change their behavior. If policies are to be developed, targeted, and monitored effectively, further investigation and understanding of the multiple facets of travel demand are required. This changing policy culture has created a need for new sources of data and new tools and procedures for retrieving this information.

This chapter has three objectives: (1) to highlight the significant contribution of leisure travel to current patterns of travel; (2) to present the hypothesis that the distinct characteristics of "discretionary" travel warrant a radically different understanding of the factors influencing this behavior; and (3) to argue the need for new approaches to data collection.

The Meaning and Growth of Leisure

The study of leisure has generated a substantial body of literature focusing on the psychology and sociology of leisure as well as the more commercial aspects of marketing and need satisfaction. There is much to be learned from these studies to inform our understanding of travel demand. In particular, notions of leisure as concomitant with freedom, choice, and opportunities for self-improvement and definition begin to contribute toward some understanding of not only why leisure travel is a sensitive issue politically, but why the formation of travel demand management policy in this area requires a detailed understanding of its distinguishing characteristics (Glyptis, 1995; Horna, 1994).

The growth in participation in all aspects of leisure is widely recognized, as is its inextricable link with increased personal mobility. However, both the growth in personal travel and the importance of leisure in participation terms are themselves a product of broader social change. Increases in disposable income and demographic factors such as an aging population with decent incomes, abundant leisure time, and increasing confidence to travel are some of the more direct and obvious factors influencing the form and structure of leisure. In addition, conventional wisdom suggests that growth in the leisure sector has been the result of a major expansion in free time, although recent research has shown that this is not necessarily the most significant factor (Martin and Mason, 1998). Indeed, since the early 1970s, the total free time available to people in the UK has increased by a modest 10 percent. More significant is the increasing amount of money that people are spending on their free time. This monetization of free time has resulted in a doubling of the annual rate of spending on leisure activity over the past twenty-five years. A parallel trend has been a change in *when* people have free time, due to a growth in flexible working practices and much greater variety in the structure of working life.

These evolving patterns of behavior have led to claims that leisure has become much more than merely what is left over after the day's or week's work has been done. Instead, leisure seems likely to become one of the crucial components of our lives, eventually resulting in what some commentators are calling a future "society of leisure" (Horna, 1994). A whole body of literature has grown purely from attempts to define what is meant by leisure and where its boundaries lie. However, no such debate of any significance has taken place with respect to the development of a meaningful definition of leisure in terms of travel purpose, consequent journey characteristics, and policy approaches. For the purposes of transport studies, the leisure journey appears to comprise all journeys that do not fall clearly into the other-well established categories of commuting, business, education, escort, and sometimes other personal business and shopping. In other words, leisure travel embraces all "discretionary" forms of travel, regardless of the fact that not everyone regards such activities as "pleasurable." The ambiguity that such a clear lack of conceptualization leads to is clear in the poor documentation of even basic leisure travel trends, let alone any deeper understanding of the factors influencing discretionary travel behavior.

Trends in Leisure Travel Demand

The transition of free time into a period for consumption and expenditure is characterized by a continual transformation in public tastes, priorities, destinations, and patterns of travel. These are manifesting themselves in travel farther from home, to, for example, increasingly numerous and dispersed visitor attractions, sports facilities, multiplex cinemas, theme parks, or travel for short or longer breaks in paid accommodations—activities that are now considered normal components of free time. The result has been an increase in total distance traveled for all lei-

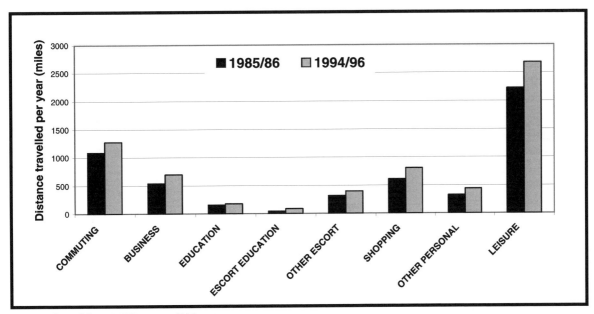

Source: Adapted from DETR, 1998a, Table 0.8, p. 10.

Figure 23.1   Journeys and Distance Traveled per Person per Year by Purpose

Table 23.1   Modal Split by Journey Purpose According to Number of Trips and Distance

	COMMUTING	ESCORT	SHOPPING	LEISURE
	NO. OF TRIPS			
Walk/bicycle	16%	48%	34%	35%
Car and other private	69%	49%	53%	57%
Public transport	14%	2%	12%	7%
	DISTANCE			
Walk/bicycle	2%	12%	5%	3%
Car and other private	81%	86%	82%	85%
Public transport	17%	2%	13%	12%

Source: Adapted from DETR, 1998a, Tables 2A and 2B, pp. 20 and 23.

sure purposes of 21 percent in the decade preceding the 1994/96 UK National Travel Survey (DETR, 1997b). This translates into 41 percent of all distance traveled, or an average of 2,685 miles per person per year out of a total average distance of 6,570 miles. This volume of travel, together with a comparison of journey purposes *not* included as leisure, can be seen in Figure 23.1.

Pure quantification of the trends in this way, however, disguises the relative car-based nature of leisure journeys. Table 23.1 shows that 57 percent of all leisure journeys are undertaken by car, as either a driver or a passenger, in addition to some travel on other private modes such as motorcycles or private bus. This proportion is slightly less than for commuting purposes, as leisure compares fa-

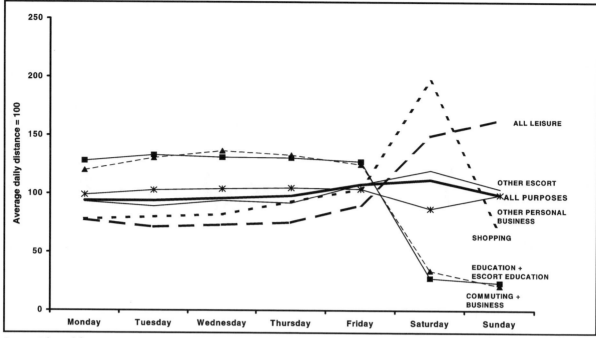

Source: Adapted from DETR, 1997a, Table 4.5, p. 37.

Figure 23.2   Average Daily Distance by Journey Purpose According to Day of the Week

vorably in the number of journeys carried out by non-motorized means. However, this figure has to be viewed in the context of the overall quantity of travel undertaken indicated above, universal participation, average journey lengths, and temporal and spatial distributions of this demand in order to appreciate the far-reaching significance of current and future leisure travel in terms of its contribution to traffic.

While the number of leisure trips taken in the aggregate has not increased significantly over the past decade, average journey length has increased by 19 percent, leading to the 21 percent increase in leisure mileage (DETR, 1998a). Furthermore, 85 percent of this distance is undertaken by private motorized means. This in turn has resulted in 60 percent of total distance per annum for all

travel purposes traveled as a car passenger, and 32 percent of car driver distance per year being accounted for by recreational trips.

In spite of the fact that leisure journeys, unlike commuting, do not generally suffer any explicit time constraints, discretionary travel is a significant cause of congestion. Analysis of traffic volumes by day of the week reveals the enormous contribution of leisure travel demand to the overall traffic situation. Saturday is clearly the busiest day for travel, closely followed by Friday and Sunday (Fig. 23.2). With respect to leisure, participation in travel for these activities is 50 percent higher on Saturday and 64 percent higher on Sunday than on other days of the week. Consequently, the already high volumes of travel demand are concentrated within a relatively short time period.

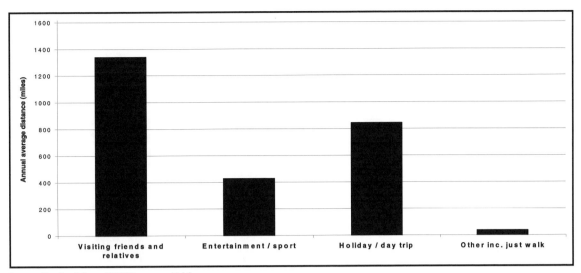

Source: Derived from DETR, 1997a, Table 2.12, p.14.

Figure 23.3   Annual Distance Traveled by Category of Leisure Travel

Another main contributor to weekend traffic is the disproportionate amount of traveling done for shopping purposes, which could be included as a leisure activity. Shopping patterns are themselves changing now that stores in the UK are open on Sundays, with the trend gradually manifesting itself in an increase in Sunday activity without a related fall-off in Saturday business. With these patterns working together, the overall peak time of the week for traffic across all modes now occurs on average on Saturday between the hours of 11:00 and 11:59 (DETR, 1997a). The nature of the weekend leisure journey, however, is relatively long-distance and "extra-urban." As a result, levels of highway congestion at least as bad as in any traditional weekday "peak time" travel period are now becoming an increasingly common occurrence on Saturday and Sunday afternoon/evening. This alone is powerful evidence of the need to recognize leisure travel as a serious factor in the adoption of strategies to manage travel demand.

DEFINING LEISURE TRAVEL

Both a contributing factor to and an implication of the neglect of leisure travel issues in transport policy-making and research is that any attempt to focus on leisure travel is beset at the outset with the vast problem of identifying what is meant by "leisure." The term appears to encompass a variety of recreational pursuits, from going out for a walk, evening entertainment, visiting friends and relatives, day trips, and short- and long-stay breaks. Even shopping can be regarded as a leisure activity and is included by some as leisure for statistical purposes. At the very least, a definition that clarifies the boundaries and a better documentation of the trends are necessary if policies are to be designed and targeted effectively.

Official UK travel statistics do offer some disaggregation of figures for leisure travel. Figure 23.3 illustrates the three most common categories used. However, even where national sources of travel statistics segregate the leisure travel category into some combination of these subcategories used in Figure 23.3, it remains difficult to formulate even a basic picture of travel behavior, as there are still many diverse activities encompassed by each category. For the purpose of designing mobility-management policies, any classification needs to address the specific demands exercised by the need to control the growth of leisure travel by car. As a basis for more detailed understanding, this necessitates identification of the broad sets of factors involved in the choice of destination and mode for each type of activity. This in turn demands some assessment of the spatial (accessibility) and temporal (fre-

Table 23.2 Content Analysis of the Recent Transport White Paper

Journey Purpose	No. of times cited in the White Paper
COMMUTING / WORK	44
SCHOOL / EDUCATION	87
LEISURE / RECREATION	16

Source: DETR, 1998b.

quency, timing restrictions, the need for planning) profiles of these activities.

THE UK TRANSPORT POLICY CONTEXT

Given the basic picture painted above of the contribution of leisure travel in its broadest terms to overall levels of traffic demand, it would be reasonable to assume that leisure travel patterns are currently assigned some importance in transport policy-making. However, *A New Deal for Transport: Better for Everyone* (DETR, 1998b), the first national government strategic policy document on transport in more than twenty years, is a more accurate reflection of the importance attached to leisure-related issues. A crude analysis of the content of this 169-page document reveals the degree to which leisure is "mentioned" within the text in comparison to other journey purposes (see Table 23.2).

Even this analysis, however, offers a generous picture of the inclusion of leisure as a policy area in the White Paper. If analyzed in qualitative terms instead, the lack of any substantive policies for recreational travel demand is more accurately revealed. For example, work journeys, telecommuting, and the journey to school all have explicit "sections" within the paper, with support pledged

for specific policy initiatives. Leisure, on the other hand, is included on a more ad hoc basis in the paper, usually with an accompanying indication of its contribution to particular traffic problems, but rarely in connection with particular policy initiatives! In this respect, the White Paper is a true reflection of the priorities attached to other journey purposes over leisure in national and the majority of regional and local transport policy-making, as well as in transport research. While there are adequate reasons to defend the emphasis of demand management policies being placed thus far on the "easier" targets of urban and inter-urban commuting and shopping, the disproportionate concentration on these journeys may not be sustainable in the face of current forecasts for recreational activity (Anable, 2000; Leisure Consultants, 1997; Mintel, 1998).

THE DISTINGUISHING CHARACTERISTICS OF LEISURE TRAVEL

The balance of push and pull factors in the decision-making process for leisure travel tends to be different from those made in, say, the case of commuting. The situational context in which decisions regarding travel mode and time are made has a greater role to play for leisure-related decisions, and the particular mix of demands involved needs to be taken into account in the design and marketing of policies to influence behavior. Using the literature, focus group research, and instinctive assessments of the leisure travel decision-making context, it is possible to make assumptions about why leisure travel should be regarded as different from other journey purposes. The following list has been compiled specifically with countryside activities in mind:

- *The psychology of leisure:* In the study of leisure sociology and psychology, most authors agree that leisure participation is an expression of identity, personal values, and attitudes. The factors closely associated with leisure conjure up notions of a state of mind often closely associated with the "love affair with the car," such as freedom of choice, freedom from obligation, liberty and free access, enjoyment, relaxation, a lack of evaluation, voluntary participation, and so on (Horna, 1994). The elicitation of these values and attitudes through behavioral research may allow identification of the necessary conditions for this state of mind to be created by using transport modes other than the car.

- *Familiarity:* As a rule, leisure travel takes place to less familiar destinations. In such cases there is no question of routine behavior. This has implications for perceptions of the possible travel alternatives and the motivation to investigate alternative travel options.

- *A derived demand?* Although most leisure journeys involve trips to and from leisure activities and are therefore a means to an end, the travel experience of the leisure journey is itself a key part of the whole activity; hence, convenience, comfort, and enjoyment are of higher importance. This renders leisure travel less of a derived demand than other kinds of travel, as it can be considered an activity undertaken partly for its own sake—indeed, often entirely for its own sake.

- *Time:* The appreciation of travel time can be reasonably assumed to differ for leisure journeys, albeit to varying degrees depending on the intended duration at the place of destination.

- *Last-minute decision-making:* There is a vast choice of where to go and what to do on, say, a Sunday afternoon. As a result, leisure journeys are subject to relatively last-minute decision-making, and this is a serious barrier to the use of means other than the car even for unfamiliar destinations. Indeed, many visitors to the countryside do not have a geographical location or a particular activity in mind when they set off. Instead, decisions about where to stop are made as they go, and the car allows plans to be spontaneously modified to meet changing circumstances. There is little time in which to inform oneself, and a greater range of factors are involved, some of which are more unpredictable than for other journey purposes (e.g., the weather, mood).

- *Multi-trips:* Many day trips involve visiting an "area" as opposed to one attraction; therefore, the multi-trip nature of this type of day out renders public transport journeys less attractive.

- *Group vs. individual travel:* Leisure trips often include children and the elderly, making the use of public transport more difficult and less economical.

- *Cost:* The appreciation of cost may be different for leisure travel, as the costs of the whole leisure experience, including the travel element, are generally evaluated together.

- *Luggage/Equipment:* Traveling to a holiday or leisure destination implies the transport of luggage and recreational equipment such as bicycles, fishing tackle, golf clubs, camping or beach equipment, pets, and picnics.

- *Weekend public transport provision:* Leisure trips on weekends tend to coincide with actual or perceived periods of infrequent public transport.

In the light of these "differentiating" factors, leisure travel may be less influenced by such factors as accessibility and price elasticity as is assumed or proven to be the case with other journey purposes. Instead, psychological issues linked with the expression of identity and practical issues concerned with the timing of decision-making and journeys take precedence. Hence, good access by train or proximity to an "urban" area may not be indicative of the number of visitors coming by alternative modes, or indeed of the size of the catchment area itself. Instead, other strategies, such as information provision and "packaged" deals, may prove to be the most effective influences on travel behavior. The marketing approach for leisure travelers will require specific market instruments as compared with other travel activities.

THE NEED FOR NEW APPROACHES TO DATA COLLECTION

Despite the invaluable role of quantitative data in the monitoring and evaluation of policy, statistics that purely measure behavior usually provide us only with indices or proof of some exemplar or trend; they don't inform us about why people desire certain things or act in a certain way. In other words, they can be seen only as the symptom rather than the cause. For example, such data sources serve mainly to reinforce our knowledge that the countryside is being invaded by tourists, that they are causing erosion, pollution, and overcrowding, that we need alternative sites and new plans for a more sustainable approach to the countryside. Moreover, many "innovative" solutions are increasingly being implemented in an attempt to influence these trends on the basis of such information. The problem is that we rarely ask why. Why are people willing to wait in line for hours in their cars to enter our national parks, or to drive for hours to reach a heritage site, walk two hundred meters, buy an ice cream, and go home?

To attempt to answer such questions is to go some way toward enabling the development of more effective solutions to the pressures placed on the countryside. Only when travel demand is understood in depth can we attempt to construct or find realistic alternatives. To do this, quantitative sustainability measures must be synthesized with behavioral indices to enable successful identification of policy packages.

To generate these "statistics of understanding" (Potter, 1997), as opposed to statistics merely of measurement, it may be necessary to shift away from "hard" scientific approaches toward softer and more socially based methods. This applies equally to any sector of travel demand. However, perhaps more than most aspects of travel behavior, our understanding of leisure travel as the fastest-growing element of demand rests on underlying perceptions and cultural tensions, particularly where the "countryside" and heritage are concerned. The cultural context suggests that it is essential to recognize the interrelationships between different tensions and identify the need for creative solutions:

> Like increasingly sophisticated direct mail advertising, policy initiatives will need to appeal to different travel needs and aspirations, rather than merely seek to reduce car travel or promote alternatives to the least car-dependent groups. (Liniado, 1996: 70)

The Focus of This Research with the National Trust

Responses to traffic dilemmas from public and private agencies responsible for countryside leisure are centered around "management" of the conflicts. This approach commands little understanding of the complexity of public attitudes toward leisure use. The National Trust also falls victim to the more general lack of understanding of car-dependent attitudes and the specific need to have a detailed grasp of the trends, values, and attitudes of its own visitors. Its attempts so far to manage the problems without a clear understanding of the trends have led to the implementation of solutions on an ad hoc and often temporary trial basis. As a result, some of the "green" transport initiatives it has introduced have not reached their potential. In this light, it is clear that this organization needs to provide more than just a tool for providing baseline figures that highlight current and future trends. Instead, it needs a method of data collection and analysis by which the most realistic and effective solutions can be assessed, designed, and targeted in a variety of situations.

Disaggregated travel surveys have begun to identify indicators of travel, such as those characteristics indicative of higher income and standards of living. However, such studies have rarely succeeded in combining socioeconomic indicators with behavioral indicators in order to look at a whole spectrum of factors that shape behavior. Much exists in the realm of cultural research or sociological studies investigating car-dependent attitudes, value systems, or environmental perspectives that shape behavior. In particular, theories of psychological behavior can provide an established framework within which to measure attitudes and behavioral intention in situations where individuals are faced with a number of choices but are constrained by perceptions, habitual responses, and barriers to behavior. Thus far, travel behavior research has generally not studied attitudes and motivations within any theoretical framework. This research will attempt to avoid this mistake by basing the data collection on a conceptual model based in turn on the Theory of Planned Behaviour (Ajzen, 1991). Constructs will be developed with the aid of this theory and focus-group research, and measured using scales to which factor analysis is applied.

In addition, much of marketing theory is based on the suggestion that there are distinct patterns of consumption associated with relatively stable "lifestyle" groups leading to similar world views, systems of evaluation, and consumption practices. Their survey methods start from the premise that there is little point in addressing the average level of car dependence or average responses to certain policies. Instead, different people must be treated differently because they are affected in different ways by policy. Change invariably takes place at the margins, and this is often ignored.

Once the relationships within the conceptual model have been tested and the salient factors in the decision-making process have been identified, it will be useful to establish whether mobility-management policy would benefit by being targeted at specific socioeconomic groups. The approach tested in this research is statistical segmentation. Segmentation techniques can be used to identify internally consistent and distinct behavioral groupings to allow individuals to be clustered on the basis of their similarities or differences on any number of characteristics. Once groups are identified using cluster analysis, it is possible to make predictions about each group's responses to various situations, marketing strategies, and types of policy to allow more creative and better targeted policies to emerge. The final results will be available early in 2002 (see Anable, 2002).

CONCLUSIONS

Despite the significance of leisure in terms of the volume of travel, little attention has been paid to its contributions to the total volume of traffic. While leisure may not feature as a priority policy area, forecasts suggest that there is every reason to believe that it should be a central tenet of the next major national transport policy framework.

For this to be done effectively, however, much work is needed to refine the definition of leisure travel in a way that assists data collection and its utility with respect to policy formation. At present, definitions are inconsistently used within and across national boundaries. For the purpose of identifying trends and designing mobility management policy, any classification needs to be able to discriminate between the broad set of factors involved in the choice of destination and mode for each type of activity (such as frequency, whether generally fixed in time, average distance, etc.). This will facilitate an assessment of the extent to which each activity exhibits potential barriers to behavioral change away from car use. Indeed, the increasing dependence on mobility management and a multitude of policy-making levels and on targets and indicators at all levels of policy-making necessitates consistency in definitions used and data collection to support this.

A main hypothesis for this research is based on the premise that in any given population, and whatever the organizational setting, a variety of market segments exist that are likely to respond in different ways to different transport policies. In this case study, a major countryside leisure supplier is struggling with the task of implementing initiatives to either encourage more existing "green" travelers or change the behavior of current car-borne visitors. However, the organization is suffering, like many, from an inadequate understanding of the motivations, constraints, and attitudes affecting the travel decisions it is attempting to influence.

The aim is to develop a data-collection tool that will aid the National Trust and other organizations like it in this task. This research utilizes established theories of behavior that provide a structured theoretical framework and shed light on the most effective methods of attitude measurement and the realistic assumptions that can be made from this sort of data. The salient factors in the modal choice process involved in undertaking a day trip to a countryside destination will be identified, and those elements that can feasibly be influenced at the organizational level will be highlighted. In addition, segmentation will allow the organization to assess how effective their efforts can realistically be, and to tailor and market policies to those people most likely to adopt alternatives to the car.

Regardless of the mobility-management context, this author advocates greater emphasis on understanding behavior, particularly by conducting research within a sound theoretical framework. However, the chosen area, day trips to countryside attractions, represents a neglected yet significant area of travel behavior. Countryside leisure in particular is one of the key arenas for conflicts between the aspirations and anxieties of car travel. In addition, notions of leisure as concomitant with freedom, choice, self-improvement, and identity render this subject an exemplary case study of current patterns of personal mobility and the barriers that influence car use in the context of social change and sustainable transport.

REFERENCES

Ajzen, I. 1991. "The Theory of Planned Behaviour." *Organisational Behaviour and Human Decision Processes* 50: 179–211.

Anable, J. 2000. "New Issues, New Methods: A Segmentation Approach to Leisure Travel Demand." Paper presented to IATBR 2000 conference, Gold Coast, Australia.

Anable, J. 2002. "Mobility Management in the Leisure Sector: The Application of Psychological Theory and Behavioral Segmentation." Unpublished doctoral thesis, Imperial College, London.

Department of Transport (DoT). 1989. *National Road Traffic Forecasts*. London: HMSO.

Department of Transport, Environment and the Regions (DETR). 1997a. *Transport Statistics Report Great Britain*. London: HMSO.

DETR. 1997b. *1994/1996 National Travel Survey Report*. London: HMSO.

DETR. 1998a. *Transport Trends: 1998 Edition*. London: HMSO.

DETR. 1998b. *A New Deal for Transport: Better for Everyone*. London: HMSO.

Glyptis, S. 1995. "Recreation and the Environment: Challenging and Changing Relationships." In D. Leslie, ed., *Tourism and Leisure: Towards the Millennium.* Eastbourne: LSA Publications.

Horna, J. 1994. *The Study of Leisure: An Introduction.* Toronto: Oxford University Press.

Leisure Consultants. 1997. *Leisure Forecasts 1997–2001.* Vol. 2: *Leisure Away from Home.* Sudbury: Leisure Consultants.

Liniado, M. 1996. *Car Culture and Countryside Change.* London: The National Trust.

Martin, B., and S. Mason. 1998. *Transforming the Future: Rethinking Free Time and Work.* Sudbury: Leisure Consultants.

Mintel. 1998. *Days Out.* Leisure Intelligence Series. London: Mintel International Group.

Potter, S. 1997. *Vital Travel Statistics: A Compendium of Data and Analysis about Transport Activity in Britain.* London: Landor Publishing.

CHAPTER TWENTY-FOUR

The Impact of Day Tourism on the Environment and Sustainability

The Northwestern Mediterranean Arc

Cristina Capineri
and Gianfranco Spinelli

INTRODUCTION

The Northwestern Mediterranean Arc has witnessed profound changes in land use and mobility patterns in the last twenty years. It is a wide area marked by cultural, social, and economic differences, which nevertheless exhibits some common features, such as landscape and tourist resources. In fact, tourism has had an important impact, which is even stronger in coastal areas characterized by a mixture of uses and activities (port activities, second homes, heavy industries, natural parks, etc.). With respect to communications, the changes have been significant not only in infrastructure but in the substance and pattern of flows and in the functional redefinition of nodes. In fact, besides the increase in traffic flow, numbers of vehicles, and gasoline use, the nodes that were the main pivots of the Mediterranean exchanges—ports—have lost their original function and organizational role in connection with global trends (de-industrialization, crisis of heavy industry, etc.) in favor of airports, which represent the new pivots of long- and medium-distance exchanges.

This chapter focuses on the impact of *short-stay* tourism on mobility. This kind of tourism has experienced strong growth in tandem with the increase in the number of private cars, the rise in living standards, and the im-

provement of communications. It plays an important role in territorial organization, in a different way than does traditional *long-stay* tourism. The analysis is an attempt to evaluate areas of day tourism by assessing the accessibility of the main resorts on the coast to the catchment basins in the inland. The results indicate areas that are likely to be subjected to the impact of day tourism and to traffic congestion and suggest policy implications.

THE RESEARCH FRAMEWORK

The following contribution is part of the work being conducted by the research unit on urban change and the environment in the northwestern Mediterranean of the Italian program HDGEG (Human Dimensions of Global Environmental Change). This unit has studied the human dimensions of environmental change with respect to urban spaces (which are predominant in this area) through the following indicators: the changing pattern of land cover and land use, urban growth (housing, infrastructure), the growing impact of motor vehicle traffic, and the response of urban planning (Cortesi, Capineri, and Spinelli, 1996).

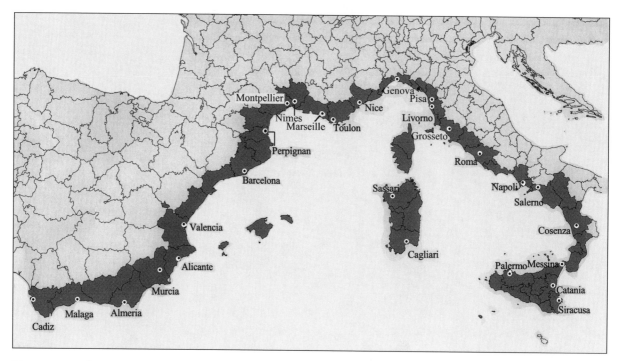

Figure 24.1 The Northwestern Mediterranean Arc

The study area is the Northwestern Mediterranean Arc, from the Strait of Gibraltar to the Sicilian Channels, which includes the most important Mediterranean islands (Sicily, Sardinia, Corsica, and the Balearic). Advanced countries are situated along the arc; the most important historical towns are concentrated there, the intensity of land occupation and use is heavy, and the flows of goods and people are growing. The demographic pressure is also very high, due to new residential choices (the sunbelt effect), tourist attractions, and immigration flows from the opposite shores of the Mediterranean. The European regions situated along the arc have much in common in terms of heritage, development patterns, opportunities, and the environmental problems they have to face; they create a sort of cultural entity[1] (Fig. 24.1).

THE PROCESS OF URBAN CHANGE IN THE NORTHWESTERN MEDITERRANEAN

Despite the huge differences deriving from their history, language, and religion, the civilizations that surround the Mediterranean have in common the fact that a large number of urban centers are established there. A network of towns and villages grew up fairly early on and has developed over thousands of years; as Gottman recalls (1984), the Mediterranean area took shape around these networks, with towns as the pivots of communication patterns, the organization of rural areas, and maritime relationships. The *Plan Bleu* (Grenon and Batisse, 1988) defined as fundamental the study of the dynamics of the Mediterranean habitat, since urban development has experienced remarkable growth in recent years and is representative of the close relationships established between demographic concentration, settlements, economic activities, and the environment. The symbiotic relationship between town and site—that is, the harmony between town and environment—featured the urban development of the arc until the end of the last century. Since then this relationship seems to have come to a halt: the environment has been a barrier to or an opportunity for growth, but is generally a resource to be used. Only recently has awareness of the limitedness of space and the fragility of the environment required closer attention to environmental issues induced by controlled urban development (congestion, pollution, land damages).

More than one-fifth of the entire population on the Mediterranean live in the Northwestern Mediterranean Arc. Population has increased by 5 million in comparison with twenty years earlier (37 million in 1970 and 42 in 1990). The increase (+13.5 percent) has been higher than in the other countries along the Mediterranean coast (+9.4 percent), and considerably stronger if compared with the rest of Europe (+4.3 percent). The coast plays a different role for each of the countries considered: only 10 percent of the French population lives on the Mediterranean coast, compared to 38 percent in Spain and 75 percent in Italy. Thus the coast has a marginal role in France, an important role in Spain, and a decisive role in Italy.

A direct consequence of population increase has been the spread of built-up areas. Housing stock increased by 7.2 million (+57 percent) between 1970 and 1990. The highest increase occurred in Spain, where housing stock has doubled, especially in the provinces of Alicante, Gerona, and Malaga. Even more meaningful are the 3 million new houses on the Italian Tyrrhenian side, where the rather low demographic increase (6.4 percent in 1970–90) has been accompanied by a 49 percent increase in housing stock. French departments reveal a balance between demographic development and housing.

Furthermore, the number of second homes has almost tripled, particularly in the recently developed tourist areas (Malaga, northern Sardinia, and Calabria) and in areas that are affected by metropolitan spillover (Tarragona and Gerona, next to Barcelona). Second home users add to the resident population, using space and resources for only a limited time (holidays, vacations, weekends). This is a relevant phenomenon, as it may be considered a proxy of residence changes: people begin using their second home as a permanent residence.

CHANGES IN TRANSPORT NODES AND PATTERNS OF TRAFFIC FLOW

Ports, once the centers of power and control in the Mediterranean area, have lost their traditional role and are now more involved with logistics of the transport cycle (e.g., Genoa) or have become industrial incubators of high-tech centers. Most of them have been replaced by airports (i.e., Barcelona, Alicante, Almeria). If traditional gateways are at a standstill, other ports are compensating (La Spezia, Livorno, Almeria, etc.), and they specialize (container traffic or particular goods) and attract SME

settlements.[2] Nowadays airports are the real gateways. The Spanish nodes have the highest level of international traffic (>60 percent of total passenger traffic), due to strong mass tourism flows, while in Italy and France the rate is much lower (35 to 45 percent). New nodes are emerging in dynamic areas (Almeria, Granada, Perpignan, Hyeres, Montpellier, Trapani), especially in connection with innovative activities (science parks or high-tech sectors) or tourism. There are still few interconnection nodes, where two or more fast transport networks (in particular rail and air) are directly linked (Pisa, Rome, and Marseille).

In the northwestern Mediterranean, the transformation has affected mobility patterns more than infrastructures, which follow the existing road and rail networks along the shoreline. Networks have developed in terms of length, but more in terms of quality (widening of roads, straightening of tracks, improvements in interconnections, etc.). Still difficult to solve are the problems associated with road networks in historic towns, town centers, and steep coastal areas. In fact, transport infrastructure requires more than 10 percent of total urban area, and in some cases as much as 40 to 50 percent of land use. But if a new town with recent urban planning can easily adapt to private cars, in historical towns of the NWM the intense use of private cars leads to a denial of freedom of movement and interaction. This is one reason why urban planning has devoted much attention to intra-urban traffic control (traffic restrictions, pedestrian areas, etc.) in order to give the town back, at least partially, to its citizens.

Most of the traffic over short or medium distances consists of private cars, which causes a concentration of flows on roads bordering the metropolitan areas, especially on highways that are also used as bypasses around city centers. Long-distance flows take place by air and generally have a north–south direction rather than a coast-to-coast (east–west) direction. The crucial areas are the junctions between the main routes heading inland and the coastal axes, where heavy local flows add to considerable national and international flows.

THE CAR INDEX AND FUEL CONSUMPTION

The worst environmental impact has been caused by the increase in the number of vehicles: in the early 1990s there were approximately 20 million cars (one for every two inhabitants), plus the numerous motorcycles and scooters that are typical of Mediterranean areas. The motor index (the ratio of inhabitants to cars) grew from 4.6 in 1970 to 2.1 in 1990. The highest rates are found in large urban areas or in areas with poorer infrastructure networks or public transport, where the car is the only alternative.

Another indicator of environmental impact is fuel consumption, as pollution is caused mainly by the emission of substances following combustion. These sources indicate the quantity of fuel sold but not the amount actually used; in fact, a detailed survey on the Ligurian coast has shown that highway traffic accounts for approximately 10 percent of total sales. It is not yet possible to establish a precise relationship between fuel consumption and pollution, but it is a useful indicator of mobility and its environmental consequences.

New Trends in Tourism

Tourism is the leading activity for most regions of the arc. It is often based on a continuity of landscapes—for example, from France to Italy—and on traditional activities (i.e., flower growing from the Maritime Alps to Liguria).[3] Nevertheless, new areas are emerging in Spain (Costa Blanca d'Alicante and Costa Brava), generally in connection with mass tourism from northern European countries, while in Italy more environmentally concerned and elite areas are emerging (south of Tuscany, Calabria, Sardegna, and Corsica). The most interesting aspect is the diversification of tourism: rural tourism, which implies an integration between the coast and the inland; and "third age" and group tourism, which require adjustments of the existing infrastructures.

Nevertheless, recent trends in tourist flows show a decrease in traditional tourism (people spending at least one night in the tourist resort, registering in hotels, camping sites, etc.). In the last twenty years, the number of hotels has decreased in most of the coastal provinces: from 9,568 in 1983 to 8,267 in 1996. The drop has occurred in places of long-established tourism, such as Liguria, the northern Tyrrhenian, and the coast of Versilia. But the number of beds is increasing almost everywhere along the coast, again in provinces of consolidated tourism: this may indicate a trend toward larger hotels.

Nevertheless, tourist flows have increased, particularly in Spain (nearly 50 percent), while in Italy and France the increase has been about 35 percent, with smaller increases in traditional tourist areas (Cote d'Azur, Riviera, Versilia). The length of stay has decreased from the typical five days of the 1970s to around four days in Spain (with higher values in the Baleares with five to six days) and about two to three days in France and Italy.

A New Way of Tourism: Day Tourism

The decrease in traditional tourism has been accompanied by another way of spending free time since the early 1970s: day tourism, or commuter tourism. The effect of day tourism is shown in the increase in demographic pressure by a population (the fourth population or city users defined by Martinotti, 1988) that exploits the coast; such pressure increases in relation to the demographic weight of the hinterland. The southern regions of Spain and Italy are still weakly affected by this process, while it is relevant on the coast of Lazio, due to the huge basin of Rome and the growing areas of Latina and Frosinone. On the other hand, the Tuscan and Ligurian coasts and the Cote d'Azur are affected by heavy commuting tourist flows that originate from the densely populated interior regions of Milan and Turin, thus increasing the saturation process of the coast. Some preconditions for the development of day tourism are second homes, car ownership, and accessibility.

The Main Features of Day Tourism

Day tourism (sometimes defined as non-tourism) refers to people who spend just a day or a weekend at a resort. It produces a heavy environmental impact, as it relies primarily on private cars as the means of travel; it uses resources (natural, environmental, etc.) very intensively; it is less linked to seasonal changes; it requires services for daily needs; it plays an important role in territorial organization in terms of facilities required; from a psychological point of view, the commuter tourist does not experience the true essence of the place visited, even less so than a second-home owner, who often becomes part of the community; and it may lead to long-stay tourism.

An Evaluation of Day Tourism

This analysis is an attempt to identify potential areas and impacts of day tourism by evaluating the accessibility of the main resorts on the coast from the catchment basins

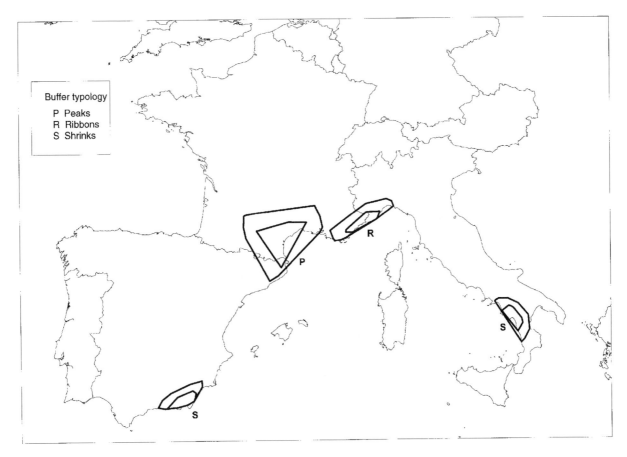

Figure 24.2   Buffer typology

situated in the inland, which are 1.5 and 2.5 hours distant by main roads (Fig. 24.2). The data used were the European road network, with speeds identified for road type and morphology; administrative boundaries (Eurostat NUTS 3 administrative boundaries); and a selection of nodes along the coast, chosen at intervals of 30 to 35 km and according to their tourist functional attributes (tourist guides, etc.).

The Buffers of Day Tourism

Considering the two buffers of 1.5 and 2.5 hours' traveling distance from the coast, three types of buffers can be identified: *peaks, ribbons,* and *shrinks.* They correspond to different ways of converging the tourist population into a resort. Peaks attract people from deep inland and from metropolitan areas and have a triangular shape; ribbons are areas with a longitudinal shape and include areas parallel to the coastline; and shrinks are smaller buffers due to the lack of a transportation network or to morphological barriers, and describe locally limited catchment areas. The typology varies at the national level and implies relationships at different scales: mainly interregional for peaks, regional for ribbons, and local for shrinks (Fig. 24.3).

The distances that can be covered in 1.5 hours and 2.5 hours from the resort differ in accordance with the shape of the buffer and with the local situation. A ribbon-like buffer has a horizontal length approximately three times

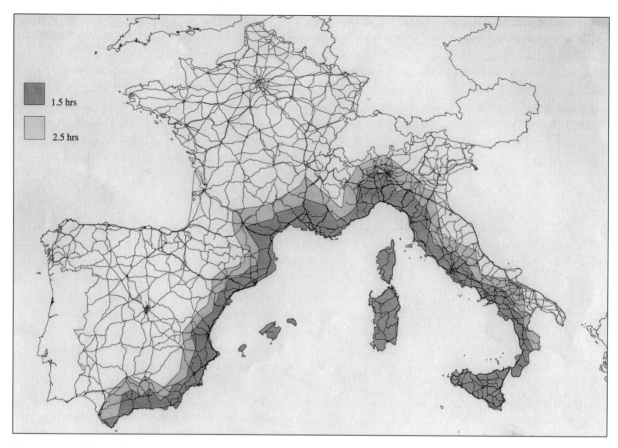

Figure 24.3   The Daily Tourism Virtual Buffers

greater than the vertical length, while peak-shaped buff-ers have a relation of less than twice the length; shrinks have a ribbon shape but smaller dimensions. The mean size of each buffer is 200 km × 90 km for the 1.5-hour buffers and 300 km × 150 km for the 2.5-hour buffers. Table 24.1 shows the mean size of the buffers. The buffers show different relationships between tourist resorts on the Latin arc and the inland. In northern Italy and France, the catchment areas develop deep inland and reach im-portant metropolitan areas, while in Spain and southern Italy they have a more ribbon-like shape, which often shrinks due to the lack of a fast road network. The pat-terns identified are strongly influenced by existing net-works and by connections with the inland.

Table 24.1   Size of the Buffers

Coastal buffers	Mean horizontal distances (km)	Mean vertical distances (km)	Mean horizontal distances (km)	Mean vertical distances (km)
	1.5 hour	1.5 hour	2.5 hour	2.5 hour
Spain	190	83	327	138
France	217	97	371	168
Italy	185	97	312	173

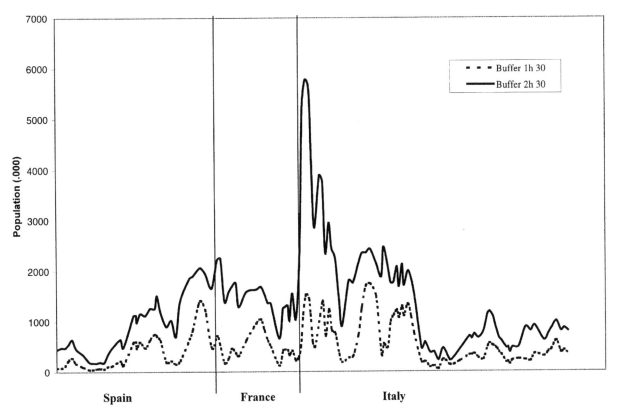

Figure 24.4   Demographic Pressure of Daily Tourism Buffers

THE EVALUATION OF VIRTUAL DAY TOURISTS

Once the catchment areas have been identified, the virtual[4] day tourists in terms of population are included in the buffers. It is difficult to evaluate the substance of this phenomenon, as day tourists do not register in hotels or in other accommodations, so the only estimate that can be achieved is the probability that a certain segment of the population will engage in day tourism. We started by selecting the active population in industrial and service activities, those between 14 and 65 years of age. We assumed that this population does not use the resource 365 days a year, but only for 50 days.[5] The resorts selected

were then classified in accordance with the number of day tourists estimated to gravitate to the node.

Figure 24.4 shows the demographic pressure of day tourism on the coast. The nodes selected for the buffers' identification, which have been calculated in relation to total road distance from Gibraltar to Reggio Calabria, are placed on the X axis. The pressure values on the Y axis are given by the evaluation of the population included in the buffers of 1.5 hours and 2.5 hours built for each node. The line of the 1.5-hour buffer highlights the most populated coastal areas (Barcelona, Marseille, Genoa, Rome, Naples); the line of the 2.5-hour buffer shows peaks corresponding to Liguria (due to the Padan Plain hinterland) and a considerable difference from the 1.5 hours

along the French coast (penetration buffer toward Tou-
louse and Lyon).

POLICY IMPLICATIONS

The identified pattern shows areas that are at risk; they
are subjected to a greater amount of unsustainable traffic
development and for this reason require management
measures. Particularly peak areas are those more subjected to congestion and strong environmental impact
due to their association with densely metropolitan areas. The ribbon areas show a local scale gravitation or
point-like accessibility through airports, for example. The
shrink areas are less subjected to the impact of day tourism
but may be subjected to point-like accessibility through
airports, for example, generally linked to mass tourism.

In all cases, a policy of loisirs[6] is needed, and it requires
that both the local level and the global level be taken into
account in order to stimulate the creation of network-
distributed tourist resources; differentiate resources and
attractions; develop new forms of tourist demand according to the new management of free time; improve
public transport even for free time, although it generally
follows personal choices and requirements; and consider
restriction and protection policies (limited numbers of
admissions, etc.).

In conclusion, the Northwestern Mediterranean Arc
is the theater of new technological paradigms (i.e., the
high-tech sector of the French coast), of regional planning policies (i.e., the high industrial decentralization
on the Italian coast, less strong in France and almost absent in Spain), of new economic location strategies (i.e.,
the diffusion of multinational enterprises), and of geo-
political factors (the new Eastern–Western European relationships) that imply new territorial organizations. The
scenarios that emerge are the following:

- *The scenario of fragmentation:* This scenario implies a
  development dynamic based on concentration and
  growth, supported primarily by current national policies.
  This leads to a reinforcement of main urban areas and
  to a decrease in peripheral areas and small and medium-
  size towns, which suffer from the concentration of powerful and high-rank services (the "intelligentsia") in a
  few privileged sites. This reduces territorial competitiveness and adds costs of dispersion and social costs. Environment protection is a residual aspect.

- *The scenario of integration:* This scenario leads to an
  equity and equilibrium scenario and to open territorial
  systems based on a diffused model of development, on
  endogenous capabilities and functional integration of
  the nodes (an example might be the French plan to
  create *"des ilots de prosperité specialisé"* on the coast or
  in the Corse region; or the *Plans d'urbanisme d'interet*
  regional to develop new tourist resorts). The environment and its protection are key issues of development
  policies, which, even if they are growth-oriented, implement planning interventions in response to environmental needs.

NOTES

1. This analysis has been based on coastal administrative units (the Spanish *provincias*, the French *département*,
and the Italian *province*), which provided the available
statistical data and allowed comparisons of situations and
results. The time considered is twenty years: changes
between 1970 and 1990 were considered sufficient to reveal
recent transformations and offer hints for future developments.

2. Small to medium enterprises.

3. From an employment point of view, we determined that tourism plays a different role in Spain, where
it accounted for 10 percent of employed people in the service sector in 1995 (particularly in the Baleari, 24 percent,
and Andalucia, 12 percent); 4 percent in France, and 5 percent in Italy.

4. "Virtual" here refers to what is *in virtus*—that is,
not real, but with the potential to become so.

5. For analytical purposes, the population has been
considered as gathered at the center of the area considered.

6. Policies related to free time, tourism, and entertainment.

REFERENCES

Capineri, C., M. Lazzeroni, and Gianfranco Spinelli. 1996.
    "Mediterranean France: In Search of Balance." In
    G. Cortesi et al., *Urban Change and the Environment:
    The Case of the North-western Mediterranean*, 65–93.
    Milano: Guerini.

Commission of the European Communities. 1994. *Com-
    petitiveness and Cohesion: Trends in the Regions.*
    Luxembourg: Office for Official Publications of the
    European Communities.

Cortesi, G., et al., eds. 1996. *Urban Change and the Environ-
    ment: The Case of the North-western Mediterranean.*
    Milan: Guerini.

Cortesi, G., C. Capineri, and G. Spinelli. 1996. "Urban

Change and Environment in the North-western Mediterranean." *Boll. Soc. Geogr. Ital.,* Serie XII, vol. I, Fasc. 1, 81–105.

Cottrell, A. J., and J. D. Theberge, eds. 1974. *The Western Mediterranean: Its Political, Economic and Strategic Importance.* New York: Praeger.

Dacharry M. 1964. *Tourisme et Transport en Méditerranée occidentale.* Paris: Presses Universitaires de France.

Gottman, J. 1984. *Orbits: The Ancient Mediterranean Tradition of Urban Networks.* Myres Memorial Lecture Series, Oxford University. London: Leopard's Head Press.

Grenon, M., and M. Batisse, eds. 1988. *Le Plan Bleu. Avenirs du Bassin méditerranéen.* Paris: Economica.

Leontidou, L. 1990. *The Mediterranean City in Transition: Social Change and Urban Development.* Cambridge: Cambridge University Press.

Martinotti, G. 1994. *Metropolis.* Bologna: Mucino.

Quinet, E., and C. Reynaud. 1990. "Les flux de transport en Europe: continuités et mutations." *Futuribles,* no. 145: 25–58.

Voiron Canicio, C. 1992. *Espace, structure et dynamiques régionales. L'arc méditerranéen.* Nice: University of Nice.

CHAPTER TWENTY-FIVE

Company Cars and Company-Provided Parking

Piet Rietveld
and Jos van Ommeren

INTRODUCTION

The private car has become the major mode of transportation in all medium- and higher-income countries. The flexibility of the car makes it suitable for many types of use, including commuting, business, shopping, and holiday travel. Many countries struggle with problems related to the growth of car use, such as congestion, noise, traffic accidents, pollution, and urban quality of life. Some countries, especially in Western Europe, have attempted to use fiscal measures (high fuel taxes) to ameliorate these problems; other countries, including the United States, rely more on environmental standards as a solution.

In this chapter we will focus on a particular aspect of car use: the role of employers in travel behavior. Employers contribute to a substantial share of total car use; some 35 to 50 percent of all kilometers traveled by car are for commuting and business trips (see, for example, Salomon et al., 1993, for European countries). The impact of the company car may even be larger, because company cars are also used for private purposes.

Companies have an impact on the travel behavior of individuals in many ways. An important aspect is the choice of location for a business; location often determines a particular choice of transport mode and travel distances for workers, customers, and other visitors. In addition to this long-run aspect, there are also business policies in which medium- and short-run consequences dominate. In this chapter, we will focus on two aspects: the financial and organizational arrangements of business trips, which is an important issue in Europe, and the provision of parking places to commuters, which has attracted much attention in the U.S.

The simplest framework within which to analyze policies to correct for the negative externalities of car use would be a consideration of two (types of) actors: car users and the government. We will broaden the scope of this analysis by including businesses as a third element. Arrangements made between a firm, its employees, and the treasury often have implications that are contrary to the official objectives of the government's transport policy. This is a serious point, because financial arrangements between firms and employees often involve large amounts of money at a macro scale. The unintended side effects of these arrangements may therefore be difficult to overcome by official transport policies.

Table 25.1   European Company Car Fleet Market, New Cars Sold in 1995

Country	Total business purchases (× 1,000)	Total market share (%)
Austria	104	37
Belgium	126	32
Denmark	45	31
Finland	31	38
France	950	46
Germany	1,520	46
Ireland	32	37
Italy	506	30
The Netherlands	193	43
Norway	29	32
Portugal	85	2
Spain	233	28
Sweden	85	50
Switzerland	109	41
UK	1,030	53
Western Europe	5,069	42

Source: The Economist Intelligence Unit.

COMPANY CARS

Data

In Europe, company cars account for a high share (42 percent) of total annual sales of new cars (see Table 25.1). The proportion of company cars in the total stock is lower, however, because company cars are usually sold to other users after a few years. Assuming that company cars are used for four years before being sold, and that the average life of a car is about ten years (ignoring differences in expected lifetime between a car that starts its life as a company car and other cars), we find that the proportion of company cars in the total stock is about 17 percent. The importance for the composition of the total national fleet is higher, of course, because in a steady state 42 percent of all cars began life as a company car. The choice of particular features on company cars, such as higher horsepower, acceleration capacity, fuel efficiency, and safety performance, remains to have its impact on aggregate figures during the whole lifetime of the car.

It should be noted that the share of total mileage traveled by company cars is higher than the figure of 17 percent mentioned above, since company cars are known to have above-average annual mileage. The well-known fact that the mileage of new cars is higher than that of older cars can thus be partly explained by the fact that many new cars are company cars.

Table 25.1 also gives information about differences between countries. High percentages of company cars are observed in the UK (53 percent) and Sweden (50 percent). Much lower percentages are found in Spain (30 percent) and Italy (32 percent). We will not go into an explanation of these differences here, but note that a variety of factors can be suggested, including the fiscal regime, the sectoral structure of the economy, the business culture, and the number of years a car is used as a company car before it is sold for non-company use.

Stakeholders

In a basic relationship between company, employees, and treasury, employees provide services to the company and receive wages as remuneration; a percentage of those wages flow to the treasury in the form of taxes.

The situation becomes more interesting when one realizes that for certain work-related activities, the employees need a car. When employees use their own car for work-related activities (Regime 1), payment by the company to the employee takes two forms: one relates to the remuneration of the use of human capital, the other to that of the private car. The treasury will tax the first component, and probably the second component as well. A possible format is that the compensation for use of the private car will be taxed when it is above a certain level. If there were no tax on the use of the private car, companies could easily evade taxes by using the car-use compensation as a substitute for the compensation of human capital.

In an alternative model (Regime 2; see Fig. 25.1), the company provides the car. This often implies that the car may be driven for personal use. In that case employees may pay for the use of the car; in addition, they probably will be taxed, depending on the amount they have to pay for personal use of the car.

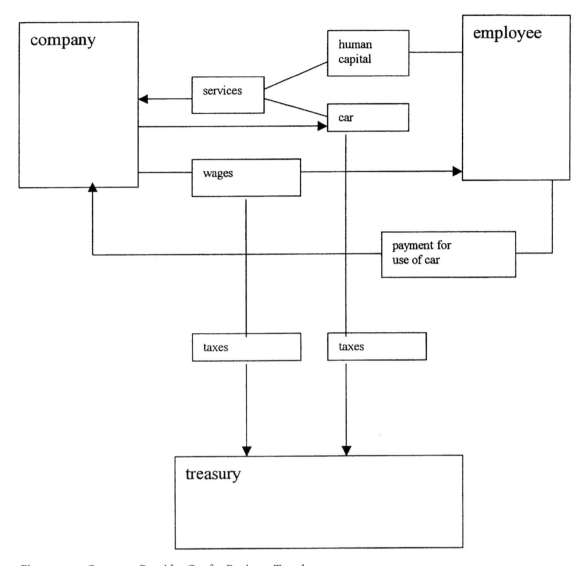

Figure 25.1   Company Provides Car for Business Travel

The relationship between the three parties in the choice of the regime is rather complex:

1. The *treasury* chooses the fiscal regimes and the various values of fiscal parameters with respect to company cars. Factors taken into account include consistency with the overall fiscal system, the potential for fraud, total tax receipts, simplicity, and possibly effects on transport (mileage). The fiscal parameters to be established relate to how the availability of a company car for private use is measured as an additional source of income. They also relate to the fiscal treatment of allowances for transport costs made for business trips with private cars (for example,

based on marginal costs of kilometers traveled versus average costs).

2. The *company* chooses a regime with respect to the options offered to employees. Some workers may be forced to use company cars; others will be excluded; some may have the option to choose between regimes 1 and 2. The factors considered by the company include use of the company car as part of a reward structure, total costs, simplicity, and the potential for fraud. Each firm will have to specify its policy in terms of rules about who is eligible for a company car, the choice of type of car when a company car is offered, the treatment of private kilo-

meters driven by company cars, the way company-related kilometers traveled in private cars are measured, the level of remuneration for such kilometers, etc.

3. With respect to the *employee,* there are two possibilities: The first is that the company does not give the employee a choice; either (s)he does not get a car at all, or (s)he gets a car chosen by the company. This is obviously not an interesting case to analyze. The other possibility is that the employee can choose the regime and/or the type of car. Relevant factors taken into account by the employee include status, costs, comfort (company cars imply carefree car use), and quality of car. The choice possibilities of employees relate to a wide variety of factors, such as whether or not to accept a company car, the choice of the type of car, the extent of use of a company car for private purposes, and the planning of business trips with a private car.

Thus we end up with a scheme in which individual decisions about work-related car use are influenced by policies set by firms and the treasury. The problem is that the major criteria of these actors are not compatible with efficient pricing policies, so that adverse effects on transport may be expected.

Fringe Benefits and Company Cars

Fringe benefits can be provided by firms in many ways, including the use of sports facilities, health services, childcare facilities, subsidized housing, low-cost mortgages, educational programs, and the opportunity to buy the firm's products at reduced prices.

An obvious reason for a company to provide fringe benefits relates to fiscal considerations. When income taxes are high and fringe benefits are not taxed, firms and employees will obviously be interested in the possibility of avoiding taxes.

Another reason is that fringe benefits may increase loyalty to the firm, leading to higher worker satisfaction, higher productivity, and a lower probability that workers will leave the firm to work for a competitor.

A third reason may be market or regulation failures. For example, fringe benefits can give firms flexibility in situations where salary systems are rigid. Also, in particular markets, firms may be in a better position than individual employees to cope with market failures. In the housing market, for example, a sufficient supply of adequate housing may be a constraint for the recruitment of workers in certain countries. Firms that invest in such housing may find it easier than other firms to recruit workers.

Fringe benefits may also be subject to economies of scale when they are provided by the company, so that the employee is better off to receive the benefit directly from the firm rather than to receive the same amount of income and then buy the product himself (assuming that he actually needs it).

With company cars, status effects seem to be involved. Those who are entitled to a company car have a higher status than those who are not. If status is indeed important, then putting a company car at an employee's disposal may be a cheaper way to improve his or her satisfaction than the payment of the equivalent amount of additional salary. Based on the ideas of a hierarchy of needs (Maslow, 1954), it makes sense that once employees have achieved a certain salary level, they start to pay more attention to the social aspects of life, including their status. The question, of course, is why company cars have this status effect, and why this effect is absent with other types of fringe benefits. This brings us to the next issue.

Status and Company Cars

What factors make a fringe benefit sensitive to status aspects? A first factor is that the status associated with a fringe benefit may be associated with that benefit's high economic value. In this respect, company cars may indeed have a substantial economic value, but low-cost mortgages may be much more important. Thus there should be other factors.

A second factor is that status is related to scarcity: when only a minority of people have a high-quality car, having such a car at one's disposal is exceptional. If everybody had such a car, then getting a high-quality car from the company would not really count (cf. Hirsch, 1977).

A third factor is that the fringe benefit should have high visibility. In this respect, company cars do a good job, because a high-quality car is visible in all spheres of life (work, private, and social). In such cases a company car seems to be superior to all other fringe benefits.

A fourth factor that makes a fringe benefit sensitive to status effects is the degree of differentiation. Given the large number of car types available, the company car scores well from this perspective.

One may wonder whether company cars are a unique fringe benefit in their status-enhancing effect. A closer inspection reveals that it is not easy to come up with alternative candidates. Consider, for example, the provision of facilities at home for telecommuting, possibly including a private home office. When we check such a proposal according to the criteria and compare it with the com-

Table 25.2   Employer-Paid Parking Spaces in the United States, 1994

Firm Size (# of Employees)	Total Number of Leased Spaces Offered Free	Total Number of Owned Spaces Offered Free	Total Number of Parking Spaces Offered Free	Share of Employer-Paid Parking in Leased Spaces
(1)	(2)	(3)	(4)	(5)=(2)/(4)
1–19	13,000,000	30,600,000	43,600,000	30%
20–49	3,200,000	10,500,000	13,700,000	23%
50 or more	3,300,000	24,200,000	27,500,000	12%
All firms	19,500,000	65,300,000	84,800,000	23%

Source: Shoup and Breinholt, 1997.

pany car, it does not seem a convincing substitute: its economic value is smaller, scarcity is not really an issue, visibility is low, and differentiation makes little sense as a consequence.

COMPANY-PROVIDED PARKING

Data on parking are not systematically collected in most countries. In low-density areas, parking is allowed everywhere at the side of the road, so that the notion of a parking place does not make much sense. In addition, little systematic attention has been paid to data on parking places and garages on private land connected to residences.

The availability of data on company-provided parking is not much better in most countries. In rural areas, company parking is again not an issue. In urban areas it is indeed an issue, but little knowledge is available at the national level on the parking situation for workers and customers of companies. An exception seems to be the U.S., where employers appear to play a large role in the supply of parking space.

For example, Shoup and Breinholt (1997) report on parking facilities offered by firms (see Table 25.2). In the U.S., firms offer about 85 million parking places free to their employees. Only 24 percent of all firms report that they do not lease or own parking places for their employ-

ees. For larger businesses, this percentage is much lower (about 8 percent), so we can conclude that a large majority of employees in the U.S. work for a firm that offers free parking.

The table shows that the majority (77 percent) of the parking spaces provided free to the workers are located on land owned by the firm; in 23 percent of the cases, the parking spaces are leased. In financial terms, companies would be indifferent about whether to use their funds to lease parking space or to give the same amount of money to those employees who decide not to make use of the parking anymore but instead look for an alternative transport mode such as carpooling. In the case of parking facilities owned by a firm, such a policy is less obvious, because it may be difficult to use the empty space in a meaningful way. The distinction between owned and leased parking space provided by companies is important in the U.S., given the plans and initiatives to require firms that lease parking facilities to cash out their parking subsidies to commuters (Shoup and Breinholt, 1997).

The basic case of the commuting trip is presented in Figure 25.2. Regime 1 is the case in which employees themselves take responsibility for parking. They may park on public roads (free parking or paid parking) or spend their own money for a parking place off the street. Companies may provide reimbursement for commuting costs, which, depending on the fiscal regime, may be subject to

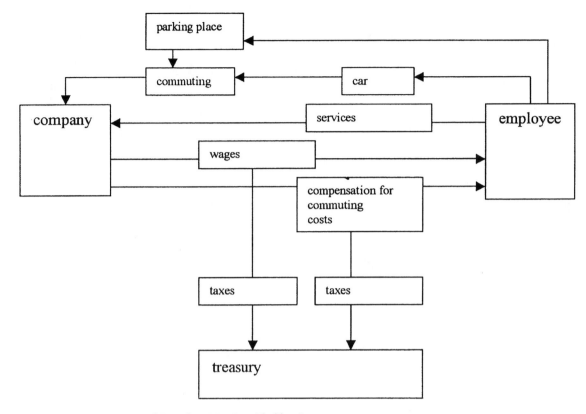

Figure 25.2   Commuting; Parking Place Not Provided by Company

taxation. We will not dwell here on the issue of compensation for travel costs, but note that it may be an important theme in several countries, since it may have substantial adverse effects.

Regime 2 occurs when companies provide parking. Here employees may be asked to pay for the use of the parking place; alternatively, if they do not pay, they may have to pay taxes for the free parking as a fringe benefit.

As indicated by Gomez-Ibanez (1997), free parking is an example of bundling. The consequence of bundling is that employees are not motivated to look for other transport modes. Cashing out parking subsidies (or imposing the obligation to pay for parking) would change the situation: employees would be motivated to use carpooling or public transport as an alternative. Whether cashing out really leads to a change in modal choice depends on the amount of money involved, and on the availability of alternatives. It is clear that in the case of jobs in large metropolitan centers, both factors are more favorable to induce such a change.

It is important to realize that in a competitive situation on the output market, firms are forced to pass on the costs of parking for workers to those workers themselves. If they provide free parking to their employees, the wage has to be adjusted in a downward direction. Therefore, one might argue that it makes no difference whether the employees have to pay the firm for the use of parking space, or whether a cash-out takes place. In reality there may be some differences, of course: fiscal treatment of wages may be different from fiscal treatment of parking money that is cashed out. In addition, from a psychological perspective, employees may interpret cashing out as more favorable ("parking remains free"), since they overlook the fact that the free provision of parking spaces implies a lower wage level. A third possible difference is that employees may display asymmetric responses toward a parking cost cash-out and a parking fee, even if the amounts of money involved would be equal. Finally, not all firms are active in competitive markets. For example, with given salary levels and a given budget for the public sector, free parking for public-sector employees plus a cash-out for employees who do not use the parking facility means that fewer employees can be employed, compared with the situation in which employees have to pay for the use of parking facilities.

In the case where companies lease parking places, it is not difficult to compute the economic value of the use of the parking area, because there is a local market for parking space. When the parking space is part of owned office buildings, such a market does not exist. Gerondeau (1997) mentions a cost of approximately US$35,000 for the construction of an underground parking place. This would give rise to an annual cost of about US$3,500 for a parking spot. If the treasury were to count it as income, it would lead to a substantial tax claim. One should realize, however, that the need for underground parking is clear only in the case of the centers of high-density urban areas. In other places no special investments are needed for parking, so the cost of supplying the place reflects only the local land price. Consider, for example, a land price of about US$100 per square meter and a need for 12 square meters per car. The total cost of land for a parking place is only US$1,200, so that, using the same approach as above, the annual costs would be about US$120, a very small amount compared with total annual income. In this case the treasury would not gain much by adding the fringe benefit of free company-provided parking to taxable income.

IMPLICATIONS FOR TRAVEL BEHAVIOR

The arrangements made between the firm, the employees, and the treasury often have implications that are contrary to the official objectives of the government's transport policy. This can be seen easily, for example, from the earlier section, where the aims of these three major actors were listed: policies related to the reduction of (the negative effects caused by) cars are not mentioned there. An empirical investigation in some countries makes

Table 25.3 Classification Scheme for Alternative Options by Firms and Countries

	alternatives	
Elements of arrangement of company cars:		
Are employees free to choose between a company car and an equivalent amount of extra income?	yes	no
Do fiscal rules motivate firms to introduce the general use of company cars?	yes	no
Do fiscal rules motivate employees to choose company cars?	yes	no
Are there adverse effects on travel behavior?	yes	no
Elements of arrangement of company-provided parking/commuting behavior:		
Are employees free to choose between a company-provided parking place and an equivalent amount of extra income?	yes	no
Do firms provide a commuting cost allowance?	yes	no
Are such allowances tax-deductible?	yes	no
Are there adverse effects on travel behavior?	yes	no

clear that adverse effects on travel behavior can indeed be observed (see, for example, Pepping et al., 1998).

This is a serious point, because financial arrangements between firms and employees often involve large amounts of money at a macro scale. The unintended side effects of these arrangements may therefore be difficult to overcome by official transport policies.

Principal-agent theory seems to be a useful framework for analyzing the adverse effects of company arrangements. A major issue is the lack of information on the company's part about the actual travel behavior of employees, the possibility of cheating, and the high contract costs related to the payment of travel expenses. This leads to arrangements involving company cars and company parking in which there is a lack of incentives for the employee to consider travel alternatives other than the private car. An international comparison of possible arrangements of company cars and company-provided parking would be welcome to identify interesting arrangements that minimize the adverse effects. The dimensions of such a comparative study are given in Table 25.3.

Information technology may help to overcome the information asymmetry between the employee, on the one hand, and the company as well as the treasury, on the other hand. For example, if cars were equipped with information technology, this would enable the company and the treasury to obtain reliable information on distances driven at various times of the day. The availability of such information might lead to changes in arrangements with smaller adverse effects.

OUTLINE OF RESEARCH PLAN

The aim of the research project is to investigate the decisions of companies, employees, and treasuries with respect to company cars, parking, and travel allowances, with special attention to adverse effects on travel behavior. The project will be carried out in an international comparative setting in order to disentangle the impacts of various factors at the macro level.

The following steps are foreseen:

- a survey of fiscal rules in countries/states;
- a survey of policies of various types of firms in countries/states;
- a survey of actual use of arrangements by employees;

- an analysis of survey results from different theoretical perspectives: principal-agent approach, cost of contract, fringe benefits;
- an analysis of unintended side effects on travel behavior; and
- an analysis of alternative arrangements to decrease unintended side effects.

REFERENCES

The Economist Intelligence Unit. *Motor Business Europe.* London: The Unit.

Gerondeau, C. 1997. *Transport in Europe.* London: Artech House.

Gomez-Ibanez, J. A. 1997. "Estimating Whether Transport Users Pay Their Way: The State of the Art." In D. L. Greene, D. W. Jones, and M. A. Delucchi, eds., *The Full Costs and Benefits of Transportation,* 149–172. Berlin: Springer.

Hirsch, F. 1977. *Social Limits to Growth.* London: Routledge.

Maslow, A. H. 1954. *Motivation and Personality.* New York: Harper and Row, 1954.

Pepping, G. C., P. Rietveld, E. T. Verhoef, and J. M. Vleugel. 1998. "Effecten van prijsmaatregelen in het personenverkeer." *Tijdschrift Vervoerswetenschap* 33: 345–362.

Salomon, I., P. H. Bovy, and J.-P. Orfeuil, eds. 1993. *A Billion Trips a Day: Tradition and Transition in European Travel Patterns.* Dordrecht: Kluwer.

Shoup, D. C., and M. J. Breinholt. 1997. "Employer Paid Parking: A Nation-wide Survey of Employers' Parking Subsidy Policies." In D. L. Greene, D. W. Jones, and M. A. Delucchi, eds., *The Full Costs and Benefits of Transportation,* 371–386. Berlin: Springer.

CHAPTER TWENTY-SIX

Can a Decoupling of Traffic and Economic Growth Be Envisaged?

Jean-Loup Madre,
Akli Berri,
and Francis Papon

INTRODUCTION

Sustainable development entails three conditions: general economic growth for the present, preservation of natural resources in the long term, and social equity. Personal transportation in the developed countries is increasingly relying on the private car. Until now, economic growth has led to income growth, which allows car ownership to increase, which in turn favors urban sprawl, which itself requires increased car ownership. Eventually, car traffic growth has followed economic growth. If this form of transportation meets the first condition for sustainable development, the other two conditions are seriously challenged. Oil depletion and the greenhouse effect are the main concerns for the long term. For the present, noise and local pollution are more of a hindrance for the less-well-off, who cannot afford to live elsewhere. Vulnerable users such as pedestrians and cyclists are involved in road accidents at a higher rate per kilometer traveled. Congestion and sprawl jeopardize the operation of public transport. Zoning of urban areas leads to social exclusion.

Thus, breaking the link between economic growth and car traffic growth would enhance sustainability. This break could result from social changes, and a change in opinion. The social changes might include some car ownership saturation in more urbanized areas, and a deceleration of urban sprawl. The numerous conferences on sustainable transport in the research sector, and the debates on the Internet (e.g., France: forum on clean transportation, ARENE, October–December 1998; U.S.: conversation list, Center for a New American Dream, January 1999) are evidence of this change of mind. But breaking the link could be facilitated by a comprehensive transportation, urban planning, and tax policy, including travel demand management measures (Papon, 1998).

AIM AND SCOPE OF THE RESEARCH

In France, passenger traffic grew rapidly during the second half of the 1980s, then showed a clear slowdown from the beginning of the 1990s, which applied as much to the general economy as to the transport sector. (The same was true in most other continental Western European countries.) As the resumption of activity seems to be confirmed, we can question the strength of the relationship that links our sector to the general economy in the long term. This is a much-debated theme, particularly with our American colleagues, who have long excluded any phenomenon of saturation, the thresholds fixed a priori being regularly exceeded. Our approach, limited to passenger transport and focusing on the private car as the dominant mode, internalizes the threshold saturation calculations and shows in the long term a trend that is increasing, although at progressively lower rates.

Our strategy is based on the combination of a demographic approach (following the behavior of successive generations) and econometric studies (on time series at the national level or on a panel of regions). It analyzes the evolution of behavior in a disaggregated way, noting the main heterogeneous dynamic factors between groups of households or motorists. We will develop two points: (1) the decomposition of the dynamics of car traffic into the number of cars and the average mileage per vehicle, and (2) the principal heterogeneity factors of behavior, particularly geographic criteria linked to population density.

REVIEW OF PREVIOUS WORK IN THIS FIELD

Our research team was in charge of the two most recent Nationwide Transportation Surveys (1981–82 and 1993–94) and has maintained two databases on automobile behavior of French households: INSEE Conjuncture survey (1972–94) and SOFRES Parc-Auto panel since 1983 (Hivert, 1998). In particular, the influence of the development of diesel cars, favored by a cheaper fuel, has been stressed (Hivert, 1996). This explains a slight increase in the average distance traveled. Predictions for the future have been made. One critical advance has been the use of demographic approaches (Madre and Gallez, 1993; Gallez, 1994a, 1994b, 1995, 1997). By following the life-cycle patterns of successive cohorts, we can identify long-term dynamics.

Car traffic forecasts are usually based on time series analysis. Bresson et al. (1997, 1998) show that the accuracy of predictions can be improved with panel data econometrics methods and a regionalization of the forecasts. The primary effect explaining car traffic is car ownership, with an elasticity not significantly different from 1. The influence of economic growth on traffic is mainly indirect, due to car ownership. The direct elasticity of car traffic to household income per capita is in the range [0.12; 0.36], an absolute value similar to the elasticity of car traffic to gasoline prices [−0.30; −0.21]. Many other studies have considered factors that influence car traffic, in particular with the aim of reducing the number of car trips to in-

crease the share of public transport trips (see CE, 1996a, 1996b): direct pricing of traffic produces a higher elasticity than do parking charges or fuel prices, and overall car ownership charges.

The last national household transport survey, conducted by INRETS and INSEE in 1993–94, and the comparison with the previous one in 1981–82 provide important data on mobility in France (RTS, 1997). Of course, the location of households outside urban areas leads to more car travel (Gallez and Orfeuil, 1998). Polacchini (1998) has shown, by comparison with housing expenditure, that it is a huge financial burden for those households.

The environmental and social issues of car travel have been shown in Hivert and Morcheoine, 1998: people who live outside urban areas pollute urban dwellers. Policy suggestions have been offered (Orfeuil and Gallez, 1997). An extensive international literature exists on these issues (e.g., Newman, 1996).

USE FOR TRANSATLANTIC COMPARISONS

Previous work by our team has included international comparisons. In particular, we compared the trends for car ownership and mobility in Paris, Grenoble (France), and Montreal (Canada) (Madre et al., 1995; Bussières et al., 1996, 1997), making a distinction between city centers, inner suburbs, and outer suburbs, and using demographic methods. A generation with maximum car ownership has been identified: those born in the 1940s in Montreal, in the 1950s in Paris, and in the 1960s in Grenoble.

Previous prospective work (Bieber et al., 1993) has envisaged three different scenarios for future regional development. The Saint-Simonian scenario is based on a stated centrality (with high-level jobs remaining in town centers) and a large potential for space expansion. The Rhine scenario has limited available expansion space, and is driven by mixed land use. The California scenario, with important potential for space expansion, is linked with liberalism, and is related more to new technology flows than to real estate values.

Several events provide opportunities for transatlantic comparisons. The annual Jacques Cartier conference, held in Lyon in December, yields substantial material from both sides of the ocean. For example, a study of car ownership is available in Orfeuil, 1998 for France, and in Wachs, 1998 for the U.S.

The scope of this chapter is limited to the French experience; however, it may be a useful base for comparisons with other work from other countries presented at this conference.

CAR NUMBERS AND MILEAGE

Our approach, which follows the behavior of successive generations over their life cycle, is particularly well adapted for describing and projecting household ownership of consumer durables, especially cars. Global income is the main factor that explains the effects of the period: its dynamic elasticity fell from 0.8 at the beginning of the 1970s to its present level of 0.5 (see Table 26.1) and will continue to decline as the saturation level is gradually approached. This strong link between car ownership and household income during the observed period cannot be extrapolated without caution from this situation onto a future where the relationship would be weaker. It is for this reason that in our econometric studies of car traffic forecasts (for total levels or by type of network, at the national or regional level) we always introduce car ownership and income as explanatory factors, although this does pose certain problems when trying to separate the effects during the observed period of two so strongly correlated variables. The income elasticities calculated in this way are fairly weak (often of the order of 0.3; see Table 26.2), except for toll-road traffic, for which the elasticity is much greater than 1. The elasticity with respect to the rate of car ownership varies according to the type of network: it is unitary (traffic growing at the same rate as the number of cars, "all other things being equal") for all traffic flows over all networks (estimated from fuel sales and fuel efficiency, that is, liters/100 km), and it is significantly less than 1 (0.8 to 0.9) for the traffic on the whole national network (freeways and A-roads, excluding local networks).

During a period in which the growth in car numbers is slowing, the intensity of use of vehicles might correspondingly increase so as to maintain the continuing growth of traffic (following the linear trend observed since the 1970s). Yet since that period, the annual average mileage per car has fluctuated between 12,000 and 14,000 km. Growing continuously since the middle of the 1980s, it is now around this upper threshold, but this is due more to price effects than to income effects. This progression was stimulated by the impact of the slump in oil prices and was continued by the move to diesel (substituting a

40 percent cheaper fuel). A simulation extending the move to diesel to 50 percent of the market of new cars shows that average annual mileage could reach 15,000 km. However, this scenario is unlikely, since this section of the market has fallen to about 40 percent since 1996, and the gap between the prices of gasoline and diesel will progressively become smaller. Besides, the aging of the stock of vehicles should put a brake on rising mileage. In any case, maintenance of the moderate traffic growth observed at the beginning of the 1990s seems improbable, since it implies that the average mileage per car will exceed 16,000 km around 2020. The potential concerning growth in mileage thus seems too weak to compensate for the expected reduction in the growth of the number of cars.

HOW DO THESE PATTERNS OF BEHAVIOR VARY ACCORDING TO THE POPULATION DENSITY?

In previous studies, notably on the Transport Surveys, we found that the most determinative geographic criterion for the evolution of patterns of traffic behavior and mobility is the division of metropolitan areas into concentric zones: (1) the city center (the most densely populated municipality in the area); (2) the suburbs (the rest of the agglomeration, defined by the continuity of the built-up area); and (3) outlying areas, including rural and agricultural zones situated outside of urban areas.

Staying within the scope of the demographic model (age-period-cohort), dynamic income elasticity increases when moving from the center to peripheral areas. Indeed, households' ownership levels are increasingly differentiated, and it can be assumed that in the densest areas, saturation is almost reached. There is thus little room for maneuver left for responding to changes in incomes. On the contrary, in rural or peripheral areas, there is much less pressure to curb rising motorization rates and car use (and therefore there are still strong responses to changes in income). In such areas car use is often indispensable (expressed by very weak price elasticities).

If we now consider the cross-section elasticities (distribution of motorization and distances traveled in relation to income per unit of consumption at a given date), the standard of living continues to determine the level of car access in dense urban areas, while this is less and less the case for inhabitants of rural areas. Clearly, this cross-

Table 26.1   The Effect of Income and Prices on French Households' Car Ownership: A Comparison between Dynamic and Cross-Section Elasticities

Dependent variable: Number of cars per adult

	Adj. R^2	Income			Purchase prices		
		Coeff.	Std Err.	Elast.	Coeff.	Std Err.	Elast.
AGE-COHORT-PERIOD MODEL 1977–1994[1]							
• France	0.882	0.272	0.019	0.48 [0.41; 0.55]	–0.035	0.008	–0.06 [–0.08; –0.04]
of which:							
• City centers	0.909	0.150	0.044	0.29 [0.12; 0.46]	–0.004	0.019	–0.06 [–0.09; –0.02]
• Inner suburbs	0.933	0.124	0.022	0.22 [0.14; 0.30]	0.005	0.009	— [>–0.02]
• Outer suburbs	0.955	0.329	0.022	0.55 [0.48; 0.62]	–0.067	0.014	–0.11 [–0.16; –0.07]
CROSS-SECTION MODELS[2]							
• France							
1977–79	0.665	0.162	0.005	0.38 [0.36; 0.40]			
1992–94	0.504	0.185	0.006	0.33 [0.32; 0.34]			
of which:							
• City centers							
1977–79	0.665	0.179	0.008	0.44 [0.40; 0.48]			
1992–94	0.505	0.206	0.011	0.40 [0.36; 0.44]			
• Inner suburbs							
1977–79	0.721	0.185	0.008	0.42 [0.38; 0.46]			
1992–94	0.552	0.220	0.011	0.39 [0.36; 0.43]			
• Outer suburbs							
1977–79	0.714	0.164	0.008	0.38 [0.35; 0.42]			
1992–94	0.601	0.166	0.010	0.28 [0.25; 0.31]			

Source: INSEE Household Conjuncture Surveys (1977–94).

Notes:

1. This model also contains dummy variables for 14 age groups and for 15 generations; income is represented by real income per unit of consumption (Oxford scale); data are grouped by age before estimation; elasticities are calculated for 1994.

For each cohort, time-series have been calculated using the "short panel" structure of the surveys (a household is interviewed for two successive years); it doubles the accuracy of elasticity estimates.

2. This model also contains dummy variables for 16 age groups; income is represented by income per unit of consumption for each zone; data are grouped by 5-year age bands and 10 income groups; as prices are supposed to be the same for all households in a given period, price effects cannot be estimated from a cross-section analysis.

Confidence intervals (with a probability of 95%) for elasticities are shown between brackets. Only one bound of an interval is mentioned if the other bound has the wrong sign (negative for income elasticities and positive for price elasticities).

Table 26.2   The Effect of Income and Prices on French Households' Car Use: A Comparison between Dynamic and Cross-Section Elasticities

Dependent variable: Average annual mileage per household

	Adj. R^2	Income			Total Cost		
		Coeff.	Std Err.	Elast.	Coeff.	Std Err.	Elast.
AGE-PERIOD-COHORT MODEL 1977–1994[1]							
France	0.840	4469	174	0.29 [0.27; 0.31]	–7111	397	–0.46 [–0.51 ; –0.41]
of which:							
• City centers	0.901	1141	389	0.09 [0.03; 0.15]	–3581	896	–0.28 [–0.42; –0.14]
• Inner suburbs	0.918	3693	329	0.24 [0.20; 0.28]	–10883	740	–0.70 [–0.79; –0.61]
• Outer suburbs and rural	0.954	7063	780	0.39 [0.30; 0.48]	–6631	879	–0.37 [–0.47; –0.27]
CROSS-SECTION MODELS[2]							
France							
1977–79	0.678	6406	178	0.59 [0.56; 0.62]			
1992–94	0.523	8646	221	0.58 [0.55; 0.61]			
of which:							
• City centers							
1977–79	0.668	5874	267	0.59 [0.54; 0.64]			
1992–94	0.523	7215	310	0.59 [0.54; 0.64]			
• Inner suburbs							
1977–79	0.717	6982	315	0.60 [0.55; 0.65]			
1992–94	0.553	9362	363	0.62 [0.57; 0.67]			
• Outer suburbs and rural							
1977–79	0.710	6960	318	0.65 [0.59; 0.71]			
1992–94	0.585	9990	410	0.58 [0.53; 0.63]			

Source: INSEE Household Conjuncture Surveys (1977–94).

Notes:

1. This model also contains dummy variables for 14 age groups and for 15 generations; income is represented by total expenditure per capita; data are grouped by age before estimation; elasticities are calculated for 1994.

2. This model also contains dummy variables for 16 age groups; income is represented by household income; data are grouped by 5-year age bands and 10 income groups; as prices are supposed to be the same for all households at the same period, price effects cannot be estimated from a cross-section analysis.

Confidence intervals (with a probability of 95%) for elasticities are shown between brackets.

Table 26.3   Evolution of Modal Split in Paris City, Inner Suburbs, and Outer Suburbs

Persons aged 6 and above, living in the Île-de-France region

Areas of residence	Modes			
	Walk	Car	Public transport	Two-wheelers
HOUSEHOLD TRANSPORT SURVEY 1976				
• Paris city	51	18	29	2
• Paris inner suburbs	42	32	20	5
• Paris outer suburbs and rural	35	43	14	8
• Île-de-France region	42	33	20	5
HOUSEHOLD TRANSPORT SURVEY 1983				
• Paris city	48	20	31	1
• Paris inner suburbs	39	37	21	2
• Paris outer suburbs and rural	32	49	15	4
• Île-de-France region	38	38	21	3
HOUSEHOLD TRANSPORT SURVEY 1991				
• Paris city	45	21	33	1
• Paris inner suburbs	36	41	21	2
• Paris outer suburbs and rural	26	57	15	2
• Île-de-France region	34	43	21	2

Source: DREIF General Transport Surveys (1976-1991).

Notes:
   Total may not equal 100% because of rounding errors.
   Walking decreases regularly in all areas of residence, but remains higher in more central locations.
   The car changes little for Paris dwellers (+3% over 15 years), but increases faster for the residents of outer suburbs (+14% over 15 years).
   Public transport is relatively stable, or slightly increasing in central areas where huge investment has occurred (RER).
   Cycling has been marginalized before 1976 in Paris, before 1983 in the suburbs.

section elasticity cannot be interpreted as a dynamic long-term elasticity, since it fell significantly between the late 1970s and the mid-1990s. It reaches a much weaker value than the dynamic elasticity. In contrast, for inhabitants of city centers, the income elasticity of motorization remains relatively stable and is not significantly different from the dynamic elasticity.

It is thus in the densest and most central urban areas that the decoupling of growth in car use and economic growth is most marked. This is because congestion and parking problems restrict the development of the car, while walking and two-wheeled transport can be used for short trips, and public transport for longer journeys (see Table 26.3 for the case of Île-de-France). In less dense areas, due to a lack of real substitutes for the car, saturation thresholds are still a long way away, and the link between income growth and increases in car use and mobility remain strong, even though they too are tending to become weaker.

The contrast in the patterns of car use according to the population density of an area should become even more marked, particularly with a strong upturn in economic activity. However, this perspective only partially relieves the threat of worsening congestion in dense urban areas. Indeed, inhabitants of peripheral zones will continue to travel to city centers, thus generating an increasing number of traffic jams, which will also reach out toward peripheral areas. Intermodal transport systems for radial traffic journeys and the development of light public transport from suburb to suburb could slow down this extension of congestion.

Conclusions and Perspectives

In conclusion, the consequences of these contrasting movements at a regional or national level will be greatly determined by the future of urban sprawl. Is it possible that the slowdown in urban sprawl that may be presently discernible (cf. differences between 1995 observations and forecasts for the 1975–82–90 trend for French departments) is linked to the depressed economic climate that began in the 1990s? If this slowdown continues, the behavior patterns of inhabitants of dense urban zones will remain dominant and the decoupling of car traffic growth and economic growth will be reinforced.

Future work by our team should provide more accurate insight into these issues. Prospective work consists in building scenarios that rely on qualitative and quantitative methods after accumulated long-period observations. Specific approaches are needed for the long term that are neither the transposition of cross-section observations nor the addition of short-term evolutions. Two projects will define the "business as usual" scenario: one, on Île-de-France, aims at completing the demographic model by estimating the effect of economic (revenue, price) and supply factors in the car/public transport competition; the second deals with the dynamics of provincial public transport networks. The building of alternative scenarios will begin with the elaboration of a system of indicators for prospective evaluation, including the three dimensions (economic, social, and environmental) of sustainable development; evaluation of the potential for maximum development of public transport in dense areas, the promotion of walking and cycling, and the adaptation of the car to the city (car sharing, carpooling, etc.); and an analysis of what new technologies can likely provide.

The implementation of one scenario not only is the result of natural trends, but can also be bent by political will. Alternative forms of transportation to the private car in urban areas are already on the political agenda, after Law 96-1236 of December 30, 1996 on air and the rational use of energy, and the compulsory elaboration of an Urban Travel Plan in urban areas. There is some underlying contradiction in the prospective work: making forecasts to detect crises that may occur in the future, and at the same time suggesting policies that can be implemented now so as to alleviate those bad trends and prove the pessimistic forecasts false.

References

Bieber, A., M. H. Massot, and J. P. Orfeuil. 1993. "Questions vives pour une prospective de la mobilité quotidienne." *Synthèse INRETS,* no. 19.

Bresson, G., J. L. Madre, and A. Pirotte. 1997. *Comparison of Forecast Performances of Car Traffic: Times Series Analysis versus Panel Data Econometrics.* IATBR, Austin, Texas, September, 31 pp.

Bresson, G., J. L. Madre, and A. Pirotte. 1998. "Régionalisation des projections du trafic automobile: une étude sur données de panel." ASRLF, Puebla, September, 30 pp.

Bussières, Y., J. Armoogum, and J. L. Madre. 1996. "Vers la saturation? Une approche démographique de l'équipement des ménages en automobile dans trois régions urbaines." *Population* 4–5: 955–978.

Bussières, Y., J. L. Madre, and J. Armoogum. 1997. "Prospective de la demande de transport dans les aires urbaines: une approche démographique à partir d'études de cas." Rencontres dans le cadre de la coopération France-Québec dans le secteur ville, INRS Urbanisation, Montréal, 24–26 September, 10 pp.

Communautés Européennes. 1996a. "Pricing and Financing of Urban Transport." *APAS* 7: 28.

Communautés Européennes. 1996b. "Effectiveness of Measures Influencing the Levels of Public Transport Use in Urban Areas." *APAS* 7: 27.

Gallez, C. 1994a. "Modèles de projection à long terme de la structure du parc et du marché de l'automobile." Thèse de doctorat en sciences économiques, Université de Paris I.

Gallez, C. 1994b. "Identifying the Long Term Dynamics of Car Ownership: A Demographic Approach." *Transport Reviews* 14, no. 1: 83–102.

Gallez, C. 1995. "Une nouvelle perspective pour la projection à long terme des comportements d'équipement et de motorisation." *RTS,* no. 48: 3–14.

Gallez, C. 1997. "Présentation des modèles de projection

à long terme du parc automobile." Note de travail présentée à l'Ademe, 23 October 1997.

Gallez, C., and J.-P. Orfeuil. 1998. "Dis-moi où tu habites, je te dirai comment tu te déplaces." In D. Pumain and M.-F. Mattei, eds., *Données Urbaines.* Paris: Diffusion Economica.

Hivert, L. 1996. "Diésélisation et nouveaux diésélistes: les évolutions récentes." Communication au colloque "Environnement, véhicules et mobilité urbaine, dix ans de coopération," ADEME/INRETS.

Hivert, L. 1998. "Le parc automobile des ménages." Etude en fin d'année 1996 à partir de la source "Parc Auto" SOFRES. Convention INRETS-ADEME. Juin. 144 pp.

Hivert, L., and A. Morcheoine. 1998. "Habiter au vert et polluer les citadins: un essai d'évaluation." *Revue Transports,* no. 388 (mars–avril): 98–107.

Madre, J. L., Y. Bussière, and J. Armoogum. 1995. "Demographic Dynamics of Mobility in Urban Areas: A Case Study of Paris and Grenoble." 7th World Conference on Transport Research, Sydney, 16–21 July.

Madre, J. L., and C. Gallez. 1993. "Equipement automobile des ménages et cycles de vie." *Sociétés Contemporaines,* no. 14/15: 59–78. Paris: Editions l'Harmattan.

Newman, P. 1996. "Reducing Automobile Dependence." *Environment and Urbanization* 8, no. 1 (April): 67–92.

Orfeuil, J.-P. 1998. "Trends in Car Ownership and Car Use in Urban Areas." In *The Future of Urban Travel: 11èmes Entretiens Jacques Cartier, Lyon, 7–9 Décembre 1998,* 1–16.

Orfeuil, J.-P., and C. Gallez. 1997. "Politiques locales et maîtrise des déplacements en automobile: une analyse des potentiels de régulation." Rapport de Convention INRETS/DTT.

Papon, F. 1998. "Implementing Travel Demand Management Is Difficult: Some Elements from the French Situation." Newcastle-upon-Tyne, July.

Polacchini, A. 1998. "Dépenses pour le logement et les transports en Île-de-France." Report INRETS/DREIF.

Recherche, Transport, Sécurité. 1997. Special issues on the French National Transport Survey, nos. 56 and 57.

Wachs, M. 1998. "The Motorization of North America: Causes, Consequences and Speculations on Possible Futures." In *The Future of Urban Travel: 11èmes Entretiens Jacques Cartier, Lyon, 7–9 Décembre 1998,* 17–30.

PART VI

Sustainability and Freight Transport

CHAPTER TWENTY-SEVEN

External Costs of Belgian Freight Traffic

A Network Analysis of Their Internalization

Michel Beuthe,
Bart Jourquin,
Fabrice Degrandsart,
and Jean-François Geerts

INTRODUCTION AND SCOPE OF THE RESEARCH

The strong expansion of freight transport throughout Europe is an important source of congestion and pollution, as well as a cause of many accidents. It is likely that this problem will only grow worse, as it is expected that freight traffic will continue to increase in the coming years. This is not a problem that can be solved by recourse to a simple and unique solution; it will require the conjunction of many different remedies. In some places a partial solution might be found in the building of enlarged infrastructures. However, spatial as well as budgetary constraints severely limit that kind of approach. A better spatial distribution of human activities should be encouraged, and various regulatory devices could contain some of the traffic expansion and its invasion of the urban environment. Another partial solution would be the promotion of transportation modes that have fewer negative effects, such as rail and waterway, and their intermodal combination with roads, in order to substitute these modes for the use of direct road transport.

Our research program is focused on this last solution. In this chapter, we present some results obtained from a detailed modeling of the Belgian multimodal freight transport network, which is part of the overall trans-European network. We outline the results of a simulation of the flows over the Belgian network in 1995, and give estimates of the corresponding pollution and congestion costs. We then present the simulated impacts of an internalization of these costs into the users' costs.

In this research, we applied the NODUS virtual network methodology (Jourquin, 1995). It allows the minimization of the total generalized cost of a transport task defined by an origin-destination (O-D) matrix over a large virtual network in which each particular transport operation is represented by a specific virtual link. It assigns each flow to the least costly mode, means, and routes and permits detailed analyses and simulation of modal choices and intermodal solutions. In contrast to the usual GIS approaches, there are no exogenous modal split functions imposed on the solution.

Thus, after this introduction, we briefly review the NODUS methodology. We then outline the modeling of the Belgian freight network and present the flow assignments and modal splits obtained for the year 1995 when only the users' costs are taken into consideration. On that basis, and using information from many different sources, in the next section we give cost estimates of the impacts of different types of pollution in 1995. The section that follows provides estimates of the cost of congestion on the road network through a computation of time lost during peak hours. Finally, we examine for the same year, 1995, the assignments that would result from an internalization of these external costs into the users' costs. The corresponding costs of pollution and congestion are computed and compared to the previous ones.

Only tentative conclusions are drawn, since this is ongoing research. The model is still a static one and does not provide an adequate spatial equilibrium solution to the problem of congestion. The definition of transport operating costs remains incomplete, since we lack information on transport attributes such as relative safety, reliability, and information that bear upon the choice of mode and means. Moreover, some estimates of external effects are certainly open to criticism, and we did not include other external costs that one may wish to consider: costs of noise, accidents, and wear and tear on infrastructure. Finally, the model does not take into account the induced effects on the matrix of origins and destinations that an internalization of external costs should have.

The NODUS Methodology[1]

A thorough analysis of freight transportation over a network, with all its alternative solutions, requires that every transport operation and its characteristics be identified separately. In the NODUS network model, all the modes and means of transportation, as well as every operation of loading, unloading, transshipping between modes, and transiting, are identified and associated with a virtual link. A fictitious expanded multimodal network, or virtual network, is thus created. As this transformation is realized automatically by NODUS on the basis of the characteristics of the underlying geographical network, this software allows very large networks to be conveniently analyzed. In the present case, there are about 17,000 geographical arcs to start with, but the virtual network is made up of about 265,000 virtual arcs.

Appropriate cost functions are attached to each virtual link defined by a specific transport operation. Altogether, the costs included in the modeling have three components: the costs directly related to the vehicles and their crew, the handling costs, and the inventory costs of the goods during transport. Obviously, the costs of successive operations must be added, the cost of every moving operation being proportional to distance. These costs are estimated on the basis of crew wages, fuel prices, main-

tenance and insurance costs, vehicles' capital annuity and speed, and the value of the transported goods. Then, given an O-D matrix, it is possible to minimize the corresponding total (generalized) cost of transportation with respect to, simultaneously, the choices of modes, means, and routes, intermodal combinations being included in the choice set.

The flow assignments are made on the basis of an "all or nothing" principle. It implies the strong hypothesis that there should be no capacity constraint, a hypothesis that is difficult to maintain across the network in the present application, but one that we will try to address in the future. The resulting assignments can be viewed as estimates of transport demand for the different modes and means under two hypotheses: that the shippers are actually minimizing the generalized cost of transportation, and that the (unknown) carriers' tariffs bear a close relationship to the operating transport cost, at least at the margin for "contestable" transports. Both hypotheses can be debated. But even if they are accepted as a good approximation, the results must be interpreted with caution, and the model must be calibrated before we proceed further, in order to take into account some elements that, for lack of information, could not be included in the minimized costs: relative safety, reliability, information, and other services characterizing the different transport solutions.

The Reference Model

The first step of the research is to create an accurate model of the actual freight flows inside and through Belgium in 1995. This "reference scenario" was set up in three steps:

1. Surveys of shippers and observations of traffic along the network were used, along with aggregated published statistical data, to create detailed origin-destination matrixes for each mode and for the ten groups of NST-R commodities.[2] A matrix for car flows was also established. The resulting matrixes provided useful information for defining some attributes of the networks. For example, along the waterways, no loading and unloading operations were allowed for certain commodities at nodes where no such operations were observed. The same kind of exclusion was introduced at some railway stations; they could also be used to exclude the handling of block trains or single-wagon operations at some stations.

2. All these matrixes were then assigned mode per mode

over the corresponding network, and the aggregated estimated flows were compared to the counts observed along the roads, railways, and waterways. This step was helpful for detecting errors in the digitized networks; also, speeds on some links could be adjusted in order to obtain a better fit between some computed and observed flows, particularly on the peripheries of large cities.

3. At that stage the matrixes relative to each freight transportation mode were merged to obtain ten matrixes corresponding to the different groups of commodities. They were used to assign the transport flows simultaneously to the modes, means, and routes through cost minimization. Finally, the cost functions were calibrated in order to obtain a better fit with the observed global modal splits.

As explained above, the model assigns the flows not only to a mode, but also to a transportation means. In this application, the model performed rather well in identifying the types of boat used (300 tons, 600 tons, 1,350 tons, and 2,000 tons or more) on the basis of their different cost functions, the capacity of each inland waterway, and the exclusions mentioned above. Likewise, the information about exclusions and cost functions included in the model allowed satisfying assignments between block trains and traditional trains. Unfortunately, the use of different cost functions for small and large trucks (7 tons and 40 tons, respectively) did not lead to correct choices between these two means. Actually, the fact is that both types of truck are used over long and short distances, according to the sizes of shipments, and no information was available about shipment sizes. We solved this problem by splitting total road flows between small and large trucks on the basis of external information about the use of the two types of truck per distance slice. A comparison of Table 27.2, which gives the detailed results of assignments realized by the model, with Table 27.1, which gives the 1995 statistics on observed modal choices, shows how well the model performed. Both tables relate to national traffic and international flows in which Belgian territory is implied.

Another way to assess the model's performance is to compute the coefficient of correlation between the observed flows and those assigned by the multimodal model. We obtained values of .92 for the waterways, .86 for the railways, and .87 and .93, respectively, for the small and large trucks. The model was calibrated in accordance with the available information on tons transported. Once that calibration was completed, it was possible to compute the

corresponding t/km per commodity group and mode. These results are given in Table 27.3 for flows over Belgian territory only.

MEASURES OF POLLUTANTS' EFFECTS AND COSTS[3]

The methodology commonly applied to assess pollutants' effects on health begins by linking the concentration of particles in the air (PM_{10}) and of tropospheric O_3 (ozone) to the emissions of pollutants, which are functions of the t/km realized by the different modes. The total health effects are then obtained by applying the relevant mortality and morbidity rates to these concentrations and multiplying by the relevant population. Concentration of PM_{10} results from emissions of particles, but also from emissions of VOC, NO_x, and SO_2, while concentration of tropospheric O_3 results from emissions of VOC and NO_x. There are some other effects on health, but the lack of data does not allow us to take them into consideration.

To obtain the monetary value of these effects, their measures in number of deaths are multiplied by the statistical value of life, estimated at 4,452,955 ECUs (European Currency Units, or euros) in 1995,[4] while their effects on the rates of various diseases are multiplied by the cost of the relevant treatment and hospitalization. Note that the effects of the traffic production of ozone in Belgium on the population of other European countries are included in the computation.

Emissions of CO and CO_2 release some carbon, which affects global warming. As for the effect on vegetation, SO_2 and NO_x emissions have a negative impact on grain harvests, while SO_2 emissions damage forests. In computing these effects in terms of monetary value, the value of lost production in the cultivated areas is taken into account.

The results of all these computations are summarized in Table 27.4, and emissions of the various pollutants in grams per t/km in 1995 are given in Table 27.5 for the different modes.

From these two tables, we infer that the total cost of pollution produced per t/km by road transport in 1995 was equal to 17.2 million ECUs, while it amounted to 7.5 and 9.5 million ECUs, respectively, for transport by rail and waterway. Multiplying the total of t/km flows for each mode, obtained from the above simulation of refer-

Table 27.1   1995 Statistics over the Full Network (tons)

	Water	Rail			Road	% Water	% Rail
Group		SW	BT	% BT			
0–9	65,859,842	18,930,991	33,592,966	63.96	465,588,204	11.28	8.99
0	3,932,810	492,649	732,467	59.79	49,618,723	7.18	2.24
1	3,528,934	1,171,755	526,938	31.02	64,476,087	5.06	2.44
2	4,706,449	1,402,576	6,682,903	82.65	5,790,638	25.33	43.51
3	10,062,680	1,232,571	955,215	43.66	22,870,753	28.65	6.23
4	4,809,562	1,643,371	7,773,560	82.55	4,963,375	25.06	49.07
5	3,241,368	6,380,784	5,044,473	44.15	28,912,266	7.44	26.22
6	27,439,906	1,685,724	1,415,778	45.65	148,044,643	15.37	1.74
7	3,614,798	194,871	606,092	75.67	10,837,438	23.70	5.25
8	3,996,431	2,825,849	452,000	13.79	42,702,124	8.00	6.56
9	526,904	1,900,841	9,403,540	83.18	87,372,157	0.53	11.40

(block trains = BT, single wagons = SW)

Table 27.2   Assigned Flows over the Full Network (tons, 1995)

	Water	Rail			Road	% Water	% Rail
Group		SW	BT	% BT			
0–9	65,802,292	19,424,746	34,394,050	63.91	475,124,181	11.06	9.05
0	4,140,610	399,201	517,541	56.45	49,718,980	7.56	1.67
1	3,912,785	1,164,644	318,870	21.49	64,307,472	5.61	2.13
2	4,659,666	2,064,780	6,064,780	74.60	5,767,463	25.11	43.81
3	10,146,089	1,295,429	1,892,309	59.36	21,787,376	28.89	9.08
4	3,626,551	1,842,912	7,921,922	81.13	6,043,059	18.66	50.24
5	3,192,463	6,639,893	5,031,532	43.11	28,730,430	7.32	26.77
6	27,565,196	1,134,132	1,236,267	52.15	148,649,488	15.44	1.33
7	3,675,127	264,962	556,769	67.76	10,756,341	24.09	5.39
8	3,922,653	2,710,122	312,117	10.33	43,031,476	7.85	6.05
9	961,152	1,908,671	10,541,943	84.67	96,332,096	0.88	11.35

(block trains = BT, single wagons = SW)

Table 27.3   Freight Transport Modal Splits in Belgium (t/km and %)

1995	Road		Waterway		Railway	
NSTR	Number of t/km (millions)	Modal split (%)	Number of t/km (millions)	Modal split (%)	Number of t/km (millions)	Modal split (%)
0	3,792	92	190	5	119	3
1	4,767	91	243	5	205	4
2	367	20	458	26	958	54
3	1,417	51	813	30	536	19
4	314	15	470	23	1,288	62
5	2,391	59	257	6	1,436	35
6	7,171	73	2,402	24	284	3
7	694	64	281	26	105	10
8	3,682	83	368	8	404	9
9	6,708	77	123	2	1,850	21
Total	31,303	71	5,606	13	7,187	16

Source: own computation.

Table 27.4   Losses per Gram of Emitted Pollutant (mECUs in 1995)[1]

Emissions of :	PM_{10}	NO_x	VOC	SO_2	CO	CO_2
Effect on health Concentration of PM_{10} Concentration of O_3	88.745	8.061 5.537	1.606 1.419	100.005		
Effect on global warming					0.009	0.006
Effect on vegetation		1.167		1.834		
Total for one gram of emitted pollutant	88.745	14.765	3.026	101.839	0.009	0.006

Source: ExternE report and Mayeres et al.
1. mECU = one ECU / 1000. Since January 1, 1999, the ECU has been renamed EURO.

Table 27.5   Emissions of Pollutants by the Three Modes (grams per t/km)

Emissions of :	PM	NO_x	VOC	SO_2	CO	CO_2
Truck	0.033	0.390	0.016	0.078	0.190	82.554
Rail	0.015	0.179	0.007	0.032	0.075	33.945
Boat	0.020	0.232	0.009	0.041	0.098	0.044

Source: Computed on the basis of Table 27.4 and the TRENEN report.

ence, by the corresponding cost of pollution per t/km provides us with an estimation of the total losses caused by the three types of transport. They amounted to 540.5 million ECUs for road transport, 54.3 million for railway transport, and 53.5 million for waterway transport.

CONGESTION

As briefly explained in the introduction, the applied methodology is a static one; it does not analyze the flows' impact on the cost of using a link, as in a possible spatial equilibrium model. We hope that further developments of the methodology will soon allow a rigorous handling of this problem over such a large network. With respect to congestion, to some extent the spatial effect of spreading flows over the network has been de facto taken into account at the calibration stage of the reference simulation. However, road traffic is slowed during the peak hours, so there is a loss of time, which induces additional labor and fleet costs, as well as an additional opportunity cost for the transported goods. On the basis of the calibrated cost functions, this overall cost of time amounts to 29.69 ECUs per vehicle/hour in 1995; it includes all the costs linked to the operation of a truck (labor, fuel, insurance, maintenance, and vehicle cost) plus the inventory cost of the goods transported. There is no congestion to speak of on Belgium's waterways. On the railway network, there are a few capacity problems on some links, but we do not have enough information at this stage to tackle the problem.

Time lost through congestion was determined in the following way: The speeds on a road during peak hours and outside peak hours are computed by using a flow-speed relation[5] applied to the respective flows.[6] The difference between these speeds translates into a loss of time for trucks traveling this road during peak hours. This loss is then multiplied by the value of time for freight transport and by the truck flows. The total loss is the sum of all the losses on the roads of the network. In 1995, it amounted to 642.9 million ECUs.

SIMULATION OF AN INTERNALIZATION OF EXTERNAL COSTS

This simulation is based on an adjustment of the transport costs per t/km according to the modes' contribution

to pollution, as computed above. The congestion cost was also included in the road cost. Beforehand, the costs per t/km of road transport were reduced by 13.2 percent to exclude the effect of indirect fuel taxes, while the costs of inland waterway transport were reduced by 12.07 percent. At this stage of our research, no such reduction was applied to rail costs.[7] Thus, this simulation aims at computing the effects that a pricing policy corresponding to the social marginal cost of transports would have on modal splits and external effects. Note that this pricing is applied to all the traffic, without distinguishing between peak and non-peak periods.

The same O-D matrixes as in the reference simulation are used for this simulation. This means that there is no consideration of the possible effects of such an internalization of external costs on the global demand for transport services. Moreover, it implies that a similar pricing policy is adopted by the neighboring countries, so that there is no skirting of Belgium by foreign traffic. Table 27.6 presents the results of this simulation.

Comparing the global modal splits of Table 27.6 to those of Table 27.3, we see that this internalization is inducing a strong shift away from road transport (from 71 percent down to 59 percent) to inland waterway transport (from 13 percent to 17 percent), and an even stronger shift to railway transport (from 16 percent up to 24 percent). This global shift does not affect all the categories of commodities in the same way. The strongest shifts affect steel products (cat. 5) toward rail, manufactured goods (cat. 9) again toward rail, petroleum (cat. 3) toward waterways, and chemical products evenly toward rail and waterways.

On the basis of these results, the total cost of pollution under this scenario of internalization could be estimated at 609.4 million ECUs—i.e., 38.9 million less than before, or a 6 percent decrease. In contrast, the congestion cost decreases much more, from 642.9 to 425.4 million. That is a 34 percent decrease, resulting from a decrease in road traffic of only 16 percent. This more than proportional decrease is the consequence of lesser flows in peak hours, hence of higher speed on the less congested roads.

CONCLUSIONS AND PERSPECTIVES OF RESEARCH

This attempt to analyze the impacts of an internalization of external costs, although still incomplete, suggests that

Table 27.6   Freight Transport Modal Splits upon Internalization (t/km and %)

1995	Road		Waterway		Railway	
NSTR	Millions of t/km	Modal split (%)	Millions of t/km	Modal split (%)	Millions of t/km	Modal split (%)
0	3,351	86	367	9	174	4
1	4,241	86	406	8	276	6
2	304	14	698	33	1,141	53
3	1,224	38	1,234	38	799	25
4	255	11	348	16	1,639	73
5	1,477	35	464	11	2,302	54
6	6,271	64	3,144	32	410	4
7	616	60	307	30	102	10
8	3,048	73	534	13	583	14
9	5,578	62	191	2	3,244	36
Total	26,365	59	7,693	17	10,670	24

Source: own computation.

such a pricing policy could be very effective in limiting road congestion and overall pollution. Obviously, however, it would not be feasible for Belgium to pursue it in isolation; it should also be applied by neighboring countries.

From a methodological point of view, this particular network approach allows us to model, with full details, every operation by the different modes and means on every segment of the network. Thus, it can take into account the particular circumstances affecting transport on a specific link. This advantage was well illustrated by the valuation of congestion costs, which were obtained from the grand total of all the congestion costs, computed separately for each segment of the network.

This is only one more step in a research program that our team is working on. Beyond completing the external costs analysis, we plan to further develop the NODUS model in order to enable it to compute a spatial equilibrium multimodal solution, spreading traffic over several routes in case of congestion. Another topic worth pursuing would be an estimation of transport services' relative qualities, in order to start the optimization with a more complete generalized cost function.

NOTES

This research is partly funded by the Services Fédéraux des Affaires Scientifiques, Techniques et Culturelles (SSTC, Belgium). Some of the data was contributed by the consultant STRATEC in the framework of a common research contract with the Ministère de l' Equipement et du Transport de la Région Wallonne. We wish to acknowledge their contribution to this research. We are grateful to B. De Borger (UFSIA), Ch. Koul A Ndjang'Ha (GTM), and, in particular, I. Mayeres (KUL) for their kind help in compiling information on external effects and costs.

1. Useful references are Jourquin, 1995; Jourquin and Beuthe, 1996; and the TERMINET report (1998).

2. This substantial work was conducted by STRATEC.

3. On this problem the reader will find abundant information in the ExternE reports of the European Commission (DG12), and in the publications by De Borger, Mayeres, and Proost.

4. This is a (1995 adjusted) value provided by Mayeres et al. (1996). It is an average value obtained from a number of stated preference European studies; it includes the value of life for relatives, the loss of revenue, and the medical and police costs.

5. Formula recommended in the COBA manual and

calibrated for Belgium by STRATEC. On average, there are five peak hours in Belgium. The car flows were taken into account for these computations.

6. The flow during one peak hour is estimated as 0.136 of the daily flow on average. This number is obtained from observations of the thirty highest hourly flows.

7. These percentages are based on numbers given in De Borger and Proost, 1997. Note that their computations of taxes and subsidies of rail transport in Belgium would have led to a positive adjustment of cost per t/km before inclusion of their external costs. As we were uncertain about this issue, we chose not to apply that adjustment. This implies that there could be a bias in favor of rail in our simulation. In any case, remember also that some additional external costs should probably be included in such a simulation.

REFERENCES

De Borger, B., I. Mayeres, S. Proost, and S. Wouters. 1996. "Optimal Pricing of Urban Passenger Transport: A Simulation Exercise for Belgium." *Journal of Transport Economics and Policy* 30, 31–54.

De Borger, B., and S. Proost. 1997. *Mobiliteit: De Juiste Prijs.* Leuven: Garant.

"External Costs of Transport in ExternE." Final Report, 1 January 1996 to 31 May 1997, European Commission DG12, Non Nuclear Energy Programme Joule 3.

ExternE. 1997. Issue 5 (July). European Commission DG12.

Jourquin, B. 1995. "Un Outil d'Analyse Economique des Transports de Marchandises sur des Réseaux Multi-modaux et Multi-produits: Le Réseau Virtuel, Concepts, Méthodes et Applications." Ph.D. thesis, FUCAM.

Jourquin, B., and M. Beuthe. 1996. "Transportation Policy Analysis with a Geographic Information System: The Virtual Network of Freight Transportation in Europe." *Transportation Research C,* no. 6: 359–371.

Mayeres, Inge, Sara Ochelen, and Stef Proost. 1996. "The Marginal External Costs of Urban Transport." *Transportation Research D* 1D, no. 2 (December): 111–130.

TERMINET Report (Deliverable D3, Feb. 1998). GIS-Presentation of Innovative Bundling Concepts, 4th Framework Program of the EU Commission.

TRENEN Project. 1995. Final Report, Joule Program of the European Commission, Verkehrwissenschaftliches Institut der RWTH-Aachen (VIA).

CHAPTER TWENTY-EIGHT

Toward Multimodal Networks and Nodes of Freight Transport in the European Union

Hugo Priemus

INTRODUCTION

The relationship between freight transport and sustainability is an uneasy one. In Europe, most freight is transported by trucks, causing environmental damage in several respects, including noise and the emission of CO_2 and NO_x. For environmental reasons, it would be preferable for there to be a larger share of green modes (train, ship, pipe), but although this policy has been a clear goal of the European Commission for many years, the share of freight transported by trucks is increasing rather than decreasing. This seems to be another example of the well-known contradiction between economic and ecological considerations. Shippers, driven by economic goals, prefer transport by truck and consider transport by train and ship to be too rigid, too slow, and inappropriate for door-to-door delivery. In this chapter we argue that multimodality can bridge the gap between economic and ecological purposes, and that the dynamics of European mainports could be strengthened by the development of corridors and multimodal networks and terminals.

We define intermodal transport as the transport of unitized loads through the coordinated use of more than one transport mode in such a way that the comparative advantages of the various modes are maximized and the transport chain is guided as a single unity (Locklin,

1972; ECMT, 1993; van Klink and van den Berg, 1998). Van Klink and van den Berg assert that Europe is now on the threshold of an intermodal revolution. Several developments may support this expectation: the elimination of borders within the European Union, increasing interactions among regions, growing congestion in metropolitan areas, the increase of scale in the transport industry, technological innovations, growing awareness of environmental problems, and government policy.

European seaports are experiencing increasing demand for the transshipment of containers and other unitized loads. The original idea of a container dates (so far as is known) from 1801, but it began to flourish only after May 1966, when Sea-land Service, Inc. moored in the harbor of Rotterdam with a container ship. The part played by the harbor authorities in the introduction and dispersal of containers has been crucial (NEA and KNV/BCT, 1998: 38).

Van Klink and van den Berg (1998: 1) assert that the major seaports are in a unique position to stimulate intermodal transport in Europe and should use intermodal systems as a tool to expand their hinterlands. Notteboom and Winkelmans (1998) also argue that there is a strong relationship between the bundling of container flows in

Table 28.1 Average Annual Growth of Container Transfer in 43 European Container Ports, Five Periods 1975–1996

Period	Annual growth of container transfer	
	1,000 TEU	percent
1975–1982	834	13.10
1982–1987	770	6.66
1987–1991	1,121	7.21
1991–1994	1,509	7.59
1994–1996	2,212	9.21

Source: Notteboom and Winkelmans, 1998: 384.

nodal points within seaport systems and transport networks in the hinterland (Mayer, 1957).

CONTAINER PORTS IN EUROPE AND HINTERLAND CONNECTIONS

Although an increase in freight flows can lead to a process of centralization or decentralization of container ports (Taaffe, Morrill, and Gould, 1963; Barke, 1986; Slack, 1990; Notteboom, 1997; Notteboom and Winkelmans, 1998), for now we consider the location and the place in the hierarchy of each of the container ports in Europe as a given (Fleming and Hayuth, 1994a, 1994b).

In the European Union, the position of Rotterdam is dominant. The emphasis is on the Hamburg–Le Havre range (11 ports), the Atlantic range (9 ports), the southern European range (18 ports on the Mediterranean Sea), and a limited British range (5 ports on the eastern and southern coasts of the United Kingdom). The ports along the Baltic Sea are omitted from the argument, as are the Scandinavian ports. Total container transfer in the European port system under consideration amounted to 27.4 million TEU (twenty foot equivalent units) in 1996, compared with 4.3 million TEU in 1975. The Hamburg–Le Havre range accounted for 14.1 million TEU in 1996, more

than half the total transfer (Notteboom and Winkelmans, 1998: 380).

The growth of container transfer in these European ports has been spectacular, as Table 28.1 makes clear. It has to be said, however, that these figures cannot compete with the even stronger growth of the large container ports in Southeast Asia. For the development of inland waterways, the courses of rivers are a determining factor. For Rotterdam, that is the course of the Rhine and, to a lesser extent, the Maas. Rotterdam is connected with Antwerp and the smaller seaports via coastal traffic. Sometimes the range of inland waterways can be increased by supplying a needed link, such as the Mainz-Danube Canal, or by increasing the capacity of a river section, but for the most part the inland waterway infrastructure is a given.

The emergence of a limited number of strategic locations for the development of multimodal barge terminals is crucial. Here maritime and continental container flows can be bundled and split, so that the inland waterway becomes a trunk line in the multimodal network of freight transport, in combination with rail and truck transport. Barge terminals can form part of the line configuration (combining and splitting of containers on ships), a collection and distribution network (mostly with feeder lines per truck), or part of a hub and spoke network (combinations of barge and rail transport).

Via the Rhine and the Maas, Rotterdam can serve parts of Germany (such as the Ruhr) and parts of France and Switzerland. But via networks of combined transport, inland shipping can also serve as the starting point for more distant destinations, such as Italy, Spain, and the Balkans. If Rotterdam were to take on this further expansion, the port authorities would become interested in terminals and transport services to these areas. If, however, Rotterdam wished to serve new markets, for example Eastern Europe, then the inland waterways would not be able to cope, and the emphasis would fall more on the railroads.

Direct shuttle trains and inland waterway routes between a container port and various destinations in the hinterland constitute the most obvious formula for the transportation by means other than trucks of containers from a seaport to its hinterland (and vice versa). Several of the main European loading centers generate thick enough freight flows to guarantee a sufficient loading level for trains and barges. For a number of places lying farther away in the hinterland, freight flows would be

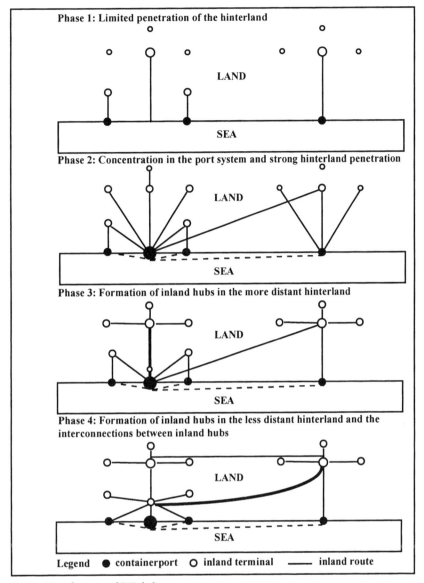

Source: Notteboom and Winkelman, 1998: 392.

Figure 28.1   Spatial Model of the Development of Mainport Related Rail Networks

too thin to make possible a system of frequent direct shuttle trains. This is even more the case for shipping connections; not all places can be reached by inland waterways, and even where they can be reached via a river or a canal, the freight flows may be too thin. Bundling of container flows can offer a future for inland hubs from which directed services could be provided via rail or inland waterway. In the finely meshed collection and distribution networks, freight trucks could again play an indispensable part.

MAINPORTS AND THE DEVELOPMENT OF RAIL NETWORKS

Figure 28.1 presents the spatial model proposed by Notteboom and Winkelmans (1998) for the development of a port-related rail network. The European intermodal railroad network can be said to be in phase 3 of this model. The hinterland network that connects with the Benelux ports actually shows clear signs of a transformation to the fourth phase, although the interconnections between the inland hubs have not yet been completely put in place.

Notteboom and Winkelmans (1998: 391–393) describe the final phases of this spatial model as follows:

> The third phase is characterized by the formation of hub and spoke systems in the outlying hinterland, so that the maritime container volumes destined for the regions concerned become totally concentrated in a few prominent corridors between the loading centers and the "master hubs" in the hinterland.
>
> The intense traffic flows over the corridors make a system of frequent, cost effective shuttle trains feasible and thus improve the competitive position of the loading centers with respect to the smaller, more distant container ports. Along the corridors new logistic nodes develop which, in the beginning phase, actually make little profit from the through rail traffic. In the last phase (phase 4) the number of these new logistic nodes grows through the development of "master hubs" in the nearby hinterland of the loading centers. . . . When the various master hubs have been interconnected via high frequency shuttle trains, the intermodal container network reaches the phase of complete integration.

MAINPORTS AND THE DEVELOPMENT OF BARGE NETWORKS

We now consider some similar developments in networks for inland waterway containers. The geographical pattern of the most important waterways in northwestern Europe is of critical importance here. The Rhineland, with its integrated rivers and canals, is by far the most important waterway in Europe. Inland shipping of containers in northwestern Europe is on the rise. In 1997, total European container traffic by barge amounted to about 2.2 million TEU, a figure that increases considerably each year (see Fig. 28.2).

Inland waterway shuttles connect the Rhine-Schelde delta ports with groups of inland terminals within each of the separate waterway areas of the Rhine (Upper Rhine, Lower Rhine, and Middle Rhine) and the Danube. In order to raise the level of service and offset the threat of competition, the inland shipping companies operate joint services on the various sections of waterway on the Rhine and the Danube through cooperative agreements,

such as the Fahrgemeinschaft Niederrhein, Penta Container Lines, and the Fahrgemeinschaft Oberrhein. In the Rhineland, particularly in Belgium and northern France, the operative principle is direct shuttle service between a port and a particular inland terminal (Notteboom and Winkelmans, 1998).

In contrast with the rail network, no one container terminal along the Rhine fulfills the function of master hub. A possible concentration of river-associated container traffic has not resulted in the formation of hub and spoke systems in the terminal network.

Inland waterway terminals focus to an increasing extent on the complementary relationship between rail and inland shipping. For example, some of the container flow between the Rhine-Schelde ports and Eastern Europe arrives by barge in Duisburg, where it is transferred to shuttle trains with destinations in the Slovakian Republic, the Czech Republic, or Poland. The same phenomenon occurs in the traffic relationships between the Benelux ports and northern Italy.

LINKAGE OF RAIL NETWORKS AND BARGE NETWORKS: TOWARD INTERMODAL NETWORKS

The inland terminals for rail and barge transport are tied together via a number of trimodal terminals. Developments on the east-west axis, for example between Rotterdam/Antwerp and Eastern European countries such as Poland, the Czech Republic, and Italy, demand a combination of inland waterway transport and rail transport.

In northwestern Europe, the pattern of freight flows seems to have reached the phase where a limited number of hub and spoke networks have been developed. Careful choice of location needs to be followed by good design of the corridors connecting the most important inland terminals to each other and to the gateways.

The development of bundling for freight shipments and the resolution of terminal problems depend in part on the development of European and intercontinental transport networks. Shippers are important players in the extension of transport services and networks into the hinterland. We foresee a process in which people will seek to move containers and other freight away from a seaport area as quickly as possible and look for consolidation at an inland terminal. Whoever is best able to resolve the

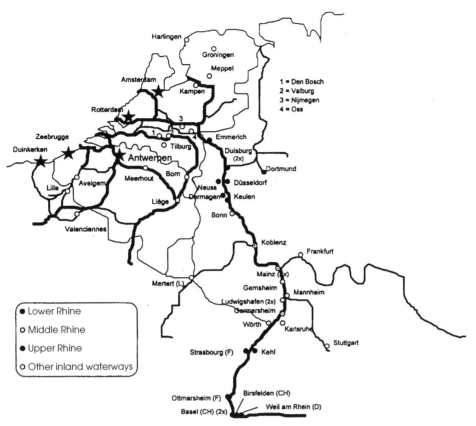

Source: Notteboom and Winkelmans, 1998: 394.

Figure 28.2   Overview of the Container Terminals for the Inland Waterways in
Northwest Europe

associated logistical problems will have the competitive edge with respect to traditional freight vehicle services.

In the trade relationships between the European Union regions (as expressed in flows of goods), the strategic position of the Netherlands, the United Kingdom, the Ruhr, northern France, and northern Italy is evident. For trade flows to continue to run efficiently, we must think more often in terms of transport chains on a European scale. Also, international transport networks must become more clearly visible, in particular networks for containers.

A condition for the successful development of multimodal terminals is their positioning in a network with sufficiently thick flows of goods, in particular goods in

unitized loads. All goods flow prognoses predict the further growth of flows of goods in the years to come, particularly in the container sector. The dematerialization frequently referred to is of great importance, but in no one realistic scenario does this phenomenon lead to a stabilization, let alone a reduction, in flows of goods.

The trend for the volume of goods flows to increase a few percentage points per year yields a favorable perspective, but is insufficient for the introduction of a new generation of fully automated terminals within the foreseeable future (say, before 2010). A reconstruction of the network will also be necessary, with a limited number of strategically placed locations functioning as a hub. Such a reconstruction would lead to shipments over longer door-

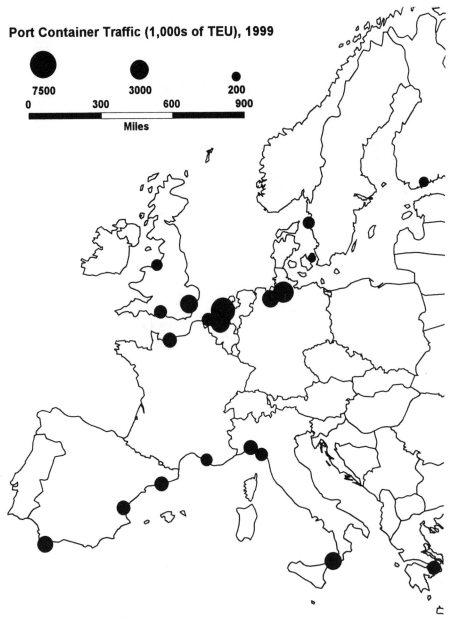

Port Container Traffic (1,000s of TEU), 1999

Data source: European Commission.

Figure 28.3   Throughput of Intermodal Terminals in Europe

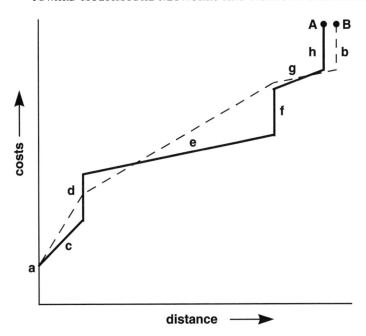

Figure 28.4   Comparison of Unimodal and Multimodal Transport Costs

to-door distances, but also higher transport frequency, faster transport speed, and in particular thicker goods flows—the basic condition for fully automated twenty-four-hour transshipment. The development of a network is necessary, within which cargo can be transshipped via a limited number of master terminals.

Figure 28.3 shows that only a few of the intermodal terminals in Europe have an annual throughput of more than 3 million TEU containers. Intermodal mainports must be developed in a manner comparable to the way that sea and air mainports have been developed. Sea mainports can serve as intermodal mainports (see Priemus et al., 1994); the same is true of air mainports. In addition, there is room for a limited number of intermodal inland logistic nodes between which very thick unitized freight flows can move. Such logistic mainports can be opened via line networks, collection and distribution networks, and hub and spoke networks. Of course, these mainports have to be located at strategic places along busy inland waterways, or at nodes in the rail networks. The greater the extent to which this multimodal goods network can be developed with logistic mainports located beyond national boundaries (a suitable task for the European Commission), the more favorable will be the starting position for the development of a new genera-

tion of automated multimodal terminals, and the greater the chance of a breakthrough in multimodal freight transport.

COMPETITIVENESS OF MULTIMODAL FREIGHT TRANSPORT

The costs of unimodal truck transport are closely related to loading level and distance. We suspect the connection to be curvilinear; the loading and unloading of trucks creates costs at the beginning and the end of the logistic chain. A break comes in the curve with a transfer from truck transport with one or two drivers. We have omitted these from Figure 28.4. The makeup of costs in multimodal transport depends on the position and nature of the transfer points, the detour factor in the logistic chain, and the nature and loading level of the established transport modes. In Figure 28.4, a CD network is supposed:

c = truck transport (collection network);
e = rail or barge transport (trunk line);
g = truck transport (distribution network).

The transfer costs in d and f can be identified (truck–rail, rail–truck or truck–barge, barge–truck). Loading and unloading are shown in the line segments a and h. Multimodal freight transport is competitive only if point A is lower than point B, or if the quality difference of unimodal truck transport can outweigh the possibly higher cost of multimodal transport. Whether this is the case is far from clear. The competitiveness of multimodal freight transport depends (among other things) on whether the depreciation of the terminal investments is included in the costs or can be omitted, as is usually the case with the road infrastructure, and on the extent to which the external costs can be internalized. Whether the transshipment accommodation is efficient is also of importance, as is the level of efficiency of the transport of the separate modalities. In particular, the efficiency of rail transport in Europe, which for decades has been run by companies that enjoy a monopoly, gives rise to considerable concern. Finally, the competitiveness that can be attained by multimodal freight transport largely determines the integration in the logistic chains. The determination of the competitiveness of multimodal freight transport will also call for extensive efforts in the next few years.

Conclusions

The strategic development described here requires, on the one hand, a new generation of inland terminals, functioning twenty-four hours a day, where freight is transshipped completely or partially automatically, rapidly, reliably, and cheaply; and offers, on the other hand, the necessary favorable conditions for the development of such terminals: thick freight flows, a restricted number of main destinations, and connection with several modalities. In addition to the European High Speed Train network, an intermodal network of freight flows should be developed in the near future, and strategic locations should be selected for advanced terminals so that bottlenecks are removed from the corridors and the barrier effect of national borders is eliminated. The changes needed to make this breakthrough toward multimodal freight transport possible are not only technological, but also social: the policies of shippers, the entrepreneurship of terminal producers and terminal managers, and—last but not least—a joint effort by European countries to reduce the impact of national barriers.

References

Barke, M. 1986. *Transport and Trade.* Edinburgh: Oliver and Boyd.

European Conference of Ministers of Transport. 1993. *Terminology on Combined Transport.* Paris: OECD.

Fleming, D. K., and Y. Hayuth. 1994a. "Concepts of Strategic Commercial Location: The Case of Container Ports." *Maritime Policy and Management* 21, no. 3: 187–193.

Fleming, D. K., and Y. Hayuth. 1994b. "Spatial Characteristics of Transportation Hubs: Centrality and Intermediacy." *Journal of Transport Geography* 2, no. 1: 3–18.

Klink, H. A. van, and G. C. van den Berg. 1998. "Gateways and Intermodalism." *Journal of Transport Geography* 16, no. 1: 1–9.

Locklin, P. D. 1972. *Economics of Transportation.* Homewood: R. D. Irwin.

Mayer, H. M. 1957. *The Port of Chicago and the St. Lawrence Seaway.* Department of Geography Research Papers, no. 49. Chicago: University of Chicago Press.

Ministry of Housing, Spatial Planning and the Environment. 1997. "Spatial Patterns of Transportation." In *Atlas of Freight Transport in Europe.* The Hague: Ministry of Housing, Spatial Planning and the Environment.

NEA Transport Research and Training and Koninklijk Nederlands Vervoer/Branchecentrum Technologie (KNV/BCT). 1998. *Diffusie van innovaties in het goederenvervoer. Eindrapport.* The Hague: Projectbureau Integrale Verkeers- en Vervoersstudies.

Notteboom, T. E. 1997. "Concentration and Load Centre Development in the European Container Port System." *Journal of Transport Geography* 5, no. 2: 99–115.

Notteboom, T., and W. Winkelmans. 1998. "Bundeling van containerstromen in het Europese havensysteem en netwerkontwikkeling in het achterland." *Tijdschrift Vervoerwetenschap,* no. 4: 379–398.

Priemus, H., E. Kreutzberger, and J. W. Konings. 1994. "Multimodaliteit: meerwaarde van de mainport" [Multimodality: Added Value of the Mainport]. Paper presented at TRAIL-congress "Mainport Rotterdam," Rotterdam, 26 October.

Slack, B. 1990. "Intermodal Transportation in North America and the Development of Inland Load Centres." *Professional Geographer* 42, no. 1: 72–83.

Taaffe, E. J., R. L. Morrill, and P. R. Gould. 1963. "Transport Expansion in Underdeveloped Countries: A Comparative Analysis." *Geographical Review* 53: 503–529.

CHAPTER TWENTY-NINE

Technological Innovations
and Spatio-Organizational Changes

Toward a Sustainable Urban Freight Transport System

Johan Visser

INTRODUCTION

Social changes and technological developments will affect the delivery of goods in the twenty-first century in many ways. The demand for goods transport in urban areas is likely to change in accordance with demographic and economic trends. Technological developments will affect how goods are bought and delivered. Innovations in information technology will play a role.

Probably the most important change at the moment is taking place in the acceptance of social costs of transport. Freight traffic in urban areas, essential to the delivery of goods, generates high social costs by producing pollution and noise. Also, from the point of view of traffic safety, freight traffic is not very welcome in urban areas.

In many urban areas, freight traffic has been restricted to specific routes and/or time periods to protect the quality of life in certain areas or to make them more attractive to visitors. On the other hand, freight traffic faces considerable accessibility problems because of congestion and restrictive measures.

These problems occur in most urban areas of the world and are as old as civilization itself. To some extent, society tries to live with them. Each stakeholder attempts to find his own solution. In most cases these solutions lead to a sub-optimal situation from a societal point of view. For this reason, governments—local as well as regional and national—are interested in the problems related to urban freight transport.

Research Attention

Urban freight transport problems have been receiving attention in the research field for quite some time. In the early 1970s, small-scale research on measures to limit freight traffic in dense urban areas was carried out in France and other developed countries (Dufour and Patier, 1997). The first experiments, such as those in the UK (Button and Pearman, 1981), started with the concept of urban distribution centers. This was the first revival of a relatively old concept, which had been abandoned when trucks began to be used in freight transport on a large scale. In the late 1980s and early 1990s, urban freight transport again became a focus of local transport research. The concept of urban distribution centers again received attention. In many countries, national and local governments tried to implement this concept, with a lot of failures and some successes. Bottlenecks included the commercial attractiveness of such terminals and the efficient solution of

235

societal problems. Dablanc and Massé (1996) present an overview of the different concepts in Europe.

Research on a European Level

European COST Action 321 is a European COST (European Co-operation in the field of Scientific and Technical Research) Action that focused on modeling and policy measures related to urban freight transport (COST 321 Action, 1997). In the Fourth Framework program, a European R & D program that started in 1994 and ended in 1998, at least three research projects focused on urban freight transport. In December 1997, the ECMT (European Conference of Ministers of Transport) organized a Round Table Meeting (Round Table 108) on "Freight Transport and the City" (see also ECMT, 1976 and 1984).

Research in the Netherlands

In the Netherlands there are two major driving forces for long-term research programs in the field of urban freight transport by the national government. First, it seems that the long-term environmental targets set out in the national environmental policy plan cannot be met because of the yearly growth in freight traffic. A large share of domestic freight transport, the dominant factor in total freight transport by road, consists of urban freight. Second, there is growing awareness that technological and organizational changes offer opportunities to make freight transport more sustainable.

In 1997 a multi-year research program was begun at the University of Delft, called Freight Transport Automation and Multimodality (FTAM). FTAM focuses on the feasibility of a modal shift in domestic freight transport, created by new logistic concepts based on intermodality and dedicated infrastructures (road, rail, or other) for freight transport within and between urban areas. The technical, logistic, economic, and environmental aspects of these new concepts are being studied now. One of the FTAM projects, "Multimodal Transfer Points and Automated Freight Transport for Urban Areas," concerns urban freight transport. In this research project, an intermodal concept will be developed that should provide a solution to the problems related to urban freight transport. An important assumption is that urban freight transport will be more sustainable when local distribution and interlocal or interregional transport are optimized separately. This means small, quiet, zero-emission vehicles in urban areas and large vehicles such as trucks and trains in interregional or long-distance transport. This kind of intermodality

will be supported in the near future by technological innovations in road and rail transportation. It is likely that automated transport systems on dedicated infrastructure above or underground will become available. One of the objectives of the research program is to develop an integral design and define an implementation strategy for this urban freight transport system.

Scope of the Research

The focus is on freight transport related to the delivery of consumer goods to shops or direct to consumers. Books on logistics refer to this kind of physical distribution as final distribution. Although the primary point of focus is freight traffic in urban areas, interregional transport will also be considered. However, no attention will be paid to other kinds of freight transport that also take place in urban areas, such as transport of building materials or garbage, or traffic generated by ports or industrial areas that happen to be situated in or near urban areas.

URBAN FREIGHT TRANSPORT AS A SUSTAINABILITY ISSUE

A European comparison study (Lewis, 1997) concluded that congestion, air pollution, noise, safety, and intrusion are regarded as the most important negative impacts of freight traffic within urban areas. It is expected that accessibility problems and environmental costs will increase. One of the concerns in the Netherlands is that the volume of freight traffic will increase from 13.3 billion vehicle kilometers in 1995 to 45.8 billion vehicle kilometers in 2020 (RIVM, 1997). According to the "Fourth National Report on the Environment" ("Nationale Milieuverkenning 4") in the Netherlands (RIVM, 1997), the national targets for reduction of NO_x emissions, noise, CH emissions, and CO_2 in the year 2010 cannot be met by current policy instruments. The emission of NO_x by freight traffic in the Netherlands is expected to be four times higher in 2010. These targets can be met only if stringent measures are implemented to reduce freight traffic volume ("volume-measures"), or if there are new technological breakthroughs (see Table 29.1).

It is also difficult to meet legislated standards for local air pollution, such as CO, NO_2, aerosols, and noise. Freight transport, particularly urban freight transport, plays an important role in this discussion. The situation in other developed countries will probably be the same.

Table 29.1   Policy Target and Expected Emissions in 2010 in Urban Areas by Freight Traffic

GC scenario [index, 1995]	Emissions in 2010			
	CO_2 emission	NO_x emission	SO_2 emission	CH emission
Van	90	76	18	41
Truck	109	73	25	66
Articulated truck	108	72	26	70
Policy target	76	23	85	44

Source: Derived from national figures from RIVM, 1997.

LOCAL POLICIES

Authorities influence the movement of goods directly or indirectly with their policies in different fields, such as spatial planning, transport environment, and business, for example the planning of shopping malls and the use of restrictions on the accessibility of certain urban zones. More and more inner-city areas are being protected from penetration by the automobile through the creation of pedestrian zones. This trend is increasing, and the areas shielded from cars are becoming larger. Time frames are enforced in these zones. The time frame is the period during the day when vehicles are allowed to enter the area—for instance, between 7:00 A.M. and 11:00 P.M. For environmental and aesthetic reasons, local authorities are planning additional or more stringent measures to reduce traffic in particular shopping areas.

Trends in Logistics and Logistic Services

The base form of logistic concepts has changed over the years and is still changing, from direct transport in the 1950s (which is still used by shops with a small range of products with a large throughput), to indirect transport with the use of intermediaries (distribution centers of retailers, wholesalers, or logistic service suppliers) in the 1980s. For the future, the evolution will probably continue. The next step will probably require a more network-based approach (Visser et al., 1998). In this approach, distribution and storage activities are carried out in a non-dedicated way by a network of interconnected, geographically spread transfer points ("brandless" distribution). Two of the main driving forces behind this scenario are outsourcing of logistics and specialization.

Van Binsbergen (1998) describes the network approach in more detail. An interesting feature of this concept is that local transport and interregional transport can be organized differently. Interregional transport will probably consist of larger sending loads ("more consolidation"), while local transport can take place more frequently in smaller quantities. This way if sufficient consolidation takes place, other modalities, such as rail and waterway, can also be used (see Fig. 29.1).

Transport Technology

Technological innovation is also taking place in the field of material use, vehicle construction, propulsion and fuel, emission reduction, and safety control. Specifically, the stringent European legislation on emissions, and in the future on noise, has become a driving force for technological innovation in road transport.

A driving force for technological innovation in other modes of transport, such as rail and waterway, is the need for a competitive intermodal transport system. Current intermodal transport concepts focus on shuttle (single-line) connections over long distances. For a competitive intermodal transport system over shorter distances (less than 120 kilometers), a more network-based approach is necessary in order to more consistently be able to provide door-to-door services. Innovations that support this approach are just beginning to emerge. A new generation of rail-transport technologies (new freight trains and rail terminals) will become available in the short term. There are some ideas about introducing small, faster freight trains for domestic freight transport. These services need to be facilitated with regional collection and distribution services.

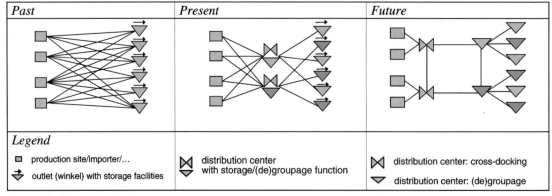

Source: Binsbergen, 1998.

Figure 29.1   Logistic Evolution

INTRODUCING INTERMODALITY

Unlike long-distance transport, which can take place by road, freight train, or barge, urban freight transport takes place only by road. Thus it is vulnerable to decreasing accessibility and to measures to restrict traffic. It is crucial to start thinking about alternative modalities that can be used in the long term. Such modalities would have to be less sensitive to congestion and traffic restrictions. At the same time, they would have to create less environmental load.

The solution to the aforementioned problems consists of the following elements: (1) separating the intra-urban part of the movement of a good from the inter-urban movement by means of introduction of a transfer point; (2) consolidating the urban goods movement; and (3) facilitating it with more efficient and sustainable transport means. Intermodal transport provides a solution when in urban freight transport the link is broken between local transport (city distribution) and long-distance transport (regional or interregional). Delinking these services makes it possible to optimize each area separately. This would be feasible if a multimodal network were to be developed for freight transport within and between urban areas. In other words, intermodal transport could be the answer if—both within and outside the city—new transport services or modalities were to be developed alongside traditional road transport. Delinking means that a transfer point will be introduced that connects the local transport to the long-distance transport.

Regional or Local Transfer Points

Regional or local transfer points, like urban distribution centers, have not been very successful in the past. The main reasons are that such transfer points do not benefit enough from consolidation to compensate for the extra transshipment costs, and that they increase the average lead time of consignments. There are three possible strategies for overcoming this problem.

The first strategy is to offset extra losses of time and costs by using faster or cheaper ways of transport. The second strategy is to move existing distribution activities to these regional locations, so that only the geographic location of the distribution centers changes. The third strategy is to integrate several logistic activities at one location, for instance by means of outsourcing to a third-party logistic service provider. Strategies two and three benefit from the fact that no extra handling activities are introduced in the logistic chain. This way no extra costs are generated. Both strategies could lead to consolidation under the condition that cooperation, outsourcing, and specialization in certain logistic services take place.

These regional or local transfer points are called intermodal freight centers, also known in other countries as Freight Villages, Güterverkehrszentren, Tradeports, Interporti, or Plat-formes Logistique. The following definition is used (Windborne International Group, 1994):

> Intermodal Freight Centres form intersections of at least two different transport modes at which independent companies from the distribution sector and other transport-

intensive business (e.g. component manufacturers) are located in a designated area. The aim is to enhance co-operation between transport modes and to improve the supply of distribution services in a region. A Freight Centre also implies an organisational element, in that individual forms co-operate or share the use of on-site facilities (e.g. through information systems) and may therefore benefit from significant synergistic effects.

The first freight centers were developed in Paris during the mid-1960s in response to urban congestion. They were created for two reasons: to facilitate logistic activities with location, space, and transport facilities, and to consolidate goods flows by developing particular transport services. The majority of existing facilities in France, Italy, and Germany were established during the 1980s and have been developed from existing locations, such as industrial sites and rail terminals. Several countries have included the development of freight centers in their national policies. Italy was the first, in 1990, followed by Germany in 1992 and France in 1993.

In the near future, special equipment and facilities will probably facilitate concepts such as urban distribution and city logistics. From the expert discussions during the COST 321 Action and Round Table 108, the following list can be derived:

- Distritrucks. In several cities in Europe, experiments are under way in which electric or hybrid vehicles, specially designed for urban distribution, are being tested. Urban distribution is already recognized as a niche market for specially designed vehicles.
- Truck routes, dedicated lanes, and shared use of bus lanes, in combination with road pricing or other kinds of selective accessibility within urban areas. In cities in Germany, such as Bremen, Cottbus, Düsseldorf, and Dortmund, specific routes for freight traffic already exist.
- Interregional freight connections by road, waterway, and rail, so-called "Corridors." It is also likely that special road or rail freight lanes will become available, which will connect regions.
- Multimodal transshipment facilities. The development of multimodal facilities demands high investments. However, spatial concentration almost guarantees an efficient use of facilities and creates a critical mass for special investments in, for instance, a rail terminal.

Underground Freight Transport Systems

New ideas on city distribution are needed for an adequate intermodal transportation system. In terms of performance, the alternatives will have to compete with direct transport. The loss of time because of extra handling should be minimized and/or offset by shorter shipping times. Likewise, the extra costs of handling should be kept to a minimum and/or offset by lower transport costs.

One way to recover transshipment costs is to improve the automation and robotization of transshipment and transport by using an underground system of pipelines or tunnels. Although in one scenario a pipeline network provides door-to-door-transport, it is also possible that more than one mode will be put in.

Underground freight transport refers to palletized or containerized consumer goods that are transported automatically through a new network of underground tunnels or tubes. The load units are relatively small. This means that the tubes, too, can be relatively small. Underground freight transport is a possible alternative for short-distance road transport in situations where combinations of accessibility problems, lack of space, and/or environmental problems occur and some concentration of transport flows take place. In general, underground systems have several advantages: (easy to realize) autonomous infrastructure with respect to other types of traffic; weather-independent transport systems; less space utilization; and fewer or no local environmental effects, such as noise, air pollution, physical hindrance, and separation.

Underground systems are expensive to build, but they have environmental and logistical advantages. Underground systems will offer higher (operational) speeds, greater reliability, and reduced energy use. There are also well-known disadvantages, such as investment costs and system safety (if an accident occurs, the consequences can be enormous). In essence, all known transport systems can be used in tunnels. In practice, there are some restrictions on propulsion and guidance that are related to tunnel characteristics. In fact, most of the requirements lead to advanced automated transport systems, which have little in common with traditional road vehicles as they are used today.

FURTHER RESEARCH

The study focuses on urban freight transport as one link in a larger collection and distribution system for the daily delivery of goods. This concept, based on new transport technologies, such as underground freight transport and intermodality, might provide the facilities for the consolidation that is necessary for sustainable development in urban freight transport. There is little evidence about whether urban freight transport and the associated problems are growing. Research is needed to provide better information. Innovations in freight transportation, such as underground freight transport and rail or other kinds of transportation, require more research and development. Research is also needed on the adoption and the impacts of these innovations. There are several reasons why this research has to take place in both Europe and the U.S.; for instance, most technical innovations and more and more trends have a global scope, including urban freight transport. This kind of research will provide a base for a better understanding of urban freight transport and how problems can be solved.

REFERENCES

Binsbergen, A. J. van. 1998. "New Logistic Concepts for Advanced Urban Freight Transport." In *Proceedings of the 26th European Transport Forum.* London: PTRC.

Browne, M. 1997. "Freight Transport and the City." CEMT, Round Table 108. Paris: Freight Transport and the City.

Button, K. J., and A. D. Pearman. 1981. *The Economics of Urban Freight Transport.* London: Macmillan.

COST 321 Action. 1997. *COST 321: Urban Goods Transport.* Final report. Brussels.

Dablanc, L., and F. Massé. 1996. "Les centres de distribution urbaine: un tableau comparatif." *Transport Urbains,* no. 91 (april–juin).

Dufour, J. G., and D. Patier. 1997. "Introduction to the Discussion Based on the Experience of the French Experimental and Research Programme." CEMT, Round Table 108. Paris: Freight Transport and the City.

European Conference of Ministers of Transport (ECMT). 1976. *Round Table 31: Freight Collection and Delivery in Urban Areas.* Paris: ECMT.

European Conference of Ministers of Transport (ECMT). 1984. *Round Table 61: Goods Distribution Systems in Urban Areas.* Paris: ECMT.

Lewis, A. 1997. *Alternative Urban Freight Strategies, Synthesis Report: Alternative Strategies for Urban Freight Transport Management.* Oxfordshire: Transport and Travel Research.

Rijksinstituut voor Volksgezondheid en Milieuhygiëne (RIVM). 1997. *Nationale Milieuverkenning 4 1997–2020.* Alphen a/d Rijn: Samson.

Visser, J. G. S. N., A. J. M. Vermunt, and A. J. van Binsbergen. 1998. *Ruimtelijke concepten ondergronds transport.* Delft/Hoeven: TRAIL Onderzoekschool.

Windborne International Group. 1994. *Intermodal Freight Centres in Europe.* Stockholm: Windborne.

CHAPTER THIRTY

The Future of Railway Transport in Europe

Toward Sustainable Development

Laurent Guihéry

Railway transport in Europe today is undergoing a fundamental reorganization that questions, on the one hand, the classical integrated structure of railway operations and, on the other hand, the sharing of responsibilities between the public sector, traditionally well represented in railroads, and the private sector, which is offering new perspectives. This trend, supported by the European Commission (Guideline 91/440/CE, Guideline 95/18/CE and Guideline 95/19/CE), affects all European countries, but it is in northern Europe—Sweden, the United Kingdom, Denmark, Germany, and the Netherlands—that such structural reform is the farthest along (Bouf et al., 1999).

On the whole, railway reform in Europe implicitly questions one of the teachings of public economics analysis, which has long considered the railway sector to be a typical example of a natural monopoly. This theory implies the existence of a unique, integrated, and controlled institution managed by public authorities. The railway sector does indeed have all the features of a natural monopoly: increasing scale activity based on large indivisible units, which occur according to functions (e.g., coordination of activities between the source and the destination of shipments) as well as techniques (e.g., integration and continuity of the network, the importance of facilities)

(Baumol and Oates, 1988; Baumstark, 1997). This railway sector is characterized, moreover, by economies of scale and scope that limit costs while widening the choice of proposed services. At the least, this sector implies, in terms of investments, numerous network irreversibilities and external effects.

The previous elements lead us to consider the railway sector to be a characteristic example of "market failure," for which a built-in monopolistic and controlled answer can be implemented. However, it appears today that this type of regulation is in crisis. This crisis of the railway institution exists on three levels: (1) The efficiency of a monopolistic solution justifies itself theoretically only with respect to a part of the monopoly, mainly the infrastructure and the network. The network then has to be analyzed separately from the railway activity, as stated in the European Guidelines. (2) In addition, the advantages of such a built-in organization must be balanced against the disadvantages that it is likely to cause. (3) Finally, a monopolistic solution is by no means a guarantee that customers' regional preferences will be taken into account. Some reform arrangements aim, then, at encouraging the consideration of citizens' regional preferences in a top-down movement of integration through the regionalization of railway passenger transport.

Table 30.1   Passengers European Union Model Split (%, in passenger/kms)

	Car	Bus	Rail	Air
1970	75.1	12.5	10.3	2.1
1980	76.9	11.4	8.5	3.2
1990	79	9	6.9	5.1
1994	79.7	8.3	6.2	5.8

Source: Nash and Stoner, 1998, p. 19.

Table 30.2   Freight European Union Model Split (%, in ton/kms)

	Car	Rail	Inland waterways	Pipelines
1970	48.6	31.7	12.3	7.4
1980	57.4	24.9	9.8	7.9
1990	67.5	18.9	8.3	5.3
1994	71.7	14.9	7.7	5.6

Source: Nash and Stoner, 1998, p. 19.

WHAT RENEWAL OF EUROPEAN RAILWAY TRANSPORT?

Railway transport offers real advantages with respect to sustainable development. It appears to be more environmentally friendly than road transport if one takes into account the negative external effects of road transport (safety issues, pollution, noise, and congestion). However, these advantages do not seem to benefit railway transport. Railroads in Europe are facing the ongoing decline of their modal share in both passenger transport and goods transport despite high levels of subsidies from the central government, which can reach close to 50 percent of the operational costs (Nash and Stoner, 1998; tables 30.1 and 30.2). What reasons can be found to explain this

decline? How can the railway institution be reformed so as to increase the efficiency of railways?

A Necessary Reorganization of the European Railway Industry

Some external or sociocultural factors (e.g., increased mobility in individual transport modes, individualistic logic) can explain this decreasing modal share, but the decline is particularly evident in the internal organization of railway transport (Kessides and Willig, 1995: 2; Nash and Stoner, 1998: 1). Thus, from one country to the next, numerous disparities exist: average revenues by employee of freight transport in the United Kingdom, France, Italy, and Germany in 1994 ranged from $43,000 in France to $19,500 in Italy and $155,000 in the United States (OECD, 1998). Traffic revenues cover 30 percent of costs in Italy, 40 percent in Spain, 46 percent in France, 50 percent in Germany, and 80 percent in the United Kingdom. Globally, with respect to the ratio of revenues to costs, disparities in Europe are important; this ratio is 20 to 25 percent in some countries, and as high as 80 to 85 percent in others (OECD, 1998).

The Internal Organization and Efficiency of Railway Operations

Before the reform, railway operations were organized in accordance with non-economic objectives, such as the guarantee of employment, regional development, protection of the environment, and maximization of the collective interest through revenues of the monopoly. Some railway operations were viewed as a "national laboratory of social progress," as in France. Japanese railroads, for example, were organized with the objective of "improving people's welfare."

The threat of the modal decline of railways and of the bankruptcy of some operators requires profound reform, which is currently taking place in Europe. However, such structural reform does not mean immediate privatization, systematic competition, and outsourcing of railway responsibilities. Reform measures implemented in England at the end of the 1980s show that in a favorable economic context, the internal differentiation of railway responsibilities, while remaining in the public sector, could lead to substantial gains in performance and efficiency. The experiences of Japan and New Zealand also confirm that internal reorganization without intramodal competition, or even without total privatization, can bring about positive results (OECD, 1998: 6). It is therefore not

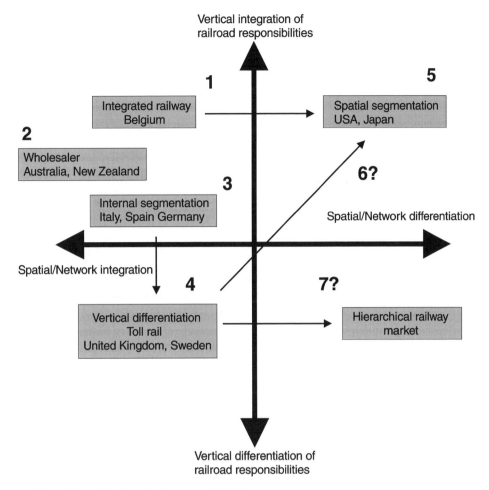

Figure 30.1   Railroad Organization: Explanatory Models

necessary to implement intramodal competition or to privatize national operations in order to achieve greater efficiency of the railways. Moreover, it is interesting to observe—contrary to the United States and to Japan, where numerous lines were closed—that the strategies employed in Europe, including the system of regional franchising in the United Kingdom, did not imply an important decrease in the railway supply. Deregulation does not mean a downturn in the railway supply, provided that public service obligations that show a deficit are covered by the public authorities, as is currently the case in the United Kingdom and generally in Europe (for example, in the organization of Regionalization Law in Germany). Nevertheless, national railway operators' losses in Europe cannot be explained by the costs of these public service obligations, which often serve officially as a justification for these losses.

THE DIFFERENT MODELS OF RAILWAY ORGANIZATION

Figure 30.1 illustrates the different models of railway reorganization throughout the world. A double perspective is expressed: on the one hand, vertical integration versus vertical differentiation of railway responsibilities—that is to say, a separation between the management of the infrastructure (network) and railroad operations; but also, on the other hand, a spatial and network differentiation, taking into account the role of the network, which can be either nationally integrated or more regionally differentiated, or even regionalized.

1. The traditional model of vertical integration of railway responsibilities—the model of the "monolithic railway" —is "production-oriented, unresponsive to market demand for services, and hierarchical yet not bloated in organizational architecture" (Kessides and Willig, 1995: 2). It often has a strong political influence on operators' choices, in return for financing through subsidies, which Nash and Stoner assess in Europe as 50 percent of operating costs. In Europe, this model has taken the form of a public monopoly, but New Zealand privatized the national operator while preserving a built-in and integrated structure, reducing relationships with the political authorities (Nash and Stoner, 1998: 2).

Such organizations have some obvious advantages in terms of industrial and technological strategies (e.g., high-speed trains), benefit from economies of scale and scope, and internalize and reduce transaction costs (Nash and Stoner, 1998: 2). This type of organization is more likely to develop long-term investments and allows a built-in scheduling of railway activities (transport planning, pricing, interconnections). Many of the advantages of this type of integration in fact correspond to advantages of centralizing responsibility: reactivity, concentration of resources on strategic objectives such as investments, internalization of spillover, and external effects. Nevertheless, the built-in model fails with respect to the issues of incentives and information: weak reactivity to demand, lack of incentive to reduce inefficiencies, lack of consideration of passengers' local or regional preferences, bureaucratic inefficiencies, lack of interest in the financial situation of the company, and close relationships with public authorities that influence commercial and company choices. The model of built-in management does not offer the opportunity for intramodal competition.

2. This built-in model can also be adapted to a "wholesaler" practice, as can be observed in Australia and New Zealand (OECD, 1998; Kessides and Willig, 1995), where strategies aim first at deregulation and intermodal competition between rail, road, and coastal transport before considering intramodal competition. In New Zealand,[1] the national railway operator therefore remains primarily built-in, in order to maintain an influence on the infrastructure, its standards, and its costs. It is also privatized; the network is open to other operators, which have to pay access charges, but this opening of the network to competition remains marginal and is not encouraged by the authorities (Nash and Stoner, 1998). In Australia, the government's strategy is also aimed at increasing intermodal competition between railroads and coastal transport, mainly over long distances. The national operator has nevertheless been divided into two internal entities, one to manage the infrastructure ("below rail") and one to manage operations ("above rail").

3. At the instigation of the European Union, European operators have moved away from a built-in structure— the "monolithic railway" (Kessides and Willig, 1995: 2)— toward a structure of "internal segmentation" (Nash and Stoner, 1998) by separating in business centers the main railway responsibilities: freight, long-distance passenger transport, regional transport, and management of the network. The objective deals often with accounts and allows a better transparency of profit centers and cost structures in order to reduce losses and inefficiencies. From a business point of view, these business centers also stick closer to the demand: better incentive and commercial reactivity, integration of services allowing economies of scale and scope, reduction of inter-agency transaction costs, and better clarity of costs. Among the weaknesses of such an organization are the common cost distribution and the lack of competitive pressure at the operational level. Following the British experience, Spain, the Netherlands, and Germany have reorganized their national operators in this direction. At the end of the 1980s, the United Kingdom recorded real gains in efficiency following such an internal reorganization. Nevertheless, this model seems to be transitory, as was the case in the UK. Germany also foresees a change to a model of vertical differentiation, by completely separating management of the infrastructure from the activities of transport.

4. This model of "internal segmentation" thus seems to be an intermediate step toward a more differentiated organization of railways by separating management from operations. This vertical differentiation model—or "toll rail," as Kessides and Willig (1995) term it—corresponds to the spirit of the European Union Guidelines and has as its objective opening the network to third parties, which can compete without discriminatory practices. Only in Sweden and the United Kingdom was management of the infrastructure completely externalized. Some European countries are reluctant to follow suit, fearing increased deficits for the national operator. The railway supply can take place through franchising or through free access and track pricing. In the United Kingdom, as well as Sweden and Germany, competition for the franchise—

"competition for the market"—allows public authorities to act on the transport plan and infrastructure policies as a whole. In France, where railway management (RFF) is officially split off from operations, the national railroad company—the SNCF—remains the only authorized operator and is responsible for building and maintaining the network. Advantages of such a differentiated organization are the competition between different operators (for track or franchise), the clarity of contractual relationships, and the increased specialization of each railway responsibility. The main weaknesses of such an organization are the difficulty of offering a nationally integrated transport plan, problems with timetables and pricing, the management of track conflicts, the possible use of bids, and the difficulty of developing investments. Once again, this model of vertical differentiation may remain incomplete, generally in terms of homogeneity of the railway transport supply and of continuity of the transport plan on a national level.

5. The built-in model can also experience spatial segmentation, as in Japan and the United States. In this model, the advantages of a built-in organization are retained, but the existence of regional monopoly zones allows significant gains in efficiency: regional monopolies can, as in freight transport in the U.S., compete for some long-distance runs, which may be achieved through alternative routes. Such spatial competition also exists in the United Kingdom within the system of regional franchising, which allows overlapping in order to offer some alternative connections for the main routes provided by separate operators. Thus, there can be four different operators between London and Birmingham. Spatial differentiation allows so-called yardstick comparison. Gains of efficiency can also be achieved if regional monopolies give reciprocal access rights to their network—which implies, as in the U.S., extensive regulations regarding the respect of common rules, reciprocal opening of the network, control of trusts and concentration, a "fair and equal basis," and management of conflicts (Kessides and Willig, 1995: 22). Nevertheless, in the United States, collusion has been observed that has required the intervention of the Surface Transportation Board (STB). In Japan, freight operators have the opportunity to operate over a network owned by a passenger operator. The Japanese reform has shown little interest in introducing competition. It is, rather, characterized by optimization of the railway operator and by the division of the national operator into six vertically built-in regional companies (the

JRses). In return for track access pricing, a freight operator can have access to the networks of the regionalized passenger operators. The Japanese reform, far from being an intramodal competition—the Shinkansen has been entrusted to a unique operator—reveals interesting results: incomes from passenger traffic rose by 46.6 percent between 1984 and 1991; costs decreased 24.4 percent within this same period; and the staff has been reduced by 45.2 percent, to 138,901 employees. In the United States, this spatial differentiation allows *interlining*, which is unusual in European railway transport. The establishment of regional monopolies combines the advantages of a centralized and built-in structure while giving incentives to operators, by using the mechanisms of a "yardstick competition" and competition for high-demand corridors.

What Are the Perspectives for Railway Reform Developments in Europe?

Does the model of vertical differentiation correspond with the outcome of railway reform? Figure 30.1 shows the possible development of European railway reform in two complementary directions.

Re-regulation and Spatial Segmentation: The American Approach

Railway reform in Europe could benefit from the American experience, as Kessides and Willig state (1995: 20):

> The U.S. experience confirms what theory predicts: decentralized market oriented decision-making that is freed from excessive regulatory control and that is energized by market incentives is the surest means of finding and implementing efficient and innovative solutions to problems posed by transportation needs.

On the one hand, if the transactions costs of differentiated management are too high, it is possible to find a way out by re-regulation and a return to a more built-in structure (phase 6 of Fig. 30.1). A trend toward re-regulation can be observed today in the United Kingdom; the reform in England has pushed the differentiation of railway responsibilities too far (Baumstark et al., 1997). Thus it is difficult to define a global transport plan in the United Kingdom. As was the case at the end of 1998, the differences in strategies between the franchisers have prevented the implementation of a global plan.[2] In this perspective, the railway sector could move toward spatial competition, with every operator having more or less a monopoly in a given region: competition then occurs in relation to interregional passenger or freight corridors. In reference to the American experience, this perspective could be implemented on the European level, with each member state opening, under a principle of reciprocity, its network to third parties while keeping a strong national, or even regional, vertical integration. True competition could thus take place, for example on the Trans-European Networks (city-to-city runs: Paris–Lyon, Paris–London, Paris–Frankfurt, etc.).

Vertical Differentiation and Spatial Segmentation of Networks: The European Approach

Another perspective of development exists in vertical differentiation combined with spatial segmentation (phase 7 of Fig. 30.1), namely a hierarchical railway market. In this perspective, networks, like operators, would be segmented and organized into a large hierarchical market with many actors. Every type of transport would have a corresponding type of network: regional networks, high-speed train networks (TEN), etc. The notion of a homogeneous transport network is changing to one of a hierarchically overlapping and segmented network that relies on strong interconnections, looking downward toward urban networks and then upward toward regional networks, high-speed networks, and the Trans-European Network. Interconnections should then play a major role. The regionalization of regional railway passenger transport in Germany—and experimentation with it in France—could lead, beyond the transfer of responsibility for regional transport to the local authorities, to a differentiation of networks, putting an end to the classically accepted idea of a unified railway network. Under this hypothesis, regionalization would affect not just the organization of transport but also the network, which would be attributed to the regional or local level. This perspective implies strong hierarchical organization of the railway network and a key role for interconnections (Bonnafous, 1993). This perspective is interesting in dense, highly congested urban areas, but it requires a large, high-quality network (Kessides and Willig, 1995: 20). Weaknesses of such railway construction concern the role of feeder of a railway integrated network and the losses of scale and scope economies.

CONCLUSION

Most of the industrialized countries have implemented a reform of railway transport, aimed at increasing efficiency and preventing, as in Europe, its decline, while road transport continues to increase. Two main trends can be highlighted: on the one hand, a vertical differentiation of railway operators, whose responsibilities—management of the network, transport, maintenance—are divided into independent units (the United Kingdom, Sweden); and on the other hand, a spatial segmentation of operators, some of which retain a built-in structure (Belgium, Australia), and others of which function in accordance with regional franchises (the United Kingdom). Across Europe, it appears that regions play a key role, as the German and French experiences proved. If they efficiently benefit from the transfer of the responsibility for managing transport planning in the region, it appears also that railway reform in Europe could lead to a regionalization of railway networks. This will imply the establishment of a hierarchical architecture of railway networks (urban, regional, interregional, and high-speed networks/Trans-European Network), in which interconnections will play a major role.

NOTES

With special thanks to Nathalie Read, Dominique Bouf, Pierre-Yves Peguy, and Yves Crozet for their comments and criticism.

1. Nash and Stoner have noticed the efficiency of the railway reform in New Zealand: a 200 percent increase in labor productivity, a 21 percent increase in average train length, and a 69 percent decrease in the number of wagons (Nash and Stoner, 1998: 10).

2. Despite the regulators' critics, British train users in December 1998 could not plan their travels after Christmas: the transport plan and interconnections had not been settled by the franchisee at this date for strategic reasons.

REFERENCES

Baumol, W. J., and W. E. Oates. 1988. *The Theory of Environmental Policy.* 2nd ed. Cambridge: Cambridge University Press.

Baumstark L. 1997. "Tarification de l'usage des infrastructures et théorie de l'allocation optimale des ressources, de la logique des coûts à la révélation des préférences." Thèse de doctorat, Université Lumière Lyon 2.

Baumstark, L., L. Guihéry, and F. Lacaille. 1997. "Process of Deregulation within the Railways Sector: Access Pricing and Institutional Organization." World Conference on Railways Research (WCRR), Firenze, September. CD-ROM.

Bonnafous, A. 1993. "Réseaux secondaires et transport intégré: promouvoir un aménagement du territoire équilibré, colloque." *Perspectives de développement du territoire de la Grande Europe,* Dresde, November.

Bouf, D., Y. Crozet, L. Guihéry, and P.-Y. Péguy. 1999. Rapport d'étape 1, contribution à l'étude du Commissariat Général du Plan: "Performance des entreprises de réseaux ferroviaires en Europe." *Laboratoire d'Economie des Transports* (January).

Kessides, I. N., and R. D. Willig. 1995. "Restructuring Regulation of the Rail Industry for the Public Interest." WPS 1506. Washington, D.C.: The World Bank.

Nash, C. A., and J. P. Stoner. 1998. "Background Notes on Railways: Structure, Regulation and Competition Policy." DAFFE/CLP (98) 1, Competition Policy Roundtable, OECD, Paris.

OECD. 1998. Working paper, DAFFE/CLP (98).

PART VII

Cultural Perspectives

CHAPTER THIRTY-ONE

Transport Culture and the Economy of Speed

Speed Limits and Changing Patterns of Accessibility in the United Sates

Donald G. Janelle

INTRODUCTION

Transport culture and the economy of speed are central concepts to understanding the role of transportation in shaping modern economies. Promoted as an economic good or service that alters the significance of distance, transport speed is reinforced by a culture that romanticizes its importance and pleasures (see Clark, 1962). Changes in speed limits on U.S. highways from 1949 to 1998 provide a context for investigating these propositions.

"Transport culture" is seen as an attribute of modernism that reinforces prevailing value systems for maintenance of our economic system. The economy is dependent on speed of movement for capital accumulation (Harvey, 1989). The implications of this dependence relate to one of the critical global societal issues of this century—the furtherance of "sustainable transportation systems." Reinforcement of a Culture of Transport by an Economy of Speed is seen as universal in capitalist societies, yet systematic investigations of this process are lacking.

A prevailing theme in social science research on transportation has been transportation's ability to transform the space economy. Examples include the work of Boubet (1986), Marconis (1985), and Plassard (1977) from Europe, and Allen, Dong, and Scott (1993), Janelle (1969), and Vance (1986) from North America. However, researchers are increasingly turning their attention to the negative externalities of transportation infrastructure that focuses too significantly on speed of movement, ranging from Ivan Illich's (1974) now classic essay *Energy and Equity* through more recent espousals for sustainable transport, most notably the work of Whitelegg (1993).

AIMS AND SCOPE OF THE RESEARCH

This research analyzes speed-limit variations and changes across the United States since 1949. Changes in travel times among a set of broadly representative cities offer a means for assessing their accessibility gains and losses in absolute and relative terms. However, the research also explores arguments of lobbyists in opposition to and in support of these changes—regarding energy savings, traffic accidents, and "just-in-time" efficiencies. Inherent political and economic controversies associated with attempts to alter speed limits are revealed by a focused interpretative documentation. Thus, distance is characterized as a contested entity, subject to political transformation through public regulatory and private economic means. Mediated by speed of movement, distance is seen as a medium of

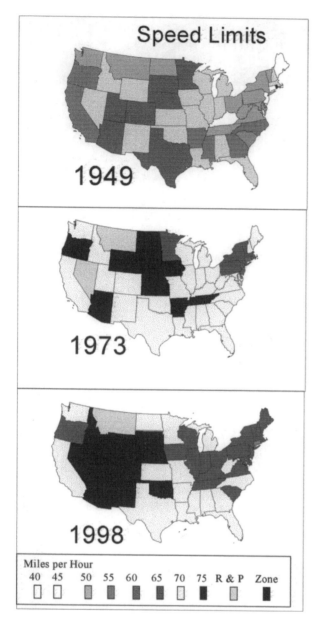

Figure 31.1   Speed Limits by States for 1949, 1973, and 1998

power in a globalizing society. A transport-speed interpretation of distance is fundamental to understanding the broader aspects of human spatial behavior, settlement system development, regional interaction, and urban-regional relationships, and to the co-evolution of sustainable transportation and settlement systems.

TRAVEL SPEEDS AND TIME-SPACE CONVERGENCE ON U.S. HIGHWAYS

For nearly three decades, controversies over speed limits on U.S. highways have generated arguments representing a clash of ideologies, resulting in considerable data for assessing trends and hypotheses. Speed zoning, the increase and decrease of speed limits, and changes in speeding behavior have been subject to intense congressional lobbying in the United States since the 1973–74 OPEC Oil Embargo. The 1974 imposition of 55 mph (89 kph) speeds on the Interstate Highway System and the withholding of highway funds from states that did not adequately enforce this measure were relaxed in 1987 to permit 65 mph (105 kph) speeds on rural sections of the system. The restoration of full state control over speed limits was enacted in 1995, yielding pronounced regional variations in regulatory responses by different states.

A selection of maps (see Fig. 31.1) provides evidence of significant spatial variations across the United States in the legislative response to setting speeds. In 1949, speeds varied from 40 to 60 mph, but the "reasonable and prudent" rule was the most popular (16 states). These speeds applied to federal and state highways in rural areas—mostly two-lane roads. A persistent pattern relates to lower speeds in the densely populated Northeast, and higher speeds in the Western Interior states. In 1973, before implementation of the National Maximum Speed Limit (55), state-imposed maximum speeds on the Interstate Highway System varied from 60 mph in the Mid-Atlantic coastal states to 75 mph in parts of the Western Interior; Montana and Nevada were the only states that allowed a "reasonable and prudent" speed—translated to mean "pedal to the metal and go like hell." In 1998, the move to higher speeds was nearly universal, but the map displays pronounced regional variations among states in the Northeast, the South, and the Western Interior and on the West Coast.

Figure 31.2 assumes uniform interstate highway speeds

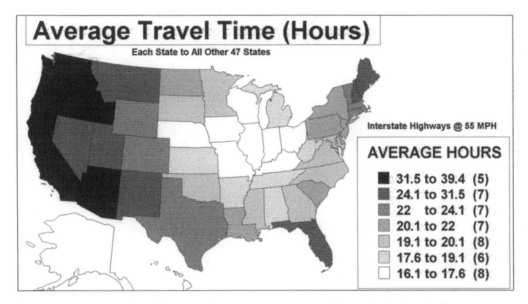

Figure 31.2   Average Travel Times in Hours from the Largest City in Each State to the Largest Cities in All Remaining 47 States

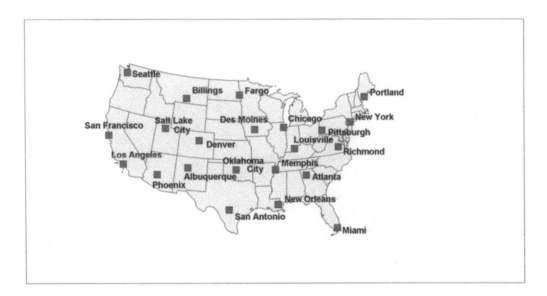

Figure 31.3   Cities Selected for Analysis

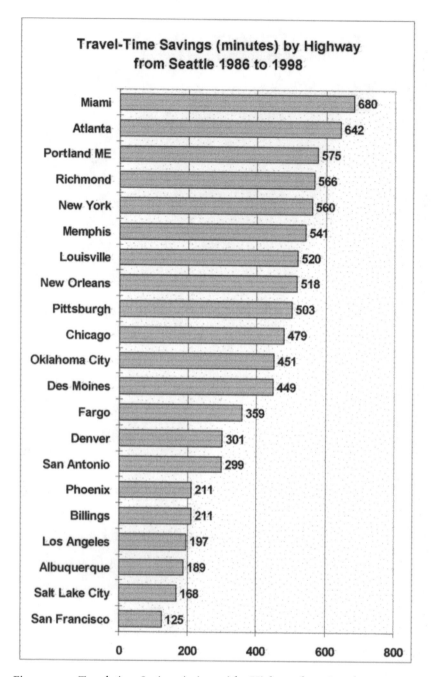

Figure 31.4   Travel-time Savings (minutes) by Highway from Seattle, 1986 to 1998

of 55 mph. It shows average travel times in hours from the largest city in each state to the largest cities in the remaining forty-seven states. All travel makes use of the quickest routes between the centers of city pairs, favoring interstate, federal, and primary state routes, but making use of local streets within cities. Congestion factors were re-flected in the assignment of lower speeds in the urbanized portions of the trip paths. The pattern shown applies to travel at legal speed limits in the period from 1974 to 1986. It depicts the basic centrality of the Midwest and the travel-time disadvantages of the West, northeastern New England, and Florida.

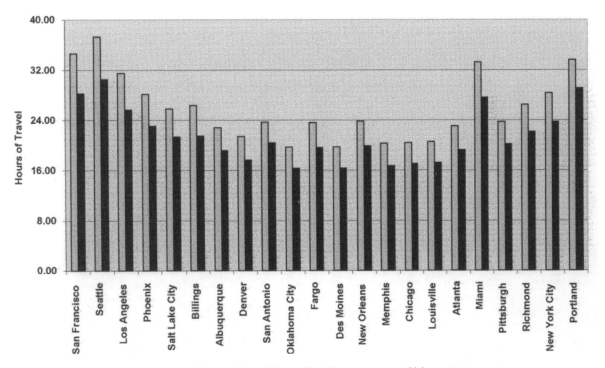

Figure 31.5   Changes in Average Highway Travel Times for Trips among 22 Cities, 1986 to 1998

The transition from 55 mph, which prevailed in law if not in practice from 1974 through 1986, has altered the economic significance of distance in the United States to an astounding degree. Yet empirical assessment of such drastic change in the temporal linkage of the space economy is limited. I will attempt to provide a brief graphical sketch of this transformation in terms of travel times for highway connections between leading cities.

A set of twenty-two cities was chosen to represent the geographical range of travel options across the country (Fig. 31.3). A comparison of travel times in 1986 (the last year of 55 mph) and January 1998, to reflect the current pattern of state-determined speed limits, illustrates the extent of change and its significance in altering highway accessibility levels for the country. Pronounced regional variations in the distribution of travel-time benefits are evident.

Figure 31.4 shows the travel-time savings (in minutes) by highway from Seattle between 1986 and 1998. In general, the savings represent 15 to 20 percent reductions in travel times since 1986, with gains proportional to distance traveled from Seattle. The calculations assume that travel through Montana is at 80 mph. In reviewing more than 200 trip measures among the twenty-two cities, some time savings approached levels of 35 percent.

Figure 31.5 depicts for each city changes in the average highway travel times to all of the remaining twenty-one cities from 1986 to 1998. The cities are arranged by longitude (west to east/left to right). This graphic illustrates the same level of Midwestern centrality shown on the map of average travel times by states in the period of 55 mph (Figure 31.2). In general, the length of the bars (hours of travel) corresponds with the average distance of each place to the remaining twenty-one cities. However, it also shows the differential benefit of higher speeds for places on the continental margins, particularly for West Coast cities and for Miami. Clearly, these places are among the big accessibility winners in the post–55 mph era.

The average time-space convergence (Janelle, 1968, 1969) among the twenty-two cities is represented in Figure 31.6 by two measures—the average minutes saved per year in travel from each place to the remaining twenty-one places (dividing travel time differences between 1986 and 1998 by 12), and the average seconds saved per mile.

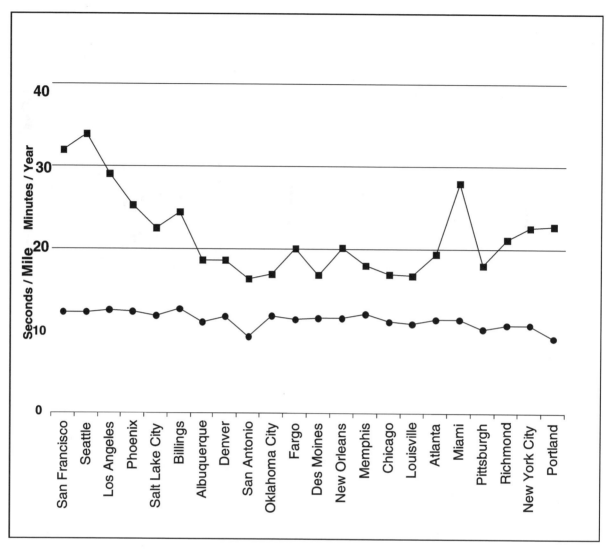

Figure 31.6   Average Time-Space Convergence among 22 Cities, 1986 to 1998

The measure of minutes saved per year represents the intrinsic value associated with higher speeds over longer distances and clearly favors the west over the east and relatively more remote places over central places. Hence, edge locations are converging more rapidly with the U.S. economic/demographic system than are more central locations. How do we factor such imbalances in the distribution of accessibility advantages into cost-benefit models? Should we?

The measure of seconds per mile factors out the distance effect and appears much more uniform throughout the country. However, there is a perceptible but slight inclination toward higher values from east to west, reflect-ing the generally higher speed limits in western states. This regional variation would appear much more significant if the measures were repeated for sets of cities within each state or by broad regions. In essence, accessibility advantages will be most apparent in the internal commerce of those states with higher speed limits. This is a truism, but it needs documentation to identify variations in the internal speed advantages among states. The impact of the political jockeying over speed limits on the macro-geography of time-space convergence processes would appear to be of fundamental significance in the comparative commercial competitiveness of different regions.

CONCLUDING COMMENTARY

This empirical analysis needs to be expanded to cover the period just prior to the implementation of the Interstate Highway System. However, a much broader range of documentation is needed to tease out significant generalizations about the recent history of highway travel times in the United States. It is evident that speed limits and travel times per se are only symbolic of more general issues reflecting the culture of transport and the economy of speed. The patterns of results are attributable only in part to technology. They also reflect the politics of special interests, contesting ideologies regarding economics, environmentalism, even life and death, with conflict outcomes mediated through lobbying, media campaigns, and legislative debate. I am currently assembling and reviewing documentation from a broad range of sources—legislative debates and court logs; public opinion polls; trade publications relating to transportation, policing, and insurance; advertising and lobbying propaganda; Web sites; planning reports; and both scholarly and popular literature. The documentation concentrates mostly on the situation in North America, but is augmented extensively with similar documentation from around the world.

Legislative debate over highway speed limits and periodic shifts in policies are particularly diagnostic of political/economic persuasion and manipulation over the significance of distance. Arguments for and against limits often pit safety and environmental concerns against the cost of doing business, the range of access to resources and markets, the coordination of production and distribution economies, and a host of other rationales that serve to contract or expand the space economy. Relating as they do to the economic prospects of firms in the retailing, wholesaling, and manufacturing sectors, speed limit regulations show sensitivity to just-in-time practices and to changes in the rationales for selecting investment locations. Countervailing arguments over the value of human life and the cost of accidents to society also provide interpretative insight into the definition of speed-based distance. Nonetheless, the just-in-time doctrine of modern business is surely a key factor in the rapidity with which the speed maps of the United States are changing.

Transportation is interwoven so tightly into the social and psychological fabric of humanity that its understanding requires more than the standard measurable parameters invoked in the model-building exercises of transportation planners and consultants. For social scientists, there is need to explore fully the meaning of speed and the role of space-adjusting technologies. Understanding the transformation of distance and space into complex physical and mental geometries and into social-spatial constructs of contesting ideologies requires careful reflection on our tool kit of algorithms. A broad perspective on the role of transportation in society remains an important dimension that lies beyond the strict purview of numerical/graphical representation and optimal solution. Approaches compatible with this view include investigations of speed in popular culture and everyday behavior by Hirano (1979) and Noguchi and Koshi (1978), reflecting a Japanese perspective, and by Barjonet (1980) from Europe.

The research draws parallels with debates over sustainable transport, particularly in Europe, as seen in geographer John Whitelegg's notions of "time pollution" and in the complete social costing of travel speed in terms of human lives and health, and with regard to atmospheric and physical environmental quality. Similarly, research on personal speed preferences, as seen in the work of Nijkamp and Baaijens (1998), and on speed behavior, represented by Rienstra and Rietveld (1996), offers empirical and theoretical perspectives for linking such concerns with policy issues.

The transportation landscape, possibly more than any other form of human landscape, exerts a dominating and often totalizing presence over both natural and social environments. Tempering its influence for a sustainable future requires a deep appreciation of its role in the transformation of space and a humanistic focus on the lure of speed in shaping new cultures and economies. The focus in this presentation, with examples from the world of speed on U.S. highways, illustrates briefly the empirical thrust of some of my current interest in this area. But the vastness of transportation, in its many forms and situations, holds an endless array of such issues for investigation.

REFERENCES

Allen, W. Bruce, Lui Dong, and Scott Singer. 1993. "Accessibility Measures of U.S. Metropolitan Areas." *Transportation Research*, *27B*, no. 6: 439–449.

Barjonet, Pierre E. 1980. "La Perception de la Limitation de Vitesse par les Conducteurs." *Transport Environment Circulation* 43: 27–34.

Boubet, Laurence. 1986. "Mesurer L'espace Temps." *Transports*, no. 323 (March): 161–164.

Clark, Arthur C. 1962. "Worlds Without Distance." *Playboy* 9, no. 8: 69–97.

Harvey, David. 1989. "The Condition of Postmodernity." Oxford: Blackwell.

Hirano, Hideaki. 1979. "Fashion and Transportation." *IATSS Research* 3: 41–47.

Illich, Ivan. 1974. *Energy and Equity.* London: Calder & Boyars.

Janelle, Donald G. 1968. "Central Place Development in a Time-space Framework." *The Professional Geographer* 20: 5–10.

Janelle, Donald G. 1969. "Spatial Reorganization: A Model and Concept." *Annals of the Association of American Geographers* 59: 348–364.

Marconis, Robert. 1985. "Rel. Inter-regionales et Disp. Intra-regionals Ref. sur l'evolutions des Rapports Espace." *Transports,* no. 307 (Sept.): 461–465.

Nijkamp, Peter, and Sef Baaijens. 1998. "Time Pioneers and Travel Behaviour: An Investigation into the Viability of 'Slow Motion.'" Manuscript, Amsterdam (Free University).

Noguchi, K., M. Koshi, et al. 1978. "Speed and Man." *IATSS Research* 2: 29–42.

Plassard, François. 1977. "Axe de Transport et Déformation de l'Espace." *International Journal of Transport Economies* 4, no. 1: 21–54.

Rienstra, Sytze A., and Piet Rietveld. 1996. "Speed Behaviour of Car Drivers." *Transportation Research D* 1, no. 2: 97–110.

Vance, James E., Jr. 1986. *Capturing the Horizon: The Historical Geography of Transportation since the Transportation Revolution of the Sixteenth Century.* New Haven: Yale University Press.

Whitelegg, John. 1993. *Transport for a Sustainable Future: The Case for Europe.* London: Belhaven Press.

CHAPTER THIRTY-TWO

Transport and Logistics in City Regions

Driving Forces for Counterurbanization?

Markus Hesse

INTRODUCTION

Urban goods movement and freight distribution processes are a key issue of urban development. The functionality and accessibility of delivery services are becoming decisive location factors in the post-Fordist urban economy. In the transportation industry, in corporate policy, and particularly in transportation planning strategies, methods and instruments are being developed to make freight traffic more efficient and more environmentally acceptable.

This chapter concentrates on a second topic within that research area: the interaction of logistics with the urban structure. Depending on certain functional requirements, suburban locations tend to be preferred for logistic and distribution centers, because of their land resources, traffic capacity, and neighborhood acceptance. This preference for the suburbs leads, in turn, to important changes in city structures. The basic research question is whether freight traffic and modern logistics are accelerating the break-up of the city and fostering counterurbanization.

The topics outlined below are part of a research project that was initiated in March 2000 for a post-doctoral degree in Urban Geography at the Free University of Berlin. The project takes a transatlantic approach, consisting of two regional case studies. One will be conducted in the Berlin-Brandenburg region, the other in the East Bay Area of California (Oakland and its environs).

AIM AND SCOPE OF THE RESEARCH

In spite of active theoretical investigation and practical efforts to improve freight transport and logistics, the nature of the interaction between logistics and urban development and the direction of the impacts are poorly understood. This study thus aims to illuminate the interrelationship of three basic processes: (1) the rationalization of logistics (of large retailers/wholesalers, manufacturers, shippers, or freight forwarders); (2) the determination of companies' locational choices according to logistical and freight transport requirements; and (3) urban development, in particular the contribution of logistics to the dispersal of urban or regional structures (see Fig. 32.1).

From the research perspective, this is virtually a new field of interest: Until now, the interaction between urban development and logistics has not been widely covered by research in the U.S. or Europe (Hanson, 1995). So far, the project promises to answer relevant questions

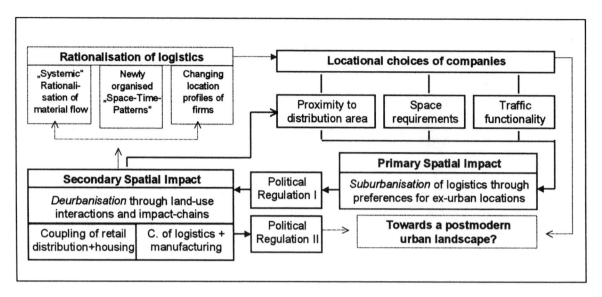

Figure 32.1   Research Model

about urban geography and urban planning, particularly as follows: What are the basic factors that determine the locational decisions of distribution firms in urban areas, particularly at the urban fringe? How do locational decisions influence further land use developments? Is the logistic function pioneering urban growth? How do these interactions fit into urban development strategies? Are there tendencies toward spatial diffusion, e.g., when residential land uses are coupled with locations of retail outlets (or commercial sites with logistics)?

The research process is divided into several steps and elements, which will be outlined further, according to methodological specifications. First, the state of the art in supply chain and logistic development has to be established, as far as it is fundamental to the goal of the study. Second, research must be conducted on the interactions of logistics modernization with locational choices of distribution companies and their significance for urban/regional development in selected regions of both Europe (Berlin-Brandenburg) and the U.S. (the East Bay Area). Third, specific paths of counterurbanization must be evaluated and assessed with regard to logistical functions and requirements. The result is expected to contribute to the determination of appropriate means of political regulation, in the context of the postmodern urban landscape.

LOGISTICS AND THE CITY: THE CONTEXT OF THE STUDY

Logistics in Transition

As part of social and economic changes in Europe, logistics have undergone a fundamental restructuring within the last ten to fifteen years. Rationalized supply chains have emerged to optimize production, distribution, and consumption processes, in response to structural change, cost competition, and rapidly changing patterns of consumption (Cooper et al., 1991; Schoenberger, 1996; Hollingsworth and Boyer, 1997).

One of the significant spatial consequences of the new logistic concepts is a reduction of stock in stores and short-term supplies of goods at points of sale (e.g., in retailing), which is made possible by new information technologies. Short-term, just-in-time delivery and large truck operations characterize cost-effective corporate rationalization strategies. Trade-offs between expensive storage and cheap transport help firms to achieve massive cost reductions, as does externalization of costs. At the same time, these trade-offs contribute to the further growth of freight transport. As the most flexible, appropriate, and competitive mode of goods movement, road freight is expected to develop dynamically.

Freight traffic seems to be much more difficult to manage than passenger transport. Realistic planning strategies must take the complex nature of logistics and goods flows into account. From an urban planning point of view, the large number of subsystems of logistics can be viewed as a result of functional fragmentation, a phenomenon that leads in turn to spatial fragmentation. The diversity of goods, the number of delivery activities and frequencies, the number of companies involved, and the specific logics of the urban distribution channels are manifold and varied. Another important urban problem derives from the functional and physical distance between the location of the enterprises and the location of the environmental damage caused by their logistical structures. The underlying decisions are being made far away from the affected area, and far away from the local problem.

Historic and Recent Trends

While the functional restructuring of corporate logistics has been investigated intensively by both economists and engineers, the nature and history of the urban consequences of this phenomenon have received little attention. Yet the emergence of cities is closely connected with their function as a marketplace (as Max Weber has pointed out). Trade and exchange contributed to the beginnings of urban development, in both Europe and the U.S., and they still characterize the classic ability of cities to concentrate people and money, culture and ideas.

Structural change as a consequence of social, economic, and technological change has played a significant role in reshaping the relationship between the city and logistics (U.S. Congress OTA, 1995). Innovations in transportation and production technology have affected the spatial distribution of the goods sector and have led to decentralization of activities away from older urban cores; I call this movement the "primary spatial impact." Many of the goods production, transportation, and distribution jobs that core cities have depended upon will continue to shift to outer suburban and exurban areas and to lower-cost smaller and mid-size metropolitan areas (cf. Fig. 32.2); in this study, that is called the secondary spatial impact.

Pawley has characterized these changes as the outcome of an abstract urbanism of trade routes:

> During the 1980s, a new city network was built in non-historic England, only it was not called a city network. . . .

All over the country millions of square metres of business park and distribution centre floorspace was being constructed at breakneck speed. Outside the old towns and cities, at 200 exits on a 1,800 mile motorway network, one thousand new commercial complexes were springing up with no reference to urban context or the supremacy of history at all. More than 100 out of town shopping centres were projected, 39 of them more than 100,000 square metres in covered area and no less than 9 of them located on the M 25 London orbital motorway. (Pawley 1994, 51)

In this context, the understanding of city or "urban" is no longer focused primarily on the central business district, but more on the dynamically changing patterns of suburbs, exurbs, and "edge cities"—a more decentralized type of urban region, with a certain amount of space developing independently from the urban core, for example as an outcome of new space-time concepts. This also reflects the meaning of the term "postmodern urban landscape" (Harvey, 1989; Dear and Flusty, 1998).

Aspects of Sustainability

As a consequence of dramatic changes in the logistic system, the growth of freight transport raises many problems for cities, which are dependent on well-functioning commercial traffic and a high quality of life. From the environmental point of view, the significance of freight transport is obvious: It creates severe noise and air pollution, it requires a lot of space, and it leads to overuse of infrastructure (Läpple, 1995). An underestimated urban problem is the increasing demand for space due to the reduction of stock in stores and the functional establishment of logistical services (forwarders, integrators). In many cases, new functions along the logistical chains require new locations, such as warehouses and distribution centers.

From the standpoint of sustainability, there is a growing conflict between the functional requirements of freight movement and commercial traffic and the significance of the city as a business location, a residential and recreational habitat. In this context, freight transport seems to be paradigmatic of a multidimensional approach to sustainability. Basic objectives for strategies of "greening" logistics are improving the efficiency of freight traffic (from the economic perspective), improving the acceptability of freight traffic (from the social perspective), and

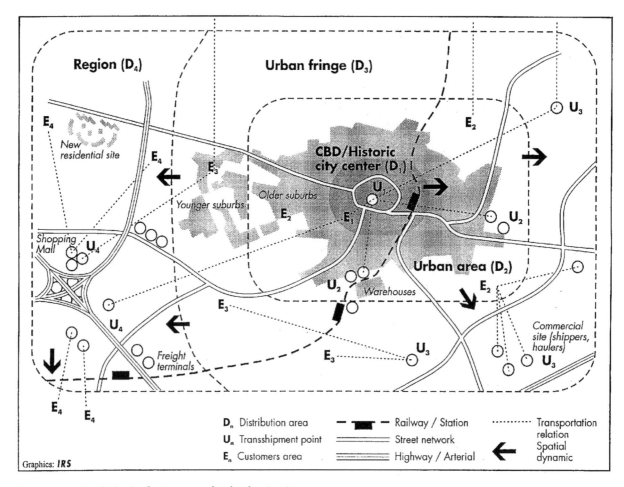

Figure 32.2   Logistics in the Process of Suburbanization

improving the sustainability of freight traffic (from the environmental perspective).

PLANNING NEEDS, POLICY TOPICS, AND LIMITS FOR ACTION

Since transportation, particularly urban goods distribution, is an important factor for the city and its environment, it is not surprising that the freight sector has been a focus of transport policy and planning since about 1990. Model projects in city or urban logistics are being launched in Germany, Denmark, Holland, and Switzerland to solve the conflict between the environment and the economy —by rerouting heavy vehicle traffic, by implementing cooperative delivery concepts, or by supporting inter-modality (combined transport, terminals). In England, a comprehensive framework named "Sustainable Distribution" has been launched to promote more acceptable modes of urban freight transport (DETR, 1999).

The practical impact of many commonly recommended "solutions" has been regarded as limited. There are several reasons for this reduced ability to solve the problems of transport and the environment. First, scant knowledge exists about the logic of logistics and freight transport, particularly as related to the city. Second, there is the matter of politics: Companies resist being regulated by public policy. Third, controlling freight traffic is crucial from the perspective of urban development: The more that restrictive urban goods policies and strategies are enforced, the more critical their economic outcome might be, and the more detrimental their impact on inner-city development could become.

These constraints are particularly visible in Europe, where the urban structure is becoming increasingly influenced by processes of dispersal and suburbanization (cf. Pawley 1994). Restrictive policy measures in urban logistics may contribute to the dissolution of cities by promoting easily accessible suburban locations. In this context, local municipalities face a triangle of conflicts: short-term economic goals (with respect to inter-urban competition), long-term balance of urban structure, and social and environmental sustainability with respect to quality of urban life, health, and ecology.

long-distance networks and large-scale infrastructure. In urban regions, a large amount of distribution will be decentralized to suburbs and exurbs.

In this context, the study contributes rather to a sustainable distribution system, combining information flows, "smart" logistic spaces, and acceptable modes of material transport. For some operations, particularly those involving more flexible and smaller-scale production and distribution, technology appears to be providing urban core areas with some niche functions. New technologies, such as those related to new modes of teleshopping and home delivery, may help to stabilize the economic functions of the CBD and develop acceptable patterns of physical distribution ("The city as a showroom").

POTENTIAL TRANSATLANTIC PROFILE OF THE RESEARCH

Comparing developments in the U.S. and Europe is useful for several reasons. The basic assumption is that experiences in the U.S. can offer worthwhile insights into possible futures both for the city and for goods distribution in Europe. The rationalization of supply chains is more advanced in the U.S. than in Europe. New information technologies, distribution concepts, and traffic management techniques have been invented and applied in the U.S.

Within the research, two case studies are being designed. One is planned in the metropolitan region of Berlin-Brandenburg, Germany, which has seen a massive suburbanization of distribution since 1990. The second case study will be conducted in the South Bay Area (San José), one of the fastest-growing urban regions in the United States. Transatlantic comparison is also justified, since there are many links in urban discourse (both in theory and in practice) between North America and Europe. Both the sprawling metropolis and the traditional European city are seen as prototypical developments.

To the extent that modern logistics redefine the historical role of the city as a distributive and economic location (marketplace), the comparison leads to specific views of possible urban futures. Assessing the findings in the context of urban development in Europe and the U.S., the reference point of the study may no longer be the vision of the central, "compact" city, with high density and mixed use. This vision is desirable, but it may be unrealistic—at least from the logistics perspective, which is characterized by

EXPECTED RESEARCH RESULTS AND PERSPECTIVES

The research is designed primarily to assess and evaluate the role of the distribution function in the (post-) modern urban landscape. The concept of sustainable development will also be exemplified in the difficult field of freight traffic. Transport and logistic research have, in theory, elaborated several measures and opportunities to make urban goods distribution more acceptable. Little of that has been successfully implemented.

In terms of sustainability, freight transport policy may not end up managing the growing transport demand as efficiently as the companies consider possible. Among the future tasks are the following:

- Minimizing the general and specific demand for transport within the overall producing-consuming-waste management chain, through the use of new instruments to estimate the demand of new production concepts or locations, through a life-cycle assessment of logistics etc.
- Avoiding additional transport and limiting transport growth, e.g., by supporting greater proximity of production and consumption or by promoting an optimized spatial division of labor. This type of division of labor need not correspond with our traditional understanding of a central city, but may also be generated within urban networks.
- Finally, every regional and local strategy requires a framework of nationally and internationally negotiated and thus accepted pricing and infrastructure policy.

Getting the prices right is one basic element for supporting a less material-intensive structural change, with more services and less energy and material consumption in the economy.

References

Bowersox, D. J. 1974. *Logistical Management.* New York, London: Macmillan.

Cooper, J., M. Browne, and M. Peters. 1991. *European Logistics: Markets, Management and Strategy.* Oxford: Blackwell.

Dear, M., and S. Flusty. 1998. "Postmodern Urbanism." *Annals of the Association of American Geographers* 88, no. 1: 50–72.

DETR/Department of the Environment, Transport and the Regions. 1999. *Sustainable Distribution: A Strategy.* London: DETR.

Fishman, R. 1990. "Unbound Megalopolis: America's New City." *Wilson Quarterly,* Winter 1990, 25–48.

Garreau, J. 1991. *Edge City: Life on the New Frontier.* New York: Doubleday.

Hanson, S. 1995. *The Geography of Urban Transportation.* 2nd ed. New York: Guilford Press.

Harvey, D. 1989. *The Condition of Postmodernity.* Oxford: Blackwell.

Hesse, M. 1995. "Urban Space and Logistics: On the Road to Sustainability?" *World Transport Policy and Practice* 1, no. 4: 39–45.

Hesse, M. 1998. *Wirtschaftsverkehr, Stadtentwicklung und politische Regulierung. Zum Strukturwandel in der Distributionslogistik und seinen Konsequenzen für die Stadtplanung.* Berlin: Deutsches Institut für Urbanistik.

Hollingsworth, J. R., and R. Boyer. 1997. *Contemporary Capitalism: The Embeddedness of Institutions.* Cambridge: Cambridge University Press.

Läpple, D. 1995. "Transport, Logistik und logistische Raum-Zeit-Konfigurationen." In D. Läpple, ed., *Güterverkehr, Logistik und Umwelt. Analysen und Konzepte zum interregionalen und staedtischen Verkehr.* Berlin: Edition Sigma.

Läpple, D. 1996. "Thesen zum Verhaeltnis von Stadt und Handel. Entwicklungstendenzen, Problemfelder und Handlungsansätze." In MSKS, ed., *Handel in der Stadt. Handeln in der Stadt,* 129–140. Düsseldorf: MSKS.

Odgen, K. W. 1992. *Urban Goods Movement: A Guide to Policy and Planning.* Aldershot: Ashgate.

Pawley, M. 1994. "The Redundancy of Space / Die Redundanz des urbanen Raumes." In B. Meurer, ed., *Die Zukunft des Raumes / The Future of Space,* vol. 1, 37–57. Der Schriftenreihe des Laboratoriums der Zivilisation—Akademie Deutscher Werkbund. Frankfurt/Main: Campus.

Schoenberger, E. 1996. *The Cultural Crisis of the Firm.* Oxford: Blackwell.

Soja, E. 1995. "Postmodern Urbanisation: The Six Restructurings of Los Angeles." In S. Watson and K. Gibson, eds., *Postmodern Cities and Spaces,* 125–137. Oxford: Blackwell.

U.S. Congress, Office of Technology Assessment. 1995. *The Technological Reshaping of Metropolitan America.* OTA-ETI-643. Washington, D.C.: U.S. Government Printing Office.

CHAPTER THIRTY-THREE

N3

*The Intersection of Transportation Networks,
Communication Networks, and Community Networks*

Barry Wellman

Looking for Community in Neighborhoods and Networks

The development of transportation networks (in the past two centuries) and communication networks (in the past century) has markedly affected the spatial distribution of community networks: interpersonal relations of sociability, support, and identity. Where community networks were once predominantly local, they are now predominantly long-distance.

For more than a century, analysts have tried to understand how large-scale social changes associated with the Industrial Revolution have affected the composition, structure, and operations of communities. Their analyses have reflected the ambivalence with which people have faced the impacts of industrialization, bureaucratization, capitalism, imperialism, and technological developments on interpersonal relations. Where religion, locality, and kinship group had some integrative claims on interpersonal relations, the shift to mobile, market societies now had the potential to disconnect individuals from the strengths and constraints of traditional societies. Although it is difficult to disentangle correlated causes, rapidly evolving transportation and communication networks have prima facie played a key role. The proliferation of widespread networks of cheap and efficient transportation and communication facilities has allowed contact to be maintained with greater ease and rapidity over longer distances: in transportation, from railroads through highways and planes; in communication, from overnight mail service, to direct long-distance telephone dialing, to the Internet. The increased velocity of transactions has fostered interactional density (Wellman, 2000).

In pre-industrial times, connectivity was principally door-to-door. Whether they lived in villages, urban neighborhoods, or traveling bands, people walked to encounter each other. Although shepherds, whores, soldiers, merchants, and seafarers traveled, most people remained in local groups, in which all knew one other. People were limited by their feet power in whom they could contact. When they visited someone, much of the group knew who was going to see whom and about what.

With such local roots, the scholarly search for community has traditionally been a search for local solidarity rather than a search for supportive ties, wherever located and however solidary. Community studies have usually been neighborhood studies of local interaction and sentiment, while neglecting the diversified non-local ties through which people obtain support, sociability, and identity. Consequently, when researchers have not found much local behavior and sentiments, they have concluded that "community" has disappeared. This does not mean that community has been lost but that it is much less likely now to be locally based, because current technological and social factors facilitate the maintenance of long-distance ties: heavy use of cars, planes, and transit; frequent residential mobility; spatially dispersed relationships and activities; efficient telecommunications and computer-mediated communication (Wellman, 2000).

The utility of a social network approach to the study of community (Wellman, 1988) is that it does not take as its starting point putative neighborhood solidarities; nor does it seek primarily to find and explain the persistence (or absence) of solidary sentiments. Most social network analyses do not treat officially defined group or neighborhood boundaries as truly social boundaries. Instead, they trace the social relationships of the persons they are studying, wherever these relationships go and whomever they are with. Social network analysts have discovered that community has not disappeared, even though it is thinly represented in its traditional neighborhood base. Except in situations of ethnic or racial segregation, contemporary Western communities rarely are tightly bounded, densely knit local groups of broadly based ties. They are usually loosely bounded, sparsely knit, spatially dispersed networks of specialized ties (Fischer, 1982; Wellman, 1999). Most community ties in the developed world stretch across a metropolitan region, with many extending across the nation or to other continents.

The Nature of Network Communities

People Are Not Wrapped Up in Traditional Densely Knit, Tightly Bounded Communities but Are Maneuvering in Specialized, Sparsely Knit, Loosely Bounded, Frequently Changing Networks

Both scholars and the public have traditionally thought of communities as composed of broadly based relationships in which each community member felt securely able to obtain a variety of help. Yet community ties are specialized, with most community members supplying only a few kinds of support (Wellman, 1999). In France, kin and neighbors engage in mutual aid, but friends and neighbors are the confidants (Ferrand, Mounier, and Degenne, 1999). In northern California, there are differences between troubleshooting kin and companionable friends (Fischer, 1982; Schweizer, Schnegg, and Berzborn, 1998).

In Toronto, those network members who provide small services or emotional aid rarely provide large services, companionship, or financial aid (Wellman and Wortley, 1990). The specialized provision of support means that people must maintain differentiated portfolios of ties to obtain a variety of resources.

Contemporary personal communities are usually sparsely knit and loosely bounded. Two Toronto studies have found that only one-third of a person's active community members have active ties with each other (Wellman, 1979; Wellman, Carrington, and Hall, 1988), and these networks become even more sparsely knit as people age and their networks become more differentiated (Wellman et al., 1997). The complex and specialized nature of personal communities means that these are fragmented networks, with clusters of relationships based on shared interests, kinship, locality, and friendship.

Communities based on voluntary selectivity can become homogeneous networks of people with similar attitudes and lifestyles. Moreover, Internet-based communication is increasing the emphasis on relationships based on shared interests (Wellman, 2000). These may be transitory, as interests change more rapidly than kinship ties or residential location.

Yet even before the advent of the Internet, few networks were stable: Only 28 percent of Torontonians' intimate ties were still intimate a decade later (Wellman et al., 1997). The tradeoff is a greater reach. Rather than locking people into one tightly bounded social circle, a person's 1,000 or so interpersonal ties connect him/her with diverse social arenas (Kochen, 1989). Although less palpably a community, these ramified connections are useful for getting jobs in China (Bian, 1999) and Chile (Espinoza, 1999), finding financial capital in Hungary (Sik and Wellman, 1999), and helping Hong Kong immigrants settle in Canada (Salaff, Fong, and Wong, 1999). Sparsely knit, fragmentary, loosely bounded communities make it possible to reach many people through short chains of "friends of friends." Yet in such sparsely knit and loosely bounded networks, people cannot depend on the goodwill or social control of a solidary community. Instead, they must actively deal with each tie separately (Wellman and Frank, 2000).

Communities Have Moved Out of Neighborhoods to Be Dispersed Networks

Contemporary communities rarely are local groupings of neighbors and kin. The residents of developed societies usually know few neighbors, and most members of their personal communities do not live in the same neighborhood (Wellman, 1992b). For example, only 23 percent of Torontonians' active community ties are with people living within one mile (Wellman, 1996), and members of personal communities are in a clear minority elsewhere: 19 percent in Japan (Otani, 1999), 10 percent in northern California (Fischer, 1982), and 20 percent in a national U.S. sample (Marsden, 1987). People maintain far-flung relationships using both telecommunications (telephones and e-mail) and transportation (based on cars, expressways, and airplanes). Rather than being door-to-door, transportation and communication are often place-to-place, with freeways and telephone networks providing little information about the territories between the places they connect. In Toronto, being within one hour's drive or within the local telephone zone—and not being in the same neighborhood—is the effective boundary for high levels of face-to-face contact and social support (Wellman, Carrington, and Hall, 1988; Wellman and Tindall, 1993). One-quarter of Toronto's socially close community ties go beyond the metropolitan area, with an appreciable number spanning the continent or the ocean (Wellman, 1979). This lack of local ties and the presence of community members living elsewhere weakens local commitment and encourages people to vote with their feet—leaving when conditions are bad rather than staying to improve things. For example, many Hong Kong emigrants rely on transpacific ties to move to North America (Salaff, Fong, and Wong, 1999).

Yet communities have not totally lost their domestic roots. Local relationships are necessary for domestic tranquility, and for getting goods and services quickly (Jacobs, 1961; Lee and Campbell, 1999; Wellman and Wortley, 1990). Thus while the ties of Torontonians are far-flung, most of their face-to-face interactions are with people who live or work near them. Moreover, much of their telephone contact is with neighbors (Wellman and Tindall, 1993; Wellman, 1996). Despite the fact that e-mail makes it cheap and easy to have long-distance ties, e-mail relationships may be more local than celebrants of the global village believe. My February 1999 pilot study of graduate students in Berkeley found that 50 percent of their interpersonal e-mail was from within Berkeley, while another 25 percent was from elsewhere in the San Francisco Bay area. Our study of a wired suburb near Toronto found Internet connectivity actively promoting neighborhood gatherings (Hampton and Wellman, 2000). Moreover, Internet users are as "glocalized" as telephone users were before the advent of cellphone, rooted by modem cable to their home and office desktops.

The development of transportation and communication networks means that accessibility, not spatial propinquity, is important for providing material aid. Accessible ties provide important goods and services. These ties are not only with people living nearby, but also with those living farther away who are co-workers or are in frequent in-person or telecommunications contact (Wellman and Wortley, 1990). However, people were as likely to get companionship or emotional support from those living elsewhere as they were to get it from those living nearby.

In contrast to the situation in developed countries, local ties are the keys to daily survival in low-income neighborhoods in Santiago, Chile (Espinoza, 1999). They provide food, shelter, short-term loans, job leads, and help in dealing with organizations. In this situation, neighbors (who are often kin) provide most everyday support. Yet such neighbors are poor themselves. To get sizable amounts of money or access to good jobs, the residents must rely on their weaker ties to wealthier, better-situated relatives who live outside the barrios. The situation fits well with the argument that weak ties often reach into other social circles to provide access to new resources, while strong ties that stay within solidary local groups are well-suited for mobilizing and conserving existing resources (Granovetter, 1982; Wolf, 1966; Wellman and Leighton, 1979).

Private Intimacy Has Replaced Public Sociability

Rather than operating out of public neighborhood spaces, contemporary communities usually operate out of private homes, where people drive, telephone, or e-mail to interact. Well into the 20th century, men customarily walked to gather in communal, quasi-public milieus, such as pubs, cafés, parks, and village greens (Roche, 1981). More accessible than private homes, such places drew their clientele from fluid networks of regular habitués. Population density, combined with the permeability of public spaces, provided many opportunities for chance encounters with friends of their friends, and to form new bonds (Wall, 1990). This public community was largely for men. Women visited privately at home (Garrioch, 1986).

Men now find community in private homes rather than in public places. The separation of work from residential localities means that co-workers commute from different neighborhoods and no longer come home from work together in sociable community groups. While men now spend more time at home instead of at bars or cafés, the high percentage of women engaged in paid work outside their homes means that women spend less time at home. Thus husbands and wives are now apt to be at home on nights and weekends, when both are available to each other (Hochschild, 1989). At the same time, zoning often places commercial areas for recreation far from home, making it difficult to go out in the neighborhood for casual sociability. Household pursuits dominate.

Rather than being accessible to others in public places, most members of Torontonians' personal communities live a median distance of 15 kilometers apart. They talk with each other an average of twice per month, as often by telephone as face-to-face (Wellman, Carrington, and Hall, 1988). The absence of well-used public spaces and nearby community members means that people cannot go out into the neighborhood to find much community. Instead, they have selective encounters, singly or in couples, with dispersed community network members. Yet the easy accessibility of local relationships means that those local ties that do exist are significant. Although people living within one mile constitute only 23 percent of the Torontonians' active ties, these neighbors engage in fully 42 percent of all face-to-face interactions with community members and 31 percent of all telephone contact (Wellman, 1996).

Despite the importance of neighborhood ties portrayed in accounts of low-income households (e.g., Liebow, 1967; Lee and Campbell, 1999; Espinoza, 1999), only a minority of community ties in the Western world operate in the public contexts of the neighborhood, formal organizations, or work. Community networks contain high proportions of people who enjoy each other and low proportions of people who are forced to interact with each other because they are juxtaposed in the same neighborhood, kinship group, organization, or workplace (Feld, 1981).

Private activity has replaced public activity. Where North Americans a generation ago often spent Saturday night going out for a movie and pizza, they now invite a few friends over to their homes to watch videos and order a pizza to be delivered. In Toronto, people watch videos at home an average of thirty times per year but go out for entertainment only three or four times a year. When North Americans do go out, they usually go out alone, in couples, or in small, informal groups (Putnam, 2000). The community of the pub in the recent television show *Cheers* is rare. Only 10 percent of adult Canadians go to a pub once a week or more.

As community has become private, contact with familiar friends and relatives has replaced public gregariousness. This privatization may be responsible for the lack of informal help for strangers who are in trouble in public spaces (Latané and Darley, 1976). People feel responsible for their "own"—the members of their community networks with whom they have strong ties—but not for the many acquaintances and strangers with whom they rub shoulders but are not otherwise connected. At the same time, people feel that they lack friends and are surrounded by strangers even when their networks are abundantly supportive (Lofland, 1998).

The privatization and domestication of relationships have transformed the nature of community. Domesticated community ties interact in small groups in private homes rather than in larger groups in public spaces. This makes it more difficult for people to form new community ties with friends of their friends, and it focuses the concerns of relationships on dealing with household problems (Wellman, 1992a). Community members help with daily hassles and crises; neighbors mind each other's children; sisters and friends provide companionship and emotional support for child, husband, and elder care (Wellman and Wortley, 1990). Yet people in these privatized milieus rarely use their community ties to accomplish collective projects of work, politics, or leisure.

Home is now the base for relationships that are more voluntary and selective than the public communities of the past. Where public communities were once men's worlds, home-based community networks now bring husbands and wives together. Married women not only participate in community, they are central to the practice of it in their households, in an ambiguous combination of assertive arrangers and unpaid service workers. With the privatization of community, community-keeping has become a part of domestic management. No longer do husbands and wives have many separate friendships. The wives' ties form the basis for relations between married couples, creating a "triple load" of domestic work, paid work, and "net work" (Wellman and Wellman, 1992).

NETWORK COMMUNITIES IN THE GLOBAL VILLAGE

With the development of transportation and communication networks, community networks have become "glocalized": global in their reach and local in their base within households. Complex community networks stretch across cities, regions, nations, and oceans. Communication has become person-to-person, ignoring the places in which people are communicating (Wellman, 2000). Yet even in an area of computer-mediated communication, transportation networks matter, as few community ties are sustained by communication alone. Neighbors still interact more than distant ties. These are network communities and not local communities. Multiple clusters and limited social control in these networks give people room to maneuver, even if the cost is that they must actively maintain their ties and scan their networks for help. The cost of escaping these bounded groups is that people think that they and the world are not well-connected. The benefit is that they have more autonomy to connect where they will.

References

Bian, Yanjie. 1999. "Getting a Job through a Web of Quanxi in China." In *Networks in the Global Village,* ed. Barry Wellman, 255–278. Boulder, Colo.: Westview.

Espinoza, Vicente. 1999. "Social Networks among the Urban Poor: Inequality and Integration in a Latin American City." In *Networks in the Global Village,* ed. Barry Wellman, 147–184. Boulder, Colo.: Westview.

Feld, Scott. 1981. "The Focused Organization of Social Ties." *American Journal of Sociology* 86: 1015–1035.

Ferrand, Alexis, Lise Mounier, and Alain Degenne. 1999. "The Diversity of Personal Networks in France." In *Networks in the Global Village,* ed. Barry Wellman, 185–224. Boulder, Colo.: Westview Press.

Fischer, Claude. 1982. *To Dwell among Friends.* Berkeley: University of California Press.

Garrioch, David. 1986. *Neighbourhood and Community in Paris, 1740–1790.* Cambridge: Cambridge University Press.

Granovetter, Mark. 1982. "The Strength of Weak Ties: A Network Theory Revisited." In *Social Structure and Network Analysis,* ed. Peter Marsden and Nan Lin, 105–130. Beverly Hills: Sage.

Hampton, Keith, and Barry Wellman. 2000. "Examining Community in the Digital Neighborhood: Early Results from Canada's Wired Suburb." In *Digital Cities,* ed. Toru Ishida and Katherine Isbister. Wiesbaden: Springer-Verlag.

Hochschild, Arlie Russell. 1989. *The Second Shift: Working Parents and the Revolution at Home.* New York: Viking Penguin.

Jacobs, Jane. 1961. *The Death and Life of Great American Cities.* New York: Random House.

Kochen, Manfred, ed. 1989. *The Small World.* Norwood, N.J.: Ablex.

Latané, Bibb, and John Darley. 1976. *Help in a Crisis: Bystander Response to an Emergency.* Morristown, N.J.: General Learning Press.

Lee, Barrett, and Karen Campbell. "Neighbor Networks of Black and White Americans." In *Networks in the Global Village,* ed. Barry Wellman, 119–146. Boulder, Colo.: Westview.

Liebow, Elliot. 1967. *Tally's Corner.* Boston: Little Brown.

Lofland, Lyn. 1998. *The Public Realm.* New York: Aldine de Gruyter.

Marsden, Peter. 1987. "Core Discussions Networks of Americans." *American Sociological Review* 52: 122–131.

Otani, Shinsuke. 1999. "Personal Community Networks in Contemporary Japan." In *Networks in the Global Village,* ed. Barry Wellman, 279–297. Boulder, Colo.: Westview Press.

Putnam, Robert. 2000. *Bowling Alone.* New York: Simon and Schuster.

Roche, Daniel. 1981. *The People of Paris: An Essay in Popular Culture in the 18th Century.* Berkeley: University of California Press.

Salaff, Janet, Eric Fong, and Siu-lun Wong. 1999. "Using Social Networks to Exit Hong Kong." In *Networks in the Global Village,* ed. Barry Wellman, 299–330. Boulder, Colo.: Westview.

Schweizer, Thomas, Michael Schnegg, and Susanne Berzborn. 1998. "Personal Networks and Social Support in a Multiethnic Community of Southern California." *Social Networks* 20: 1–21.

Sik, Endre, and Barry Wellman. 1999. "Network Capital in Capitalist, Communist and Post-Communist Countries." In *Networks in the Global Village,* ed. Barry Wellman, 225–254. Boulder, Colo.: Westview.

Wall, Helena. 1990. *Fierce Communion: Family and Community in North America.* Cambridge, Mass.: Harvard University Press.

Wellman, Barry. 1979. "The Community Question." *American Journal of Sociology* 84: 1201–1231.

Wellman, Barry. 1988. "The Community Question Re-evaluated." In *Power, Community and the City,* ed. Michael Peter Smith, 81–107. New Brunswick, N.J.: Transaction Books.

Wellman, Barry. 1992a. "Men in Networks: Private Communities, Domestic Friendships." In *Men's Friendships,* ed. Peter Nardi, 74–114. Newbury Park, Calif.: Sage.

Wellman, Barry. 1992b. "Which Types of Ties and Networks Give What Kinds of Social Support?" *Advances in Group Processes* 9: 207–235.

Wellman, Barry. 1996. "Are Personal Communities Local?" *Social Networks* 18: 347–354.

Wellman, Barry, ed. 1999. *Networks in the Global Village.* Boulder, Colo.: Westview.

Wellman, Barry. 2001. "Physical Place and Cyber Place: The Rise of Networked Individualism." *International Journal of Urban and Regional Research* 252: 227–252.

Wellman, Barry, Peter Carrington, and Alan Hall. 1988. "Networks as Personal Communities." In *Social Structures: A Network Approach,* ed. Barry Wellman and S. D. Berkowitz, 130–184. Cambridge: Cambridge University Press.

Wellman, Barry, and Kenneth Frank. 2000. "Network Capital in a Multi-Level World." In *Social Capital: Theory and Research,* ed. Nan Lin, Karen Cook, and Ronald Burt. New York: Aldine DeGruyter,

Wellman, Barry, and Barry Leighton. 1979. "Networks, Neighborhoods and Communities." *Urban Affairs Quarterly* 14: 363–390.

Wellman, Barry, and David Tindall. 1993. "Reach Out and Touch Some Bodies: How Social Networks Connect Telephone Networks." In *Progress in Communication Sciences,* ed. William Richards, Jr. and George Barnett, 63–93. Norwood, N.J.: Ablex.

Wellman, Barry, Renita Wong, David Tindall, and Nancy Nazer. 1997. "A Decade of Network Change." *Social Networks* 19, no. 1: 27–51.

Wellman, Barry, and Scot Wortley. 1990. "Different Strokes from Different Folks." *American Journal of Sociology* 96: 558–588.

Wellman, Beverly, and Barry Wellman. 1992. "Domestic Affairs and Network Relations." *Journal of Social and Personal Relationships* 9: 385–409.

Wolf, Eric. 1966. "Kinship, Friendship and Patron-Client Relations." In *The Social Anthropology of Complex Societies,* ed. Michael Banton. London: Tavistock.

PART VIII

Alternative Solutions

CHAPTER THIRTY-FOUR

Implementation of Pricing Measures for Sustainable Transport

Investigating Economic Efficiency and Social Acceptability

Erik T. Verhoef
and Eric Pels

INTRODUCTION

Economists have widely recognized that Pigouvian marginal external cost pricing in principle offers an efficient, first-best means of dealing with transport externalities, the main external cost categories being congestion, accidents, noise, and pollution. According to most analysts, it would offer the socially most cost-effective means of inducing the behavioral and social changes that are necessary in order to achieve an efficient and sustainable transport system. This holds for changes in both the shorter run (route choice, mode choice, trip suppression, rescheduling) and the longer run (choice of vehicle technology, work, leisure, and residential locations, etc.). With the ongoing increase in external costs of transport in general, and peak hour road transport in urbanized areas in particular, this economic principle also seems to be gaining political and perhaps even social acceptability, in addition to the growing technical feasibility (e.g., automatic vehicle identification). This is illustrated in recent policy plans in the field of transport and sustainability; witness, for instance, the principles underlying the EU document "Towards Fair and Efficient Pricing in Transport" (Commission of the European Communities, 1995) and, specific to the Dutch situation, the current plans for introducing electronic road pricing during peak hours in

the Randstad (2001), and on the basis of a flat kilometer charge throughout the country (2002). In aviation, likewise—another sector with rapidly increasing traffic volumes—increased congestion, noise, and emissions are often cited as a motivation for a more active use of the price mechanism in the regulation of external costs.

Such charges offer a practical application of Pigou's (1920) ideas on optimal externality taxes in (road) transport. Although the economic theory of externality charges in road transport has developed considerably since the days of Pigou (Button and Verhoef, 1998 offer a recent collection of papers), the theoretical and empirical modeling of (road and air) traffic congestion, emissions, and road pricing is still a fruitful area of scientific research. This holds in particular for modeling the various complexities of real-life traffic: dynamics, in terms of traffic flows as well as of consumer and producers scheduling; network issues, such as route choice and spillovers under non-optimal pricing; and heterogeneity of users, in terms of, for instance, (desired) speeds, emissions, and values of time. Such detailed analyses are indispensable both for determining first-best and (more realistic) second-best optimal road charges in reality, and for more accurately predicting the behavioral impacts and economic welfare effects of implementing various possible pricing regimes. They are also indispensable for a more reliable assessment and evaluation of the actual behavioral impacts and economic welfare effects of the currently limited number of practical applications of pricing instruments.

Apart from these "efficiency aspects" of first-best and second-best pricing, another major issue surrounding the introduction and use of price instruments for achieving a more efficient, sustainable transport system is social and political acceptability, which is often limited. There seems to be ample scope for innovative theoretical and empirical research concerning these questions as well.

This chapter offers some reflections on possible transatlantic research initiatives on sustainable transport pricing in general, and on road traffic and aviation in particular. Especially now that road charging is becoming a realistic possibility, and an increasing number of airports are facing capacity restrictions, research in these fields can be expected to yield important insights for practical policy-making in both the U.S. and the EU. The necessity for the U.S. and the EU to pool research on this topic is also increasing. In particular, many problems encountered both in the modeling of marginal external cost pricing (for the purpose of policy advice and evaluation) and in practical applications (for instance, the question of how to obtain a sufficient level of public acceptance) may be very similar across the two nations.

Aim and Scope of the Research

In light of the foregoing, this project aims at (1) providing an inventory of the state of the art in research on the main methodological and empirical questions surrounding marginal cost pricing in transport; (2) assessing future research needs on this topic; and (3) stimulating joint research initiatives by U.S. and EU researchers and institutions interested in this field.

Although the contexts in which transport pricing might be implemented may be quite different in the EU and the U.S. (without implying that conditions would be nearly similar within the two countries), there is still a lot to be gained from sharing knowledge of and experience with both the modeling aspects and the empirical analysis of revealed or stated preference data relating to the use and effects of transport pricing. According to economic theory, marginal social cost pricing is an indispensable part of efficient policy packages that aim at bringing about the

social and behavioral changes needed to achieve a sustainable transport system. The general themes of the project are therefore at the heart of the Social Change and Sustainable Transport discussion.

The exact research themes to be selected during the project will depend, of course, on the consortium to be formed, but there are a number of proposed themes, including the following: behavioral impacts and economic welfare effects of first-best and (more realistic) second-best pricing; equity impacts, social feasibility, and tax revenue allocation issues of pricing measures in transport; modeling pricing in dynamic transport network models; pricing and public versus private ownership of infrastructure; and political and institutional barriers to implementing pricing measures. It is important that both theoretical and empirical approaches to these research questions be addressed in the project.

Context in the Existing Research Literature[1]

Pigou's original idea of using economic instruments to regulate transport externalities has given rise to a substantial body of literature. Seminal works include Wardrop (1952), Walters (1961), and Vickrey (1969). Pigou's insights were extended to the regulation of transport externalities other than congestion, in particular environmental degradation, noise, and accidents—all those unintended side effects that make current transport systems unsustainable.

However, the stringent assumptions for first-best regulation of transport externalities are rarely met in practice. Economic distortions elsewhere in the system (which can be a unimodal transport network, a multimodal transport network, a closed economy, an open economy, etc.), reflected in non-optimal prices, prevent "naive" marginal cost pricing from being a truly welfare-maximizing transport policy. Second-best alternatives to first-best Pigouvian "benchmark" policy have therefore received ample attention in the recent literature. Two classic examples on second-best regulation in road transport are Lévy-Lambert, 1968 and Marchand, 1968, which studied optimal congestion pricing with an untolled alternative, an issue that was more recently discussed also by Braid (1996), Verhoef et al. (1996), and Liu and McDonald (1999). Other studies on second-best regulation in road transport include Arnott et al., 1990; Arnott, 1979; Sullivan, 1983; Braid, 1989;

d'Ouville and McDonald, 1990; and Wilson, 1983. Nilsson, 1992 looks at second-best problems in rail transport, and Daniel, 1995 and 2000 study airport congestion pricing.

"Second-best" pricing—often considered the realistic counterpart of the hypothetical benchmark of first-best pricing—still faces great scientific research challenges. For example, what is the optimal toll if not all links/nodes on a network can be charged? What is the optimal pattern of a toll when it cannot be adjusted continuously and/or perfectly to prevailing traffic conditions? What is the optimal level of a tax when externalities caused by different departure times or places differ across users? What is the optimal tax if there are only a small number of players active in the network, responsible for a large number of interdependent movements? For realistic situations, such questions may be answered only through the use of suitable models, e.g., dynamic transport network models, a research field that is still rapidly evolving (Ran and Boyce, 1996; Nagurney, 1998).

Optimal transport pricing, although economically desirable and frequently suggested by economists, has rarely been adopted by policy-makers. Various practical applications have demonstrated that it is technically possible to operate an electronic road pricing scheme successfully (Dawson and Catling, 1986; Hau, 1992), but the use of this approach in practice remains limited. Suggested road pricing in the Randstad in the Netherlands (Verhoef et al., 1996) has still not been implemented, and still faces plenty of opposition, despite the fact that the congestion problem continues to worsen. When Boston Logan Airport tried to restructure its pricing scheme, regional airlines and general aviation argued that the new plan violated federal laws, according to which airports should be available for public use on fair and reasonable terms and without discrimination. The Court of Appeals agreed, and effectively prohibited fee structures based on social costs of operation (Daniel, 2000). Lave (1995) summarizes the problem: "It has been a commonplace event for transportation economists to put the conventional diagram on the board, note the self-evident optimality of pricing solutions, and then sit down waiting for the world to adopt this obviously correct solution. Well, we have been waiting for seventy years now, and it's worth asking what are the facets of the problem that we have been missing. Why is the world reluctant to do the obvious?"

Redistributional effects of transport pricing and equity considerations may contribute to this problem, and have received due attention in the literature. Segal and Steinmeier (1980) argue that the redistributional effects of transport pricing override the efficiency gains. Because of these effects, Andrew Evans (1992) questions the desirability of (road) pricing and points out the possibility of monopolistic pricing. But when heterogeneity of consumers (for example, due to income differences) is allowed for, some transport infrastructure users may benefit from pricing. Richardson (1974), Layard (1977), Glazer (1981), and Arnott et al. (1994) all conclude that road pricing is likely to be regressive. Foster (1975), on the other hand, argues that road pricing can be progressive, in particular when society is divided into richer car owners, on the one hand, and poorer non–car owners, on the other. The regressive incidence of road pricing generally reported results from the fact that higher-income drivers typically suffer disproportionately from unregulated congestion because of their higher value of time. It is questionable, though, whether the progressive incidence of welfare losses due to unregulated congestion provides a sound basis for allowing this inefficiency to continue. Both Andrew Evans (1992) and Small (1983, 1992) discuss redistribution of pricing revenues, so that as many actors as possible benefit, and how it can play a vital role in the discussion of feasibility of pricing schemes. Verhoef et al. (1997), on the basis of a survey of road users in the Randstad, also found the redistribution of revenues to be an important factor in the acceptance of road pricing. Sheldon et al. (1993), from an interview study of London residents, find that a simple road pricing from which the revenues are used in a transparent and equitable manner is more likely to be accepted. However, as pointed out by May (1992), it may be that inequities are intrinsic to any form of road pricing. "The key is to keep these to a minimum." Else (1986) mentions the possibility of giving road users a choice between paying a toll or waiting in line. Such a scheme was recently suggested in the Netherlands as an alternative to road pricing. Some (political) parties, however, referred to the tolled alternative as "a racetrack for the rich." Daniel (2000) argues that "equity concerns favor imposition of airport congestion pricing." Using a common weight-based pricing scheme, private aircraft operators (using small aircraft) impose delays on commercial aircraft passengers without having to pay the social cost of these delays. Redistribution of revenues can ensure welfare improvement of all types of aviation.

Despite problems of social and political feasibility, road pricing in various forms has been, or soon will be, introduced in a number of cities (see also Small and Gomez-

Table 34.1 Some Prejudices on Possible Differences between U.S. and EU Contexts of Transport Pricing

U.S.	EU
Greater reliance on car	Greater role of alternative transport modes
Smaller public involvement in collective transport	Greater public involvement in collective transport
"Urban sprawl"	"Stronger concentration in cities"
Pricing more often by private companies	Pricing by public institutes
Greater tradition in dynamic transport modeling	Traditionally using static network models
Higher average travel distances	Lower average travel distances
Single national government	Multiple national governments
Predominantly national aviation market	Predominantly international aviation market

Ibañez, 1998). A number of types of road pricing exist, some of which involve the private operation of so-called pay-lanes (as in California). It seems worthwhile, therefore, for the U.S. and the EU to pool their experiences with pricing, both in modeling and in practical applications, in a transatlantic research project under the SCAST flag.

POTENTIAL COMPARATIVE EUROPEAN
AND NORTH AMERICAN PROFILES
OF THE RESEARCH

The questions raised above are particularly suited for an interesting comparison between European and North American experiences. In Table 34.1, we sketch some of the notable expected differences between the two, on the basis of pure intuition/expectation; a thorough investigation would be one of the first interesting tasks to be carried out during the project.

A comparative study might therefore provide unique insights into the impact of "background variables" upon the impacts of (and scope for) using pricing instruments to obtain (more) sustainable transport, as well as provide a platform for an exchange of research experiences between the U.S. and the EU. Third, of course, analysis of

the various possible barriers (social, political, institutional, etc.) in both areas to the implementation of pricing policies in transport, and the possibilities for overcoming these, would also be interesting, both from a scientific and from a policy-making perspective. Fourth, the sharing of road- and aviation-oriented research may prove fruitful in terms, for instance, of cross-fertilization in modeling work in the field of transport network modeling for assessments of social, political, and institutional barriers to the implementation of marginal cost pricing in transport.

EXPECTED RESEARCH RESULTS
AND PERSPECTIVES

The project should provide (further) insights into the behavioral impacts, economic welfare, and equity effects of the use of pricing instruments in the quest for sustainable transport, into theoretical and empirical research on these matters, and into the role of public versus private ownership of infrastructure, as well as of political, social, and institutional barriers in the implementation of marginal social cost pricing, from a comparative transatlantic perspective. Depending on the eventual composition of the research consortium, certain priorities in this as yet rather broadly defined set of goals will be set. The tangible results should be working papers, journal articles, and perhaps a joint book.

A proposed research strategy would be to have a number of workshops, the first to be dedicated to an identification and definition of key research questions to be addressed and an overview of research and knowledge currently available; the second one to discuss joint comparative research to be carried out; and a third one, open to a larger audience, for the presentation and discussion of final results. Apart from these workshops, a number of working visits of researchers from participating institutes may be helpful in improving the quality and coherence of the research to be carried out.

Note

1. This section draws on a literature review in the introduction to Button and Verhoef (1998).

References

Arnott, R. J. 1979. "Unpriced Transport Congestion." *Journal of Economic Theory* 21: 294–316.

Arnott, R., A. de Palma, and R. Lindsey. 1990. "Economics of a Bottleneck." *Journal of Urban Economics* 27: 11–30.

Arnott, R., A. de Palma, and R. Lindsey. 1993. "A Structural Model of Peak-Period Congestion: A Traffic Bottleneck with Elastic Demand." *American Economic Review* 83, no. 11: 161–179.

Arnott, R., A. de Palma, and R. Lindsey. 1994. "The Welfare Effects of Congestion Tolls with Heterogeneous Commuters." *Journal of Transport Economics and Policy* 28: 139–161.

Arnott, R., A. de Palma, and R. Lindsey. 1998. "Recent Developments in the Bottleneck Model." In K. J. Button and E. T. Verhoef, eds., *Road Pricing, Traffic Congestion and the Environment: Issues of Efficiency and Social Feasibility.* Cheltenham: Edward Elgar.

Braid, R. M. 1989. "Uniform versus Peak-Load Pricing of a Bottleneck with Elastic Demand." *Journal of Urban Economics* 26: 320–327.

Braid, R. M. 1996. "Peak-Load Pricing of a Transportation Route with an Unpriced Substitute." *Journal of Urban Economics* 40: 179–197.

Button K. J., and E. T. Verhoef, eds. 1998. *Road Pricing, Traffic Congestion and the Environment: Issues of Efficiency and Social Feasibility.* Cheltenham: Edward Elgar.

Commission of the European Communities. 1995. *Green Paper towards Fair and Efficient Pricing in Transport: Policy Options for Internalising the External Costs of Transport in the European Union.* Brussels: Directorate-General for Transport.

Daganzo, C. F. 1995. "A Pareto Optimum Congestion Reduction Scheme." *Transportation Research* 29B, no. 2: 139–154.

Daniel, J. I. 1995. "Airport Congestion Pricing: A Bottleneck Model with Stochastic Queues." *Econometrica* 63, no. 2: 327–370.

Daniel, J. I. 2000. "Distributional Effects of Airport Congestion Pricing." Working Paper, Department of Economics, University of Delaware.

Dawson, J. A. L., and I. Catling. 1986. "Electronic Road Pricing in Hong Kong." *Transportation Research* 20A, no. 2: 129–134.

De Meza, D., and J. R. Gould. 1987. "Free Access versus Private Property in a Resource: Income Distributions Compared." *Journal of Political Economy* 95, no. 6: 1317–1325.

Else, P. K. 1981. "A Reformulation of the Theory of Optimal Congestion Taxes." *Journal of Transport Economics and Policy* 15: 217–232.

Else, P. K. 1982. "A Reformulation of the Theory of Optimal Congestion Taxes: A Rejoinder." *Journal of Transport Economics and Policy* 16: 299–304.

Else, P. K. 1986. "No Entry for Congestion Taxes?" *Transportation Research* 20A, no. 2: 99–107.

Evans, Alan W. 1992. "Road Congestion: The Diagrammatic Analysis." *Journal of Political Economy* 100, no. 1: 211–217.

Evans, Andrew W. 1992. "Road Congestion Pricing: When Is It a Good Policy?" *Journal of Transport Economics and Policy* 26: 213–243.

Evans, Andrew W. 1993. "Road Congestion Pricing: When Is It a Good Policy? A Rejoinder." *Journal of Transport Economics and Policy* 27: 99–105.

Foster, C. 1975. "A Note on the Distributional Effects of Road Pricing: A Comment." *Journal of Transport Economics and Policy* 9: 186–187.

Glazer, A. 1981. "Congestion Tolls and Consumer Welfare." *Public Finance* 36, no. 1: 77–83.

Goodwin, P. B. 1989. "The Rule of Three: A Possible Solution to the Political Problem of Competing Objectives for Road Pricing." *Traffic Engineering and Control* 30, no. 10: 495–497.

Hau, T. D. 1992. "Congestion Charging Mechanisms: An Evaluation of Current Practice." Preliminary Draft, Transport Division, The World Bank, Washington, D.C.

Hills, P. 1993. "Road Congestion Pricing: When Is It a Good Policy? A Comment." *Journal of Transport Economics and Policy* 27: 91–99.

Jones, P. 1991. "Gaining Public Support for Road Pricing through a Package Approach." *Traffic Engineering and Control* 32, no. 4: 194–196.

Lave, C. 1995. "The Demand Curve under Road Pricing and the Problem of Political Feasibility: Author's Reply." *Transportation Research* 29A, no. 6: 464–465.

Layard, R. 1977. "The Distributional Effects of Congestion Taxes." *Economica* 44: 297–304.

Lévy-Lambert, H. 1968. "Tarification des services à qualité variable: application aux péages de circulation." *Econometrica* 36, no. 3–4: 564–574.

Liu, N. L., and J. F. McDonald. "Economic Efficiency of Second-Best Congestion Pricing Schemes in Urban Highway Systems." *Transportation Research* 33B: 157–188.

Marchand, M. 1968. "A Note on Optimal Tolls in an Imperfect Environment." *Econometrica* 36, no. 3–4: 575–581.

May, A.D. 1992. "Road Pricing: An International Perspective." *Transportation* 19, no. 4: 313–333.

Mun, S.-I. 1998. "Peak-Load Pricing of a Bottleneck with Traffic Jam." *Journal of Urban Economics* 46, no. 3: 323–349.

Nagurney, A. 1998. *Network Economics: A Variational Inequality Approach.* Dordrecht: Kluwer.

Nash, C. A. 1982. "A Reformulation of the Theory of Optimal Congestion Taxes: A Comment." *Journal of Transport Economics and Policy* 16: 295–299.

Newell, G. F. 1988. "Traffic Flow for the Morning Commute." *Transportation Science* 22: 47–58.

Nilsson, J.-E. 1992. "Second-Best Problems in Railway Infrastructure Pricing and Investment." *Journal of Transport Economics and Policy* 26: 245–259.

d'Ouville, E. L., and J. F. McDonald. 1990. "Optimal Road Capacity with a Suboptimal Congestion Toll." *Journal of Urban Economics* 28: 34–49.

Pigou, A. C. 1920. *Wealth and Welfare.* London: Macmillan.

Ran, B., and D. Boyce. 1996. *Modeling Dynamic Transportation Networks: An Intelligent Transportation System Oriented Approach.* 2nd ed. Berlin: Springer.

Richardson, H. W. 1974. "A Note on the Distributional Effects of Road Pricing." *Journal of Transport Economics and Policy* 8: 82–85.

Segal, D., and T. L. Steinmeier. 1980. "The Incidence of Congestion and Congestion Tolls." *Journal of Urban Economics* 7: 42–62.

Sheldon, R., M. Scott, and P. Jones. 1993. "London Congestion Charging: Exploratory Social Research among London Residents." In *Proceedings of Seminar F of the PTRC 21st Summer Annual Meeting*, 129–145.

Small, K. A. 1983. "The Incidence of Congestion Tolls on Urban Highways." *Journal of Urban Economics* 13: 90–111.

Small, K. A. 1992. "Using the Revenues from Congestion Pricing." *Transportation* 19, no. 4: 359–381.

Small, K. A., and J. A. Gomez-Ibañez. 1998. "Road Pricing for Congestion Management: The Transition from Theory to Policy." In K. J. Button and E. T. Verhoef, eds., *Road Pricing, Traffic Congestion and the Environment: Issues of Efficiency and Social Feasibility*, 213–246. Cheltenham: Edward Elgar.

Sullivan, A. M. 1983. "Second-Best Policies for Congestion Externalities." *Journal of Urban Economics* 14: 105–123.

Verhoef, E. T., P. Nijkamp, and P. Rietveld. 1996. "Second-Best Congestion Pricing: The Case of an Untolled Alternative." *Journal of Urban Economics* 40, no. 3: 279–302.

Verhoef, E. T., P. Nijkamp, and P. Rietveld. 1997. "The Social Feasibility of Road Pricing: A Case Study for the Randstad Area." *Journal of Transport Economics and Policy* 31, no. 3: 255–276.

Vickrey, W. S. 1969. "Congestion Theory and Transport Investment." *American Economic Review* 59 (Papers and Proceedings): 251–260.

Walters, A. A. 1961. "The Theory and Measurement of Private and Social Cost of Highway Congestion." *Econometrica* 29, no. 4: 676–697.

Wardrop, J. 1952. "Some Theoretical Aspects of Road Traffic Research." *Proceedings of the Institute of Civil Engineers* 1, no. 2: 325–378.

Wilson, J. D. 1983. "Optimal Road Capacity in the Presence of Unpriced Congestion." *Journal of Urban Economics* 13: 337–357.

CHAPTER THIRTY-FIVE

Consumer E-Commerce, Virtual Accessibility, and Sustainable Transport

Jane Gould
and Thomas F. Golob

The growth of the Internet has rekindled interest in the relationship between communications and travel. New communication technologies have expanded the range, the type, and the number of transactions that can take place without travel. A number of promotions capture the new trade-offs between communications and travel: initially, the Internet was referred to as "the information superhighway," and Microsoft ran an ad campaign dubbed "Where do you want to go today?" The connection between travel and bytes has been summed up as "the death of distance" (Cairncross, 1997).

A parallel evolution in telecommunication and transportation was envisioned more than 150 years ago with the invention of the telegraph and telephone. The telephone was expected to "speed the movement of perishable goods," "reduce the travels of salesmen," and "let (itinerant) workers stay at home to be phoned for jobs" (Pool, 1983).

Today, the Internet has fueled similar expectations, and many of them center on travel-related issues. The Internet might relieve demand for new road capacity, slow down the rate of new vehicle ownership, and divert existing travel trips to less congested times. The Internet might help create more sustainable growth in transportation by providing virtual accessibility. In this chapter, we explore the transportation aspects of consumer electronic commerce (e-commerce). Shopping activities are currently automobile-intensive in many countries, and increases in e-commerce could portend important changes in transportation patterns and activities.

THE GROWTH OF CONSUMER E-COMMERCE

Currently, consumer e-commerce represents a small but rapidly growing proportion of retail sales. It is estimated that 17 million U.S. households shopped online in 1999 (Forrester, 2000), and consumer e-commerce revenues in the U.S. were estimated to be US$20 billion, up dramatically from US$4 billion in 1997 (IDC, 1999). Europe and the rest of the world are catching up to the U.S. in terms of online shopping, and there are forecasts of worldwide consumer e-commerce revenues of US$200 billion by 2002 (IDC, 1999). Growth in e-commerce will be driven by anticipated advances in information technology. Some of these advances (discussed in Golob, 2000) include (1) improvements in Internet speed and capacity involving the next-generation Internet Protocol, (2) wide-band and satellite home Internet connections, (3) handheld Internet devices ("smart phones"), (4) television set-top Internet devices and other simplified "Internet appliances," (5) Extensible Markup Language (XML), (6) smart agents (software "bots") for comparing products and prices, and (7) voice-over Internet Protocol (VoIP) for multimedia and human-assisted shopping.

Consumer e-commerce today is concentrated in items such as books, software, music, travel (e.g., airline tickets), hardware, clothing, and electronics. In the U.S., most of the online sales take place during the holiday season. However, there is also a developing e-commerce sector in groceries and household goods. It is estimated that this part of e-commerce might reach US$11 billion in sales by 2003, but this will still be only 2 percent of the total grocery market (Forrester, 2000). Restricted geographic location, high development and maintenance costs of online inventory display, and high delivery costs are cited as factors impeding the growth of grocery e-commerce. E-merchants in this sector are attempting to establish one of two types of markets: household replenishment or specialty luxury items (Forrester, 2000).

Online shopping for groceries and household goods is of particular interest to transportation planners, because this activity is much more repetitive than other types of shopping, and many shopping trips are linked to trips for other purposes. More sustainable transportation networks might be developed if e-commerce substituted for certain types of trips. For example, there might be less demand for new suburban centers with acres of parking, and e-commerce could reduce congestion during peak shopping periods (Golob, 2000). E-commerce could also radically change both the location of transshipment centers and the patterns of vehicle movement for physical goods distribution.

Another benefit for sustainable transportation is that e-commerce might induce more neighborhood, pedestrian-based commerce, particularly in Europe (ESRC, 1995). Local corner shops, village centers, or high-street stores could serve as pickup points, with regular scheduled deliveries by truck of perishables and drygoods ordered through e-commerce.[1] This would reduce the difficulty of making daytime deliveries to working households, and provide new opportunities for small shopkeepers. The opportunity has not been overlooked by oil companies and operators of gasoline stations, who envision existing neighborhood gasoline/food courts as pickup centers.

Although electronic commerce will not eliminate travel trips for shopping, it could affect the type and number of vehicles on the road. The need for advanced logistics and delivery vans will surely increase, and household transportation needs might change. Fewer shopping trips might reduce demand for personal vehicles that are capacious, designed to accommodate both passengers and shopping cargo. There might be a gradual shift toward smaller, alternative-fuel vehicles, since there could be less reliance on personal vehicles for transporting groceries, boxes, and bulky durable goods. A growth in electronic commerce might also slow a trend toward acquiring a second, and in some cases a third, household vehicle.

The aim of this chapter is to explore the interrelationships between personal shopping trips and transportation. We begin by examining the role of the personal vehicle for shopping trips, with an emphasis on fully employed workers, in both the U.S. and the UK. We choose to look at fully employed workers because they have opportunities to access e-commerce from work and home computers. We also know that many of these workers, particularly female heads of households, have very busy schedules (Golob and McNally, 1997; Gould and Golob, 1997).

RESEARCH INTO DEMAND FOR SHOPPING TRAVEL

It is estimated that shopping trips account for one out of every five person trips and one out of every seven person miles traveled in the U.S. (NPTS, 2000). Shopping trips in the U.S. account annually for 1,700 miles per car, a figure that has increased by 88 percent since 1969 (Edmondson, 1994, citing the 1990 U.S. Nationwide Personal Transportation Survey). Travel trips by women are of particular note. Between 1983 and 1990, the number of miles driven by women increased by 49 percent, with women ages 20 to 34 driving the most. This is partly explained by the overall increase of women in the labor force. Pisarski (1992) notes the dependence of working women on cars, and observes that in Los Angeles, working women have a multiple-function commute, which, in addition to work, includes dropping off children at school or daycare, stops at grocery stores, pharmacies, and so forth.

It is likely that conditions in the UK, and throughout Europe, are similar for women workers, although the distances they drive are not as great, due to different land use. The National Travel Survey for the UK indicates that

Table 35.1   Trends in UK Shopping Trips

	Shopping trips per person per year	Average miles per trip	Annual mileage*	Percentage of households owning cars	Number of shopping centers	Real consumer expenditure (billion £)
1965	77	3.5	268	42%	50	218.3
1975	115	3.8	440	53%	300	270.2
1985	125	4.6	557	62%	500	323.4
1995	145	5.2	747	68%	990 (1992)	405.6 (1993)

*excludes shopping trips < 1 mile.
Sources: Social Trends, 1997; UK DOT, 1996.

there has also been a steady gain in the number of personal journeys where shopping is defined as the main purpose (Table 35.1). In 1965, about 13 percent of all trips were for this purpose, and that figure had risen to about one in five trips around 1995. These data are not broken down by gender. For both the U.S. and the UK, shopping accounts for about 20 percent of the average household's annual trips by vehicle, and the majority of these trips are probably made by women.

Even today, however, many aspects of shopping do not involve travel and evoke other levels of involvement. For example, Salomon and Koppelman (1988) observed that purchasing goods is just one part of a shopping trip. Gould (1998) and Salomon and Mokhtarian (1998) noted that there can be a recreational aspect to shopping-related travel. Gould and Golob (1997) broke shopping activities down into two components, the time engaged in actual shopping and the time spent traveling to and from the shopping sites. Using a structural equation model of activity patterns, they found that recouping time spent in travel for shopping purposes would be particularly useful for busy working women with families. For these women, that travel time could be used for other pressing activities or demands. This result is consistent with earlier NPTS (1994) data, which suggests a pattern of increasing com-

plexity in women's travel trips. In order to explore the future role of e-commerce, it is useful to understand more about the travel patterns of busy working women: When do they schedule their shopping? To what extent do they chain their shopping trips to work and other activities? For many reasons, working women are likely to be one of the first groups to adopt e-commerce, because they are technologically adept, they must make continual trade-offs between in-home and out-of-home activities, and they make the majority of household purchases and transactions.

Transportation researchers are beginning to explore the impacts of e-commerce (e.g., Kilpala et al., 2000; Marker and Goulias, 2000; Martens and Korver, 2000). These recent studies are guided by a series of earlier works that predated the Internet as we know it today (e.g., Koppelman et al., 1991; Salomon, 1985, 1990; Salomon and Koppelman, 1988, 1992; Salomon and Schofer, 1988). But it is difficult for travel behavior researchers to keep up with the pace of development. Studies of consumer e-commerce are outdated, in that they are relevant to virtual opportunities that are obsolete before the studies are completed. Lacking relevant up-to-date e-commerce data, here we explore what can be learned from investigating existing activity patterns.

SHOPPING CHAINED WITH THE WORK TRIP

An activity and travel study involving a large and representative sample was conducted for the Portland Metropolitan Area in 1994–95. This is the only recent multi-day travel diary in the U.S. that includes a spatial distribution of stores and households. The spatial distribution is a key variable for studying the influence of virtual accessibility. The survey, of 3,891 households, achieved a distribution of households similar to the 1990 Census, although there was a tendency for low-income households to be under-

represented. There were 6,919 persons in the sample age 16 or over, and of these, 1,669 were women who worked outside the home for four hours or more on one of the survey diary days. This segment represents 46.7 percent of the 3,573 women in the full data set.

We first examine the frequency with which workers engage in a work tour that includes at least one shopping trip. More specifically, we count as a work/shopping tour any journey to or from work that is interrupted by at least one shopping activity. As expected, women are far more likely than men to engage in work/shopping tours. Less than 10 percent of all male workers engage in combined work/shopping trips, compared to about 15 percent of all women. We did not find much indication that women in lower-status professions ran a greater number of errands or engaged in more work-related shopping tours than did women in higher-status jobs (Table 35.2). Across all job categories, women shopped more than their male counterparts.

We constructed a logistic regression model that distinguishes between two types of home-based trip chains involving away-from-home work destinations: (1) any chain not involving shopping, and (2) any chain involving shopping. There are 6,790 work-involved trip chains, 12.1 percent (822) of which involve at least one shopping sojourn.

The logit model results are listed in Table 35.3. The strongest predictors of shopping attached to work trips

Table 35.2   Percentage of Workers in Select Professions Engaging in Work/Shopping Tours

Occupation	Gender	
	Men	Women
Managerial/Professional	10.5	16.4
Sales/Administration	9.3	16.3
Service	7.6	11.8
Labor/Manuf./Repair	17.3	—
Factory	6.3	16.4

Table 35.3   Is a Shopping Sojourn Included in the Home-Based Work Trip Chain? (0 = shopping not included; 1 = shopping included)

Exogenous Variable	Coefficient	z-statistic
Gender (+ = female)	.561	6.71
Age	.066	3.00
Age^2	−.000692	−2.74
Possession of driver's license	.634	2.41
Annual household income > $60,000	.358	3.69
Number of children in household under 6 years old	−.403	−3.55
Number of children 12 to 17 without license	−.287	−2.44
Number of drivers	−.227	−3.34
Constant	−4.44	−8.59
Initial −2 log likelihood	4079.9	
Final −2 log likelihood	3969.0	
Model Chi-square (degrees of freedom)	110.97 (8)	

Table 35.4 Is a Shopping Sojourn Included in the Home-Based Work Trip Chain?, with consideration of spatial factors (0 = shopping not included; 1 = shopping included)

Exogenous Variable	Coefficient	z-statistic
Gender (+ = female)	.568	6.76
Age	.0709	3.17
Age^2	–.000716	–2.82
Possession of driver's license	.627	2.39
Annual household income > $60,000	.343	3.53
Number of children in household under 6 years old	–.371	–3.26
Number of children 12 to 17 without license	–.269	–2.28
Number of drivers	–.166	–2.35
Accessibility to zonal employment weighted by auto travel times (from destination choice models)	.0068	4.00
Accessibility to total employment within 1 mile of home location (GIS data)	–.0059	–1.90
Constant	–5.06	–9.15
Initial –2 log likelihood	4079.9	
Final –2 log likelihood	3952.8	
Model Chi-square (degrees of freedom)	127.13 (10)	

are possession of a driver's license and gender. Female workers are more likely to shop on the way home from work or during breaks in the workday. Household size, as measured by the number of small children, the number of older children, and the number of drivers in the household, is a negative indicator of work-related shopping. The maximum value of the non-linear age function occurs at age forty-eight.

We next tested whether accessibility associated with household location affected shopping attached to work trips. Four different accessibility indices were used. Two of the indices are based on detailed land use and transportation network data compiled in a geographical information system (GIS) database maintained by Metro, the metropolitan planning organization responsible for the Portland Metropolitan Area. For each household location, GIS was used to compute total employment and total retail employment within one mile of the household. These indices are at the neighborhood level, capturing accessibility by walking or bicycling or by using personal vehicles for short trips.

The other two accessibility indices are derived from destination choice models used in a traditional (four-step) urban transportation planning system. These measures are computed for every traffic analysis zone and are assigned to the households that reside in that zone. They are the travel time–weighted sums over all zones of logs of attractions from multinomial logit destination choice models. One index used total employment as the attraction, and the second index used total households as the attraction. These indices capture accessibility on a broader scale utilizing the arterial road and mass transit networks. Two of these accessibility indices added significant explanatory power to the logit model shown in Table 35.3. The expanded model is shown in Table 35.4.

The improvement in model goodness of fit, as measured by the –2 log likelihood chi-square, is 16.2 with 2 degrees of freedom, which is significant at any reasonable confidence level. The index with the greatest explanatory power was the one that measures access to total regional employment from the home zone. This accessibility is positively related to the propensity to shop when going to or from work. The second index, total employment within one mile of the home location, is marginally negatively significant. That is, controlling for all other effects, persons living in denser areas with mixed land uses are less likely to chain their shopping with their work trips.

DISCUSSION

Our results have implications for the future location of stores (land use planning issues) and for the choice of transportation to reach these stores. As a baseline, the Portland data establishes that people who live in higher-density areas engage in fewer chained shopping trips. Presumably these people can make relatively short shopping trips from home, thus avoiding the need to shop on their way home from work.

E-commerce could be channeled as a virtual substitute for the high-density neighborhood. This has important implications for environmental policies that promote mixed development and greater residential densities. In residential areas with fewer stores and outlets, the local gas station or corner store could become an afternoon pickup site for groceries and sundries ordered earlier in the day. This virtual substitute is dependent, however, on reasonably priced, efficient, and timely package delivery.

The development of localized e-commerce could provide more opportunity for sustainable transport. Commuters could become less car-dependent if personal vehicles were not needed to make multiple after-work stops and carry goods home. These commuters might also find that they could use public transport or carpools more readily.

For working women, e-commerce holds the greatest promise, providing that there is growth of a reasonable, timely, and efficient package-distribution system. Working women run more errands on the way home than others; in addition to shopping trips, women may pick up young children from school or daycare, or go to after-school activities. E-commerce is one aspect of the multi-stop commute, but it might make the number of stops fewer, and less frequent.

It is worth mentioning that the type of merchandise available will also determine whether e-commerce evolves as a virtual alternative for the high-density neighborhood. The majority of Internet purchases are currently less frequently purchased items, such as books, software, and music. However, it is the more routine things of daily commerce—postage stamps, dry-cleaning, fill-in groceries, diapers, and pharmacy runs—that can usefully be consolidated in a single drop-off. For the most part, these must be provided by local fulfillment centers or middlemen in order to meet same-day delivery requirements.

AGENDA FOR FUTURE RESEARCH

In light of the growth of e-commerce, transportation planners should reopen the issue of what defines accessibility. Can accessibility gains be attained by entirely new electronic means? Salomon and Mokhtarian (1998) question whether accessibility attained through (traditional) land use planning or temporal policies (such as alternate work schedules) should be considered socially efficient.

Policy-makers may wish to consider to what extent the development of e-commerce is socially desirable: Will it help to reduce congestion, lessen the need for new roads, and perhaps provide greater flexibility for workers to use mass transit to travel to and from work? If e-commerce is considered to be socially desirable, what actions and policies can facilitate it? Relatedly, we need to examine the logistics delivery system in various countries to determine the issues involved in enhancing the on-demand delivery service.

E-commerce can also be a catalyst in breaking dependence on the car for shopping, particularly in the U.S. (Handy, 1993). Potentially, those who use mass transit will be among the first group to benefit from e-commerce and virtual accessibility. Commuters who favor mass transit and carpool or vanpools might be studied to see if their travel patterns and activity space are enhanced by travel-less shopping.

NOTES

The research was sponsored in part by the University of California Transportation Center. The authors wish to thank Keith Lawton and his staff at Portland Metro for providing data and encouragement. The opinions expressed are those of the authors, who are solely responsible for any errors of commission or omission.

1. McKinnon and Woodburn (1994) estimate that the contents of one single lorry (i.e., truck) will dispense with 670 car trips.

REFERENCES

Cairncross, F. 1997. *The Death of Distance.* London: Orion Publishing Group.

Edmondson, B. 1994. "Alone in the Car." *American Demographics* 16 (June).

ESRC Transport Studies Unit. 1995. "Car Dependence." A report for the RAC Foundation.

Forrester. 2000. "B2B Insights: eMarketplaces." Cambridge, Mass.: Forrester Research. http://www.forrester.com/

Golob, T. F. 2001. "TravelBehavior.Com: Activity Approaches to Modeling the Effects of Information Technology on Personal Travel Behavior." In D. A. Hensher, ed., *Travel Behaviour Research: The Leading Edge*, 145–184. Oxford: Pergamon.

Golob, T. F., and M. G. McNally. 1997. "A Model of Household Interactions in Activity Participation and the Derived Demand for Travel." *Transportation Research B*, 31: 177–194.

Gould, J. 1998. "Driven to Shop? The Role of Transportation in Future Home Shopping." *Transportation Research Record*, no. 1617: 149–156.

Gould, J., and T. F. Golob. 1997. "Shopping without Travel or Travel without Shopping? An Investigation of Electronic Home Shopping." *Transport Reviews* 17: 355–376.

Handy, S. 1993. "A Cycle of Dependence: Automobiles, Accessibility and the Evolution of the Transportation and Retail Hierarchies." *Berkeley Planning Journal* 8: 21–43.

IDC. 1999. *The State of the Internet Economy: Trends Forecast, 1998–2003.* Framingham, Mass.: International Data Corp.

Kilpala, H. K., P. N. Seneviratne, and S. M. Pekkarinen. 2000. "Electronic Grocery Shopping and Its Impact on Transportation and Logistics with Special Reference to Finland." Presented at Annual Meeting of the Transportation Research Board, January 9–13, Washington, D.C.

Koppelman, F., I. Salomon, and K. Proussalogou. 1991. "Teleshopping or Store Shopping? A Choice Model for Forecasting the Use of New Telecommunications-Based Services." *Environment and Planning B* 18: 473–489.

Marker, J. T., and K. Goulias. 2000. "A Framework for the Analysis of Grocery Teleshopping." Presented at 79th Annual Meeting of the Transportation Research Board, January 9–13, Washington, D.C.

Martens, M. J., and W. Korver. 2000. "Forecasting the Mobility Effects of Teleservices Using a Scenario Approach." Presented at Annual Meeting of the Transportation Research Board, January 9–13, Washington, D.C.

McKinnon, A., and A. Woodburn. 1994. "The Consolidation of Retail Deliveries: Its Effect on CO_2 Emissions." *Transport Policy* 1, no. 2: 125–136.

Mokhtarian, P. L. 1997. "Now That Travel Can Be Virtual, Will Congestion Virtually Disappear?" *Scientific American* (October). http://www/sciam.com/1097issue

NPTS. 1994. *NPTS Urban Travel Patterns.* Washington, D.C.: Federal Highway Administration, U.S. Department of Transportation.

NPTS. 2000. *Our Nation's Travel: 1995 NPTS Early Results Report.* National Personal Transportation Survey, U.S. Department of Transportation, Washington, D.C. http://www-cta.ornl.gov/npts/1995/Doc/publications.shtml

Pisarski, A. E. 1992. "New Perspectives on Commuting." Report prepared for U.S. DOT, FHWA. Office of Highway Information Management, Washington, D.C.

Pool, I. de Sola. 1983. *Forecasting the Telephone: A Retrospective Technology Assessment.* Norwood, N.J.: Ablex Publishing Corporation.

Salomon, I. 1985. "Telecommunications and Travel: Substitution or Modified Mobility." *Journal of Transport Economics and Policy* 19: 219–235.

Salomon, I. 1990. "Telematics and Personal Travel Behavior, with Special Emphasis on Telecommuting and Teleshopping." In H. H. Soekka et al., eds., *Telematics, Transportation and Spatial Development*, 67–89. Utrecht: VSP.

Salomon, I., and F. Koppelman. 1988. "A Framework for Studying Teleshopping versus Store Shopping." *Transportation Research A* 22: 247–255.

Salomon, I., and F. Koppelman. 1992. "Teleshopping or Going Shopping: An Information Acquisition Perspective." *Behaviour and Information Technology* 11: 189–198.

Salomon, I., and P. L. Mokhtarian. 1998. "What Happens When Mobility-Inclined Market Segments Face Accessibility-Enhancing Policies?" *Transportation Research D* 3: 129–140.

Salomon, I., and J. Schofer. 1988. "Forecasting Telecommunications-Travel Interactions: The Transportation Manager's Perspective." *Transportation Research A* 22: 219–229.

UK Office for National Statistics. 1997. *Social Trends 27.* London: The Stationery Office.

UK Department of Transport. 1996. *Transport Statistics.* London: The Stationery Office.

CHAPTER THIRTY-SIX

Uncertainty in the Adoption of Sustainable Transport Technology

The Electric Vehicle

Marina van Geenhuizen

SETTING THE SCENE

The demand for transport in Europe is increasing, especially in those sectors that are relatively most polluting, road and air transport (ECMT, 1997). Over the past twenty-five years, private car use in Europe has more than doubled, while road freight has increased by 160 percent. Transport by air has shown an even more spectacular rise. Extrapolation of current trends would lead not only to critical bottlenecks and high environmental decay, but also to serious disparities in accessibility of regions and cities. Thus, the overall picture is rather negative. The demand for transport services is rapidly growing, while causing increasing stress on the environment and quality of life due to traffic congestion, pollution, and use of non-renewable resources.

Environmental damage by transport can be reduced by new technology or a better application of existing technology. We can divide sustainable transport technology into two categories, on the basis of how damage is prevented (e.g., Geerlings, 1997): end-of-pipe technologies, designed to clean or filter the waste or emissions before the actual damage can occur; and process-integrated technologies, aimed at preventing damage by making adjustments in the processes—process-integrated measures often require a fundamental change in the processes at hand.

Process-integrated technologies now on the horizon as realistic possibilities, such as the hydrogen-powered fuel cell vehicle, suggest that technology may be able to reduce pollution to almost zero. Few of the sustainable transport technologies are without disadvantages or trade-offs, however. For example, there is a trade-off in setting environmental objectives, meaning that improvements in the reduction of gas emissions may worsen the outcome on other aims, such as noise. In addition, improving fuel efficiency may have the unintended effect of increasing mobility in terms of longer distances, because of the decrease in operating costs. There is also a trade-off with respect to economic policy. For example, the liberalization of world trade and freight transport affects the transport sector but will likely have adverse impacts on the environment. The time scale is also important in this context. For the short term, particular problems can be solved by technology such as local air pollution, but global air pollution and poor urban quality of life cannot.

In order to avoid some trade-offs, we may move in the medium and long term to technological solutions that integrate the transport sector with other sectors such as energy, spatial planning, and architecture. For example, in such an approach vehicles may be fueled by electricity from hydro, wind, or solar power that is produced in small units in the residential areas of cities. There may also be a redefinition of the role of individual motorized transport in a mobility system in which public transport is a high priority (Weber and Hoogma, 1998; Schoonman, 1998). A broader and integrated policy, however, would mean a fundamental break with the past and concomitant uncertainty and complication of the formulation of policy strategies.

A FOCUS
ON UNCERTAINTY

Policy for the adoption of new transport technology is surrounded by different types of uncertainty. The following types can be distinguished (van Geenhuizen et al., 1998; Rowe, 1994):

- Temporal uncertainty about the future of the transport system. Knowledge may be lacking about the shape of that future and about the probability of particular trends and policy impacts.
- Structural uncertainty about the complexity of the system in modeling. This uncertainty depends on the number of parameters and the interaction used in models; and accordingly, the issue is usefulness or the extent to which the models represent reality.
- Metrical uncertainty about difficulties in measurement of the system. Central issues here are precision and accuracy.
- Translational uncertainty about the communication and explanation of results. This type often follows on measurement and modeling (prediction) in policy stages where goals, values, and capabilities of actors affect the interpretation of results.

All four types of uncertainty occur in any situation, but their relative dominance may vary. Furthermore, they may reinforce each other in many situations. When focusing on the fields (sources) where uncertainty occurs, the following distinction can be made (Friend and Hickling, 1997; van Geenhuizen et al., 1998; Mulder et al., 1996):

Time-related aspects:
- when the new technology is available
- the period of introduction of the technology

Systemic factors (obstacles):
- opposing forces from old, dominant technologies
- opposing forces from new, competing technologies
- opposing institutional forces
- behavior of actors on the supply side of the new technology
- behavior on the demand side: willingness to pay for environmental gains and to bear inconvenience costs

Policy-related aspects:
- selection of the appropriate policy measures
- policy decisions in related fields

Impact-related aspects:
- contribution of the technology to sustainable transport
- emergence of (unwanted) side effects
- outcomes of related policy decisions

Policy-makers tend to perceive the many types of uncertainty differently and to react differently to them (e.g., Friend and Hickling, 1997; van Geenhuizen et al., 1998). They may reduce uncertainty through forecasting attempts (modeling). An alternative is to learn about uncertainty, as in critical events and bottlenecks, through such approaches as scenario analysis and Delphi studies. A more comprehensive strategy is to incorporate uncertainty into policy-making, i.e., in flexible and adaptive procedures. By contrast, policy-makers may ignore uncertainty and implement measures at random, or do nothing in the hope that uncertainty will be reduced over time.

The ability to cope with uncertainty is influenced by culture and the institutional environment (Stough and Rietveld, 1997). This situation would imply that policy measures pertaining to sustainable transport differ between countries—for example, between those with a relatively rigid and top-down planning tradition and those with a more flexible and bottom-up tradition. Aside from this, we have to keep in mind different macro-economic factors and factors concerning the sector where the new technology is adopted. A further interesting point of difference may be the reactions and decisions of consumers (households).

This chapter addresses cross-country differences in policies for sustainable transport technology by using electric vehicles as an example. The underlying aim of comparative research is to learn from other countries about the efficiency and effectiveness of policies. This chapter is not the end result of a thorough reflection on the subject but merely a starting point for such activity.

VALUE ORIENTATION

Transport, mobility, and communication tend to be positively valued around the globe as contributing to individual welfare and economic development. However, there are considerable differences in the processes and content of the policies that governments adopt to try to solve transport problems. For example, the need for broad policy support among citizens may be different between countries, leading to different policy-making procedures. Similarly, countries may differ in their political views on taxation, environmental standards, government interference in land use, privacy, and so forth, all leading to different types of policy measures (de Jong, 1997; Stough and Rietveld, 1997).

Policy-making is partly influenced by the value orientation of the organizations involved. Values are a strong force in the creation and maintenance of institutions as rule structures in countries. Cross-country comparison of value orientations is generally not an aim in itself but a way to reflect on one's own position, particularly to identify strong and weak points in one's own policy practices in order to learn. The importance of differences within countries (between regions) is not detrimental to this learning but can contribute to it.

Various research has been carried out on the value orientations of countries. Hofstede (1997) evaluates cultural attitudes in terms of the following dimensions: power distance, individualism, masculinity, uncertainty avoidance, and long-term orientation. The two dimensions that are closely related to attitudes toward uncertainty are power distance and uncertainty avoidance. Power distance indicates the degree to which less powerful members of institutions (organizations) in a country expect and accept that power is unequally distributed. In cultures with a small power distance, power is considered a fundamental societal fact that tends to overrule the choice between good and evil. Uncertainty avoidance is the degree to which the members of a culture feel threatened by uncertain (unknown) situations. This feeling expresses itself in such things as a need for predictability (rules). On the basis of differences in value orientation, the following clusters of countries can be distinguished (Hofstede, 1997):

- an Anglo-Saxon cluster: low power distance, high individualism, low uncertainty reduction, and a short-term orientation (e.g., the UK and the U.S.);
- a Roman cluster: very high power distance, relatively low individualism, average masculinity, and high uncertainty reduction (e.g., Belgium, Italy, and France);
- a Germanic cluster: low power distance, relatively low individualism, high masculinity, relatively high uncertainty reduction, and a long-term orientation (e.g., Germany and Austria); and
- a Scandinavian cluster: low power distance, low individualism, very low masculinity, very low uncertainty reduction, and a long-term orientation (e.g., Sweden and Norway).

The Netherlands is more or less a mix of these types. It may be concluded that the broad range of variation between countries is sufficient indication of the challenge of comparative research on national policies aimed at the adoption of sustainable transport technology.

THE CASE OF ELECTRIC VEHICLES

In electric vehicles, power is transmitted to the wheels by an electric motor. At present the most common energy source is an electrochemical battery, recharged from the electricity grid. Although battery research is yielding promising results for the near future, current battery types are relatively expensive and perform poorly, with a limited range (to 100 km) and limited speed (90 to 100 km per hour). Battery life is three to four years. Of particular concern is the chance for a dead battery and the time required for recharging.

Electric vehicles are priced much higher than comparable versions of conventional vehicles. In the pilot introduction project in Mendrisio, Switzerland, despite a subsidy of 50 percent, price differences remain as high as 25 to 30 percent for most cars (Peugeot, Citroen, and Renault). Only the VW Golf is cheaper. In fact, a substantial portion of the price of most electric vehicles is for the battery (30 to 35 percent). This problem has been solved in France by counting battery costs as operating costs. Accordingly, the battery is not included with the vehicle but is rented after purchase. The adoption of such a procedure in other countries, however, may face problems in the legal and fiscal areas. Other energy sources for electric vehicles are combustion engines (in hybrid cars) and fuel cells. The latter sources are not yet competitive but may become so in the near future. Fuel cell systems today pro-

Table 36.1   A Preliminary Overview of Uncertainty in the Adoption of Electric Vehicles

---

SOURCES OF UNCERTAINTY (a)

Time-related aspects

- The time that high-performance batteries, fuel cells, and EVs are available at a competitive price (M, T)
- The period necessary for the introduction of EVs (projects) (M, T, Tr)
- In the introduction: the period necessary for adaptation of consumer behavior and habits in driving EVs and recharging the battery (M, T, Tr)

Systemic aspects

- Opposing influence from actors in the conventional car manufacturing and gasoline fueling industry, potentially working on alternative solutions of cleaner combustion engines (T, S)
- Incompatibilities within the EV area, such as between the type of battery system (i.e., low and high temperature) and charging system (conductive versus inductive) (S, T, Tr)
- Opposing institutional forces, e.g., in the case of leasing the battery (guarantee of battery and value-added taxes) (S, T, Tr)
- Behavior of actors on the supply side, such as EV manufacturers, battery and fuel cell manufacturers, energy companies (S, T, Tr)
- Behavior of actors on the demand side, i.e., willingness to pay extra and willingness to bear inconvenience in favor of environmental gains (S, T, Tr)

Policy-related aspects

- Selection of the right policy, e.g., sequence of measures, type of measures, and costs (S, T, Tr)
- Selection of the right market segment (S, T, Tr)

Impact-related aspects

- Contribution of EVs to sustainable development, e.g., concerning emissions and energy use (S, Tr)
- Measurement bias of impacts due to differences between laboratory situations, simulation, and reality, e.g., due to topography, recharging habits, style of driving, etc. (M, Tr)
- Unwanted side effects, e.g., increase of car ownership (small substitution) (S, T)

---

a.   Uncertainty types are in brackets: M = Metrical; S = Structural; T = Temporal; Tr = Translational.

---

duce energy at a price of $5,000 per kW, whereas such systems become competitive only at a price of approximately US$200 (van Geenhuizen and Schoonman, 1999).

The use of electric (or hybrid) vehicles helps the environment in three ways: it improves air quality in cities; it reduces emissions of greenhouse gases if the electricity is generated by nuclear, solar, or hydro-power; and it increases the energy efficiency of motor vehicles. In most European countries, electric vehicles are niche technologies (Weber and Hoogma, 1998).

Resistance to the use of electric vehicles comes from the conventional car industry and the gasoline industry, in a situation that can be seen as a case of "lock-in" of a dominant technology (Cowan and Hulten, 1996). This situation causes various uncertainties (Table 36.1). As of now, resistance can also be expected from potential consumers because of the cars' relatively weak performance and high market price. An important issue is uncertainty about when the electric vehicle will become economically viable, in the sense that the cost will be similar to that for conventional cars. It seems relatively easy to predict how many cars must be manufactured for the price to drop to this level, dependent on a decrease in production costs and costs for research. However, it is difficult to foresee when and under which conditions this will happen (Sperling, 1996).

Table 36.2   Factors Advancing EV Adoption and Government Roles

Country	Factors	Role of Government
France	*ADVANCING* Need for outlet for nuclear power Air pollution in cities Centralized government structure Industry monopoly	Coordination of initiatives Subsidy for EV purchase Funding of R&D
Sweden	*ADVANCING* EV matches environmental policy EV is nearly zero emission (high public appreciation) Low price of electricity	Support of R&D Support of demonstration and procurement programs
Switzerland	*ADVANCING* EV matches environmental policy EV is zero emission (high public appreciation)	Clean Air Act Coordination and subsidization of pilot programs Subsidy for EV purchase
Germany	*PROHIBITING* Full emission: energy from coal-fired plants Decentralized government structure Fragmented electricity industry	Small involvement

We can observe different approaches to uncertainty in government-funded research on electric vehicle adoption. Some studies aim to reduce uncertainty by prediction, whereas others strive to learn about uncertainty and the future (AssoVEL, 1998; Cheron and Zins, 1997; Golob et al., 1996). In the remaining section we broadly compare four national policies for the adoption of electric vehicles to identify factors that influence such policies (IAEA, 1996; Weber and Hoogma, 1998) (see Table 36.2).

The situation in Germany has apparently been very different from that in France and Sweden, leading to a low level of government involvement with electric vehicles in the former. Recently, however, greater involvement on the part of the government was prompted by a perceived threat of foreign competition in the emerging international electric vehicle car industry. Switzerland is an important example of a country in which the use of electric vehicles is favored by a situation of nearly zero emission, and where the government has established a Clean Air Act. The goal of the latter policy is for electric vehicles to make up 8 percent (about 200,000) of the overall vehicle fleet by 2010. The Swiss government, together with the Kanton, supports demonstration programs and subsidizes the purchase of electric vehicles in designated pilot introduction areas. In contrast to Germany, the decentralized structure of government has not been an obstacle in government involvement in Switzerland.

The Netherlands compares with Germany in that electric vehicles are powered with electricity from non-sustainable sources (coal and gas), a situation in which the environmental gains of the technology can be questioned. The government is fairly reluctant here as far as individual transport is concerned, but subsidizes pilot projects for electric buses in public transport.

RESEARCH LINES

This chapter has addressed the variation in national policies for adoption of sustainable transport technology. Policy-making in this area is subject to the value orientation of a society and, connected with this, to structural factors such as the model of governance. By focusing on electric vehicles, the chapter has identified other important nation-specific factors, such as public appreciation of the environmental gains of the technology and dynamics in the industry sectors at hand. In this context, we can distinguish three avenues of cross-comparative country (state) research: adoption policies of national (state) government (process and content); adoption decisions by households; and efficiency and effectiveness of adoption policies, according to ex-post and ex-ante design.

In cross-comparative research on the adoption of sustainable transport policies, a first question would deal with differences in those policies themselves regarding various dimensions. One dimension is how policy-makers cope with uncertainty. A second is the role of the government, for example, as a coordinator, initiator, or investor. Another important dimension is the differentiation in policy measures over time, based, for example, on a model of how adoption ideally develops.

Decisions about the adoption of sustainable transport take place at the level of the national (or state) government and at the level of households. There is, of course, an interplay between the two. The behavior of households and this interplay form a second research path within cross-comparative research of countries (states). Such research may focus on the values attached to cars and to mobility, and on related constraints for the adoption of new transport technology.

In a third path of cross-comparative research, the focus would be on the efficiency and effectiveness of adoption policies, including research programs, pilot introductions, and subsidization. In this context, a first step would be to establish a number of relevant evaluation criteria. With regard to effectiveness, we might think of the scale of actual adoption after various years and the size of environmental gains. Efficiency criteria might focus on costs, budget use, and public support for the policies.

With regard to the research design, it is important that the research identify most clearly the impact of national policy. It is difficult, however, to control in evaluation studies for important non-policy factors such as public appreciation of environmental gains and structure of the relevant industries, because government policies make use of such circumstances.

A final remark pertains to the type of transport technology in the research. Electric vehicles can be seen as a technology that involves relatively few fundamental changes. It might be interesting to establish a research design with contrasting technologies causing different amounts of uncertainty, in order to explore the robustness of results.

REFERENCES

AssoVEL. 1998. "Large Scale Fleet Test with Lightweight Electric Vehicle in Mendrisio." 2nd interim report. Mendrisio, Switzerland.

Cheron, E., and M. Zins. 1997. "Electric Vehicle Purchasing Intentions: The Concern over Battery Charge Duration." *Transportation Research A* 31, no. 3: 235–243.

Cowan, R., and S. Hulten. 1996. "Escaping Lock-In: The Case of the Electric Vehicle." In *Technological Forecasting and Social Change* 53, 61–79.

ECMT. 1997. *Trends in the Transport Sector.* Paris: ECMT.

Friend, J., and A. Hickling. 1997. *Planning under Pressure: The Strategic Choice Approach.* Oxford: Butterworth-Heinemann.

Geenhuizen, M. van, P. Nijkamp, and H. van Zuylen. 1998. "Limits to Predictability." In *Proceedings of the PTRC European Transport Conference 1998*, 291–302. London: PTRC.

Geenhuizen, M. van, and J. Schoonman. 1999. "Sustainable Transport Technology: A Policy View on the Adoption of Electric Vehicles." In *Proceedings of the CONAT '99: The IXth International Conference.* Brasov: Transylvania University of Brasov (Romania).

Geerlings, H. 1997. "Towards Sustainability of Technological Innovations in Transport: The Role of Government in Generating a Window of Technological Opportunity." Ph.D. thesis, Erasmus University, Rotterdam.

Golob, T., et al. 1996. *Forecasting Electric Vehicle Ownership and Use in the California South Coast Air Basin.* Irvine: Institute of Transportation Studies.

Hofstede, G. 1997. *Culture and Organizations: Software of the Mind.* New York: McGraw Hill.

IAEA (The International Energy Agency). 1996. *Imple-*

menting Agreement for Electric Vehicle Technologies and Programs. Paris: IAEA.

Jong, M. W. de. 1997. *An International Comparison of Decision Making on Infrastructures.* The Hague: Ministry of Transport and Waterworks. (In Dutch.)

Mulder, K., C. van de Weijer, and V. Marchau. 1996. "Prospects for External Sources of Vehicle Propulsion: Results of a Delphi Study." *Futures* 28, no. 10: 919–945.

Rowe, W. D. 1994. "Understanding Uncertainty." *Risk Analysis* 14, no. 5: 743–750.

Schoonman, J. 1998. *Decentralized Production and Storage of Electricity for Large Scale Application of Renewable Energy.* Delft: Delft University of Technology.

Sperling, D. 1996. "The Case for Electric Vehicles." *Scientific American* (November): 54–59.

Stough, R., and P. Rietveld. 1997. "Institutional Issues in Transport Systems." *Transport Geography* 5, no. 3: 207–214.

Weber, M., and R. Hoogma. 1998. "Beyond National and Technological Styles of Innovation Diffusion: A Dynamic Perspective on Cases from the Energy and Transport Sectors." *Technology Analysis & Strategic Management* 10, no. 4: 545–566.

Closing Thoughts and a Look toward the Future

William R. Black
and Peter Nijkamp

Since the SCAST conference, there have been some very interesting developments in the general area of social change and sustainable transport. The transatlantic nature of this problem has been given attention by the European Union under their Fifth Programme, which will govern research over the next five years. A special call for thematic networks on this theme has been issued. There is also a growing body of literature in this area, where a decade ago there was nothing.

There have been technological changes as well. Perhaps the most important of these has been the introduction of fuel cell automobiles and hybrid (gasoline-electric) vehicles into the marketplace. These promise increases in fuel efficiency by a factor of two or three, and there is much optimism regarding these developments. At the same time, we must not lose sight of the fact that transport growth in the developing world may very well absorb any fuel or emissions savings from these new technologies.

Social changes are also occurring, but these are less favorable to solving the sustainability problem. It is estimated that 12 million Americans flew to Europe in 2001, attracted by the weaker currency there and a disregard for the pollution generated or the fuel used in the process. Applications for passports on the American side are at an all-time high. Globally, tourism is at record levels and is becoming a substantial component of gross domestic product (GDP) for many nations in the developing world.

Ford Motor Company recently noted conflicts between its current business, consumer choices, and sustainability. The company produces sports utility vehicles in response to consumer demand, which enables it to meet its economic goals, but at the same time this makes its environmental goals more difficult to reach. Ford officials argue that they are responding to consumer demand, and if they did not do it, one of their competitors would. Although there appears to be a bit of corporate spin at work here, the rationale they offer is undoubtedly correct. There is a need for change in our culture, a change away from automobiles as the dominant transport mode.

The automobile culture must end in the United States and Europe. In the U.S., the problem is a bit more complex. Even if it were possible to re-educate the public away from automobiles, there is simply no mass transit alternative to the private motor vehicle. Eliminating the automobile would eliminate mobility. In Europe we are seeing the fulfillment of a latent demand for motor vehicles that may go back to the middle of the twentieth century. Taxes have done little to decrease the demand for motor vehicles there. In effect, both areas seem destined to have more automobiles and trucks along with the sustainability problems that naturally accompany these modes.

Globalization of industrial production is also proceeding at a rapid pace, and there seems to be nothing that will decrease its spread. It should be recognized that much of the freight transport generated by globalization would have been unnecessary in its absence. Unfortunately, there seems to be no way of reversing this process in the near term, and even less incentive to do so in the long term.

Awareness has grown that in the past decades the industrial, economic, and social organization of our societies has exhibited a new form of architecture, in which interaction, communication, and association play a prominent role. This new configuration, often coined "the network economy," has a multimodal and open structure, in which nodal centers act as the core of the network infrastructure concerned. This applies to both physical and virtual networks.

This new phase in the economic history of the industrialized world provokes three intriguing research challenges: What are the socioeconomic, institutional, and technological drivers of this modern development? What are the implications of the worldwide transition to a network economy for human behavior, for the spatial and mobility patterns of human activity, and for the industrial organization of our world? What are proper policy responses to this new mega-trend in terms of adjusted strategies or new institutions (including private-public arrangements)?

Clearly, the above research questions need a cross-national systematic framework of a multidisciplinary nature. Disciplines to be involved are, inter alia, economics, management science, sociology, political science, psychology, and law. The study of the network economy is concerned with many dimensions, and hence a dedicated set of focal points in research is necessary.

It has been noted that Americans always believe that a technological solution will emerge to solve problems, while Europeans tend to lean more toward the use of policy instruments. This is probably an accurate assessment of activities for most of the last century. It seems that the problem of transport sustainability will not necessarily be solved by either approach, but will require the development of new technologies and the application of different policy approaches. One thing that seems quite certain is that the population on both continents must be willing to try new technologies and, in some cases, even give up some of the mobility they have had in the past. This will be necessary, given the social changes discussed here, if transport in the developed world is to be sustainable.

Contributors

JILLIAN ANABLE is with the Huxley School of the Environment, Imperial College, London, UK.

DAVID BANISTER is Professor in the Bartlett School of Planning, University College London, UK.

JÖRG BECKMANN is with the Sociologisk Institut, Kobenhavns Universitet, Kobenhavn, Denmark.

AKLI BERRI is a doctoral student working on the project on Prospective Mobility in Metropolises with the Transport Economy and Sociology Department of the National Institute for Research on Transportation and Transportation Safety, Arcueil, France.

MICHEL BEUTHE is Professor with Group Transport and Mobility, Facultés Universitaires Catholiques de Mons, Mons, Belgium.

WILLIAM R. BLACK served as North American co-chair of the NSF-ESF Social Change and Sustainable Transport project and is Professor of Geography and Public and Environmental Affairs at Indiana University, Bloomington, Indiana, USA.

KENNETH BUTTON is Professor of Public Policy with the Institute of Public Policy at George Mason University, Fairfax, Virginia, USA.

CRISTINA CAPINERI is with the Dipartimento di Storia–Sezione Geografia, at the Università di Siena, Siena, Italy.

FABRICE DEGRANDSART is with Group Transport and Mobility, Facultés Universitaires Catholiques de Mons, Mons, Belgium.

ERAN FEITELSON is Senior Lecturer in the Department of Geography at the Hebrew University of Jerusalem, Jerusalem, Israel.

BIRGITTA GATERSLEBEN is with the Department of Psychology, University of Surrey, Guilford, UK.

MARINA VAN GEENHUIZEN is a member of the Faculty of Technology, Policy and Management at the University of Delft in Delft, the Netherlands.

JEAN-FRANÇOIS GEERTS is with STRATEC S.A., Brussels, Belgium.

RICHARD GILBERT is a transportation consultant affiliated with the Centre for Sustainable Transportation, Toronto, Canada.

ANDY GILLESPIE is Director of the Centre for Urban and Regional Development Studies at the University of Newcastle at Newcastle-upon-Tyne, UK.

GENEVIEVE GIULIANO is Professor of Urban Planning and Development at the University of Southern California in Los Angeles, Los Angeles, California, USA.

THOMAS F. GOLOB is a Full Researcher with the Institute of Transportation Studies at the University of California at Irvine, Irvine, California, USA.

ROGER GORHAM is a transportation consultant in Lenox, Massachusetts, USA.

JANE GOULD is with the Future Media Programme, London Business School, London, UK.

DAVID L. GREENE is Senior Energy Economist with the Oak Ridge National Laboratory, Oak Ridge, Tennessee, USA.

LAURENT GUIHÉRY is with the Laboratoire d'Economie des Transports, Université Lumière Lyon, Lyon, France.

MARKUS HESSE is with the Department of Geography, Free University of Berlin, Berlin, Germany.

DONALD G. JANELLE is Research Professor and Program Director of the Center for Spatially Integrated Social Science, University of California at Santa Barbara, Santa Barbara, California, USA.

BART JOURQUIN is Associate Professor with Group Transport and Mobility, Facultés Universitaires Catholiques de Mons, Mons, Belgium, and Limburgs Universitair Centrum, Diepenbeek, Belgium.

TSCHANGHO JOHN KIM is Professor in the Department of Urban and Regional Planning at the University of Illinois at Urbana-Champaign, Champaign, Illinois, USA.

HELI A. KOSKI is with ETLA, the Research Institute of the Finnish Economy in Helsinki, Finland.

HANS KREMERS is with the Department of Spatial Economics, Faculty of Economics and Econometrics, Free University Amsterdam, Amsterdam, the Netherlands.

LARS LUNDQVIST is with the Department of Infrastructure and Planning, Division of Transport and Location Analysis unit of the Royal Institute of Technology, Stockholm, Sweden.

JEAN-LOUP MADRE is Research Director and the moderator on the project on Prospective Mobility in Metropolises with the Transport Economy and Sociology Department of the National Institute for Research on Transportation and Transportation Safety, Arcueil, France.

BRIAN A. MIKELBANK is a graduate student in the Department of Geography, The Ohio State University, Columbus, Ohio, USA.

PATRICIA L. MOKHTARIAN is Associate Professor of Civil and Environmental Engineering and Faculty Associate with the Institute of Transportation Studies, University of California at Davis, Davis, California, USA.

PETER NIJKAMP served as European co-chair of the NSF-ESF Social Change and Sustainable Transport project and is President of the Governing Board of the Netherlands Research Council.

MORTON E. O'KELLY is Professor of Geography in the Department of Geography, The Ohio State University, Columbus, Ohio, USA.

JOS VAN OMMEREN is with the Cranfield School of Management, Cranfield, Bedfordshire, UK.

FRANCIS PAPON is in charge of research on the project on Prospective Mobility in Metropolises with the Transport Economy and Sociology Department of the National Institute for Research on Transportation and Transportation Safety, Arcueil, France.

ERIC PELS is with the Department of Spatial Economics, Free University Amsterdam, Amsterdam, the Netherlands.

HUGO PRIEMUS is with OTB Research Institute for Housing, Urban and Mobility Studies, Delft University of Technology, Delft, the Netherlands.

PIET RIETVELD is on the Faculty of Economics at Vrije Universiteit, Amsterdam, the Netherlands.

AMANDA ROOT is Research Officer with the Transport Studies Unit, University of Oxford, Oxford, UK.

GEORG RUDINGER is with the Psychologisches Institut of the Universität Bonn, Bonn, Germany.

ILAN SALOMON is Professor of Geography with the Department of Geography, The Hebrew University of Jerusalem, Jerusalem, Israel.

KARIN SANDQVIST is with the Department of Child and Youth Studies, Stockholm Institute of Education, Stockholm, Sweden.

LAURIE SCHINTLER is a Research Assistant Professor with the Institute of Public Policy, George Mason University, Fairfax, Virginia, USA.

GIANFRANCO SPINELLI is with the Dipartimento Economia Aziendale, Università del Piemonte Orientale, Novara, Italy.

PETER STEEN was with the Environmental Strategies Research Group of the National Resources Management Institute, Stockholm, Sweden. He passed away in May of 2000.

KARIN TILLBERG is with the Institute for Housing Research in Gaevle, Uppsala University, Sweden.

DAVID UZZELL is with the Department of Psychology, University of Surrey, Guilford, Surrey, UK.

ERIK T. VERHOEF is with the Department of Spatial Economics, Free University Amsterdam, Amsterdam, the Netherlands.

JOHAN VISSER is with the OTB Research Institute for Housing, Urban and Mobility Studies, TRAIL Research School, Delft University of Technology, Delft, the Netherlands.

MARTIN WACHS is Director of the Institute for Transportation Studies at the University of California at Berkeley, California, USA.

PAUL WADDELL is Associate Professor with the Evans School of Public Affairs and the Department of Urban Design and Planning, University of Washington, Seattle, Washington, USA.

MICHAEL WEGENER is Director of the Institute of Spatial Planning at the University of Dortmund, Dortmund, Germany.

BARRY WELLMAN is Professor of Sociology with the Centre for Urban and Community Studies, University of Toronto, Toronto, Ontario, Canada.

Index

Aalborg Charter, 36

accessibility, 173–174, 176–177, 185, 187; community and, 267; of delivery services, 259; of highways, 255; Internet and, 279; shopping travel and, 283; underground freight transport and, 239

accidents, 3, 35, 82, 120, 220; costs of, 13; economy of speed and, 251; older drivers and, 161; preventing, 11; pricing policies and, 273; risk of, 137; in underground freight transport, 239; victims of, xi, 37, 209

acid rain, 36

adventure seeking, 175

AEMEÏS project, 157–163, 158t

aging. See elderly (aging) people

agriculture, 36, 77, 110

air pollution, xi, 11; automobiles and, 35; control equipment for, 85; decrease in, 19, 23, 25; health effects of, 137, 145, 221, 223t; microsimulation modules and, 130; as nuisance, 89. See also pollution

air travel, 76

airports, 8, 21, 193; congestion at, 79; day tourism and, 198; as exchange pivots, 191; pricing policies and, 275

alternative routing, 12

American Association of State Highway and Transportation Officials (AASHTO), 18

Applied General Equilibrium (AGE), 79–80, 81fig.

architecture, 287, 296

Atlanta, 95

Australia, 108, 111, 117, 177, 244, 246

Austria, 289

automobiles: appeal of, 8, 118–120t, 118–121; attitudes toward, 175; automobile industry, 5, 107, 290; automobilization as mobility paradigm, 101–102, 104; car use as commons dilemma, 137–138; catalytic converters in, 85, 86; company cars and parking, 201–208; consumer society and, 166; culture of, 106, 295–296; dependence on, 23, 31, 68, 107–114, 188, 284; disembodied automobilization, 102–103; downsizing of, 11; drawbacks of, 35; drive-alone mode, 94, 96;

emission standards for, 19; fuel-cell, 295; fuel consumption of, 193–194; invention of, 17; leisure travel and, 183, 183t; mileage, 211; ownership rates, 24, 95, 108, 117, 118–123, 177, 210; public transport and, 51; rise in use of, 27, 30; spatio-temporal abstractions of, 103–104; stages of automobility, 117–118; as universal objects, 104–105. See also motor vehicles

aviation industry, 5, 9

backcasting, 63–64, 69, 72

barge transport, 51, 228, 230–231, 231fig., 233, 234

Baudrillard, Jean, 112–113

behavior, 6–8, 15; adjustment of, 125; company-provided parking and, 207–208; of elderly drivers, 159–160; policy and, 11; routine, 187; technology and, 12; Theory of Planned Behavior, 188

Belgium, 79, 219–226, 230, 246, 289

bicycling. See cycling

biodiversity, 21

brainports, 10

"brandless" distribution, 237

Britain. See United Kingdom (UK)

Brotchie triangle, 89

Brundtland Commission, xi, 149

buffers, travel and, 175, 195–196, 195–196fig., 196t, 197fig.

bundling, 12, 206, 229

bureaucracy, 265

bus transportation, 94–95, 144, 292

business-as-usual (BAU) scenario, 64–66, 215

CAFE standards, 38

California, 25, 210, 266, 267, 276

Canada, 38, 40, 66, 117, 150; community ties in, 266, 267, 268; fuel prices in, 39. See also North America

capitalism, 146, 251, 265

carbon dioxide (CO_2), 36, 40, 86, 221; EST criteria for, 64; freight transport and, 236, 237t; Kyoto agreements and, 56; reduction of emissions, 75t, 87t; transportation emissions and, 149

carbon monoxide (CO), 19, 36, 150, 221, 236, 237t

care work, 7, 12

carpooling, 7, 10, 94, 215; company-provided parking versus, 205, 206; e-commerce and, 284; trust and, 138

cars. See automobiles

Castells, Manuel, 49

CEEC countries, 76, 77

cellular automata (CA), 126

central business district (CBD), 93, 94, 95, 110, 145, 263

chains, 13

chaos models, 12–13

Chicago, xiii, 27; commuting congestion in, 95; economy of speed in, 254–256fig.; land use/transport in, 86, 87, 88t, 89

children, 37, 93, 122–123; automobile accidents and, 137; caring for, 7, 150; chauffeuring of, 118, 280, 284; dependency motif and, 112; EST criteria and, 67, 68; freedom of, 31; household formation and, 127, 128; leisure travel and, 187; mobility of, 167–168; women's mobility and, 152

Chile, 266, 267

China, 266

cities: air pollution in, 19; automobile dependence and, 107, 108; congestion in, xi, 79; density of, 166; dependence on transport, 35; goods delivery in, 11; growth of, 191; in Northwestern Mediterranean Arc, 192–193; population densities, 38; postmodern urban landscape, 261; public transport and, 22–23; road pricing in, 275; spatial patterns of, 17, 27–29; speed limits in, 254fig., 255; transport logistics in, 259–264, 260fig., 262fig.; urban distribution, 239; urban planning, 193; urban sprawl, 209, 215

City Planning and the Problems of Congestion conference (1909), 23

civil liberties, 112

class, 146, 153

Clean Air Act (Swiss), 291

Clean Air Act (U.S.), 18, 38, 85

Clean Water Act, 20